BEST AMERICAN
CRIME WRITING
2003

BEST AMERICAN
CRIME
WRITING
2003

INTRODUCTION BY **JOHN BERENDT**

EDITED BY **OTTO PENZLER** AND **THOMAS H. COOK**

VINTAGE BOOKS

A DIVISION OF RANDOM HOUSE, INC. • NEW YORK

A Vintage Original, August 2003

Copyright © 2003 by Otto Penzler and Thomas H. Cook
Introduction copyright © 2003 by John Berendt

ISSN 1542-0558

ISBN 0-375-71301-8

Book design by Debbie Glasserman

www.vintagebooks.com

Printed in the United States of America
10 9 8 7 6 5 4 3 2 1

CONTENTS

PREFACE

As might be expected, American crime writing in 2002 was deeply influenced by the events of September 11, particularly in regard to the number of articles that dealt in one form or another with terrorism. There were investigations of the September 11 terrorists and of the societies from which they came. There was a race to second-guess anyone who might have been able to foresee or prevent the attack, as well as those who responded to it, both at the actual moment of the emergency and later, as the nation, and particularly the presidential administration, began first to formulate and then to implement its response. As a predictable result, American crime writing evidenced a distinct internationalism, with stories that took readers far beyond our shores in order to portray people and places we could ignore only at our peril.

The selection was large, as was the scope, and as editors we were challenged by both the magnitude and the quality of these offerings. Indeed, so much magazine and newspaper space was devoted in one way or another to the aftermath of September 11 that we easily could have produced a volume whose individual contributions dealt with nothing else. In the end, however, we chose those pieces that most focused on individuals, both terrorists and those who seek to bring them to justice, both suicide bomber and homicide victim.

We also felt that to concentrate on the events of September 11 would require that we ignore the wide variety of human feloniousness and malfeasance that last year's collection so clearly established. Certainly, the cloud of September 11 hung heavily over American crime writers during the past year, but not so heavily as to obscure the fact that for the most part human beings, criminal and otherwise, either returned to their normal patterns of behavior with astonishing speed or had never really abandoned them.

Thus, during the year following September 11, Americans witnessed the usual caravan of malefactors, everything from the most highly paid business executives to the most humble connivers, from men whose greed knew no bounds to a woman who wished only to be someone else. September 11, for all its profound impact, could not in the least alter the ironclad reality of human frailty, nor its occasional transcendence. Buildings fell and lives were lost, but life itself, both social and individual, moved steadily onward along a wholly predictable continuum of noble and debased intent.

Consequently, within these pages, you will find a crusading brother, a determined journalist, and a renowned sports figure. You will find a hustler, a pimp, and a specialist in decaying flesh. You will find a "terrible" boy who seems hardly terrible at all, along with another such boy who became at last an equally terrible man. You will find cowardice and courage, honesty and trickery, people whose selfishness will astonish you, and others of measureless self-sacrifice. In short, you will find your fellow men and women in their depravity and in their glory, their bottomless capacity both to harm and to heal each other.

And so, more than anything, the distinguished writers of this year's collection of *Best American Crime Writing* continue to demonstrate the dual nature of human potential, the good and the evil men and women can do. In the year following September 11, what could be more in keeping with our experience or more instructive in our ongoing need to balance fear with determination, freedom with security, faith with doubt, pessimism with hope, as our Founding Fathers did so many years ago, and thus by the darkest of visions fashioned the brightest of lands.

. . .

In terms of the nature and scope of this collection, we defined American crime reporting as any factual story involving crime written by an American or a Canadian and published in the United States or Canada during the calendar year 2002. We examined a very wide range of publications, which included all national and regional magazines and nearly two hundred so-called little magazines, reviews, and journals.

We welcome submissions by any writer, publisher, editor, or other interested party for *Best American Crime Writing 2004*. Please send a tear sheet with the name of the publication in which the submission appears, the date of publication, and if available, the address of the author. If first publication was in electronic format, a hard copy must be submitted. Only articles actually published with a 2003 publication date are eligible. All submissions must be made by December 31, 2003, and should be sent to Otto Penzler, The Mysterious Bookshop, 129 West 56th Street, New York, NY 10019. Those wishing verification that their submission was received should provide a self-addressed, stamped postcard or envelope. Submitted material cannot be returned.

Thomas H. Cook
Otto Penzler
New York
January 2003

There was a time, pre-9/11, when you could read about crime with a certain detachment, as you would a novel or a short story. No matter how serious or frightening or infuriating the crime, reading about it was essentially a form of entertainment, because the criminals and their victims were generally at a comfortable remove from you, the reader.

The sudden rise of terrorism has changed all that. As the weapons of choice among criminals have morphed from knives and guns (which kill individuals) into chemicals, germs, and atoms (which kill everybody), you the reader have suddenly become a possible victim. So reading about crimes has taken on somewhat greater immediacy, at least when the subject is terrorism—and it often is these days.

But wait, you have not only been cast in the role of victim; you have also become a *suspect*. If that sounds preposterous—you, a suspected terrorist—then what else would you call yourself when you are compelled to empty your pockets at airport security gates, walk through metal detectors, submit to electronic frisking, stand by while a uniformed guard rummages through your carry-on luggage, and take off your shoes so they can be inspected for explosives?

Nor does it end there. In addition to being victim and suspect, you have also been deputized as a cop. In January 2002, President Bush announced the formation of a volunteer Citizen Corps that would wage war against terrorism at the grassroots level, and that means you. A highlight of the program was to be Operation TIPS, in which millions of Americans would act as informers—especially people who had access to other people's homes—and would report any suspicious activity to the authorities.

The very notion that millions of people would be playing Miss Marple and Big Brother, looking under furniture and pawing through garbage, stirred vociferous opposition. Uneasy comparisons were made to the East German secret police, the Stasi. So the administration quickly took back the part about spying inside people's homes and said the spying would stop at the front door. In any case, the FBI was soon flooded by calls from thousands of amateur private eyes with raw information. Writing for the online magazine Salon.com, Dave Lindorff reported that when he called the Justice Department to ask what citizens were supposed to do if they had terror tips to pass on, he was given a telephone number that he was told had been set up by the FBI. When he called the number, a female operator greeted him cheerily with the words "*America's Most Wanted*, good afternoon." Lindorff expressed his surprise, and the lady said, "No, this is not the FBI. This is the TV program *America's Most Wanted*. We've been asked to take the FBI's tips for them." The propriety, not to mention the legality, of the FBI's farming out its intelligence-gathering duties to a privately produced TV show never became an issue, because Operation TIPS never quite got off the ground.

Crime writers, who are ordinary citizens like the rest of us, have also been pulled into the game as victims, suspects, and cops, but their work as reporters has been even more deeply affected by the aftermath of 9/11, and not at all for the better. Since 9/11, there has been a rush within the government to classify all sorts of formerly accessible information on the grounds that its release would endanger national security. Within two months of 9/11, an informational black hole had swallowed entire universes of data. Reporters found their sources slipping away, closing down, evaporating.

The Justice Department, for example, arrested and detained a thousand people on American soil but refused to say who they were or what charges they faced. At the same time, all U.S. immigration and deportation proceedings were declared secret and closed to the public. Access to the INS reading room was closed except by appointment and with an escort. President Bush signed an order restricting public access to the papers of past presidents, and the White House even took the unusual step of paring the list of congressional leaders approved for classified law enforcement briefings. The announcement of these moves, it should be noted, triggered objections in Congress and lawsuits by the press and citizens' rights groups, and as a result some of the measures were rolled back a bit. Still, the clampdown on information has continued unabated.

Reporters have been caught in a whipsaw. Deprived of information on the one hand, they are finding their own private notes being construed as public property. In July 2002, for example, federal judge T. S. Ellis III agreed with government lawyers who argued that CNN reporter Robert Young Pelton was acting as a government agent when he interviewed John Walker Lindh, the American captured with the Al Qaeda in Afghanistan. The judge ruled that Pelton would have to surrender his notes.

What we have here is a reaction to September 11 that, while understandable under the circumstances, has seriously altered the dynamics of crime fighting, crime reporting, and crime itself. Two pieces of sweeping legislation passed by Congress since 9/11 lie at the core of this seismic shift—the USA Patriot Act and the Homeland Security Act.

The first to be voted into law was the USA Patriot Act, an acronym for Uniting and Strengthening America by Providing

Appropriate Tools Required to Intercept and Obstruct Terrorism Act. It was rushed through Congress in six weeks with abbreviated hearings and almost no debate; it was then approved by the House, 357–66, and the Senate, 98–1. This is breathtaking, considering that the Patriot Act vastly expands the surveillance capabilities of the government without providing the customary judicial restraints designed to protect civil liberties.

Of all the provisions in the Patriot Act, the ones of greatest concern to journalists, especially journalists who write about crime, are Sections 213 and 215. These two sections enable law enforcement officers to break into newsrooms and journalists' homes in order to search for and seize materials they believe may constitute "evidence of a criminal offense in violation of the laws of the United States." The wording is dangerously broad; the "criminal offense" is not limited to terrorism, and the target of the break-in need not be suspected of any crime at all. This means, essentially, that under the guise of fighting terrorism, the government has given itself the right to burglarize independent news organizations if they think they might find information (presumably in the form of a reporter's research) about a crime, whether or not it has anything to do with terrorism. Furthermore, the government does not have to inform the victim of the break-in that it ever occurred, and anyone who may happen to know about the break-in is forbidden to tell anybody else. This break-in provision, known as the "sneak and peek" clause, is eerily reminiscent of the Watergate plumbers operation and seriously weakens the Fourth Amendment protections against unreasonable search and seizure.

The Patriot Act also enables law enforcement agencies to get around many of the restrictions on intercepting electronic communications. Until now, for example, the Wiretap Statute has set a very high standard of proof for court-ordered wiretaps in domestic criminal cases: The government had to show probable cause that (1) the target of the surveillance was committing a specific crime; (2) the communications being intercepted would bear directly on that crime; and (3) the actual phone being tapped was the one being used in connection with the crime.

A lower standard of proof was required for tracing the telephone numbers of incoming and outgoing calls, because the information captured did not include the actual content of the phone conversation, just the phone numbers. Government attorneys needed only to certify that the telephone numbers would be "relevant to an ongoing criminal investigation." The Patriot Act expands this "trap and trace" law to include the Internet, and this is a significant broadening of the government's invasive power. The difference is that the nature of the information gathered from tracing Internet activity is much more revealing than mere telephone numbers and comes very close to content. For example, among the data captured from an Internet surveillance would be all the searches a crime reporter (or anybody else) made on Google, all the web addresses visited in browsing the Internet, and addresses of incoming and outgoing e-mails. And the only requirement for an intercept warrant under the "trap and trace" law is that the information gathered would be relevant to a crime. Again, the crime does not have to involve terrorism.

Section 206 of the Patriot Act goes even further than intercepting the electronic communications of individuals. It permits the FBI to put a monitor on any public Internet facility that they think a terrorist might use, and that includes libraries, cyber cafés, and university computer laboratories. *All* the users of these facilities would be monitored, not just the suspects, and the operator of the facility would be prohibited from informing its patrons that their activities were being monitored by the FBI.

The Homeland Security Act, which was passed in November 2002, created a whole new federal bureaucracy and redoubled the government's powers to amass information about individuals. But it also put crucial information out of reach of the public by undermining the Whistleblower Law, which prohibits reprisals against people who come forward to reveal corruption, malfeasance, or any criminal activities within government or private businesses. The Homeland Security Act exempts from the Freedom of Information Act any information provided voluntarily to the government as long as it relates to "infrastructure vulnerabilities or other vulnerabilities to terrorism." Exactly what these vulnerabilities are is not made clear, and the vagueness of the wording invites the broadest interpretation. So any company or agency that is about to have a whistle blown against it need only pass the pertinent information about itself on to the FBI voluntarily, claiming that it affects infrastructure vulnerability, and it will automatically become secret, immune to Freedom of Information requests by inquiring reporters. Such a cover-up could have an impact on the environment, the economy, public health and safety, and the public's right to be informed, but the Homeland Security Act would make it a crime to tip off a reporter.

On the other hand, the information the government *does* put out may become increasingly suspect if Defense Secretary Donald Rumsfeld's announcement of the formation of the Office of Strategic Influence (OSI) is any indication of what's to come. The business of the OSI, Rumsfeld said in February 2002 when he announced its formation, would be to influence public opinion by planting disinformation in domestic and foreign media, thereby using the press as dupes. The public outcry was so great that the very next day Rumsfeld said the OSI would *not* put out false information, and a week later he announced he was closing the short-lived OSI altogether. But nine months after *that*, feeling his oats at a press conference, Rumsfeld boasted to reporters that although he had been forced to close the Pentagon's OSI, he had not abandoned its mission. "And then there was the Office of Strategic Influence," he said. "You may recall that. And 'oh my goodness gracious, isn't that terrible, Henny Penny, the sky is going to fall.' I went down that next day and said fine, if you want to savage this thing, fine, I'll give you the corpse. There's the name. You can have the name, but I'm gonna keep doing every single thing that needs to be done, and I have." At the same time Rumsfeld made this remark, reports in the press indicated that he intended to make information warfare a major Pentagon strategy.

One saving grace in all the legislation following 9/11 is the repeated proviso in the Patriot Act that surveillance in any of its forms will be permitted only if "such investigation of a United States person is not conducted solely upon the basis of activities protected by the First Amendment to the Constitution." In other words, writing or speaking unpopular sentiments or criticizing the government is not yet considered sufficient reason to spy on American citizens.

But there is still cause for concern. Every year, the First Amendment Center, together with the *American Journalism Review*, conducts a survey to gauge how Americans view the free-speech protections of the First Amendment. A year before 9/11, 22 percent said they thought the First Amendment went too far in the rights it guarantees. By 2002, after 9/11, that percentage had more than doubled—to 49 percent. As for how the public views the press in its coverage of the war on terrorism, 49 percent do *not* think the American press has been too aggressive in asking government officials for information. But almost as many, 48 percent, think it has. If this trend continues, then the result will be an uninformed public, shorn of its privacy and right of free expression—a democracy's nightmare and a terrorist's dream.

—John Berendt

BEST AMERICAN
CRIME WRITING
2003

BIG SHOT

PETER RICHMOND

He steers the van over the rolling folds of country Route 579, a two-lane road flanked by fields once neatly tilled and sown, now increasingly given over to development. But the landscape still carries the flavor of open country in the deep dead of night. His headlights find the sign for Woolf Road, and he turns down a curving, narrow lane; here the trees lean in close on both sides. A half mile later, he takes another left and creeps down a blind driveway, curling right, until his beams alight on an incongruous sight in the wooded blackness: two ornate white gates. Sculpted lions perch atop the columns that anchor them. The letter *J* is patterned into the gate on the left, a W into the other. Between the gates stands a brick wall. Set into the brick is a plaque. From a distance, it looks like a Hall of Fame plaque, Cooperstown bronze, but this plaque is slightly different. It depicts a man's head and shrugging shoulders, his hands held out, palms up, as if to say, Who knew? And these are the very words printed below: WHO KNEW? ESTATES.

The gate on the right swings open, and Gus Christofi steers the van past the expressionless gaze of the lions, down another driveway, and slows at the house, 31,000 square feet of star shrine, the centerpiece of a sprawling fiefdom that shoves the Jersey woods aside. It is a building quite unlike anything Gus has ever seen.

Who knew, indeed? That he'd ever arrive at such a place? That a man who'd busted into other people's homes in search of things to fence would ever see such a door as this, unlocked, welcoming him in? That a man who had shuttled for so many years from jail cell to jail cell would one day come face-to-face with such an ornate and pearly gate?

Then again, who knew how false the facade would turn out to be? How slick an Oz-land stage set could look? As Gus strolls toward Jayson Williams's front door, he doesn't see it, not for what it really is: a gateway back into a world he's spent seven years desperately trying to escape.

The funny thing, the surprising thing, is how much they have in common, at least at first glance. Jayson hails from the Lower East Side of Manhattan—a cocky kid who hung with "a bunch of Italian tough guys," who did jail time as a teen for hitting a cop, who muddied his life with alcohol. Gus was raised across the Hudson River on the dark streets of Paterson, New Jersey. He dropped out of school after sixth grade, ran with a bad crowd, spiraled into addiction by the age of 16.

Both had reclaimed their lives. Both had realized their promise. And now both had moved on to a most unfamiliar landscape—the woods and horse fields of northwestern New Jersey—Gus, at 55, seeking a clean and sober place, Jayson, at 33, in search of a clean escape.

When you think of all the ways their paths could have crossed, it's remarkable that they were as yet unacquainted. They easily could have met on the back roads of Hunterdon County—Gus driving his limo, Jayson piloting his new motorcycle, the one with the absurdly large engine. They might have met in a sports bar when their drinking days had overlapped. Or on the set of the United Way commercial that featured Gus telling the tale of his recovery, filmed on the leafy grounds of his rehab center.

And yet, given how much Gus loved his work and given how much Jayson loved a good time, it only stood to reason that they'd meet this way. On this night. When Gus was on the job. And Jayson was throwing a party.

It's Jayson's brother who makes the call to the dispatcher at Seventy Eight Limousine on the evening of February 13: He hires a car to pick up several people just over the Pennsylvania state line in Bethlehem, where the Harlem Globetrotters are playing a charity game at Lehigh University. Jayson will be at the game with some friends. He has invited the Globetrotters to join him for dinner. They'll need a limo ride to the restaurant.

A few minutes later, Gus returns to the office. His workday has officially ended, but he leaps at the Williams job when the dispatcher offers it. Gus is a serious sports fan, and Gus is a workaholic, and Gus deserves to catch a break. He'll reel in a considerable tip on top of $65 per hour. He'll get to meet the local All-Star.

Sam Nenna, the owner of Seventy Eight Limousine, clears Gus's schedule for the next day. Nenna figures this will be a long night. Jayson has used the services of Seventy Eight Limousine before, for trips to the casinos in Atlantic City. No telling when Gus's evening will end. It doesn't begin until 10:30, when he steers the company's silver van to the Comfort Suites in Bethlehem to collect four Globetrotters: two former Nets, Benoit Benjamin and Chris Morris, and two men Jayson has never met, Curley Johnson and Paul Gaffney.

Jayson will drive his own car. In all, there will be thirteen for dinner, and on this night they'll be treated to first class. The best food. The best company. Jayson's old friends Benjamin and Morris will meet his new ones, Kent Culuko, 29, a former Jersey prep star, and John Gordnick, 44, a middle school basketball coach. The star of the evening, of course, will be Jayson. Center stage is a place in which he has long been comfortable. In his prime, he was a force on the court; off it he took to the limelight with ease, feeding a public ever hungry for over-the-top behavior. His best-selling memoir, *Loose Balls*, paints a portrait of a man who has spent his entire life gleefully Bigfooting all convention, demanding respect at every turn, dispensing frontier justice to anyone foolish enough to defy him, desperate to prove his manhood by whatever display necessary.

Two years ago, a series of playing injuries pulled him off the hardwood stage. Since then he's had little trouble finding other outlets for his act: MTV. The game-day studio at NBC. The taverns in and around his new neighborhood. Even the sprawling grounds of Jayson's estate are not vast enough to rein him in.

A man spends more than half his life imprisoned by addiction, supporting his own demands in the company of no one but himself—well, when he's freed from those bonds it stands to reason he would want to make amends. And so Gus Christofi has decided to dedicate his life—as sappy as it sounds—to helping others. He makes up for the years in solitude by embracing everyone around him. The photographs are legion: Gus, the stout figure with the fold-lined face of a bulldog who has long given up the fight, his arm draped around this guy, that guy, a buddy's kid; he's like Zelig—someone takes a picture, Gus is in it. He is driven, it seems, to weave himself into the fabric of society. Determined to make things easier for the retired pharmaceutical executive who insists on Gus as his driver and for the homeless guy on the streets of Manhattan, hitting up good-hearted Gus with a goofy scam. Gus can't pass a stranded motorist, even on a busy interstate, without tapping the brakes, whether it's a day laborer in a broken-down beater or a state senator on his knees, struggling to fix a flat.

Gus's fares will testify to the depths of his new soul. Along with the recovering addicts he counsels at Freedom House, they provide the simple joys in a life now measured in small blessings. He smothers them with attention: bags of their favorite candy stowed in the trunk, jokes, card tricks he learned in jail. If he drives someone to the medical center to visit a sick relative, a card arrives in the fare's mail a few days later. From Gus. Hoping everything turned out for the best.

He doesn't do it for profit. He does it because he likes people. And people invariably like him. By the time he has chauffeured the Globetrotters to the Mountain View Chalet in Asbury, they are so charmed that one invites him in.

The Mountain View rings high-class for a restaurant hard by the asphalt of I-78. Behind the Mountain View's doors, diners enjoy an evening of rural upscale: $20 entrées. Haute cuisine sauces. Etched-glass partitions.

During the next few hours, according to one source, the Williams party will run up a tab of $1,800. Gus sits to one side, drinking coffee. According to one account of the evening, though, he is not entirely excluded from the revelry, for at one point Jayson says something to Gus, something sealed away in court files, an offhand remark with a nasty overtone.

Gus lets it wash over him. He does not have a violent streak. Even as a kid, he shied away from fights. Maybe in the young and troubled Jayson he sees something of his former self as well.

The barb does not surprise anyone who knows Jayson, knows of his hair-trigger temper, the trip wire tied to the volatile influence of alcohol. The catalog of Jayson's early-career explosions is substantial: a 4:00 A.M. street fight after a play-off game; two men maced, another one beaten outside the bar Jayson had bought in Manhattan; a busted head in Chicago; a tag-team melee with Charles Barkley. "Part-time player, full-time party animal" is how Rick Barry put it once to an acquaintance, who passed his words on to Jayson, who promptly took it out on Barry's son. Roughed the kid up for four full quarters. Knocked him down. Cross-wired justice, the Jayson Williams way.

These days in Hunterdon County, just about anyone you meet will furnish a tale about Jayson's antics, though none are as outlandish as the anecdotes in *Loose Balls*. The story about the kid Jayson knocked out, then tried to shove from a fourth-story window in high school. The one about his father planting a bullet in the posterior of a boy who had given his son trouble—the father whose license-plate holder carried the legend .45 MAGNUM, reflecting the caliber of the weapon he routinely carried. Those of us searching for clues to Jayson's behavior need only look at the picture his memoir sketches of his childhood years in New York and South Carolina: The day one brother shot another. The day his mother shot at his father after she'd been told he was cheating on her. The day his half sister was brutally attacked. The day she learned the hospital blood transfusion had given her HIV. The day she passed it on to another sister through a shared needle. Both sisters died. Jayson was only a rookie when he adopted a son and a daughter left behind by his sisters. As Jayson tells it, after the man who'd beaten his sister was released from prison, Jayson hunted him down. Wanted to kill him. But let him go.

Some of the stories in the book reek of hyperbole. On this night, though, there's a very real court appearance awaiting Jayson, the result of an incident three months ago at a suburban tavern favored by softball teams, local professionals, bikers, and laborers. A clean, well-lit venue offering a glut of TVs and every Irish beer on the market. Cryan's is a lousy place for an angry soul to find himself late on a Wednesday night. A man who saw Jayson at the bar recalls, "He was pretty tuned up. He'd had a few." Some kids started taunting the washed-up All-Star, says the witness, and Jayson took the bait. He lunged. Got himself into a scuffle. Ended up in cuffs. The Branchburg Police Department charged him with obstructing its investigation by twice shoving a policeman.

The incident did not appear to trouble Jayson's employer, NBC, which, in the fashion of so many of his employers through the years, felt no need to put undue emphasis on his transgressions. If this is the history of a man constantly flirting with disaster, cry-

ing out for help, it is also the story of a man favored by constant forgiveness.

One of the reasons he built his own well-appointed theme park,
said an allegedly older and wiser Jayson in his memoir, was his
desire to protect the outside world when he felt the need to go a little crazy. And so on this evening, when dinner at the Mountain
View ends, close to 2:00 A.M., Jayson decides to move the party to
his place. The Globetrotters beg off. But Jayson insists. He will
drive them himself. Gus will transport the others in his van. For
what good is a trophy house when there's no one there to see it?

The hallways run for half a football field. The walls harbor a basketball court, a theater, a billiards room, and an indoor pool. A col-
umned balcony overlooks the outdoor pool, two par-3 golf holes,
and a sweeping vista of landscaped real estate. Tucked away on the
130-acre grounds are a duck pond, riding stables, an ATV track,
and a pasture with a gated entrance, also decorated with the initials
JW, for his prize cattle, which graze in its shade.

When Gus's van reaches the end of the driveway, it's Jayson's
friend Kent Culuko who invites Gus into the house. Gus grabs his
camera. For a man whose home is a small apartment shared with
a fellow recovering addict, the sheer size of the place is incomprehensible. It almost feels cold. But the grand scale is also revealing, a physical manifestation of the owner's need to appear larger
than life.

The truth is, Gus's apartment is a whole lot more comfy. It's on
the ground floor of an anonymous two-unit home eighteen miles
north, in a dull western New Jersey town bruised by the passage of
time. The furnishings in Gus's place pale compared to the expensive appointments in Jayson's place, but they reflect the soul of the
man. The mirror, for instance, that Gus salvaged from a Dumpster.
It took him months to restore. He placed his picture on it, then

wrote a poem, "The Man in the Mirror," because he too had been reclaimed, through the efforts of an army of folk: the counselors at Freedom House, his probation officer, his best friend, Joe Armstrong—all had helped salvage and polish the person you see today.

Joe lives on the second floor. He volunteers as a counselor at Freedom House, too. Together he and Gus received the rehab center's achievement award in 1999. Joe used to give Gus grief about the mirror. Spare me the sentimental stuff, he would tell Gus. Gus would call Joe a cynic. Joe would call Gus a sap. So when Gus wanted to play for Joe the audiotape he'd made on Christmas morning 1999, Joe said no. No sentimental shit. But Gus made him listen to it anyway. Something had come over him, a moment of clarity, and Gus had to get it on the record. He spoke from the heart while sitting at the kitchen table, with a gospel version of "Silent Night" in the background as a syrupy sound track.

"Almost five years ago, around this time, I was released from Middlesex County Jail," Gus says. There's some gravel to his disembodied voice. Some world-weariness, too, but it's not confessional. It is a matter-of-fact recitation.

"I weighed about 170 pounds and had about half a garbage bag of clothes. I wanted to change the way I had lived for the past forty years. I was 47 years old, no direction, no clue how to live a sober, meaningful life. No true friends to speak of. I was lost, alone, and scared I was going to die.

"I used to think about all the things other people had," says the voice on the tape. "But now I choose to speak of the things for which I am grateful." And one by one, he lists them: his sobriety. His God. His job. The family members who are back in his life. His friends.

"There are too many things to list," says the voice. "It would take ten sheets of paper."

If he'd made that tape today, Gus may have added one more

thing: the credit card he had finally obtained. The first he ever owned. It was one of the proudest moments of his life, proof of his new standing in society.

Jayson had had something of an epiphany himself a few years earlier, after another NBA star and St. John's alumnus, Chris Mullin, explained the economics of sobriety. Mullin told Jayson he had decided to give up drinking. If I stick with alcohol, he said, I'll end up back on the streets with nothing to show for my work. If I sober up, it'll translate into nearly $30 million over ten years. With a return like that, why not put the high life on hold for at least a decade?

These figures, this logic, they intrigued Jayson, a man forever obsessed with money. How much he had. How much others had. So he cut back on the party scene. Even suggested inserting a no-alcohol clause into his 1996 contract. No more public scandals. No more tipsy brawls.

Smarter, soberer, more mature, Jayson became a near-great player, the best rebounder in the NBA. He was selected to the Eastern Conference All-Star team. The year his Nets made the play-offs, this was when all the promise was finally fulfilled. The Nets rewarded Jayson with an astounding $86 million contract, which spawned an estate measured by equally astounding numbers: more than $100,000 a year in property taxes. Proof that a former outlaw can be made clean and shiny and new.

As the guided tour of Who Knew? stretches into the early-morning hours, Jayson's blood alcohol level, according to a source close to the investigation, is conservatively estimated at .19. He is animated. Witnesses say that at one point he bares his torso to show off how buff he is; at another, for the second time that evening, he addresses Gus. Puts him down. Half good-naturedly.

Why Gus? Maybe because he's neither a player nor a groupie.

Maybe because he's the clear-cut comic foil in this late-night tableau, which is by now replete with all the makings of a Jayson Williams theatrical performance: alcohol, money, attitude. The only thing missing is a gun—the most obvious manifestation of a man's need to prove his manhood.

Tales of athletes and firearms are hardly unusual in this day and time, but there's nothing routine about Jayson's love of guns, not if one anecdote in his book is grounded in any semblance of truth. The scene was an after-hours gathering at Manute Bol's home. Jayson and his buddy Franco were drinking with Bol and his uncle from the Sudan. Fueled by a couple of Heinekens, Bol's uncle started giving Jayson a hard time. "You the one they call Mr. Capone? You not so tough." When Bol's uncle donned a necklace of crow feet, rooster feet, and turtle heads to prove that Jayson's tough-guy act was no match for his charms, they all had a good laugh. But Bol's uncle kept pushing. It was around 3:00 A.M. when Jayson fetched a pistol from his BMW, pointed it at Bol's uncle, and scared the man half to death.

These days Jayson's tastes run toward shotguns. He shoots skeet, as if he has tamed his family's legacy of Wild West shoot-outs. Turned his frontier sensibility into a rich man's game. Truth be told, though, he nearly blew New York Jets receiver Wayne Chrebet's head off by accident once, not the kind of gunmanship a hunt club looks for in a man.

In fact, it's remarkable that Jayson is permitted to own guns, considering the night in 1994 when he was charged with reckless endangerment and unlawful possession of a weapon in the parking lot outside the Nets' arena. Prosecutor John Fahy claims Jayson fired a SIG Sauer .40-caliber automatic pistol over the heads of teammates. Jayson says he never fired the gun. No one was hurt. Over Fahy's vigorous objections, the judge dropped the charges after Jayson agreed to enter a pretrial program and to spend a year lecturing children about the dangers of guns. As part of his rehabilitation, he purchased newspaper ads in the *Bergen Record*. "Shoot for the top. Shoot for your future. Shoot Baskets, not Guns."

The rack on the wall in Jayson's enormous bedroom holds several shotguns. It is one of the first things Gus sees when he enters the room between 2:30 and 3:00 A.M. along with Jayson and three Globetrotters. Gus does not have to know that some of the guns are loaded to feel uneasy; he hates all guns. He has hated them since his father tried to teach him to hunt as a child. Back then Gus would not touch his father's shotgun. Even the replica pistols his friend Joe used to collect gave him the creeps.

According to witness accounts, evidence at the scene, and sources close to the investigation, this is what happens next: With Culuko in the doorway behind him, Williams opens the glass case—which is unlocked—and takes out a twelve-gauge double-barreled Browning shotgun. He cracks the gun open, lowers the barrel, and peers inside. Turning toward Gus, who stands three feet away, he flicks the gun shut with a snap of his wrist. The moment the barrel clicks into place, the shotgun discharges. All twelve pellets enter the left side of Gus's chest. They open a hole large enough to swallow a silver dollar. Gus Christofi falls, coming to rest on the floor on his left side. The life bleeds out of him, a good life, fifty-five years in the making and a few minutes in the ending.

It is not likely that he is conscious after the pellets tear into his chest. It is not likely he is able to reflect on the profound and futile and sorry unfairness of it all: that seven years spent fleeing his previous life led him back to a world worse than any he'd left. That there are some sins for which you never stop paying.

According to witness accounts, the blast awakens Jayson's half brother, who rushes in from a distant bedroom. John Gordnick comes from the downstairs gym, where he was playing ball with his two young sons. Williams and Culuko confer. Culuko instructs the witnesses to tell the police it was a suicide. Jayson wipes down the gun. And then he takes the hand of Gus's dead body, still warm, and tries to imprint Gus's fingerprints on the stock.

Jayson takes off his clothes and tosses them to Gordnick to dispose of before the police arrive. He goes downstairs and dives into the pool to wash himself clean, wipe away any trace of what he has done, and when his body emerges, six feet ten inches of finely tuned athlete, it glistens, free of all sin—renewed, restored, absolved. He drapes it in a fresh set of clothes and awaits the arrival of the authorities. He will plead innocent to seven charges, including aggravated manslaughter, a crime that carries a penalty of ten to thirty years in prison.

On February 20, Gus Christofi's body is lowered into the ground, accompanied by Joe Armstrong's seven-year-sobriety medallion. Gus himself didn't make it to seven. But perhaps in death he will right one more life, the life of Jayson Williams, as Jayson sits and ponders his misdeeds, maybe in a jail cell, a cell Gus used to call home. Who knew?

———

Jayson Williams's book wasn't your average athlete's bio. Jayson Williams's book boasted of the usual—his tough-childhood-to-rural-estate rise through the ranks; his basketball skills; his predictably defiant attitude. But it also boasted of some very odd stuff. Like his swaggery abuse of alcohol. Like the night he pointed a pistol at a teammate's uncle. The night he inadvertently discharged a shotgun so close to another athlete's head that the other guy was knocked unconscious. Jayson Williams was always a popular guy as a player. No surprise his book became a best-seller. Some must have loved it for its comic content. Me, I found it fascinating as a grim, dead-serious cry for help. For someone to save him from himself. But there must have been a lot of people who hadn't read it, judging from the widespread response in the days after a limo driver was shot dead in Jayson's bedroom after a night of revelry. Jayson? Jayson the doer of good works? Kind-hearted and funny as hell? Jayson couldn't have blown the guy away. Jayson the national TV commentator? Former All-Star? But he had: with one of the shotguns he kept loaded in an unlocked case on his bedroom wall. After a night of drinking.

To lifetime chroniclers of modern professional sport, there was nothing unusual about the story of Jayson Williams and the night he pointed his shotgun at and took the life of Costas "Gus" Christofi. Like so many before him, vaulted to a place in society for which he was entirely unprepared, Jayson Williams was unable to make a seamless transition when injuries cut a spectacular career short, and his other passions took over. For firearms. For drinking. For boasting. What was unusual was the nature of the victim. Gus Christofi, former addict, former thief, former all-time loser, had done something astounding: He had entirely turned his life around. Sober for years, he was a model counselor at his rehab clinic. The favorite driver of just about every client of the limo company that employed him. Huge sports fan. And gentle? He always walked away from a fight, even as a kid on the mean streets of Paterson. And he had a deathly, lifelong fear of guns.

The night of his death, he'd volunteered for the job. Because he loved sports and admired athletes. Because he'd get to meet Jayson Williams. And he did. Very briefly—but long enough to see how wrong he'd been about thinking that stardom could make a man something special. As Gus bled out his life through his chest on Jayson's bedroom floor, did he understand the larger message? That as we celebrate our athletes unto godhood, we are also stunting them? No. Gus undoubtedly forgave Jayson with all of his heart, or what was left of it. He left it to the rest of us to take a larger lesson from his

death: that until we start paying as much attention to our superstars'
psychological frailties as we do to their physical triumphs, there will
be more victims. For Jayson Williams was a train wreck coming from
a long, long way off. Anyone could have seen it coming. If they'd
wanted to.

In February of this year, Williams and the family of Christofi settled a civil lawsuit filed by the family in October of 2002. Terms were
not disclosed.

The criminal trial was scheduled to start in February, one year
after the shooting. But it was postponed when Williams' attorneys
appealed the original indictment, arguing that the original indictment was flawed: The prosecutor's presentation to the grand jury,
they said, had been misleading.

But before a state appellate court could hear arguments on that
appeal, the prosecutors trumped the defendants' counsel, obtaining a
second indictment from a different grand jury—a stronger one,
which carries a maximum term of 55 years, instead of the original 45,
because of an added weapons charge.

A new trial date has not been set.

THE DAY TREVA THRONEBERRY DISAPPEARED

SKIP HOLLANDSWORTH

ELECTRA, TEXAS—1985

She was a pretty girl, thin, with a spray of pale freckles across her face and light brown hair that curled just above her shoulders. The librarian at the high school called her "a quiet-type person," the kind of student who yes-ma'amed and no-ma'amed her teachers. She played on the tennis team, practicing with an old wooden racket on a crack-lined court behind the school. In the afternoons she waitressed at the Whistle Stop, the local drive-in hamburger restaurant, jumping up on the running boards of the pickup trucks so she could hear better when the drivers placed their orders.

Her name was Treva Throneberry, and just about everybody in that two-stoplight North Texas oil town knew her by sight. She was never unhappy, people said. She never complained. She always greeted her customers with a shy smile, even when she had to walk out to their cars on winter days when the northers came whipping off the plains, swirling ribbons of dust down the street. During her breaks, she'd sit at a back table and read from her red Bible that zipped open and shut.

There were times, the townspeople would later say, when they did wonder about the girl. No one had actually seen her do anything that could be defined, really, as crazy. But people noticed that she would occasionally get a vacant look in her blue eyes. One day at school she drew a picture of a young girl standing under a leafless tree, her face blue, the sun black. One Sunday at the Pentecostal church she stumbled to the front altar, fell to her knees, and began telling Jesus that she didn't deserve to live. And then there was that day when Treva's young niece J'Lisha, who was staying at the Throneberry home, told people that Treva had shaken her awake the previous night and whispered that a man was outside their room with a gun—which turned out to be not true at all.

But surely, everyone in town said, all teenage girls go through phases. They get overly emotional every now and then. Treva was going to turn out just fine. She didn't even drink or smoke cigarettes like some of the other girls in town.

Then, that December, just as the Electra High School Tigers were headed toward their first state football championship and the town was feeling a rare surge of pride, Treva, who was sixteen years old, stopped working at the Whistle Stop. She stopped coming to school. "She disappeared," a former classmate said. "And nobody knew where she went."

VANCOUVER, WASHINGTON—1997

The new girl arrived at Evergreen High School wearing loose bib overalls, a T-shirt, and tennis shoes, and her hair was braided in pigtails. She was fuller-figured than most teenage girls, wide-hipped, but she had an appealing, slightly lopsided smile and a childlike voice tinged with a southern drawl. She was carrying a graphite tennis racket and a Bible.

Her name, she told school officials, was Brianna Stewart. She was 16 years old, she said, and for almost a year she had been living in Portland, Oregon, just across the Columbia River from Vancouver, walking the streets during the day and sleeping in grim youth shelters at night. She started attending services at Vancouver's charismatic Glad Tidings Church, where she met a young couple who took her into their home after hearing her testimony. The couple, who had accompanied Brianna to school that morning, said that she was full of potential, determined to succeed—and that all she needed was a chance to get over her past.

"What is your past?" asked one of the school's counselors, Greg Merrill.

For a moment Brianna said nothing, as if she was trying to maintain her composure. Then she told Merrill that she had been raised just outside Mobile, Alabama, by her mother and her Navajo stepfather, a sheriff's deputy. Brianna said that when she was a child, her mother had been murdered, and after that she lived with her stepfather. At about the age of 13, she ran away, hitchhiking from state to state. Because Brianna remembered her mother telling her that her real father lived somewhere in the Northwest, she had come to the area hoping that she could find clues to her past.

It was the most unusual case Merrill had ever heard in his thirty years of counseling students. When he asked about her education, she told him she had only been homeschooled, but she promised she would be a good student. "I've never had a normal life," she said. "That's all I want—to be a normal teenager like everyone else."

She was enrolled in the tenth grade at the 1,900-student school. One of her first classes was Algebra I. She walked in and was given a seat toward the back, where she pulled out a notebook and began listening intently to the teacher. Then she glanced over at the boy sitting next to her.

"Hi," said Ken Dunn, who couldn't stop smiling at her.

She giggled shyly. "Hi," she said. "I'm Brianna. I'm new here."

ELECTRA, TEXAS—1985

It didn't take long for the rumor to spread through town that Treva Throneberry had last been seen down at the police station, where she had given a statement claiming that her daddy, holding a gun in his hand, had raped her. She added that her mother had only laughed when she found out what had happened.

A stunned police officer called child welfare, which quickly sent a social worker to Electra to whisk Treva away, and a judge entered emergency protection orders temporarily preventing Treva's parents from seeing their daughter or even finding out where she was. Soon, Electra was buzzing: Was it possible that Carl Throneberry had raped his own daughter?

Carl and his wife, Patsy, were known as good country people. They lived in a small frame home decorated with a photo of John Wayne on one wall and a rug that depicted the Last Supper on another. Carl was a big, lumbering man, a truck driver in the oil fields. He had met Patsy in the early fifties at a soda fountain in Oklahoma, and after a few weeks of courting, they had driven to the A&P supermarket in Wichita Falls, where the butcher, who was also a preacher, had wiped his hands on his apron, pulled out a small pocket Bible, and performed their wedding ceremony out in the A&P parking lot while the couple sat holding hands in the back seat of Carl's Chevy.

Yes, Carl admitted, he sometimes had trouble making ends meet, but he had always made sure his children—one son and four daughters, of whom Treva was the youngest—were well fed and dressed properly for school. In fact, Carl said, his older brother Billy Ray often dropped by to give the four Throneberry girls presents. After the older girls had left home, Billy Ray especially doted on Treva, bringing her candy bars, buying her clothes from the dollar store, and taking her on drives in his car.

In court Carl and Patsy insisted that Treva had made up the entire story, and their attorney went so far as to demand that Treva be given a lie detector test. Treva's sisters also gave affidavits saying they too believed that their father was innocent.

If anyone had raped Treva, Carl told police officers and social workers, it was one of those fanatical members of Electra's Pentecostal church. He knew for a fact, he said, that they had been trying to brainwash her into becoming a missionary. The church members, in turn, said they had only been trying to help a young girl who was obviously in great distress. They said that in the weeks leading up to her rape allegation, Treva had been telling them that she was scared of being at her home and that she had been slipping out at night to sleep in an abandoned house next door or even on a pew at the church itself. What was also perplexing to social workers was Treva's behavior at the foster home in Wichita Falls where she had been taken. Her foster mother, Sharon Gentry, a middle school science teacher, said that she would often find Treva at night curled in a fetal position in the corner of her bedroom, the bedcovers pulled over her head. On other nights Gentry would find her banging her head against the wall, murmuring in her sleep, "Please don't hurt me. I'll be a good girl."

Like so many who had known Treva, Gentry was touched by the girl's gentleness. Around the house, she was soft-spoken and exceedingly polite. She began attending Wichita Falls High School, where she developed a reputation as a diligent, thoughtful student. She regularly read her Bible, and she wrote soulful teenage poetry in her notebook. One poem began:

Raining tears, flowing down my face
Yours forever, a lost case
No one cares or sees you fall
No one hears you when you call.

As the weeks passed, however, Treva started to leave disturbing handwritten notes on the ironing board for Gentry. "Sometimes I wish I were dead," she wrote in one note. "Sometimes I don't. Life seems impossible and death seems eternal. I will have no life after death." She came out of her bedroom one morning and told Gentry that she had been dreaming about shooting herself. In the dream, she said, she could see the bullet entering her head. She later told her a story about how she had been kidnapped in Electra and taken blindfolded by members of a satanic cult to an abandoned oil field, where she was tied to a stake. People in black robes danced around her, she said, then slit the throats of black cats and dogs and forced her to drink their blood.

In May 1986 Treva went to see her counselor at Wichita Falls High School and said in an eerily calm voice that she was thinking about jumping off the third floor of the building to kill herself. Police officers sped to the school, handcuffed Treva, and drove her to the old redbrick Wichita Falls State Hospital at the edge of the city. There she spent long periods of time by herself, sitting in the dayroom of the adolescent unit, looking out through large windows on the neatly mowed lawns. According to hospital reports, she was often seen crying. She rarely ate. Her face was blank, her cheeks sunken, her hair flat. Doctors and therapists arrived to give her various tests, including the Woodcock-Johnson Psychoeducational Battery. They sat beside her and asked if she felt detached, if she felt hostile, if she felt withdrawn, if she felt lonely. They prescribed Xanax, for anxiety, and Trilafon, which was designed to combat what they called thought disorders, and Tofranil, an antidepressant. They put her in a weekly group therapy session, where she and other adolescents sat in a circle on vinyl-covered chairs.

But she said little. She did write a few sad letters to Gentry and a boy from Wichita Falls High School who had once taken her on a date to Six Flags Over Texas. "I feel like a living robot," she wrote to him. "I walk when they say walk. I sit when they say sit. I do everything they say because I have to. I can't take it anymore. I have to die."

Needing to put something in their reports, the baffled doctors described Treva's condition as a "characterological disorder." "She's kind of quiet and secretive and she may have a personality problem," wrote one therapist. Perhaps to get a better clue of what had happened to her, staffers finally arranged for her to meet with her parents, who had been coming to the hospital demanding to see her. (The district attorney's office ultimately dismissed the sexual assault charges against Carl, saying there was no evidence to prosecute.) Treva sat with Carl and Patsy in the presence of a social worker and a therapist as her parents told her to admit that she had been lying about the rape. Treva rose and said that they were the ones who were the liars, that they didn't love her, and then she announced that she had nothing more to say and that she wished to return to her room.

VANCOUVER, WASHINGTON—1997

Brianna Stewart seemed so grateful just to have the chance to be at Evergreen High. Each morning, she rode a city bus to the school, her backpack crammed with her textbooks and her Bible. Like a lot of students she had trouble with algebra, but she shone in English. She was able to quote entire passages of *Macbeth* from memory, the Shakespeare play the sophomore class was required to read, and for extra credit she wrote poems and stories, including one about a little girl who had only imaginary friends as playmates.

Almost every day she came to school in the same outfit—overalls, a T-shirt, and tennis shoes—and she wore pigtails, a serious teenage fashion faux pas. One afternoon a classmate named Cheyanne McKay asked Brianna if she would like to go to the mall with a group of other girls. On the way there Cheyanne cranked up the stereo, and she and a couple of other girls in the car started dancing. When Brianna tried to dance along, she moved in jerky, arrhythmic ways, as if she had never danced to that kind of music in her life.

To most of the Evergreen kids, Brianna was the classic teenage wallflower. But for Ken Dunn, an amiable sandy-haired sophomore, Brianna was unlike any other girl he had ever known. "I like the way she walks, and I really like the way she talks," he told his friends, referring to her southern accent. In algebra he began imitating the way she wrote sevens on her homework, adding a short horizontal line through the middle of the number. He escorted her from class to class, and he smiled encouragingly at her during tennis practice, despite the fact that she was easily the worst player on the girls' team. He spent much of his time helping her work on her lines for her drama class. Brianna was a hopelessly awkward actress, yet she still tried out for all the school plays. Perhaps out of pity, the drama teacher put her in the chorus of the school's production of *Man of La Mancha*, where she moved leadenly across the stage, smiling bravely, making stilted gestures, and nearly colliding with the other performers.

Soon, Ken and Brianna were swapping flirtatious notes. ("Hi!" Brianna wrote. "What's up? I know—the great blue sky!!! . . . You're the best guy I've ever known as a friend. You're more than that to me . . . Class of 2000 rules!") In his 1978 brown El Camino, known around school as the Turd Tank, Ken began taking Brianna on little dates—to the bargain stores in downtown Vancouver, to the roller rink, and to the mall, where they sat in the food court and talked. He attended services with her at the Glad Tidings Church and went with her to the Thursday-night youth group meetings, where she often gave her testimony. He was amazed at the amount of Scripture Brianna knew. He told his parents that she must have studied the Bible for years—for years!

Initially, Brianna told Ken only a few details about her past. But sitting at the food court one day, Brianna took a deep breath and told Ken stories she said she hadn't told anyone. She said she had watched her stepfather stab her mother to death and carry the body away. He then made tapes of himself and his friends raping her, which he sold on the black market. When she became pregnant at the age of 11 or 12, he pushed her down a flight of stairs to force her to miscarry. She went to the police station to turn him in, but no one would believe her. They called her stepfather to come pick her up, which is why she knew she had to flee.

And there was one more thing, Brianna said, her voice softer than ever. Earlier that summer, just before coming to Evergreen, she had gotten to know a security guard who worked in downtown Vancouver. One day while the two of them were sitting in his car, she said, he pulled down his pants, then pulled down her pants, and forced her to have intercourse. "He raped me. He raped me. He raped me," she repeated over and over, tears streaming down her face. "I wanted to kill myself. I began to think about standing on an overpass and jumping off."

"Here was this beautiful girl who had been forced to endure unimaginable atrocities," Ken would later say. "And yet here she was at Evergreen, wanting to make something of herself in life. I wanted to help. I wanted to make her happy. I wanted her to know that someone cared for her."

He took her to the school's Sadie Hawkins dance, where they dressed in matching blue overalls and crimson shirts. When the disc jockey played Shania Twain's "You're Still the One," he escorted her onto the dance floor, looked her in the eyes, and said, "I love you."

"I love you, too," Brianna replied.

Ken pushed her hair back and kissed her on the mouth. Then he kissed her again.

"I was sixteen, and she was sixteen," he recalled. "It was the perfect teenage romance. I couldn't imagine that anything could go wrong."

WICHITA FALLS, TEXAS—1986

After Treva had spent five months at the state hospital, the doctors declared that she was no longer suicidal or severely depressed. Her biggest issue, said her adolescent-unit therapist, was that she was "unpredictable." She was discharged in October 1986, yet even then no one was sure what to do with her. Treva begged her social workers not to return her to her parents, which suited Carl and Patsy just fine. They didn't want her home, they said, until she recanted her rape story.

It was finally decided that Treva would be sent to the Lena Pope

Home, the Fort Worth residential treatment center for troubled adolescents. There, counselors came up with a therapeutic plan to improve her skills in "self-confidence" and "to develop and maintain interpersonal relationships." She was enrolled at nearby Arlington Heights High School so that she could finish her senior year.

In June 1987 she wore a beautiful blue graduation gown as she walked across the stage to receive her diploma, smiling politely at the principal. Treva had just turned 18, and by law she could no longer be under juvenile supervision. She was completely on her own. When her counselors at Lena Pope asked what she would do next, she said she planned to apply to a Bible college that didn't require an SAT test. "All I want is to be and to feel normal," she wrote to one of her social workers before she left state care. "I want to live life, but I want it to be normal and most of all, I want to live a normal life."

Treva did return to Electra for a couple of days. Although she refused to go to her parents' home, she visited with her three older sisters—Carlene, Kim, and Sue. "Treva, honey, what you said about Daddy is still breaking his heart," said Carlene. "You need to go apologize."

Treva did not respond. She kept her eyes locked on the floor.

Each of the sisters asked Treva what was bothering her, but the truth was that they didn't really need to be told. They knew why Treva didn't want to return to that house. They knew what she had endured there—because they had endured it themselves. When they were children, they too had lain awake in their own beds at night, praying that he would not come to touch them.

"He" was not their dad. "He" was their father's older brother, Uncle Billy Ray. He was a Vietnam veteran, divorced and a heavy drinker, and he often stayed at the Throneberry home. Sometimes he'd ask one of the girls if she wanted to go with him to the store. "Go on," their dad would say. He adored his older brother. "Let Billy Ray buy you something nice."

According to the statements that Carlene, Kim, and Sue would give years later, long after Billy Ray had died, they didn't just receive cute presents from their uncle. On the nights that he stayed at their home, he'd slip out of his bed and tiptoe to where his nieces were sleeping, moving from one bed to another, running his hands restlessly, endlessly, over their bellies, thighs, and bottoms. He'd put his hands up their shirts to feel their undeveloped breasts, and he'd put them down their panties to feel between their legs. His breathing would get faster and faster. "Keep your mouth shut," he'd say, his breath stinking with liquor. Sometimes he'd grab them for just a few seconds; other times, for minutes. No matter how long it lasted, the girls would shut their eyes, their teeth clenched, and they would make no sound at all—no scream, not even a whimper.

"We didn't know what to do," Carlene recalled. "We were just children—uneducated small-town girls. I know you're not going to understand this, but those times were different. We were too scared to say anything because we thought people would make us feel ashamed and tell us it was our fault. We had tried to let Momma and Daddy know what he was doing—at least we thought we had. But we didn't come out and say anything outright because Billy Ray had told us that if we ever did, he'd have Momma and Daddy killed, and then he'd have us all to himself. What were we supposed to do? We thought, and I know this sounds so terrible, that this was the way things worked, that this was how everyone lived."

As they got older, Carlene, Kim, and Sue still didn't say anything—"We had been trained from an early age not to talk about it, not even to each other," said Sue—but they did everything to keep their distance from Billy Ray. They worked double shifts at their waitressing jobs. Sue ran away once, and when she was caught in the Panhandle town of Childress, she was too scared to tell her parents why she had left. All three of them got married as teenagers so they could live in their own homes.

Which meant that Treva was left alone, the sweetest and the quietest of all the Throneberry girls—and the favorite of Uncle Billy Ray. Each of the older Throneberry girls believe that Billy Ray turned into an even greater predator with Treva. When Sue came back to the house one day, she saw little Treva sitting on Billy Ray's lap. His hips were squirming back and forth, his hand underneath her shirt. Sue froze, torn between the desire to race forward and grab her little sister and the fear she had of her uncle.

When Carlene was 16 and already married, she asked Treva, who was then 10, if she needed any help with Billy Ray. "You know what I mean, don't you?" Carlene asked. But Treva said she liked Billy Ray's presents. "She still didn't understand what was happening to her," Carlene said. "I'll never get over the shame that I didn't do something for her right then." Carlene paused. "I'll never get over that shame."

When Treva reached the age of 16 and accused her father of rape, the sisters assumed that she too had finally reached the point where she had to make her own escape. "She knew child welfare would get her out of there if she accused Daddy," Carlene said. "I think she was just like us, too scared about what people might say or believe if she told the truth."

The sisters also assumed that she would handle the rest of her life the way they had handled theirs—suffering in silence, praying to God that they could get through a day without the memories returning. But as they talked to her, they began to wonder if Treva's escape had come too late. They listened in disbelief as Treva began to tell them stories that seemed, well, crazy. She told Kim the story about being kidnapped by a satanic cult, which forced her to drink blood and participate in infant sacrifices.

"Treva, why are you talking like that?" Kim asked.

But she could not tell if Treva was listening to her. That vacant look had returned to Treva's eyes, as if she were somewhere else entirely.

Soon after her arrival in Electra, Treva left. She never did go to college. She lived briefly in the Fort Worth area with a woman who was raising three children, and then reportedly she went to live at a YWCA. On one occasion Sharon Gentry received a collect phone call from Treva, who said she was working at a run-down motel in Arlington. She called again and said she was living on the streets. And then she disappeared.

"We never really did look too hard for her," said Sue. "It wasn't that we didn't want to see her. We figured that she wanted to get away, to get a new start. At least that's what we hoped she was doing—that she was alive somewhere, doing her best."

VANCOUVER, WASHINGTON—1998

By the fall of 1998, her junior year, Brianna Stewart had become a well-known figure at Evergreen High. Most of the kids had heard the stories of her tormented childhood. They had learned that she had courageously gone to the Vancouver police to file rape charges against the security guard, who had pleaded guilty to "communicating with a minor for immoral purposes." Whenever students would see her in her oversized overalls and her pigtails, they'd say, "Hi, Bri"—she preferred the shortened version of her name, pronounced "Bree"—and she'd shyly smile back and tell them to have a nice day.

Brianna said her goal in life was to become a lawyer, focusing on children's issues. She spent her free time in the library reading books about law or researching elaborate reports she would turn in to her teachers bearing the titles "Society's Missing Youth," "Child Abuse," and "Adjustive Behaviors." For an English class she wrote a poignant short story titled "Betrayed" about a girl named Jessica who has no idea where she came from. In it the police and the FBI conduct a DNA test that proves that Jessica was abducted as a child.

The story was not unlike Brianna's own search for her past. As she told almost anyone who would listen, she desperately needed a Social Security number that identified her as Brianna Stewart. If she could just get one, then she would be able to move on with her life—obtain a driver's license, apply for college, find a job. The problem was that the federal government would not issue her a new Social Security number unless she could track down her birth certificate or find her real father—or at least find some evidence to show that he, and she, existed.

What complicated the search was that Brianna was hazy about many parts of her past. The mental health professionals in Vancouver who had interviewed her believed she suffered from amnesia or some sort of post-traumatic stress syndrome. Brianna, for instance, was not even sure what her real name was. She knew only that when she was a little girl her stepfather had started calling her Brianna, which he had told her meant "Bright Eyes" in Navajo. "I probably wasn't always Brianna Stewart," she told a sympathetic reporter from a weekly Portland newspaper who interviewed her in 1999. "I may not know who I was before I was three." But then she added adamantly, "I do know who I am now."

Numerous people were more than willing to help her. A state social worker conducted exhaustive governmental record searches looking for any evidence of Brianna, her mother, or the man she said was her stepfather. A staffer from Indian Health Services, who had been unable to get Brianna off his mind since meeting her, scoured national databases of missing children and even asked her to give blood in hopes of finding a DNA match. She reportedly asked an FBI agent in Portland to investigate whether she was the victim of an unsolved kidnapping in Salt Lake City and visited a Montana sheriff's office to find out if she was a girl who went missing in 1983.

Everyone came up empty-handed. Undeterred, Brianna took time off from school in January 2000 and rode the bus to Daphne,

Alabama, where she said she had been raised. A police detective from Daphne spent several days driving her around, hoping she would see something that would jog her memory. She saw a swing set at a park that she remembered playing on. She saw a table at a McDonald's where she believed she had once sat. Nevertheless, no one could find any evidence that she had ever lived there.

One possible clue came when she visited a dentist in Portland. The dentist later told a social worker that he was surprised to notice that Brianna's wisdom teeth had been extracted and that the scars had healed—highly unusual for a 16-year-old girl. When the social worker asked Brianna about the dentist's statement, she responded with a blistering five-page, single-spaced letter criticizing those who would doubt her story. "My word means much to me," she wrote, "and when I give my word that I am doing and being as honest and upfront as I can with the information about myself, I mean it."

When Brianna talked to Ken about the dentist's story one afternoon while they cruised around in the Turd Tank, he found himself, to his astonishment, under attack when he asked if there might be anything to what the dentist was saying. "How dare you think that I'm not sixteen?" Brianna said, furious. "How dare you even ask that? How can you even say you love me?"

Ken tried to put the confrontation out of his mind. He knew deep down that she loved him. Just a few weeks earlier she had worn a dress to the homecoming dance that his mother had made using yards of the most expensive gold lamé that she could find at Fabric Depot. To show that he still loved her, he bought her a sterling silver ring for Christmas, the inside of which was engraved with her favorite line from the new *Romeo and Juliet* movie, starring Leonardo DiCaprio: "I love thee."

But at the end of their junior year, something happened that devastated him. By then Brianna was staying with the Gambetta family, whose son was good friends with Ken. (She had told him that she needed a new place to live because the church families could no longer afford to keep her.) The Gambettas had been treating her like a daughter, giving her the spare bedroom, where she could put her tennis posters on the wall, and providing her with an allowance of $10 a week. Everything, in fact, seemed idyllic—until Brianna called the police in May 1999 and said that David Gambetta, the father of the household, had been spying on her. She said he had put miniature cameras in the light fixtures in her room and was making videotapes of her as she undressed.

After a quick investigation the police decided that the accusations were groundless, and the Gambettas ordered Brianna to move out. Yet Brianna, who soon found new lodging with the mother of a police officer, kept insisting she was telling the truth. For the first time, Ken didn't believe what she was saying. In fact, he began thinking back on all the dramatic stories she had told him. "My God," he said to one of his friends, "what if Brianna has been making everything up?"

ELECTRA, TEXAS—1992

As the years passed and nothing more was heard from Treva Throneberry, many people in town assumed she had been killed. Carl and Patsy maintained a $3,000 burial insurance policy on their daughter. In 1993 a rumor swept through Electra that Treva had died in the fire at the Branch Davidian compound near Waco. Sharon Gentry even sent Treva's dental records to the authorities investigating the fire to see if one of the burned bodies might be Treva.

Treva was not there. But in the little town of Corvallis, Oregon, two thousand miles away, there was a teenager named Keili T. Throneberry Smitt working at a McDonald's and staying with a family she had met at a church. She told people she preferred the name Keili Smitt. In fact, she went to court in Corvallis to change her name legally to Keili Smitt because she said she was hiding from her father, who lived in Dallas. She told Corvallis police officers that he had already found her once in Oregon, forced her into his car, and raped her.

But the police could never find Keili's father, and eventually she disappeared. The next summer she surfaced in Portland, telling the police there that she was on the run from her sexually abusive father. This time she said that her father was a Portland police officer. Once again, an investigation was begun, and once again, Keili disappeared.

She reappeared in the summer of 1994 in the town of Coeur d'Alene, Idaho, where she told the police her name was Cara Leanna Davis. She said her mother had been murdered and her father, a police officer, had been a member of a satanic cult and had repeatedly raped her. After two months in Coeur d'Alene, she vanished. Later that year she arrived in Plano, a suburb north of Dallas. She told rapt police officers and social workers that her name was Kara Williams, that she was 16 years old, and that she had been born and raised in a satanic cult, where she had been taught that her destiny was to honor Satan and to die in a lake of fire. She said that many of the children she had grown up with had been sacrificed, stabbed to death with daggers. Her own mother had been murdered by her father, a cult leader who happened to be a police officer in Colleyville, another Dallas suburb. He also raped her repeatedly, she said, and at bedtime would force her to chant prayers to Lucifer.

One female detective was so determined to discover who had harmed Kara that she drove to Colleyville and asked the police chief if he knew of any officer who might have any kind of special interest in the study of satanic activities. A volunteer for a social work agency took it upon herself to show Kara the outside world, taking her to malls and to Six Flags. Social workers shuttled her from various foster homes and youth shelters around the Dallas area, trying to find a place where she would feel safe. At one shelter she accused a young male staffer of sexually molesting her, which led her to be moved again. With each move she was enrolled in a new high school. In the spring of 1995 alone, Kara attended high schools in Sadler, Sherman, and Dallas, joining the tennis team at each new place. The Child Protective Services worker supervising Kara's case, Susanne Arnold, went so far as to buy her a new tennis racket to help her play better.

But in September 1995 Arnold received a call at home from a staffer at the residential treatment center where Kara was staying. The staffer, who just happened to be from the little town of Electra, said, "Susanne, I think Kara is actually a twenty-six-year-old woman named Treva Throneberry."

Days later Kara was confronted at the treatment center with records, photographs, and handwriting samples that proved her identity. Yet she confessed to nothing. Her protests were so adamant, and so tearful, that more than one person watching her came to the conclusion that she truly believed what she was saying. After a court hearing discharged her from government supervision, Arnold handed her a quarter and gave her the phone numbers for the state's mental health office and for a homeless shelter. "Please get some help," Arnold said. But as Kara got on an elevator, she told Arnold one last time that she was not Treva Throneberry, and she disappeared again.

In June 1996 a 16-year-old teenager named Emily Kharra Williams arrived in Asheville, North Carolina, where she told police officers she was on the run from a cult in Texas. In August 1996 a 16-year-old girl named Stephanie Williams came to Altoona, Pennsylvania, where she told the police she was on the run from her father in Memphis, Tennessee, who was involved in a cult and a child pornography ring. A social worker spotted a reference in the girl's notebook to a Susanne Arnold in Texas, and some phone calls and records checks proved that the girl was Treva Throneberry. She was arrested and sent to jail for nine days for providing a false report to law enforcement. At one point an Altoona social worker called Carl and Patsy and asked them to speak to their daughter, to remind her who she was.

"Hi, baby," said Carl. "It's your daddy."

"You sound like an awful nice man, and I wish you were my father, but you're not," Treva replied. "I'm not who you think I am."

"Honey, you'll be Treva Throneberry until the day you die," Patsy said in a wobbly voice. "Now stop playing games."

"Oh, no," she said. "You got me mixed up with someone else. But someday I may just get that way to see you."

And once again, after her release from the Altoona jail, she was on the road, making appearances in Louisiana, New Jersey, and Ohio, where she'd show up at youth shelters carrying some luggage, a teddy bear, a Bible, a flute with sheet music, and algebra homework. She kept reenacting the same scenario, looping back in time. She found her refuge in high school: eating cafeteria food, playing on the tennis team, studying *Macbeth* in English, and memorizing quadratic equations in algebra year after year after year. She kept trying to get back to the one place every teenager wants to leave.

Why? Why had Treva Throneberry used at least eighteen teenage aliases since the early nineties, and why had she spun such gruesomely outlandish tales? Was she nothing more than a con artist, pretending to be a downtrodden teenager to receive free foster care and a free education? Was she afflicted with what doctors call psychiatric Munchausen syndrome, in which she intentionally feigned intense emotional distress to receive extra attention?

Or was she slowly descending into an irreparable insanity, the likes of which no one had ever seen before? Was it indeed possible that by the time she entered Evergreen High School in 1997, she had completely forgotten the girl she had once been in 1985?

VANCOUVER, WASHINGTON—2000

In June 2000 Brianna Stewart wore a beautiful green graduation gown as she walked across the stage to receive her diploma from Evergreen High School, where she earned a 2.33 grade point average. At a graduation party Ken Dunn approached her. Although he and Brianna had broken up after the Gambetta "hidden camera" episode, no one had ever affected him in the way she did. As the head-banger band Burner played in the background, the two talked about her plans to attend a community college in Vancouver. The financial aid office at the college would allow Brianna to enroll with a tuition scholarship despite the fact that she had no Social Security number. Ken, who would leave Vancouver for a job at Disney World that fall, said, "You're going to do great, Brianna, and I mean it."

She spent the summer of 2000 working as a volunteer answering phones for the Ralph Nader presidential campaign, but most of her time was devoted to getting a Social Security number. She wrote a six-page letter to the governor of Washington asking for help. She also enlisted the services of two lawyers—one in Portland and one in Vancouver, neither of whom knew what the other was doing. The attorney in Vancouver sued the state to force the Vital Records Office to issue Brianna a birth certificate. To support the claim, he provided letters from school officials, Brianna's high school transcripts, her state picture identification, and medical statements about her mental health. The attorney in Portland chose to petition the federal government directly, asking it to issue Brianna a Social Security number. Before filing the petition, however, he had asked Brianna to submit to a fingerprint test just to make sure there was no chance she could be someone else.

Weeks later the Vancouver attorney was informed by a state deputy attorney general that the state would not oppose Brianna's petition for a birth certificate. All Brianna would have to do was appear for a simple court hearing set for March 2001. Brianna's three-year fight for an identity was finally over. She was about to officially become known as Brianna Stewart.

But on March 22, a week before the hearing, a Vancouver police detective arrested Brianna on charges of theft and perjury. He told her that she was a 31-year-old woman and that she had fraudulently received free foster care and free public education from the State of Washington. When Brianna told the detective that there had to be some mistake, he said that her fingerprints, which had been requested by her Portland attorney, had matched those of a woman from Altoona, Pennsylvania, by the name of Treva Throneberry.

Ken Dunn's mother called him in Disney World with the news. He nearly dropped the phone. "Mom, I went to homecoming with a woman twelve years older than me," he said. Most of the Evergreen kids were convinced that Brianna had brilliantly hoodwinked them all. They thought she had deliberately acted awkward in her drama class, where she received a D, and had lost all of her tennis matches against girls half her age as part of her plot to deceive. But others weren't so sure about her motives. They were fascinated, for example, that she still couldn't make an A in algebra despite fifteen years of high school. "It just goes to show you how algebra can really suck," one girl said.

Just as curious was the reaction of the community itself. Although Clark County senior deputy prosecutor Michael Kinnie said that Treva needed to be treated as a common criminal—"What we are dealing with here is a woman who knows exactly what she's doing," he said—a writer for the Vancouver newspaper suggested that Treva's behavior "doesn't suggest maliciousness so much as misery." As for Kinnie's contention that Treva was dangerous—after all, a Vancouver security guard went to jail because of her accusation of rape—the writer reminded his readers that the security guard pleaded guilty. "Even though his record has since been cleared because no minor was actually involved," the writer's editorial pointed out, "he apparently thought there was, so he might not be without guilt himself."

Letters to the editor from Vancouver's citizens came in that favored Treva's getting psychiatric help rather than being sent to prison. One angry writer said that the authorities were "spending far more taxpayer money through the legal system than Throneberry's relatively harmless scam cost."

There was an even greater outpouring of sympathy for Treva after her sisters told reporters about the sexual abuse she, and they, had suffered. "This case is not about fraud but about a tremendous emptiness, a need, a trauma very early in her life," one of her court-appointed attorneys told reporters. If Treva was truly a con artist looking for financial gain, the attorney added, she could have picked a far better ruse than wandering the country as a homeless youth.

But for many, the greatest mystery about the story was why Treva Throneberry—after being caught in Plano, Texas, in 1995; Altoona, Pennsylvania, in 1996; and now Vancouver, Washington, in 2001— still refused to admit who she was. From her jail cell she declared in letters to the judge and in interviews with the news media that she had never before heard of Treva Throneberry. When her niece J'Lisha wrote her, she says that Treva responded with a letter of her own: "Dear J'Lisha Throneberry . . . I'm sorry to tell you this. I don't know who you are."

How much Treva actually remembered about her past had become a topic of enormous interest to psychiatrists, psychologists, and social workers. Some experts speculated that her past abuse from her uncle had been like a physical trauma, disconnecting memories in her brain. One professor of psychology said the abuse could have set off what is known as a dissociative fugue, a type of amnesia in which she didn't know how she got where she was or why she was there. Others suggested she could have a multiple personality disorder, in which she had created several personalities over the years to deal with her sexual abuse. A psychologist who had examined her for several days in 1995 when she was in Texas pretending to be Kara Williams was intrigued by her sincerity when she talked of satanic rituals and gang rape. "There was nothing in her behavior or presentation to suggest that she was knowingly misrepresenting the facts," the psychologist had written in his report.

What baffled everyone in Vancouver was her decision to give her fingerprints to the attorney. If she had been thinking rationally, she would certainly have known that the fingerprints would link her to Altoona. It was equally odd that, after her arrest, she demanded that her DNA be compared with the DNA of Carl and Patsy Throneberry. She said that she was certain such a test would prove she was not their child. (The DNA tests showed a 99.93 percent likelihood that she was.) And why did she try so hard to get people to look into her past, to discover her real identity? If she was deliberately trying to con people, why would she set herself up to be discovered?

There was little in medical or psychological literature that came close to helping the experts understand what had happened to Treva. "If it is what people think—a woman needing to go back to a certain age and relive it again and again—then it would be one for the books," said Kenneth Muscatel, a Seattle psychologist who had been hired by the court to examine Treva. "Here is a woman who invents stories to get the love and affection she had never known in her home, yet a woman so profoundly disturbed that she ends up turning on the very people who are trying to help her, accusing them of abuse."

Other than J'Lisha, no one from Treva's family tried to contact her after her arrest. Carl said he didn't write Treva because he had dropped out of school in the sixth grade and didn't know how to spell. He did want it known, however, that he was angry that "completely untrue stories" about Treva and his brother had made the newspapers. Patsy said she didn't write because she was still hurt by the way Treva had turned her back on the family. She did say that she believed that Treva hadn't forgotten about her entirely. At the funeral of her own mother, in 1998, Patsy said there was an elderly lady sitting at the back, wearing an old faded dress. The lady brushed against her as everyone was leaving the funeral parlor. Patsy noticed she was wearing a gray wig and granny glasses, and she had loads of pancake makeup on her face. "In my heart," she said, "I know it was Treva."

Treva's arrest did motivate her sisters to start talking to one another for the first time about their own feelings of shame about the past. But they didn't write Treva either. "We thought that maybe it would be best to just let her continue pretending to believe that she was a teenager," said Sue. "If she thought she was living in a better place, then so be it."

The prosecutor offered Treva a plea bargain—a recommendation of two years in prison in return for her admitting who she was. She wouldn't take the deal. She then fired her court-appointed attorneys when she learned that they were planning to argue that even though she was indeed Treva Throneberry, she had no idea she was committing a crime because she really did believe that she was Brianna Stewart. Treva told the judge that she wanted to exercise her constitutional right—which she apparently had read about in a law book at the library—to defend herself. She said she wanted to convince the jury that she truly was Brianna Stewart. "It is very important for me to clear my name," she said at a hearing. The judge could not say no. By law, to act as her own counsel Treva only had to demonstrate that she understood the nature of the charges against her and their potential punishment. Her nemesis, prosecutor Michael Kinnie, snarled to the press that Treva was perfectly competent. "She's graduated from high school at least twice," he said.

When Muscatel told the judge that he could not find sufficient mental problems to prove her incompetent, the stage was set for a disaster.

VANCOUVER, WASHINGTON—2001

Her trial began in mid-November, and each day, Treva shuffled into the courtroom, carrying a stack of law books and notebooks. Although she often kept her hair braided in her usual pigtails, she had traded her overalls for denim skirts that came down to her ankles. Before testimony began, she always smiled at Superior Court judge Robert Harris and said in her little girl's voice, "Hi." The esteemed judge was completely discombobulated by Treva. At one point he said, "Hello, Miss Stewart, Miss Throneberry, whatever."

He had one of her court-appointed attorneys sit beside her to answer any questions she might have about courtroom procedure and other points of law, but Treva seemed perfectly comfortable in her role as defense attorney. "Objection, relevance," she often called out, beaming at the judge. After several such objections, Kinnie, a serious, bearded fellow, began clenching his fists, trying to control his anger. When an investigator from the prosecutor's office took the stand and explained the complexities of fingerprint evidence, Treva nodded thoughtfully and, in her cross-examination, asked several pointless questions about ridge patterns on particular fingers. It was as if she were back in a high school science class asking a teacher how an experiment worked. Later, when another law enforcement officer told the jury about the way Keili Smitt in Corvallis, Oregon, used numerous aliases, she seemed mystified. "Why would someone come up with so many names?" she asked. "It makes no sense." This time, she turned and beamed at the jury. The officer just shrugged, staring at her.

Kinnie was so adamant about proving that Brianna really knew her true identity that he called to the stand a woman from a Vancouver convenience store. She said that she had remembered Brianna once coming in with some other teenagers to buy a pack of cigarettes and that Brianna showed an identification card with the name Treva Throneberry. The Evergreen teenagers who had been close to Brianna, however, were convinced that the clerk was lying. They said that Brianna never smoked, and no one could remember going to that store with her.

To further bolster his case, Kinnie had flown in Sharon Gentry, Treva's foster mother from fifteen years ago, to testify that she had known Treva in 1985, when she was 16 years old. Gentry's unexpected appearance led to a moment in the trial that can only be described as heartbreaking. After she answered some perfunctory questions from Kinnie, Treva rose slowly from the defense table, approached the witness, and asked to see some photos that Gentry had brought with her. For the first time Treva seemed ill at ease. She stared at the photo of herself and Gentry on the beach at Port Aransas for spring break; then she stared at a photo of herself with the high school boyfriend from Wichita Falls who had taken her to Six Flags. After a long silence Treva said, "This Treva in these pictures. What was she like?"

Gentry glanced around. She wasn't sure what to say. "She was a very polite young lady," she finally said. "She enjoyed church. She enjoyed tennis. She had a wooden tennis racket. She was always very appropriate, very thankful. She always apologized if she hurt my feelings."

There was another long silence. Treva stared down at her notebook, her eyes blinking. Was it possible that the past was returning—that she was remembering the girl she once was?

"Was Treva smart?" Treva asked.

"Oh, yes. She loved to read and really enjoyed school activities. She made good grades."

Another silence. "Did she work hard?" Treva asked.

It was clear that Gentry was now struggling to control her emotions. She would later say that she almost stood up at that moment and leaned across the witness box so that she could wrap her arms around Treva. "She worked very hard," Gentry said. "She tried hard. Treva was a wonderful young woman."

"Oh," said Treva. "Thank you."

As the trial hurried to its conclusion, Treva presented little evidence to counter Kinnie's case. She attempted to introduce a report from a therapist in Vancouver who had once guessed that Brianna Stewart was about 20 years old, but the judge ruled the report inadmissible. She called her former teachers and counselors to the stand to testify that she had only wanted a Social Security number so that she could continue her schooling. "I wanted to go to college so I could take care of myself, isn't that right?" she asked her former Evergreen counselor, Greg Merrill. "And not have someone take care of me?"

"All of our conversations were about you being self-sufficient," Merrill replied stiffly, obviously embarrassed that he had believed Brianna's story for so long.

In his final argument Kinnie was merciless. He loomed over the jurors and said, "If you feel sorry for her, we don't give a damn about your tears. That's not why we're here." He then mimicked Treva's voice, telling the jury that she just wanted to remain a "pampered child" and that she wanted a free financial ride.

For her final argument Treva stood before the jury and read a short speech that she had handwritten in one of her notebooks. "I still say I am Brianna Rebecca Stewart," she said, polite as always. "I don't pretend to be anyone else but me."

It was a slam dunk of a case, of course. The jury quickly found her guilty, and the judge sentenced her to three years in prison. The attorney who had been assisting Treva, Gerry Wear, made a last-minute request for the judge to state for the record whether he thought that Treva was competent to stand trial. "There's no question in my mind, having spent as much time with her as I have, that she is of the opinion that she is Brianna Stewart," Wear said. But it was too late. Judge Harris said he wished he could send her to a state hospital for treatment, but his only legal option was prison. The problem with prison in Washington State, he admitted, was that there were limited mental health services available for inmates. Nor was there any supervision for nonviolent offenders after their release. When Treva completes her sentence, she will be sent out the front door with a little money and perhaps a phone number for a women's shelter. And without any help, she might resume her cross-country odyssey.

Treva told the judge she would immediately file an appeal. Before she walked out of the courtroom for the last time, she looked out a window. Rain was beginning to fall outside. With no wind, it came down in a sprinkling whisper, little drops flicking through the last of the maple leaves hanging on the trees. "It's so unfair," she said. "It's so unfair."

A reporter standing nearby said, "What's unfair? Are you talking about what happened to you a long time ago?"

She looked at the reporter quizzically; then she gathered her law books and sheets of paper. "My name," she said, "is Brianna Stewart, and I am nineteen years old."

As bailiffs led her into an elevator, she said once again, in a much louder voice, to the crowd who had gathered to see her, "I'm nineteen! I'm not guilty of anything except being a teenager!"

━━━━

In March 2001, I read a one-paragraph newspaper story about a 31-year-old woman, born in a small Texas town, who had been arrested in the state of Washington for fraud because she was pretending to be a high school student: taking classes, playing on the tennis team, and acting in school dramas. Why, I wanted to know, did a grown woman desperately want to be back in the one place, high school, that most teenagers wanted to escape? And thus began my year-long journey into the bewildering life of Treva Throneberry.

Because Treva wouldn't talk to me about many episodes in her life, I had to do far more reporting than I thought I would need. I interviewed dozens of people from around the country, filed records requests in various states to get court documents, begged social workers to let me see their files, and finally traveled to Treva's hometown in the windswept plains of North Texas, talking to almost anyone I could find, looking for evidence of long-held secrets. But it wasn't just the mystery of Treva's life that absorbed me. I realized that with this story I could try something rarely seen in nonfiction. Instead of creating a traditional narrative, I kept readers jumping back and forth through most of the story between the lives of two teenage girls who seemed to have nothing to do with one another whatsoever. Then slowly and inevitably I brought those two lives together.

SEX, LIES, AND VIDEO CAMERAS
RENE CHUN

From the corner of Broadway and Canal Street, SoHo Models looked like any other boutique modeling agency: the converted loft building; the flag with the agency logo billowing in the wind; the engraved brass plaque mounted above the intercom. Seeing all this, scores of would-be models rang the bell, proceeded to the elevator, and obeyed the sign that read, ALL MODELS PLEASE REPORT DIRECTLY TO THE THIRD FLOOR.

But once the elevator doors opened, the meticulously crafted illusion crumbled. There were no bookers working the phones. No photographers showing portfolios. Not even a dog-eared copy of *Vogue*.

Which isn't to say there weren't attractive girls. There were. Their names were scrawled in grease pencil on two large schedules opposite the reception desk: HOT LIPS, POISON IVY, CANDY ASS.

The girls worked in cubicles in an adjoining room. The 5-by-8-foot cells were just big enough to hold a twin bed, a wall-mounted Hi-8 video camera, a flat-panel screen, a keyboard, and a mouse. Somewhere in cyberspace, a prospective customer bought a block of time with a credit card, entered a chat room, selected a mate, and typed out instructions:

STRIP.

SPREAD YOUR LEGS.

TOUCH YOURSELF.

The girl in the cubicle read the instructions on her screen, complied, and tapped out a response:

HOW'S THE VIEW, BIG BOY?
I'M PUTTING ON "BOLERO."
BUY SOME MORE MINUTES.

Although SoHo Models was clearly no ordinary modeling agency, it had the potential to be an incredibly lucrative operation, with a projected annual gross of $3 million, or even $6 million. These fantastic figures ultimately proved meaningless. By the time SoHo Models closed its doors last in December of 2001, its cash flow had slowed to a trickle. One night before the end, only three of the twenty booths were occupied. Depeche Mode played as models sprawled on cheap mattresses, staring vacantly at their flat panels. From time to time they composed offers of companionship. Finally a reply came back from the ether:

I WANT YOU TO STICK A BLACK DILDO UP YOUR ASS.

Just another day in the glamorous world of modeling.

Sex scandals have always plagued the modeling business. They're usually fairly routine stuff: Milanese playboys booking talent for orgies at Lake Como, Parisian agents deflowering underage girls from the American heartland, coke-addled photographers demanding head for head shots.

But SoHo Models was something new—a fictitious agency used to recruit attractive young women for online porn. Even hardened veterans of the business were appalled. "This is the worst possible thing, because it undermines legitimate modeling agencies," says

Robert J. Hantman, a Manhattan lawyer whose firm specializes in fashion-industry litigation. "It's outrageous."

Yet the names of fashion insiders who were deceived by SoHo Models, or willing to suspend disbelief, reads like the guest list for a Bryant Park runway show. This is a testament to the persuasive powers of Jason Itzler, 35, who got his start with a phone-sex service in Miami, then took aim at New York with SoHo Models. Armed with little more than the backing of two clueless investors from New Jersey, the lease on a soaring loft space in downtown Manhattan, and a bottomless capacity for generating hype, he succeeded beyond his most overheated fantasies. "I was surprised big-time," Itzler says from the jail in Newark, New Jersey, where he has been held since August 2001. "I thought to myself, this is a field wide open to be taken over."

In many ways, he was right. Itzler blew into town at a time when fashion was in a slump. Budgets were being slashed; modeling agencies were downsizing. The charismatic agents who had presided during the glamour years had left the stage, replaced by joyless money managers. "There aren't too many personalities in the business since Eileen Ford and I and a few other characters left," laments John Casablancas, retired president of Elite. "The modeling scene is kind of dull."

Itzler saw it the same way, and he was determined to remedy the situation.

Jason Itzler didn't start out as a flimflam man. He didn't even start out as Jason Itzler. He was born Jason Sylk in 1967, a nice Jewish kid from a good Philadelphia family. His mother, Ronnie Lubell, was a dark-haired beauty from Queens and "a bit of a Jewish Mafia princess," Itzler says. He claims she gave him everything: brains, looks, charm, even his taste in women. "My mother was absolutely gorgeous," he says. "Growing up, everybody made comments about how they wanted to sleep with her. And if your mom happens to be drop-dead gorgeous and sexy, and you get comfortable interacting with that type of woman, those are the type of people you're comfortable with."

Itzler's father, Lenny Sylk, is the son of the founder of the Sun Ray drugstore chain. The Sylks lived outside Philadelphia in a 120-year-old mansion with an eighteen-car garage, a helicopter pad, and maids and butlers who attended to domestic chores. But Ronnie and Lenny's marriage had unraveled by Jason's second birthday.

After the divorce, Lenny dropped out of the picture and Ronnie got custody of Jason. She moved back to New York, where she met and married a bankruptcy lawyer named Ron Itzler. A partner in the powerful Manhattan law firm Fishbein, Badillo, Wagner & Itzler, Ron raised Jason from then on. Jason would later acknowledge this by changing his name to Itzler.

Jason Itzler was shuttled through a series of exclusive private schools. The only thing he recalls about his early academic years is his celebrity classmates: Mira Sorvino ("tall with big boobies") and Brooke Shields ("really pretty, classy, and elegant"). Curiously, though, he left them behind and graduated instead from a public high school in Tenafly, New Jersey. "I wanted to experience the real world," he explains.

In 1985, Itzler enrolled at George Washington University. Born a Sylk, he had inherited expensive tastes. Now, living away from home for the first time, he felt liberated to indulge them—he drove a 280 ZX, appreciated fancy restaurants. To finance his lifestyle, Itzler says, he exploited the collegiate demographic in every way he could think of. He promoted fraternity keg parties and wet-T-shirt contests. He did a brisk business in fake IDs and scalped concert tickets. ("It was a little shady," he admits.) And he dabbled in publishing. His most memorable title was *The World's Greatest Pick-up Line*. Advertised in the back of *Rolling Stone* for $5, the book contained exactly one page, printed with a fill-in-the-blank exercise: "Do you know _____? Hi, I'm _____."

After graduation, he bowed to pressure from his parents and went to law school. During his first year at Nova Southeastern University in Fort Lauderdale, Itzler launched 1-900-REVENGE ("Press 1 for revenge on a wife. Press 2 for revenge on a teacher . . ."). The take—$5,000 a month—wasn't much by the standards of an industry then at its peak, but it did give Itzler a vision of his future life. "My whole attitude was, anything's easier than being a lawyer," he says.

Soon after REVENGE folded, he was approached by an investor who wanted to start a 900 number offering legal advice. Itzler's eyes glazed over. He countered with a proposal to do a sex line, something that had been percolating in his mind for months. His money-man acquiesced. Christened Boss Entertainment, this would be Itzler's first big score.

What set Boss Entertainment apart from the competition were the ads, which ran in *Penthouse* and *Hustler*. Instead of listing the 900 number, Itzler promised a "free live call." Prospective customers would dial a toll-free number and talk to a woman who pretended to be in the same town. After chatting up the lovesick chump for several minutes, she'd then ask him to call her back at a 900 number, where the meter would run at $5 a minute.

It was the first time anyone had used the "free live" rubric, an angle that made Itzler's ads "fifty times more profitable than a standard 900-number ad," according to one industry expert. Within sixty days, Boss Entertainment was grossing $600,000 a month. Although there were many larger players in the industry, Itzler, ever the self-promoter, declared that he was the "Phone-Sex King." But just as Boss was hitting its stride, Itzler says, he was edged out of the business by his partner.

Itzler graduated from Nova in 1993 with a 2.03 grade point average. Since he had no intention of practicing law, he bypassed the bar exam. (Still, a remarkable number of people seem to be under the impression that Jason is a lawyer, including, at times, Jason himself.) Instead, he would ask his stepfather to help stage his triumphant return to the phone-sex business. According to Jason, Ron Itzler told one of his bankruptcy clients, Mel Roslyn, about his son the phone-sex king, and Roslyn cut a check for $100,000. M2 Communications was launched in 1993, and within three years, Jason claims, it was grossing between $1.2 and $1.4 million a month.

As the money poured in, Jason Itzler gave his college sweetheart a six-carat heart-shaped engagement ring from Harry Winston. They flew to Las Vegas and were married at the Little White Chapel, but the union would last only nine months. Lenny Sylk blames his son for the breakup. "The first thing he did was get her a nose job," Sylk says. "The second thing he did was get her a boob job. And then he made her crazy. We just felt bad for her, because she was such a lovely, sweet girl." He sighs. "Jason's a sick kid."

To fill the void in his life, Itzler dated strippers, leased exotic sports cars (including a $400,000 Aston Martin Virage), gambled (blackjack at the Hard Rock Casino), shopped for real estate (a luxury high-rise apartment in the Oceania on Collins Avenue in Miami Beach). He says he was making $2 million to $3 million a year and spending half of it on "lifestyle."

All true, says a former M2 employee: "Jason spent 80 to 100 grand a month on his Platinum Amex card alone. The kid would go into the Disney store and spend $13,000 on ceramic statues of the Seven Dwarfs. He'd spend $1,000 a night in strip clubs. His place in the Oceania was decorated with a waterfall and a smoke machine. It was like a Vegas show." One friend who visited Itzler at the Oceania describes the decor as "early-nineties Miami coke den. There were low-rent models and blow everywhere."

Women were a significant expense. For Itzler, there was no such thing as a cheap date. He showered them with gifts: Cristal champagne. Chanel frocks. Bulgari jewelry. Breasts. By one ex-girlfriend's estimate, Itzler referred at least ten girls a year to Lenny Roudner, a local plastic surgeon whose flair for breast implants has earned him the nickname "Dr. Boobner." Itzler praises Roudner as an "amazing artist"; Roudner, returning the compliment, billed Itzler the preferred-customer rate, $3,500 a set.

During Itzler's shopping spree, Mel Roslyn was told M2 hadn't turned a profit yet. He was starting to wonder whether he would ever see a return on his $100,000 investment, so he did some investigating and discovered that M2 was a raging success. The silent partner suddenly became very vocal. He sued not only Ron Itzler but his law firm as well. Needless to say, the firm was not pleased that one of its partners was involved in a phone-sex service with a client, and Ron resigned.

The legal fees cut into M2's profits, and that wasn't the only drain. The company was bridging the gap between accounts payable and accounts receivable with loans that carried exorbitant interest rates—as high as 36 percent. Even with its torrential cash flow, M2 couldn't keep up. Itzler lost the company and all his business assets, including his most prized possessions. Back when the Internet was still a gleam in Al Gore's eye, Itzler had had his minions registering every dirty domain name they could think of. "He was a visionary in that respect," one employee says. Now, with M2 in ruins, he had to give up the rights to blowjobs.com and pussy.com.

In 1997, Itzler left Miami, acutely depressed. Some time later, he turned up in New York and began to ponder his next move. He'd been toying with the idea of breaking into the Internet-sex business, selling video feed to online porn sites. All you needed were naked girls, web cams, and a T1 line. And the field had its perks. While operators at 900 lines were hired for their voices, not their bodies, Internet-sex girls were hot.

Itzler, who estimated he'd need at least $250,000 to get his cyber-sex company up and running, somehow persuaded his stepfather to find new investors. Ron Itzler thought of Fred Baum, a 49-year-old housing developer with a Ferrari collection and a short temper. Baum thought Jason was obnoxious as hell, possibly even a little crazy. But he was willing to make allowances because he was convinced that the young man was a computer-savvy marketing genius who was going to make him absurdly wealthy.

Baum was so certain of this that he called his longtime friend and business partner Bruce Glasser. Glasser made a good living in textiles, but like Baum, he'd always been receptive to investment opportunities that provided an escape from his more mundane ventures. This one certainly fit the bill.

Contracts were drawn up. For this new venture, to be called Baum Multimedia, Glasser fronted $100,000 (a loan, he says); Baum put up $150,000. Company documents indicate that each of the three men owned a third of the business. Glasser, however, now claims that he and Itzler were consultants and only owned options; Baum, he says, was the sole proprietor.

Itzler set out to secure a suitable location. By late 2000, he'd found just the thing in a landmark cast-iron building at 415 Broadway. The third-floor space covered 7,000 square feet, featured majestic fifteen-foot ceilings, and was drenched in sunlight. ("The space gave the project instant credibility," says Richard Renda, a stylist and video producer who worked briefly at SoHo Models. "It's what got me and a lot of other people interested and excited.")

The loft was so grand that it seemed a shame to use it for nothing more than porn. A streaming-video business, after all, could get along just fine in a basement. Then Itzler had a vision. Since beautiful women draw more customers, why not create a phony model-ing agency and use it to attract a superior grade of prospective tal-ent? Glasser objected that the models would flee for their lives once they learned they were being hired to masturbate in front of a web cam. "Not if we tell them they can make $5,000 a week," Itzler countered.

In honor of his favorite New York neighborhood, Itzler named the ersatz agency SoHo Models Management. He began to hype it around town, handing out sleek, glossy business cards everywhere he went. The cards gave his name as Jason Sylk. He claims that the name change was prompted by a falling out with his stepfather, and besides, he says, Sylk is "a beautiful name." Others insist his motives were simpler. "Jason's made so many enemies and burned so many bridges that he had to change his name," says one former M2 employee.

Next on the agenda was to assimilate himself into the New York fashion culture. One of the first people he hooked up with was Ed Feldman. By way of introduction, Feldman mentioned that he was listed in the modeling world's definitive Who's Who: the index of Michael Gross's *Model: The Ugly Business of Beautiful Women.* Had Itzler checked the index and turned to page 241, he would have read that Feldman had wielded a heavy wooden mallet on an agent named Jeremy Foster-Fell in 1981, sending him to the hospital.

"Someone once asked me to name the three most rotten bas-tards in the whole industry," one grizzled fashion veteran recalls. "I said, 'That's an easy list: Ed Feldman, Ed Feldman, Ed Feldman,' Nobody else comes close."

Like everyone else who met Itzler, Feldman was intrigued. This kid from Miami with a fortune to spend on a new modeling agency was almost too good to be true. Feldman began to act as Itzler's mentor, freely sharing his Rolodex, making introductions, and advising his new protégé every step of the way. Feldman asked Joey Grill, who was overseeing operations at the Click agency, to "teach

Jason the modeling business." Grill complied, giving him a Cliffs Notes overview of the industry.

The list of fashion victims who met with Itzler—and believed his story—goes on and on: I.D. Models owner Paolo Zampolli ("I thought the guy was loaded with millions"); Q Models owner Jeff Kolsrud ("I think that Jason *does* have money"); photographer Marco Glaviano ("I said, 'Send me the girls when you open'").

"Everybody thought it was legit," says Lee Kalt, Itzler's first hire at SoHo Models. "I would see him pulling the wool over their eyes. It amazed me the way people believed Jason."

One of those people was the photographer Peter Beard. Itzler says he offered Beard 10 percent of the agency in exchange for his "expertise." What he really wanted, though, was Beard's imprimatur. Although Beard wasn't the fashion-world force he had been when he was shooting for *Vogue* in the sixties, his name still opened doors. After an impromptu business meeting, Itzler invited him to inspect the 415 Broadway property. Later that evening, Itzler took Beard to the roof. Here, stoned and feeling more confident than he had since the old M2 days, Itzler had another flash of inspiration: SoHo Models would be a bona fide modeling agency.

"I was going to do a whole different type of agency," Itzler explains. "It was going to be hip, stylish, and trendy. One that people talk about and that had an element of European class." Think of Elite in the early nineties, but with models who went all the way on the first booking. "In three weeks, the project went from the concept of a bait and switch to me saying, 'Fuck that! I'm going to kick ass at this modeling agency!'"

Itzler saw no potential conflict in having a modeling agency on the same floor as an Internet-sex service. On the contrary, he actually envisioned a synergy between them. "The models would hear how much the Internet girls were making, and they'd check out Baum," he says. "And if the Internet girls were pretty enough, they'd be able to cross over to SoHo Models."

Itzler needed all the synergy he could get. Baum Multimedia had promised to provide content 24/7, which meant finding enough girls to fill the twenty booths for three eight-hour shifts each day. He composed a vague help-wanted ad that ran in *The Village Voice* and *New York Press* classified sections: "Make $3,000 a week!! + benefits & the most flexible schedule you could want." Some ads even promised applicants that they'd be able to watch MTV while they worked.

When respondents realized that the position entailed performing sex acts live on the Internet, many stomped off in a huff. The rest filled out applications. Models who were already working for established agencies like NMK, Next, Click, Major, and I.D. began showing up, books in hand. A surprising number of them accepted jobs. "We got a lot of innocent girls coming off the street saying, 'Yes, I'm here for the modeling agency,'" one former Baum employee recalls. "And Jason would say, 'Sure! Come on in.'"

Itzler says he was conducting between sixty and seventy interviews a day, in the privacy of his on-site living quarters just a few feet from the booths. "I built a gorgeous bedroom with a marble Jacuzzi, two-head shower, and everything," he says. "Two smoke machines, disco lights—it was a combination bedroom-disco." In his interviews, Itzler would tell the applicants to strip and pose for Polaroids; sometimes he'd smoke pot with them. "It's not like you're hiring accountants. You're hiring these crazy young girls that are doing very open-minded stuff."

One stripper, who sees herself as a "Kate Moss type," interviewed with Itzler because she thought she might be able to cross over to SoHo Models. "Once he mentioned the modeling agency, tons of thoughts and hopes were running through my head," she says. Itzler told her that he needed to see how she would perform on camera. "He tried to have sex with me," she says. "I kept my bottoms on at all times, but he touched me everywhere else. We started smoking pot, then he took off his clothes. When I noticed he was aroused, I told him, 'You're not putting that in me!'" She stops suddenly, then confesses, "I was broke. That's why I let it progress as far as it did."

"Absolutely untrue," Itzler responds. "There was only one girl that I ever touched during an interview; when she got naked for the interview, she said she had milk in her boobs because she'd had a baby recently. And I asked her if I could taste some. She said okay. So I drank out of her boob for about a minute. And I ended up dating her for a little bit. But that's the only girl I ever touched during an interview."

A number of former employees of Baum Multimedia complain about Jason's liberal interpretation of the term *human resources*. "I busted him the first time for having sex with one of the girls," says Jennifer, a model who moonlighted at Baum six nights a week. (Like many of the women who worked there, she asked that her last name not be used.) "I walked in his room and saw a girl in the bed beating him with a belt." According to Jennifer, Itzler was a masochist: "One girl that came in for an interview got so mad at him that she hit him in the face, and he asked her to do it again. She did it five or six times before she walked out of the interview. He liked it."

Itzler says that he's no masochist, that no interviewee ever hit him in the face, although one did "smack me on the ass with a belt, which is no big deal." He denies using Baum Multimedia as his personal matchmaking service, claiming that he dated only women who were no longer in Baum's employ. "I never slept with one of the girls at the sex place while she was working with us. I slept with all the wannabe models. The girls who worked for Major Models, Elite, Click—those are the girls I slept with." Claims to the contrary are "hearsay and rumor," he says. "I'm so professional about this stuff. I'm a lawyer. I would never." But in a later conversation, he recalls having sex with one of the workers in her booth while she was performing on the Internet.

Baum Multimedia went online in May 2001. To inaugurate the new venture, Itzler threw a twenty-six-hour party featuring naked women and Grammy-nominated DJ Danny Tenaglia. The drug-fueled party provoked at least four visits from the NYPD. "Tenaglia played while girls were masturbating online in the booths," Itzler says. "It was a very funny evening."

The humor escaped Fred Baum. With the festivities still in progress, he sent an enforcer to shut down the party. Baum's messenger, whom Itzler describes as "a fat guy with a killer's eyes," burst in, cut the power to the 30,000-watt sound system, and locked Tenaglia in a room. Itzler says the man then hauled him up to the roof, slapped him around, dangled him over the edge of the building, and informed him that Fred Baum was, as of that moment, terminating his employment. He told Itzler to clear his belongings out of the bedroom, because he was taking it over, along with his job.

"Jason's a talented young man, but we had fundamental business differences," Baum says diplomatically. "My belief is that you spend money after you make money. He wanted to spend money on crazy Tenaglia parties and make money later."

Despite their differences, though, Itzler and Baum reconciled only days later. The tough-love management style of Baum's new hired hand wasn't working out. More important, Glasser and Baum didn't have the faintest idea how to run the business they'd bought into. For the moment, it seemed that they needed Itzler on board if they were to have any chance of recouping their investment.

Baum Multimedia was run like a Chinatown sweatshop. Six-day workweeks were mandatory; many women worked seven days, with no lunch or coffee breaks. To increase production, they operated two keyboards at once.

And the pay was atrocious. A handful of "top hostesses" pulled down about $200 a week, but the average weekly salary was closer to $100, and double-digit checks weren't unusual. Cecilia Lagos, the office manager, said the hardest thing she'd ever had to do was to hand an employee a $6.50 paycheck. As if this weren't bad enough, some checks would bounce, and others never materialized. "Sometimes we wouldn't get paid for weeks at a time," complains one of the women. "I only collected four checks from Baum in the two months I worked there."

Glasser and Baum point out that salaries were based on commission for time spent online, so if an employee's paycheck was low, it was simply because she was a lousy salesperson. Customers would chat with a woman briefly, then had to buy more minutes to continue. According to Baum, no more than 20 percent of the women who worked for him knew how to sell themselves with the right combination of sultry looks, dirty chat, and whatever other intangibles thrill the heart of the solitary porn surfer.

Yet the Internet connection between Baum and its customers was frequently interrupted, a common problem with the technology. In interviews, at least eight former sex workers complained that their paychecks didn't fully credit them for the terminated calls. "For every hour online, I only got paid for 30 minutes," says Christina Cruz, 20. Glasser maintains the charge is untrue; Baum says that such glitches were "one of the problems of the business. We were working on it."

As the $30 paychecks continued to bounce, girls began to exit en masse. "Some girls worked three weeks without a check," Christina Cruz recalls. "It was like they were working for free. These financial problems, combined with self-esteem problems, reduced a lot of the girls to tears." Adding to the humiliation, the Baum girls were put on display in a kind of porno petting zoo. In the evenings, Itzler would bring men to Baum Multimedia to party, and they would invariably end up prowling around the space in an altered state. "It was horrific going into that chat room," Cruz says. "Every guy there wanted you to do something or show them something."

Fred Baum insists that Baum Multimedia was a desirable place to work. "I have a number of girls who say it's the best job they've ever had," he says. "Because they really don't have to do anything. They just sit down and chitchat. Then for thirty minutes they get to play with themselves and make money."

One would think that with its low payroll, Baum Multimedia would have turned a handsome profit. But it was hemorrhaging money. Fred Baum says that the company received an infusion of capital from a new source. "The Mob had about fifty, sixty grand into it," he says. "Absolutely not true," Glasser responds. "Fred Baum is out of his mind."

Hoping that some fresh hype would help business, Itzler pitched his story to the *New York Post*'s Page Six. The item ran on May 31, 2001, under the headline MODELS ATOP A PORNO PARLOR. It reported that Jason Sylk ("a lawyer by trade") and photographer Peter Beard had teamed up in a new venture called SoHo Models. The kicker was that the agency would share office space with an interactive online sex service. Nobody took the piece seriously except Bruce Glasser and Fred Baum, who weren't keen on the extra attention.

Itzler's short but fulfilling career at Baum Multimedia was over for good this time. His erratic behavior had become intolerable. "It was quite apparent that if Jason Itzler wasn't removed permanently, all the employees were going to quit," Glasser says.

Itzler negotiated a settlement that required him to relinquish his interest in Baum Multimedia, hardly a significant concession considering the state of the business. He would retain the SoHo Models name and receive a $50,000 buyout. (Itzler ultimately received only a fraction of that amount.)

Then, in July, someone began calling Baum employees at home. Almost all the women were working secretly; many were young and lived with their families or with boyfriends. The phone calls, by turns obscene, threatening, and more than a little psychotic, caused many of the girls to quit. Jason is convinced that Glasser and Baum suspected him.

On July 27, Itzler received a voice-mail message on his cell phone accusing him of "corporate espionage." "I think you better turn yourself in to the police," the message said. "Freddie has new partners. They're very, very serious people. They're coming after you, Jason. You better get out of the city and the state of New York. You're in a lot of trouble, kid."

Itzler wasn't buying it. He'd been threatened before, and he was still standing. But the next day, he got a second message, and this time he began to think the threat was real. "Jason, we know it's you," the voice said. "You're going to have the shit. . . . You're going to be in bad shape. You're an asshole."

Prudently, Itzler decided to leave New York. He flew to Amsterdam and spent his money getting high in the tourist cafés and getting laid in the red-light district. While he was getting stoned one day, he had what passed for a moment of clarity: Running away was crazy. Threats or no threats, he would return to the States and open an Internet-sex service in Miami. Now that he had learned how *not* to run one, it would be easy. Then he'd take the profits, return to New York, hire the best booker in town, and relaunch SoHo Models.

With his remaining $3,000, Itzler bought around 4,000 ecstasy tablets. By the time he was ready to go home, several days later, he says, he had 3,869 left, which had a street value back in New York of more than $116,000. He put the pills in a plastic bag, strapped the bag to his body, and boarded a flight bound for Newark International Airport. When he landed in Newark on August 1, Itzler was fidgeting and sweating profusely. Drug-sniffing dogs and steely-eyed Customs police were everywhere. Itzler was arrested during a routine search. "I must have looked nervous," he says.

Itzler was charged with possession of narcotics and possession with intent to distribute. Shortly after his arrest, he was swearing "on his mother's memory" that his only intent was to kill himself by blending the 3,869 ecstasy pills in an extra-large chocolate milk shake. "I already tried it with 100 pills, and all that happened was that I woke up groggy. I wanted to make sure this time." Although the story is not quite as implausible as it sounds—after all, he had once tried to commit suicide by stabbing himself in the chest with a steak knife—he's apparently had second thoughts about it. He now says that he was an ecstasy addict, and that the pills were for his "personal consumption."

According to Glasser, Baum Multimedia was essentially out of business by September 2001, although it limped along until December, when the computers and equipment were stolen. Unable to raise the $25,000 bail, Itzler has been locked up in Essex County Jail in Newark since August, enjoying the company of some of New Jersey's finest gang members. "It's been terrible," he says. "I've been beaten up by Bloods and Crips five times. Once a Crip punched me really hard in the kidneys. I was pissing blood."

Itzler has no regrets about his brief but memorable excursion through the fashion world. "When I was running the agency, I'd never had more fun in my life," he says. "I was meeting thirty new gorgeous girls a day. It's just paradise. It's like being Hugh Hefner, with the girls warming themselves up all day."

And he knows what he'll do when he's paid his debt to society: head back to Manhattan and reopen SoHo Models. He might even find some old friends willing to give him a second chance. Peter Beard, for one. "Modeling agencies are horrible bussinesses with dykes that demand sexual favors from the girls," Beard says. "This is the cheap-shit industry that you've seen exposed over and over. Amongst all this bullshit, I'd just as soon listen to good old Jason."

Itzler's time in jail has not been completely wasted: He has been writing a memoir. So far, he has twenty-seven chapters and a title: *Ecstasy.* "I think I'm going to sell two million copies and get enough money to start life over again," he says. "Although my story isn't a positive one with a hero emerging at the end, I've never read anything more interesting than the shit I've been through. It's action, action. Up, down. Kill myself, live. My shit's cool."

He adds that anyone interested in buying the film rights should contact him through his lawyer. Then, a few days later, he reports that he has fired his lawyer and is trying to persuade Lenny Sylk to hire "the Johnny Cochran and Bruce Cutler of Newark." He's confident he will be back in action before long.

The State of New Jersey apparently has other ideas. When prosecutors presented Jason's case to a grand jury earlier this year, they added a third count: possession with intent to manufacture, distribute, and dispense. A first-degree felony usually levied against drug kingpins, this new charge carries a mandatory minimum sentence of ten years.

In some ways, jail has changed Jason Itzler. His street swagger is virtually gone, replaced by the first inklings of a sense of responsibility. "I did something stupid," he says, "and now I have to pay the price."

He is stunned when he learns of the new charge and the prosecutor's assertion that he is looking at "significant time," even with parole. There is a long silence while he considers this. The seconds tick by on his collect call. For a moment, it almost seems that he is chastened, humbled by the news. And then:

"Is this going to be a cover story?"

———

Like all great journalism, "Sex, Lies, and Video Cameras" started out as a Page Six item. I remember the salacious headline vividly: "MODELS ATOP A PORNO PARLOR." The gossip item told the heartwarming tale of a millionaire entrepreneur from Miami, known as the Phone-Sex King, who had come to New York to open up a combination modeling agency/porn website. What's not to like about this story? I thought to myself between chuckles. I immediately clipped the item from the New York Post and pinned it to the wall.

The pitch was money: Johnny Casablancas meets Larry Flynt with a gritty Elmore Leonard vibe. The fact that a hustler from South Beach was hawking this rather unorthodox business model around town wasn't that interesting to me. Far more intriguing was that Mr. Itzler had evidently managed to wrangle a top photographer as a business partner and was taking meetings with some of the key players within the fashion industry. I reread the item: fashion models, online sex, a gorgeous SoHo loft where all of this seductive commerce was to take place. Something didn't smell right. This is a good thing. As any journalist will tell you, the best stories are the ones that smell slightly gamy at the start. This one was still fresh and already it was stinking up the town like a runny wedge of Limburger. That's when I decided to do the story.

Jason Itzler didn't disappoint. He is a flimflam man from the old school: charismatic, earnest, and always working a new scam. There's no telling how far he would have gone if he had decided to peddle, say, California real estate instead of desperate girls and ecstasy tablets. Groupies will be pleased to know that Mr. Itzler was released from the New Jersey State Correctional System in January 2003 after serving seventeen months and one week of a five-year stretch. Collection agencies, cuckolds, and IRS agents can reach the former Phone-Sex King through the New Jersey Parole Board. He is currently looking for venture capital funds and is available for interviews.

THE COUNTERTERRORIST
LAWRENCE WRIGHT

The legend of John P. O'Neill, who lost his life at the World Trade Center on September 11, begins with a story by Richard A. Clarke, the national coordinator for counterterrorism in the White House from the first Bush administration until last year. On a Sunday morning in February 1995, Clarke went to his office to review intelligence cables that had come in over the weekend. One of the cables reported that Ramzi Yousef, the suspected mastermind behind the first World Trade Center bombing, two years earlier, had been spotted in Pakistan. Clarke immediately called the FBI. A man whose voice was unfamiliar to him answered the phone. "O'Neill," he growled.

"Who are you?" Clarke said.

"I'm John O'Neill," the man replied. "Who the hell are you?"

O'Neill had just been appointed chief of the FBI's counterterrorism section, in Washington. He was 42 years old, and had been transferred from the bureau's Chicago office. After driving all night, he had gone directly to headquarters that Sunday morning without dropping off his bags. When he heard Clarke's report about Yousef, O'Neill entered the FBI's Strategic Information Operations Center (SIOC) and telephoned Thomas Pickard, the head of the bureau's National Security Division in New York. Pickard then called Mary Jo White, the United States attorney for the Southern District of New York, who had indicted Yousef in the bombing case.

One of O'Neill's new responsibilities was to put together a team to bring the suspect home. It was composed of agents who were working on the case, a State Department representative, a medical doctor, a hostage-rescue team, and a fingerprint expert whose job was to make sure that the suspect was in fact Ramzi Yousef. Under ordinary circumstances, the host country would be asked to detain the suspect until extradition paperwork had been signed and the FBI could place the man in custody. There was no time for that. Yousef was reportedly preparing to board a bus for Peshawar. Unless he was apprehended, he would soon cross the Khyber Pass into Afghanistan, where he would be out of reach. There was only one FBI agent in Pakistan at the time, along with several agents from the Drug Enforcement Administration and the State Department's diplomatic security bureau. "Our ambassador had to get in his car and go ripping across town to get the head of the local military intelligence," Clarke recalled. "The chief gave him his own personal aides, and this ragtag bunch of American law enforcement officials and a couple of Pakistani soldiers set off to catch Yousef before he got on the bus." O'Neill, working around the clock for the next three days, coordinated the entire effort. At 10:00 A.M. Pakistan time, on Tuesday, February 7, SIOC was informed that the World Trade Center bomber was in custody.

During the next six years, O'Neill became the bureau's most committed tracker of Osama bin Laden and his Al Qaeda network of terrorists as they struck against American interests around the world. Brash, ambitious, often full of himself, O'Neill had a confrontational personality that brought him powerful enemies. Even so, he was too valuable to ignore. He was the point man in the investigation of the terrorist attacks in Saudi Arabia, East Africa, and Yemen. At a time when the Clinton administration was struggling to decide how to respond to the terrorist threat, O'Neill, along with others in the FBI and the CIA, realized that Al Qaeda was relentless and resourceful and that its ultimate target was America itself. In the last days of his life, after he had taken a new job as the chief of security for the World Trade Center, he was warning friends, "We're due."

"I *am* the FBI," John O'Neill liked to boast. He had wanted to work for the bureau since boyhood, when he watched Efrem Zimbalist, Jr., as the buttoned-down Inspector Lewis Erskine in the TV series *The FBI*. O'Neill was born in 1952 and brought up in Atlantic City, where his mother drove a cab for a small taxi business that she and his father owned. After graduating from Holy Spirit High School, he got a job as a fingerprint clerk with the FBI. During his first semester in college, he married his high school sweetheart, Christine, and when he was 20 their son, John P. O'Neill, Jr., was born. O'Neill put himself through a master's program in forensics at George Washington University by serving as a tour guide at the FBI headquarters. In 1976, he became a full-time agent in the bureau's office in Baltimore; ten years later, he returned to headquarters and served as an inspector. In 1991, he was named assistant special agent in charge in the Chicago office. In 1994, he received the additional assignment of supervising VAPCON, a national investigation into violence against abortion providers. The following year, he transferred to headquarters to become the counterterrorism chief.

John Lipka, an agent who met O'Neill during the VAPCON probe, marvelled at his ability to move so easily from investigating organized crime and official corruption to the thornier field of counterterrorism. "He was a very quick study," Lipka told me. "I'd been working terrorism since '86, but he'd walk out of the Hoover building, flag a cab, and I'd brief him on the way to the White House. Then he'd give a presentation, and I'd be shocked that he grasped everything I had been working on for weeks."

O'Neill entered the bureau in the J. Edgar Hoover era, and throughout his career he had something of the old-time G-man about him. He talked tough, in a New Jersey accent that many loved to imitate. He was darkly handsome, with black eyes and slicked-back hair. In a culture that favors discreet anonymity, he cut a memorable figure. He favored fine cigars and Chivas Regal and water with a twist, and carried a 9-millimeter automatic strapped to his ankle. His manner was bluff and dominating, but he was always immaculately, even fussily, dressed. One of his colleagues in Washington took note of O'Neill's "nightclub wardrobe"—black double-breasted suits, semitransparent black socks, and ballet-slipper shoes. "He had very delicate feet and hands, and with his polished fingernails, he made quite an impression."

In Washington, O'Neill became part of a close-knit group of counterterrorism experts which formed around Richard Clarke. In the web of federal agencies concerned with terrorism, Clarke was the spider. Everything that touched the web eventually came to his attention. The members of this inner circle, which was known as the Counterterrorism Security Group (CSG), were drawn mainly from the CIA, the National Security Council, and the upper tiers of the Defense Department, the Justice Department, and the State Department. They met every week in the White House Situation Room. "John could lead a discussion at that level," R. P. Eddy, who was an NSC director at the time, told me. "He was not just the guy you turned to for a situation report. He was the guy who would say the thing that everybody in the room wishes he had said."

In July of 1996, when TWA Flight 800 crashed off the coast of Long Island, there was widespread speculation in the CSG that it had been shot down by a shoulder-fired missile from the shore. Dozens of witnesses reported having seen an ascending flare that culminated in an explosion. According to Clarke, O'Neill, working with the Defense Department, determined the height of the aircraft and its distance from shore at the time of the explosion, and demonstrated that it was out of the range of a Stinger missile. He proposed that the flare could have been caused by the ignition of leaking fuel from the aircraft, and he persuaded the CIA to do a video simulation of this scenario, which proved to be strikingly similar to the witnesses' accounts. It is now generally agreed that mechanical failure, not terrorism, caused the explosion of TWA Flight 800.

Clarke immediately spotted in O'Neill an obsessiveness about the dangers of terrorism which mirrored his own. "John had the same problems with the bureaucracy that I had," Clarke told me. "Prior to September eleventh, a lot of people who were working full-time on terrorism thought it was no more than a nuisance. They didn't understand that Al Qaeda was enormously powerful and insidious and that it was not going to stop until it really hurt us. John and some other senior officials knew that. The impatience really grew in us as we dealt with the dolts who didn't understand."

Osama bin Laden had been linked to terrorism since the first World Trade Center bombing, in 1993. His name had turned up on a list of donors to an Islamic charity that helped finance the bombing, and defendants in the case referred to a "Sheikh Osama" in a recorded conversation. "We started looking at who was involved in these events, and it seemed like an odd group of people getting together," Clarke recalled. "They clearly had money. We'd see CIA reports that referred to 'financier Osama bin Laden,' and we'd ask ourselves, 'Who the hell is he?' The more we drilled down, the more we realized that he was not just a financier—he was the leader. John said, 'We've got to get this guy. He's building a network. Everything leads back to him.' Gradually the CIA came along with us."

O'Neill worked with Clarke to establish clear lines of responsibility among the intelligence agencies, and in 1995 their efforts resulted in a presidential directive giving the FBI the lead authority both in investigating and in preventing acts of terrorism wherever Americans or American interests were threatened. After the April 1995 bombing in Oklahoma City, O'Neill formed a separate section for domestic terrorism, but he concentrated on redesigning and expanding the foreign-terrorism branch. He organized a swap of deputies between his office and the CIA's counterterrorism center, despite resistance from both agencies.

"John told me that if you put the resources and talents of the CIA's counterterrorism center and the FBI's counterterrorism section together on any issue, we can solve it—but we need both," Lipka recalled. In January 1996, O'Neill helped create a CIA station, code-named Alec, with a single-minded purpose. "Its mission was not just tracking down bin Laden but focusing on his infrastructure, his capabilities, where he got his funding, where were his bases of operation and his training centers," Lipka said. "Many of the same things we are doing now, that station was already doing then."

The cooperation that O'Neill achieved between the bureau and the CIA was all the more remarkable because opinions about him were sharply polarized. O'Neill could be brutal, not only with underlings but also with superiors when they failed to meet his expectations. An agent in the Chicago office who felt his disapproval told me, "He was smarter than everybody else, and he would use that fine mind to absolutely humiliate people."

In Washington, there was one terrorist-related crisis after another. "We worked a bomb a month," Lipka recalled. Often O'Neill would break for dinner and be back in the office at ten. "Most people couldn't keep up with his passion and intensity," Lipka said. "He was able to identify those people who shared his work ethic, and then he tasked the living shit out of them, with e-mails and status briefings and phones and pagers going off all the time, to the point that I asked him, 'When do you sleep?'" O'Neill began acquiring nicknames that testified to his relentlessness, among them the Count, the Prince of Darkness, and Satan.

But many in the bureau who disliked O'Neill eventually became devoted followers. He went to extraordinary lengths to help when they faced health problems or financial difficulty. "He was our Elvis—you knew when he was in the house," Kevin Giblin, the FBI's head of terrorist warning, recalled.

. . .

O'Neill's tenure in the FBI coincided with the internationalization of crime and law enforcement. Prior to his appointment as the bureau's counterterrorism chief, the FBI had limited its involvement to operations in which Americans had been killed. "O'Neill came in with a much more global approach," Lipka told me. One of his innovations was to catalogue all the explosives used by terrorists worldwide. "He thought, 'When a bomb goes off in the Egyptian embassy in Islamabad, even though no Americans were killed, why don't we offer our assistance, so that we can put that information on a global forensic database,'" Lipka said. Since 1984, the FBI had had the authority to investigate crimes against Americans abroad, but that mandate had been handicapped by a lack of cooperation with foreign police agencies. O'Neill made a habit of entertaining every foreign cop or intelligence agent who entered his orbit. He called it his "night job."

"John's approach to law enforcement was that of the old Irish ward boss to governance: you collect friendships and debts and obligations, because you never know when you're going to need them," Clarke told me. He was constantly on the phone, doing favors, massaging contacts. By the time he died, he had become one of the best-known policemen in the world. "You'd be in Moscow at some bilateral exchange," Giblin recalled, "and you'd see three or four men approach and say, in broken English, 'Do you know John O'Neill?'"

The need to improve relationships with foreign police agencies became apparent in November 1995, when five Americans and two Indians died in the bombing of an American-run military training center in Riyadh, Saudi Arabia. The FBI sent over a small squad to investigate, but the agents had scarcely arrived when the Saudis arrested four suspects and beheaded them, foreclosing any opportunity to learn who was behind the operation.

In the spring of 1996, Jamal Ahmed al-Fadl, who had supported a plot by Al Qaeda against American soldiers in Somalia four years earlier, arrived at the American embassy in Asmara, Eritrea. The CIA debriefed him for six months, then turned him over to the FBI, which put him in the witness protection program. Fadl provided the first extensive road map of the bin Laden terrorist empire. "Fadl was a gold mine," an intelligence source who was present during some of the interviews told me. "He described the network, bin Laden's companies, his farms, his operations in the ports." Fadl also talked about bin Laden's desire to attack Americans, including his ambition to obtain uranium. The news was widely circulated among members of the intelligence community, including O'Neill, and yet the State Department refused to list Al Qaeda as a terrorist organization.

On June 25, 1996, O'Neill arranged a retreat for FBI and CIA agents at the bureau's training center in Quantico, Virginia. "We had hot dogs and hamburgers, and John let the CIA guys on the firing range, because they never get to shoot," Giblin recalled. "Then everyone's beeper went off." Another explosion in Saudi Arabia, at the Khobar Towers, a military housing complex in Dhahran, had killed nineteen American soldiers and injured more than five hundred other people, including Saudis. O'Neill assembled a team of nearly a hundred agents, support personnel, and members of various police agencies. The next day, they were on an Air Force transport plane to Saudi Arabia. A few weeks later, they were joined by O'Neill and the FBI director, Louis Freeh.

It was evening when the two men arrived in Dhahran. The disaster site was a vast crater illuminated by lights on high stanchions; nearby lay charred automobiles and upended Humvees. Looming above the debris were the ruins of the housing complex. This was the largest bomb that the FBI had ever investigated, even more powerful than the explosives that had killed 168 people in Oklahoma City in 1995. O'Neill walked through the rubble, greeting exhausted agents who were sifting the sand for evidence. Under a tarp nearby, investigators were gradually reconstructing fragments of the truck that had carried the bomb.

In the Khobar Towers case, neither the Saudis nor the State Department seemed eager to pursue a trail of evidence that pointed to Iranian terrorists as the likeliest perpetrators. The Clinton administration did not relish the prospect of military retaliation against a country that seemed to be moderating its anti-Western policies, and according to Clarke, the Saudis impeded the FBI investigation because they were worried about the American response. "They were afraid that we would have to bomb Iran," I was told by a Clinton administration official, who added that that would have been a likely course of action.

Freeh was initially optimistic that the Saudis would cooperate, but O'Neill became increasingly frustrated, and eventually a rift seems to have developed between the two men. "John started telling Louis things Louis didn't want to hear," Clarke said. "John told me that, after one of the many trips he and Freeh took to the Mideast to get better cooperation from the Saudis, they boarded the Gulfstream to come home and Freeh says, 'Wasn't that a great trip? I think they're really going to help us.' And John says, 'You've got to be kidding. They didn't give us anything. They were just shining sunshine up your ass.' For the next twelve hours, Freeh didn't say another word to him."

Freeh denies that this conversation took place. "Of course John and I discussed the results of every trip at that time," he wrote to me in an e-mail. "However, John never made that statement to me. . . . John and I had an excellent relationship based on trust and friendship."

O'Neill longed to get out of Washington so that he could "go operational," as he told John Lipka, and supervise cases again. In January 1997, he became special agent in charge of the National Security

Division in New York, the bureau's largest and most prestigious field office. When he arrived, he dumped four boxes of Rolodex cards on the desk of his new secretary, Lorraine di Taranto. Then he handed her a list of everyone he wanted to meet—"the mayor, the police commissioner, the deputy police commissioners, the heads of the federal agencies, religious and ethnic leaders," di Taranto recalled. Within six months, O'Neill had met everyone on the list.

"Everybody knew John," R. P. Eddy, who left Washington in 1999 for a job at the United Nations, told me. "You would walk into Elaine's or Bruno's with him, and everyone from the owner to the waiters to the guy who cleaned the floor would look up. And the amazing thing is they would all have a private discussion with him at some point. The waitress wanted tickets to a Michael Jackson concert. One of the waitstaff was applying for a job with the bureau, and John would be helping him with that. After a night of this, I remember saying, 'John, you've got this town wired.' And he said, 'What's the point of being sheriff if you can't act like one?'"

O'Neill was soon on intimate terms with movie stars, politicians, and journalists—what some of his detractors called "the Elaine's crowd." In the spring of 1998, one of O'Neill's New York friends, a producer at ABC News named Christopher Isham, arranged an interview for a network reporter, John Miller, with Osama bin Laden. Miller's narration contained information to the effect that one of bin Laden's aides was cooperating with the FBI. The leak of that detail created, in Isham's words, "a firestorm in the bureau." O'Neill, because of his friendship with Isham and Miller, was suspected of providing the information, and an internal investigation was launched. The matter died down after the newsmen denied that O'Neill was their informant and volunteered to take polygraphs.

In New York, O'Neill created a special Al Qaeda desk, and when the bombings of the American embassies in Kenya and Tanzania occurred, in August 1998, he was sure that bin Laden was behind them. "He was pissed, he was beside himself," Robert M. Blitzer, who was head of the FBI's domestic terrorism section at the time, remembered. "He was calling me every day. He wanted control of that investigation." O'Neill persuaded Freeh to let the New York office handle the case, and he eventually dispatched nearly five hundred investigators to Africa. Mary Jo White, whose prosecuting team subsequently convicted five defendants in the case, told me, "John O'Neill, in the investigation of the bombings of our embassies in East Africa, created the template for successful investigations of international terrorism around the world."

The counterterrorist community was stunned by the level of coordination required to pull off the simultaneous bombings. Even more troubling was the escalation of violence against civilians. According to Steven Simon, then a terrorist expert at the NSC, as many as five American embassies had been targeted—luck and better intelligence had saved the others. It was discouraging to learn that, nearly a year before, a member of Al Qaeda had walked into the American embassy in Nairobi and told the CIA of the bombing plot. The agency had dismissed this intelligence as unreliable. "The guy was a bullshit artist, completely off the map," an intelligence source said. But his warnings about the impending attacks proved accurate.

Moreover, key members of the Al Qaeda cell that planned the operation had been living in one of the most difficult places in the Western world to gain intelligence: the United States. The FBI is constrained from spying on American citizens and visitors without probable cause. Lacking evidence that potential conspirators were actively committing a crime, the bureau could do little to gather information on the domestic front. O'Neill felt that his hands were tied. "John was never satisfied," one of his friends in the bureau recalled. "He said we were fighting a war, but we were not able to fight back. He thought we never had the tools in place to do the job."

O'Neill never presumed that killing bin Laden alone would be sufficient. In speeches, he identified five tools to combat terrorism: diplomacy, military action, covert operations, economic sanctions, and law enforcement. So far, the tool that had worked most effectively against Al Qaeda was the last one—the slow, difficult work of gathering evidence, getting indictments, hunting down the perpetrators, and gaining convictions.

O'Neill was worried that terrorists had established a beachhead in America. In a June 1997 speech in Chicago, he warned, "Almost all of the groups today, if they chose to, have the ability to strike us here in the United States." He was particularly concerned that, as the millennium approached, Al Qaeda would seize the moment to dramatize its war with America. The intelligence to support that hypothesis was frustratingly absent, however.

On December 14, 1999, a border guard in Port Angeles, Washington, stopped an Algerian man, Ahmed Ressam, who then bolted from his car. He was captured as he tried to hijack another automobile. In the trunk of his car were four timers, more than a hundred pounds of urea, and fourteen pounds of sulfate—the makings of an Oklahoma City–type bomb. It turned out that Ressam's target was Los Angeles International Airport. The following day, Jordanian authorities arrested thirteen suspected terrorists who were believed to be planning to blow up a Radisson Hotel in Amman and a number of tourist sites frequented by Westerners. The Jordanians also discovered an Al Qaeda training manual on CD-ROM.

What followed was, according to Clarke, the most comprehensive investigation ever conducted before September 11. O'Neill's job was to supervise the operation in New York. Authorities had found several phone numbers on Ressam when he was arrested. There was also a name, Ghani, which belonged to Abdel Ghani Meskini, an Algerian, who lived in Brooklyn and who had travelled to Seattle to meet with Ressam. O'Neill oversaw the stakeout of Meskini's residence and spent much of his time in the Brooklyn command post. "I doubt he slept the whole month," David N. Kelley, an assistant United States attorney and chief of organized crime and terrorism for the Southern District, recalled. A wiretap picked up a call that Meskini had made to Algeria in which he spoke about Ressam and a suspected terrorist in Montreal. On December 30, O'Neill arrested Meskini on conspiracy charges and a number of other suspected terrorists on immigration violations. (Meskini and Ressam eventually became cooperating witnesses and are both assisting the FBI's investigation of the September 11 attacks.)

O'Neill was proud of the efforts of the FBI and the New York Joint Terrorism Task Force to avert catastrophe. On New Year's Eve, he and his friend Joseph Dunne, then the chief of department for the New York City police, went to Times Square, which they believed was a highly likely target. At midnight, O'Neill called friends at SIOC and boasted that he was standing directly under the giant crystal ball.

After the millennium roundup, O'Neill suspected that Al Qaeda had sleeper cells buried in America. "He started pulling the strings in Jordan and in Canada, and in the end they all led back to the United States," Clarke said. "There was a general disbelief in the FBI that Al Qaeda had much of a presence here. It just hadn't sunk through to the organization, beyond O'Neill and Dale Watson"— the assistant director of the counterterrorism division. Clarke's discussions with O'Neill and Watson over the next few months led to a strategic plan called the Millennium After-Action Review, which specified a number of policy changes designed to root out Al Qaeda cells in the United States. They included increasing the number of joint terrorism task forces around the country; assigning more agents from the Internal Revenue Service and the Immigration and Naturalization Service to monitor the flow of money and personnel; and creating a streamlined process for analyzing information obtained from wiretaps.

Many in the FBI point to the millennium investigation as one of the bureau's great recent successes. A year earlier, O'Neill had been passed over when the position of assistant director in charge of national security became available. When the post of chief of the New York office opened up, in early 2000, O'Neill lobbied fiercely for it. The job went to Barry Mawn, a former special agent in charge of the Boston office. As it happened, the two men met at a seminar just after the decision was announced. "I got a knock on the door, and there was John holding two beers," Mawn recalled. O'Neill promised complete loyalty in return for Mawn's support of his work on counterterrorism. "It turns out that supporting him was a full-time job," Mawn said.

O'Neill had many detractors and very few defenders left in Washington. Despite occasional disagreements, Louis Freeh had always supported O'Neill, but Freeh had announced that he would retire in June 2001. A friend of O'Neill's, Jerry Hauer, of the New York–based security firm Kroll, told me that Thomas Pickard, who had become the bureau's deputy director in 1999, was "an institutional roadblock." Hauer added, "It was very clear to John that Pickard was never going to let him get promoted." Others felt that O'Neill was his own worst enemy. "He was always trying to leverage himself to the next job," Dale Watson said. John Lipka, who considers himself a close friend of O'Neill, attributes some of O'Neill's problems to his flamboyant image. "The bureau doesn't like high-profile people," he said. "It's a very conservative culture."

The World Trade Center had become a symbol of America's success in fighting terrorism, and in September 2000, the New York Joint Terrorism Task Force celebrated its twentieth anniversary in the Windows on the World restaurant. The event was attended by representatives of seventeen law enforcement agencies, including agents from the FBI and the CIA, New York City and Port Authority policemen, United States marshals, and members of the Secret Service. Mary Jo White praised the task force for a "close to absolutely perfect record of successful investigations and convictions." White had served eight years as the United States attorney for the Southern District, and she had convicted twenty-five Islamic terrorists, including Yousef, six other World Trade Center bombers, the blind cleric Sheikh Omar Abdel Rahman, and nine of Rahman's followers, who had planned to blow up the Lincoln and Holland Tunnels, the United Nations headquarters, and the FBI offices.

O'Neill seemed at ease that night. Few of his colleagues knew of a troubling incident that had occurred two months earlier at an FBI preretirement conference in Orlando. During a meeting, O'Neill had been paged. He left the room to return the call, and when he came back, a few minutes later, the other agents had broken for lunch. His briefcase, which contained classified material, was missing. O'Neill immediately called the local police, and they found the briefcase a couple of hours later, in another hotel. A Montblanc pen had been stolen, along with a silver cigar cutter and a lighter. The papers were intact; fingerprint analysis soon established that they had not been touched.

"He phoned me and said, 'I gotta tell you something,'" Barry Mawn recalled. O'Neill told Mawn that the briefcase contained some classified e-mails and one highly sensitive document, the Annual Field Office Report, which is an overview of every counterterrorist and counterespionage case in New York. Mawn reported the incident to Neil Gallagher, the bureau's assistant director in charge of national security. "John understood the seriousness of what he had done, and if he were alive today he'd tell you he made a stupid mistake," Gallagher told me. Even though none of the information had been compromised, the Justice Department ordered a criminal inquiry.

Mawn said that, as O'Neill's supervisor, he would have recommended an oral reprimand or, at worst, a letter of censure. Despite their competition for the top job in New York, Mawn had become one of O'Neill's staunchest defenders. "He demanded perfection, which was a large part of why the New York office is so terrific," Mawn said. "But underneath his manner, deep down, he was very insecure."

On October 12, 2000, a small boat filled with C4 explosives motored alongside a U.S. destroyer, the *Cole*, which was fueling up off the coast of Yemen. Two men aboard the small craft waved at the larger vessel, then blew themselves to pieces. Seventeen American sailors died, and thirty-nine others were seriously wounded.

O'Neill knew that Yemen was going to be an extremely difficult place in which to conduct an investigation. In 1992, bin Laden's network had bombed a hotel in Aden, hoping to kill a number of American soldiers. The country was filled with spies and with jihadis and was reeling from a 1994 civil war. "Yemen is a country of eighteen million citizens and fifty million machine guns," O'Neill reported. On the day the investigators arrived in Yemen, O'Neill warned them, "This may be the most hostile environment the FBI has ever operated in."

The American ambassador to Yemen, Barbara Bodine, saw things differently. In her eyes, Yemen was the poor and guileless cousin of the swaggering petro-monarchies of the Persian Gulf. Unlike other countries in the region, it was a constitutional democracy—however fragile—in which women were allowed to vote. Bodine had had extensive experience in Arab countries. During the Iraqi invasion and occupation of Kuwait, she had been the deputy chief of mission in Kuwait City, and she had stayed through the 137-day siege of the American embassy by Iraqi troops until all the Americans were evacuated.

Bodine, who is on assignment from the State Department as diplomat in residence at the University of California at Santa Barbara, contends that she and O'Neill had agreed that he would bring in a team of no more than fifty. She was furious when three hundred investigators, support staff, and marines arrived, many carrying automatic weapons. "Try to imagine if a military plane from another country landed in Des Moines, and three hundred heavily armed people took over," she told me recently. Bodine recalled that she pleaded with O'Neill to consider the delicate diplomatic environment he was entering. She quoted him as responding, "We don't care about the environment. We're just here to investigate a crime."

"There was the FBI way, and that was it," she said to me. "O'Neill wasn't unique. He was simply extreme." According to Michael Sheehan, who was the State Department's coordinator for counterterrorism at the time, such conflicts between ambassadors and the bureau are not unusual, given their differing perspectives; however, Bodine had been given clear instructions from the outset of the investigation. "I drafted a cable under [then Secretary of State] Madeleine Albright's signature saying that there were three guiding principles," Sheehan said. "The highest priorities were the immediate safety of American personnel and the investigation of the attack. Number three was maintaining a relationship with the government of Yemen—but only to support those objectives."

O'Neill's investigators were billeted three or four to a room in an Aden hotel. "Forty-five FBI personnel slept on mats on the ballroom floor," he later reported. He set up a command post on the eighth floor, which was surrounded by sandbags and protected by a company of fifty marines.

O'Neill spent much of his time coaxing the Yemeni authorities to cooperate. To build a case that would hold up in American courts, he wanted his agents present during interrogations by local authorities, in part to ensure that none of the suspects were tortured. He also wanted to gather eyewitness testimony from residents who had seen the explosion. Both the Yemeni authorities and Bodine resisted these requests. "You want a bunch of six-foot-two Irish-Americans to go door-to-door?" Bodine remembers saying to O'Neill. "And, excuse me, but how many of your guys speak Arabic?"

There were only half a dozen Arabic speakers in the FBI contingent, and even O'Neill acknowledged that their competence was sometimes in question. On one occasion, he complained to a Yemeni intelligence officer, "Getting information out of you is like pulling teeth." When his comment was translated, the Yemeni's eyes widened. The translator had told him, "If you don't give me the information I want, I'm going to pull out your teeth."

When O'Neill expressed his frustration to Washington, President Clinton sent a note to President Ali Abdullah Saleh. It had little effect. According to agents on the scene, O'Neill's people were never given the authority they needed for a proper investigation. Much of their time was spent on board the *Cole*, interviewing sailors, or lounging around the sweltering hotel. Some of O'Neill's requests for evidence mystified the Yemenis. They couldn't understand, for instance, why he was demanding a hat worn by one of the conspirators, which O'Neill wanted to examine for DNA evidence. Even the harbor sludge, which contained residue from the bomb, was off limits until the bureau paid the Yemeni government a million dollars to dredge it.

There were so many perceived threats that the agents often slept in their clothes and with their guns at their sides. Bodine thought that much of this fear was overblown. "They were deeply suspicious of everyone, including the hotel staff," she told me. She assured O'Neill that gunfire outside the hotel was probably not directed at the investigators but was simply the noise of wedding celebrations. Still, she added that, for the investigators' own safety, she wanted to lower the bureau's profile by reducing the number of agents and stripping them of heavy weapons. Upon receiving a bomb threat, the investigators evacuated the hotel and moved to an American vessel, the USS *Duluth*. After that, they had to request permission just to come ashore.

Relations between Bodine and O'Neill deteriorated to the point that Barry Mawn flew to Yemen to assess the situation. "She represented that John was insulting, and not getting along well with the Yemenis," he recalled. Mawn talked to members of the FBI team and American military officers, and he observed O'Neill's interactions with Yemeni authorities. He told O'Neill that he was doing "an outstanding job." On Mawn's return, he reported favorably on O'Neill to Freeh, adding that Bodine was his "only detractor."

An ambassador, however, has authority over which Americans are allowed to stay in a foreign country. A month after the investigation began, Assistant Director Dale Watson told *The Washington Post*, "Sustained cooperation" with the Yemenis "has enabled the FBI to further reduce its in-country presence. . . . The FBI will soon be able to bring home the FBI's senior on-scene commander, John O'Neill." It appeared to be a very public surrender. The same day, the Yemeni prime minister told the *Post* that no link had been discovered between the *Cole* bombers and Al Qaeda.

The statement was premature, to say the least. In fact, it is possible that some of the planning for the *Cole* bombing and the September 11 attacks took place simultaneously. It is now believed that at least two of the suspected conspirators in the *Cole* bombing had attended a meeting of alleged bin Laden associates in Malaysia, in January 2000. Under CIA pressure, Malaysian authorities had conducted a surveillance of the gathering, turning up a number of faces but, in the absence of wiretaps, nothing of what was said. "It didn't seem like much at the time," a Clinton administration official told me. "None of the faces showed up in our own files." Early last year, the FBI targeted the men who were present at the Malaysia meeting as potential terrorists. Two of them were subsequently identified as hijackers in the September 11 attacks.

After two months in Yemen, O'Neill came home feeling that he was fighting the counterterrorism battle without support from his own government. He had made some progress in gaining access to evidence, but so far the investigation had been a failure. Concerned about continuing threats against the remaining FBI investigators, he tried to return in January of 2001. Bodine denied his application to reenter the country. She refuses to discuss that decision. "Too much is being made of John O'Neill's being in Yemen or not," she told me. "John O'Neill did not discover Al Qaeda. He did not discover Osama bin Laden. So the idea that John or his people or the FBI were somehow barred from doing their job is insulting to the U.S. government, which was working on Al Qaeda before John ever showed up. This is all my embassy did for ten months. The fact that not every single thing John O'Neill asked for was appropriate or possible does not mean that we did not support the investigation."

After O'Neill's departure, the remaining agents, feeling increasingly vulnerable, retreated to the American embassy in Sanaa, the capital of Yemen. In June, the Yemeni authorities arrested eight men who they said were part of a plot to blow up the embassy. New threats against the FBI followed, and Freeh, acting upon O'Neill's recommendation, withdrew the team entirely. Its members were, he told me, "the highest target during this period." Bodine calls the pullout "unconscionable." In her opinion, there was never a specific, credible threat against the bureau. The American embassy, Bodine points out, stayed open. But within days American military forces in the Middle East were put on top alert.

Few people in the bureau knew that O'Neill had a wife and two children (John, Jr., and his younger sister, Carol) in New Jersey, who did not join him when he moved to Chicago, in 1991. In his New York office, the most prominent pictures were not family photographs but French Impressionist prints. On his coffee table was a book about tulips, and his office was always filled with flowers. He was a terrific dancer, and he boasted that he had been on *American Bandstand* when he was a teenager. Some women found him irresistibly sexy. Others thought him a cad.

Shortly after he arrived in Chicago, O'Neill met Valerie James, a fashion sales director, who was divorced and was raising two children. Four years later, when he transferred to headquarters, in Washington, he also began seeing Anna DiBattista, who worked for a travel agency. Then, when he moved to New York, Valerie James joined him. In 1999, DiBattista moved to New York to take a new job, complicating his life considerably. His friends in Chicago and New York knew Valerie, and his friends in Washington knew Anna. If his friends happened to see him in the company of the "wrong" woman, he pledged them to secrecy.

On holidays, O'Neill went home to New Jersey to visit his parents and to see his children. Only John P. O'Neill, Jr., who is a computer expert for the credit card company MBNA, in Wilmington, Delaware, agreed to speak to me about his father. His remarks were guarded. He described a close relationship—"We talked a few times a week"—but there are parts of his father's past that he refuses to discuss. "My father liked to keep his private life private," he said.

Both James and DiBattista remember how O'Neill would beg for forgiveness and then promise better times. James told me, "He'd say, 'I just want to be loved, just love me,' but you couldn't really trust him, so he never got the love he asked for."

The stress of O'Neill's tangled personal life began to affect his professional behavior. One night, he left his Palm Pilot in Yankee Stadium; it was filled with his police contacts all around the world. On another occasion, he left his cell phone in a cab. In the summer of 1999, he and James were driving to the Jersey shore when his Buick broke down near the Meadowlands. As it happened, his bureau car was parked nearby, at a secret office location, and O'Neill switched cars. One of the most frequently violated rules in the bureau is the use of an official vehicle for personal reasons, and O'Neill's infraction might have been overlooked had he not let James enter the building to use the bathroom. "I had no idea what it was," she told me. Still, when the FBI learned about the violation, apparently from an agent who had been caught using the site as an auto repair shop, O'Neill was reprimanded and docked fifteen days' pay. He regarded the bureau's action as part of a pattern. "The last two years of his life, he got very paranoid," James told me. "He was convinced there were people out to get him."

In March 2001, Richard Clarke asked the national security adviser, Condoleezza Rice, for a job change; he wanted to concentrate on computer security. "I was told, 'You've got to recommend somebody similar to be your replacement,'" Clarke recalled. "I said, 'Well, there's only one person who would fit that bill.'" For months, Clarke tried to persuade O'Neill to become a candidate as his successor.

O'Neill had always harbored two aspirations—to become a deputy director of the bureau in Washington or to take over the New York office. Freeh was retiring in June, so there were likely to be some vacancies at the top, but the investigation into the brief-case incident would likely block any promotion in the bureau. O'Neill viewed Clarke's job as, in many ways, a perfect fit for him. But he was financially pressed, and Clarke's job paid no more than he was making at the FBI. Throughout the summer, O'Neill refused to commit himself to Clarke's offer. He talked about it with a number of friends but became alarmed when he thought that headquarters might hear of it. "He called me in a worked-up state," Clarke recalled. "He said that people in the CIA and elsewhere know you are considering recommending me for your job. You have to tell them it's not true." Clarke dutifully called a friend in the agency, even though O'Neill still wanted to be a candidate for the position.

In July, O'Neill heard of a job opening in the private sector that would pay more than twice his government salary—that of chief of security for the World Trade Center. Although the Justice Department dropped its inquiry into the briefcase incident, the bureau was conducting an internal investigation of its own. O'Neill was aware that the *Times* was preparing a story about the affair, and he learned that the reporters also knew about the incident in New Jersey involving James and had classified information that probably came from the bureau's investigative files. The leak seemed to be timed to destroy O'Neill's chance of being confirmed for the NSC job. He decided to retire.

O'Neill suspected that the source of the information was either Tom Pickard or Dale Watson. The antagonism between him and Pickard was well-known. "I've got a pretty good Irish temper and so did John," Pickard, who retired last November, told me. But he insisted that their differences were professional, not personal. The leak was "somebody being pretty vicious to John," but Pickard maintained that he did not do it. "I'd take a polygraph to it," he said. Watson told me, "If you're asking me who leaks FBI information, I have no idea. I know I don't, and I know that Tom Pickard doesn't, and I know that the director doesn't." For all the talk about polygraphs, the bureau ruled out an investigation into the source of the leak, despite an official request by Barry Mawn, in New York.

Meanwhile, intelligence had been streaming in concerning a likely Al Qaeda attack. "It all came together in the third week in June," Clarke said. "The CIA's view was that a major terrorist attack was coming in the next several weeks." On July 5, Clarke summoned all the domestic security agencies—the Federal Aviation Administration, the Coast Guard, Customs, the Immigration and Naturalization Service, and the FBI—and told them to increase their security in light of an impending attack.

On August 19, the *Times* ran an article about the briefcase incident and O'Neill's forthcoming retirement, which was to take place three days later. There was a little gathering for coffee as he packed up his office.

When O'Neill told ABC's Isham of his decision to work at the Trade Center, Isham had said jokingly, "At least they're not going to bomb it again." O'Neill had replied, "They'll probably try to finish the job." On the day he started at the Trade Center—August 23—the CIA sent a cable to the FBI saying that two suspected Al Qaeda terrorists were already in the country. The bureau tried to track them down, but the addresses they had given when they entered the country proved to be false, and the men were never located.

When he was growing up in Atlantic City, O'Neill was an altar boy at St. Nicholas of Tolentine Church. On September 28, a week after his body was found in the rubble of the World Trade Center, a thousand mourners gathered at St. Nicholas to say farewell. Many of them were agents and policemen and members of foreign intelligence services who had followed O'Neill into the war against terrorism long before it became a rallying cry for the nation. The hierarchy of the FBI attended, including the now retired director Louis Freeh. Richard Clarke, who says that he had not shed a tear since September 11, suddenly broke down when the bagpipes played and the casket passed by.

O'Neill's last weeks had been happy ones. The moment he left the FBI, his spirits had lifted. He talked about getting a new Mercedes to replace his old Buick. He told Anna that they could now afford to get married. On the last Saturday night of his life, he attended a wedding with Valerie, and they danced nearly every number. He told a friend within Valerie's hearing, "I'm gonna get her a ring."

On September 10, O'Neill called Robert Tucker, a friend and security company executive, and arranged to get together that evening to talk about security issues at the Trade Center. Tucker met O'Neill in the lobby of the north tower, and the two men rode the elevator up to O'Neill's new office, on the thirty-fourth floor. "He was incredibly proud of what he was doing," Tucker told me. Then they went to a bar at the top of the tower for a drink. Afterward, they headed uptown to Elaine's, where they were joined by their friend Jerry Hauer. Around midnight, the three men dropped in on the China Club, a nightspot in midtown. "John made the statement that he thought something big was going to happen," Hauer recalled.

Valerie James waited up for O'Neill. He didn't come in until 2:30 A.M. "The next morning, I was frosty," she recalled. "He came into my bathroom and put his arms around me. He said, 'Please forgive me.'" He offered to drive her to work, and dropped her off at 8:13 A.M. in the flower district, where she had an appointment, and headed to the Trade Center.

At 8:46 A.M., when American Airlines Flight 11 crashed into the north tower, John O'Neill, Jr., was on a train to New York, to install some computer equipment and visit his father's new office. From the window of the train he saw smoke coming from the Trade Center. He called his father on his cell phone. "He said he was okay. He was on his way out to assess the damage," John Jr., recalled.

Valerie James was arranging flowers in her office when "the phones started ringing off the hook." A second airliner had just hit the south tower. "At nine-seventeen, John calls," James remembered. He said, "Honey, I want you to know I'm okay. My God, Val, it's terrible. There are body parts everywhere. Are you crying?" he asked. She was. Then he said, "Val, I think my employers are dead. I can't lose this job."

"They're going to need you more than ever," she told him.

At 9:25 A.M., Anna DiBattista, who was driving to Philadelphia on business, received a call from O'Neill. "The connection was good at the beginning," she recalled. "He was safe and outside. He said he was okay. I said, 'Are you sure you're out of the building?' He told me he loved me. I knew he was going to go back in."

Wesley Wong, an FBI agent who had known O'Neill for more than twenty years, raced over to the north tower to help set up a command center. "John arrived on the scene," Wong recalled. "He asked me if there was any information I could divulge. I knew he was now basically an outsider. One of the questions he asked was 'Is it true the Pentagon has been hit?' I said, 'Gee, John, I don't know. Let me try to find out.' At one point, he was on his cell phone and he was having trouble with the reception and started walking away. I said, 'I'll catch up with you later.'"

Wong last saw O'Neill walking toward the tunnel leading to the second tower.

———

Until September 11, 2001, I had more or less abandoned my career as a journalist and turned to writing films. One of them, The Siege, which I cowrote with director Edward Zwick and his writing partner, Menno Menjes, eerily prefigured the events that took place on that day. Because I had lived in the Arab world—I taught English at the American University in Cairo more than thirty years ago—and because I had in some sense pre-imagined the tragedy, I felt an obligation to learn what events had led to the attack on America and why. During the week that followed, as I was reporting for The New Yorker, I began scanning online obituaries, hoping to find some character whose life and death would help me tell the story. As soon as I saw John O'Neill's name and read the brief details of his life—he was head of the FBI's counterterrorism force in New York until he resigned over a trivial embarrassment, and then took a job as the head of security for the World Trade Center—I knew that he would lead me into the secret world of intelligence. The obit left one with the impression that O'Neill was a bit of a disgrace. I just knew there was more to it. That brief obit has led me into the book about terrorism I am presently writing, in which O'Neill will play a prominent role—as he did in life.

THE BOY WHO LOVED TRANSIT
JEFF TIETZ

Before leaving his girlfriend's apartment in Crown Heights, on the morning of his nineteenth arrest for impersonating and performing the functions of New York City Transit Authority employees, Darius McCollum put on an NYCTA subway conductor's uniform and reflector vest. Over his feet he pulled transit-issue boots with lace guards and soles designed to withstand third-rail jolts. He took transit-issue work gloves and protective goggles. He put a transit-issue hard hat on his head. In his pockets he carried NYCTA work orders and rerouting schedules and newspaper clippings describing his previous arrests: for driving subway trains and buses and various other vehicles without authorization, possessing stolen property, flagging traffic around NYCTA construction sites, forging documents. He also carried a signed letter on NYCTA letterhead:

To: All Concerned Departments
From: Thomas Calandrella
        Chief Track Officer
Re: Darius McCollum

Effective this date of January 10, 2000, Darius McCollum is a member of a special twelve-member Special Study Group; and will analyze the operations of track safety and track operations. SSG will report directly to this office and will be issued all

related gear for the respected purposes of this department and
will receive assistance of any relating department.

To his belt Darius clipped a flashlight and a key ring the size of
a choker. From this ring six smaller rings hung like pendants. Along
the curves of the small rings, 139 keys climbed symmetrical and fan-
like. Each key granted access to a secure area of the train, bus, or subway system of the New York City Transit Authority. The collection
was equivalent to the number of keys an employee would acquire
through forty years of steady promotions. Just before he left the apartment, Darius picked up an orange emergency-response lantern.

Six weeks earlier, Darius had been paroled from the Elmira
Correctional Facility, near Binghamton, New York, where he had
served two years for attempted grand larceny—"attempted" because
he had signed out NYCTA vehicles for surface use (extinguishing
track fires, supervising maintenance projects) and then signed
them back in according to procedure. Darius has never worked for
the NYCTA; he has never held a steady job. He is 37 and has spent
a third of his adult life in prison for victimless offenses related to
transit systems.

He was at work by 7:20, eating buttered rolls and drinking coffee
in a GMC pickup with a small signal crew above the Nostrand
Avenue stop on the Number 3 line. The truck was hitched to an
emergency generator temporarily powering the station lights; during a repair job Con Edison had spliced into the wrong cable. Traveling through the system three days earlier, Darius had encountered
the crew members and told them that he was a track-department
employee waiting for his truck to be fixed. In the meantime, he
said, his only responsibility was the occasional street-flagging operation. The signal guys were on what they, and therefore Darius,
called "a tit job": babysitting the generator and periodically reporting on the electrical work. Darius sat in the station with the signal
guys, surveying the Con Ed work and watching girls.

That slow morning there was a lot of conversation about the transit union. Its president, Willie James, was on his way out. Darius, who is voluble and almost perpetually affable, was deferentially critical of James, who, he said, "came from buses and favored the bus guys." Darius voiced or echoed complaints about the effects of union inaction: low pay, retirement after twenty-five years instead of twenty, the difficulty of getting basic equipment. For nearly two decades Darius had attended NYCTA workers' rallies and union meetings. At the meetings he had argued for, among other things, better lighting in tunnels and the right to wear earplugs against ambient noise. He had agreed that positive drug tests should result in mandatory ninety-day suspensions and counseling but objected to withholding salary during that time. He took detailed notes as he traveled through the system so that he could accurately critique management actions.

At noon Darius volunteered to go to his girlfriend's apartment and bring back lunch for the crew. Darius had met his girlfriend a week earlier, on the subway. It was a snowy night; they were alone in the car. Darius said she looked cold. She nodded and smiled and pointed to his uniform. He told her where he worked in the track department and how he approached various kinds of emergency situations and that he did street flagging and drove heavy equipment. She didn't understand anything he said because she was from Ecuador and didn't speak English. Her name was Nelly Rodriguez. She was 45 and had five children and worked as a seamstress in a garment factory. They exchanged phone numbers; later her sister translated for them.

Within a week Nelly had asked Darius for his Social Security number and invited him to move in. Several months later they would be married, and Darius would confess to Nelly, having fabricated a story about his nineteenth arrest, that he was a lifelong subway impostor, and she would say, through her sister, "If it's your problem it's our problem, and I'm not going to tell anybody," and then successfully inveigle him into signing over the rights to his story to a small Manhattan production company for a relatively tiny sum (several newspapers had covered his arrest). Eventually a lawyer hired by Darius's parents would void this agreement, and Darius would yield to their unremitting pressure and request a divorce. When he is asked now if he worried about his quick start with Nelly, Darius says, "No, because I had already said a long time ago that I had not planned to get married until I was at least in my thirties. . . . I wanted to get married when I was a little more settled, when I had a little better insight."

In Nelly's kitchen, Darius ate a plate of the fish and rice and beans that she had cooked the night before. He sealed the rest in Tupperware and brought it back to the crew. He told the guys to take their time finishing up; he had to check on his truck at fleet operations. Then he left to visit a friend, a token booth clerk at 57th Street in Manhattan.

Darius's friend was at lunch when he arrived, so he let himself into the station's command tower to wait. The control room had a big signal board that tracked train movement and a tinted picture window with a platform view. The vacant tower had recently been automated, but Darius remembered when the seven empty lockers had been full and when, in the recessed kitchen with its miniature sink and stove, there had been pots in the bottom cabinet and food in the top. He had often stopped by to chat about work, or read the newspaper, or get a doughnut and a cup of coffee.

Darius sat surveilling the lights on the board: a clear-skinned dark black guy of average height in an unusually complete Transit Authority uniform. Darius is only slightly overweight, but everything about him appears tender and fleshy: the heels of his hands and the little underhung bellies of skin between the knuckles of his fingers, his small paunch, the cushions of his cheeks, his chubby iridescent lips. His movements are almost always leisurely—when he's being chased by transit cops he lopes onerously, counting on his knowledge of the system's crannies—and he stands slightly stooped, the shallow curve of his back in conformity with all the small padded curves of his body. Darius has big circular eyes that quickly admit delight, a serene form of which he was feeling as he absorbed the scrupulous, luridly represented shuttling of the trains. He can't explain why, but he is always content in the subway: elementally content, at unrivaled ease, unable to think about anything outside the system.

Darius grew up near the 179th Street yard, the terminus of the F train, in Jamaica, Queens. He was a bright, early-talking child. His obsession with the subway manifested itself as soon as he began riding trains with his mother, at age three: His desire to see a train's headlights materialize in the tunnel black always threatened to propel him over the platform edge. The force of this attraction never diminished. Darius did well in school, but an opaque inwardness isolated him from other children and worried his teachers; he never formed enduring friendships or felt comfortable in class.

Darius spent hundreds of hours watching trains at 179th Street. He estimated the angle of every track intersection in the yard. By the time he was eight, he could visualize the entire New York City subway system. (Later he memorized the architecture of the stations.) Family and friends with subway questions began calling the McCollum household and asking for Darius. In small notebooks he recorded arrival and departure times at various stations, and documented whatever he observed: the shrill, keyed-up atmosphere an emergency stop instantly creates on a platform, the presence of transit police, mechanical problems ("E train to Canal st 0015 L.C. Delay of train leaving Parson's Blvd Door Trouble"), passengers riding between cars ("A train to 81st L.C. 4112—Girl riding in between cars approx. 17 Brown Coat Blue Pants Brown Shoes"). He hasn't abandoned this note-taking. His logs—

0210 D train 169st N.P.C. Meal
0217 S/B F 169th st L.C. 586
0230 S/B F Woodhaven D train
0311 N/B F 71st F.H. L.C. 1200
0317 N/B E Kew Gardens L.C. 1134 . . .

—span twenty-five years.

When Darius was 11, a classmate, unprovoked, stabbed him in the back with a pair of scissors. The scissors punctured a lung and came within an inch of his heart. The boy opened and closed the scissors as he pulled them out, creating a wound in the shape of an irregular star. At the hospital, doctors pumped blood out of Darius's lung and reinflated it. He didn't speak that day or the next: He just stared at his parents with awestruck eyes. At night he paced in his sleep or lay awake. When he went back to school, he would sit only with his back against the wall.

Not long after the stabbing, Darius began disappearing into the subway system for days at a time:

> 3/30/81 7:30 didn't go to school, but then I went on the J train up to Chambers st . . . 11:30 I went back on the J train and went to catch the D train to Brighton Beach at approx 12:45. Transf to M train and went to Stillwell at 1:05 and went to the bathroom (no food dur this time) back on the M, return to Brighton and took D train to pacific st (Bklyn) approx 2:00 took the #2 train transfered to the #6 to 28th street to Girls Club at 3:30 pat, angie, rosemary. They gave me a sandwich and milk and then left 3:45. . . .

> 4/2/81 I left to #6 to Grand Central took #7 to 5th ave and took F for the rest night, and slept on the F train Balance of night till approx 6:30 am.

Darius counted on certain relatives in Queens and Brooklyn: He would stop by to eat and spend the night and then return to the subway. He often went home for provisions when his parents were asleep or at work. Samuel and Elizabeth McCollum worked long hours, but they tried to stay up later than their son and wake up before him. They tried to lock him in and lock him out; they talked to NYCTA supervisors; they called his school and arranged for morning escorts; they tried different schools; they had him hospitalized for psychiatric treatment. But each remedy had its limit, and ultimately they found that they could only interrupt his journeying. Mrs. McCollum tracked her son's movements. On one of her calendars, the word "out," meaning "location unknown," fills fourteen day-boxes in January of 1981, when Darius was first arrested for driving a train. The four days from the twenty-seventh to the thirtieth read: *late for school—in at 10:00 a.m.; home; out—drove train; court.*

By this time Darius had cultivated a constellation of admirers at the 179th Street yard. Darius has always been deeply disarming. His charm resides in his peculiar intelligence, his perpetual receptivity to transporting delight, and his strange, self-endangering indifference to the consequences of his enthusiasm. Darius never curses. He has no regionally or culturally recognizable accent. He has a quick-to-appear, caricaturishly resonant laugh, like the laugh ascribed to Santa Claus, and he can appreciate certain comedic aspects of what he does, but he often laughs too long or when things aren't funny, as when he mentions that he briefly worked on the LIRR route that Colin Ferguson took to slaughter commuters. Darius litters his speech with specialized vocabulary ("BIE incident," "transverse-cab R-110") and unusually formal phrases ("what this particular procedure entails," "the teacher didn't directly have any set curriculum studies"). He frequently and ingenuously uses the words "gee," "heck," "doggone," "gosh," and "dang."

It is difficult to find anyone who knows Darius well and does not express an abiding protective affection for him. Cops always refer to him by his first name, and often with wistful amusement, as if he were a wayward godson. In discussing his cases, they have called him "great," "endearing," and "fabulous." They mention his honesty and abnormally good memory. Sergeant Jack Cassidy, a high-ranking transit cop who has interviewed Darius more often than anyone else in the NYPD, told me, "You'll be talking to a fantastic person when you talk to Darius, and I hope prison never changes that. Give him my best. But don't tell him where I am, because he'll probably come visit me." (Darius has paid Sergeant Cassidy several friendly, unannounced visits at his office, in full transit gear.)

Darius's apprenticeship began with a motorman he called Uncle Craft, who drove the first train Darius took regularly. When Craft began working at the 179th Street yard, he taught Darius to drive along the generous stretch of track between the yard and the last F stop. Darius learned how to ease a train into a station, aligning it with the markers that match its length, how to read signals while simultaneously observing the track connections the signals predict (he was taught never to assume the infallibility of signals), and how to understand the timers that govern the signals. Darius was an exceptional, methodical student: He learned quickly and thoroughly, building on each skill he acquired and instantly memorizing terminology. Soon he was doing yard maneuvers and taking trains into passenger service, as both a train operator and a conductor. (By the time of his first arrest, he had driven trains dozens of times.)

To broaden his knowledge, Darius visited employees from 179th Street who had taken up new positions elsewhere. He learned to drive garbage trains and de-icer trains and to repair the electrical boxes that control signals. In renovation shops he learned how to dismantle trains and reassemble them. In control towers he learned how to direct traffic: routing trains around obstructions, replacing late trains, switching ABD trains ("abandoned due to malfunction") out of service. The more he learned, the more he volunteered to do, and the easier he made the lives of the people who taught him. By the time he was 18, TA employees had begun calling him at home and asking him to pull shifts.

Darius was given his first uniform at 15: "I can't compare that feeling to anything. I felt official. I felt like this is me, like this is where I belong." Darius discusses his work in the subway with professional pride, generally using the first-person plural ("Sometimes we didn't feel that management should be doing certain things . . ."). His vision of himself as an NYCTA worker is officious and uncompromising: "I'm a very good train operator. Even though I drive fast, don't get me wrong: I believe in coasting, I don't believe in excessive speeds. Even if you're late don't speed, because eventually you'll catch up. As a conductor, I give a whole announcement before and during stops. . . . That's just me. Sometimes they'll make part of an announcement: 'Next stop is Queens Plaza.' Okay, the next stop is Queens Plaza, but what do we *do* there?"

The question of how Darius's immutable sense of belonging has never been damaged by all the skillful impersonation and fakery it depends on is not one that he can answer. I spent almost fifteen hours sitting across a table from him, and I asked this question several times. He looked bemused, his eyes wandered, he half smiled, he said he just thought of himself as a part of the system, that he felt safer and more content there than anywhere else, that for reasons he doesn't understand this paradox never occurs to him until he is behind bars for a while. He always stressed that he improved service to the "riding customers," and that, given his ability and care, he would never endanger anyone. (During one of these conversations, he said, "Oh—in the article could you put that my title is Transportation Captain? That's the title the employees gave me, because I move around the system so well.") Eventually Darius began taking the skills tests the NYCTA requires for employment, but by then he was notorious.

.   .   .

Reclining in the tranquillity of the 57th Street tower, Darius heard the descending scale of a train losing its charge. He sat up and waited. He knew something had tripped the train's emergency brake, and he knew the operator would reset the brake and try to recharge the train. When the recharge attempt failed, he picked up his helmet, his vest, his gloves, his lantern, and his flashlight. He was thinking only of the train. The first four cars had made it into the station. Darius questioned the train operator and lent him his flashlight so that they could begin the routine debris search. Darius was inspecting the tracks when over the train radio he heard Command Center order an evacuation, so he unhooked the chains between the fourth and fifth cars, climbed up and unlocked the two sets of car doors, made the standard evacuation announcement, and continued down the train this way until the last passengers walked off. (After opening each car, he stood by the doors to make sure everyone got through safely.) When the train was empty, he briefly examined its rear brakes and then resumed his debris search. Two transit cops arrived; Darius hurried back to help explain the situation.

The cops, Officers Cullen and Morales, saw passengers exiting the train in a neat stream, and they saw Darius conscientiously inspecting the track with a flashlight. They had just begun questioning the conductor and train operator when Darius rushed up and co-opted an answer: "Yeah, the train went BIE and we think it caught some debris, so we're evaluating the track—the rear brakes checked out, the passengers are all clear." When Darius had gone back to work, the train operator pulled the cops aside and whispered, "This guy's not one of us. He's an impostor."

They found that hard to believe. Everything about Darius—his gear, his carriage, his total comfort with protocol—suggested authenticity. But the train operator had recognized Darius from a Transit Authority wanted poster, and he told the cops to ask for ID. Darius produced his study-group letter, which essentially convinced them that he was legitimate (they had encountered track-study notices many times before), but the operator was adamant, and they asked Darius to have his supervisor come vouch for him. Darius led Officer Cullen back to the tower, unlocking the door and turning on the lights and telling Officer Cullen to sit down and make himself comfortable. Darius got a drink from a water cooler and sat down at a desk to call a friend. Cullen, short and thick-limbed, with a gelled part in his hair and multiple tattoos and nine years on the force, felt faintly guilty for inconveniencing Darius.

On the phone, Darius asked to speak to someone and then said, "Oh, okay, I'll try back." His boss was out to lunch, he said. Cullen said not to worry, they could wait, and apologized for the annoyance. Out the tower window Darius glimpsed an unfriendly superintendent conferring with the train operator. Darius started laughing. He said, "All right, you got me." Officer Cullen asked him what he was talking about. Darius—now narrowly smiling and incipiently prideful—said, "You got me! I don't work for the TA. The letter's a forgery. I stole the letterhead and did the letter myself. The uniform and keys I got from people I know. I've been doing this for a long time. It's actually easy if you know what you're doing." Officer Cullen stood silent and staring, suspended in his disbelief. "Here's some articles about me," Darius said.

On the way to a formal interview with Assistant District Attorney Michael Dougherty at 100 Centre Street, Darius offered unsolicited, sophisticated descriptions of the NYCTA surface crews the police car passed. Cullen and Morales wondered how he knew so much about the minutiae of surface work; Darius responded with monologues about his mastery of the system. To the officers it seemed that he couldn't speak fast enough, that his confession had energized him and elevated his self-regard. The sight of the Brooklyn Bridge reminded Darius that he had plans to go to a barbecue the next day on the Manhattan Bridge: It was a Friday tradition of a bridge crew he had been working with. He asked if there was a chance he would get out in time. Officer Cullen said that, whether or not he got out, it might not be such a great idea.

At Centre Street, Darius was interviewed by ADA Dougherty and Detective Martin Mullen. He gave no sign that he knew a transgression had occurred, that there was a permanent divide in the room and that he was alone on one side of it. With a single exception, neither interviewer noted any change in his demeanor, which was one of subdued bliss. According to Detective Mullen, "emotionally Darius was even-keeled the entire time. The fact that he was carrying these articles from his previous arrests—it was almost like he dug the publicity, like there was some prestige in the experience."

The exception came when ADA Dougherty suggested that Darius might have had something to do with the train's emergency stop. The absurd, pejorative idea that he would ever compromise service quality and passenger safety disturbed Darius. "That's exactly what I'm trained *not* to do," he said. He explained that stopping the train would have required both override permission from the City Hall control tower and access to the switch room in the back of the 57th Street tower. Neither was available to him—though, as he admitted, he probably could have guessed the location of the switch-room key. City Hall later confirmed Darius's story, and evidence indicated that he had never been in the switch room. His theory of the event—a wheel-detector device had tripped the train's emergency brake because the train had exceeded the posted speed—was later determined to be the most plausible.

Once it became clear that Darius wouldn't plead to the charge of reckless endangerment, Dougherty and Mullen decided to let him talk. He talked for two hours and seemed willing to talk indefinitely. He was cagey when it came to identifying collaborators or detailing certain methods whose secrecy was essential to his freedom of movement; otherwise, almost any question elicited long tales of his exploits that gave way episodically to ornate, unnecessary digressions. Once I asked Darius what he was doing at 57th Street before his arrest. My question implied that he'd been in the station. His answer began like this: "No, no. I was mainly in the tower, not the station. Now: Towers are for what is known as train-traffic control. The board lights tell you where everything is at. All right? Okay. So every single train from Fifth Avenue, on the N and the R, down to Canal Street. Not only that but there's a communications box for listening to the crew on every train. You also have what is known as fire watch. I watch the board for anything relating to a fire condition. Now, if it's something minute, I can hopefully go down and end the problem without having to call the fire department. If it's close to the third rail, use a dry chemical. If it's something major, call the fire department, call Command, have the power turned off for that section because otherwise the fire department cannot go on the tracks, that's part of their protocol. . . . And if need be you can have EMS on standby, just in case. So you always take all necessary precautions. Okay! Now on this particular day, I'm in the tower . . ."

Darius's obsession has always been concentrated on the subway, but a long interview with him will teach you how far beyond it he has roamed. He may describe his experiences as a substitute engineer on the freight trains of Conrail, Norfolk Southern, Delaware & Hudson, or CSX. ("CSX is definitely my favorite. Every single engine is freshly painted.") He may tell you now to manipulate the employee-transfer protocol of the Metro bus system to get a job as a shifter (cleaning and prepping buses at depots), and how to use that position to take buses out on express routes. He might explain Job 179 (conductor) on the Long Island Railroad: what track you'll be on (17 or 19), how to let the crew know when you've finished preparing the train for departure (two buzzes on the intercom), how you return to Penn Station "as equipment" (without passengers).

It is unlikely that Darius will omit the year he spent wearing an

NYCTA superintendent's shield. While he was doing a stint as a conductor, he discovered that he could have a shield made in a jewelry store. He began wearing it on a vest he pulled over his TA-specified shirt and tie. He had a hard hat and pirated ID. Darius considered himself a track-department superintendent, so he signed out track-department vehicles and radios and drove around the city, supervising track maintenance and construction projects and responding to emergencies. He was sensitive to the threat of close scrutiny by superiors, but given his high position and network of allies, that was rare. Darius worked regular hours: eight to four from Tuesday to Thursday, seven in the evening to three in the morning on Friday, and three until eleven on Saturday morning. That way he was off from Saturday morning until Tuesday morning. "Because of my title and my position," Darius told me, "I figured I had the seniority to do it."

At the end of the Centre Street interview, Darius was facing felony charges to which he had confessed. He had twice been convicted of felonies. He had just dramatically violated his parole, and he had multiple parole and probation violations on his record. But he never asked Detective Mullen or ADA Dougherty about his legal situation. He shook their hands and was led out in handcuffs, his still face showing contentment.

On that day Darius's parents, who had retired from New York to North Carolina, awaited him uncertainly in their house outside Winston-Salem. Since his release, Mr. and Mrs. McCollum had prevailed on him to apply for a parole transfer and recommence his life in North Carolina, where Mrs. McCollum's nephew had found him a job through a state program for parolees. Darius stayed with them for a few weeks, and then went up to New York for a parole hearing. But weeks had passed; Darius's aunt, with whom he'd been staying, no longer knew where he was or what he was doing.

What he was doing, while sleeping and eating and showering at Nelly's or in NYCTA crew rooms, was driving a de-icer train from Coney Island to Prospect Park on the D line; putting out track fires (a train dripping battery acid caused a small explosion at 34th Street and Sixth Avenue; a tossed cigarette butt kindled a small rubbish fire in Brooklyn); investigating a busted water main at 110th Street on the A line; flagging traffic, on weekends, around a transit construction project at Queens Plaza ("The guys from transit that do street flagging, they look as if they're stiff, and see, when I do it, I look like I'm with DOT, because I make it look so efficient—I know how to do the hand signs"); assisting the track crew he mentioned to Cullen and Morales with inspections of the Manhattan Bridge on Mondays, Wednesdays, and Fridays; and entirely repainting a crew room after hearing a supervisor say that it would make a good project for someone. This all happened, Darius says, because he ran into some old friends at Queens Plaza soon after he got back to New York and they invited him to hang out and take some of their shifts, and he thought he could do a few and go back to North Carolina, "but it just kept going, and that was it."

Elizabeth McCollum is unreserved and accurately judgmental and dresses well and cannot discuss her son without becoming fervent; she retired a decade ago from an administrative job at a textbook company. Samuel McCollum, a former plant supervisor, is bulky and skeptical, has an impulsive falsetto giggle, and tries, when discussing the actions of others, to discover decent motivations that have been obscured by mistakes or cruelties. Like his wife, he has been injured by the experiences of his only child: "Darius won't open up and talk about anything. He would never elaborate on an answer. That's all we ever wanted. Now, how do you get somebody like that in touch with himself?" On the day of the final arrest, Mrs. McCollum was still hopeful: "You can't let negativism cloud you, because with Darius, once that comes in, forget it." She and Mr. McCollum talked about the life Darius might have in

North Carolina, and thought about getting him a driver's license
and a pickup truck, which he had always wanted. They didn't say it,
but they were each thinking that in their house Darius grew restless
immediately.

The McCollum house stands at the edge of a rural two-lane, on
a four-acre grass lot that runs to a curtain of hardwoods. The neighboring houses, similarly situated, occasionally give way to graz-
ing horses. When I visited, the only thing in one big field down
the road was a tethered mule. The problem for Darius was that
he couldn't walk out the front door and easily go anywhere. The
McCollums had furnished their house ardently: Chiming clocks
and porcelain figurines and hand-stitched antimacassars and
graven glassware and pictures of sunset-silhouetted African kings
left no blank space. Emptied from many rooms in many homes
over a lifetime and now tensely converged in this final house, these
encroaching objects in their familiarity had become largely invisible to Mr. and Mrs. McCollum, but in an attempt to understand
the propensities of her son, Mrs. McCollum had preserved every
document—subway notes and journals, school reports, letters from
prison—that might explain him, and this expanding collection
never entirely disappeared from her or her husband's awareness.
Much was boxed; much lay around, visible and frequently handled;
the things that Mrs. McCollum liked to look at every few days
remained enshrined in convenient places. One was a letter from
prison, dated June 12, 1987:

> Its me again saying hello along with a thought . . . my thought
> goes like this. There once lived a young man and a very bright
> man. This young man had . . . such good parents . . . they did
> everything that they saw was good for this guy. . . . The guy was
> actually great until he [got] into his teenage years and started
> hanging out around trains, trucks and buses, but one day it all

caught up with him and this young man was confused. . . . This guy is away somewhere to where he can't runaway from and has to face his problems. He is sorry for everything and wants to forget about everything he has done. That is the end of that story. This is a beginning step. I am wondering what is going to happen when this young man comes home. . . . I'm sure there will be some changes but what I mean is will he be able to find his destiny.

Darius's call from Rikers Island didn't surprise Mr. and Mrs. McCollum. They had long since learned how to entertain ambitious plans for him while anticipating legal dilemmas. They replaced his court-appointed attorney with a family friend named Tracey Bloodsaw. Bloodsaw decided on a psychiatric defense and got the access order required for an examination, but corrections officers at Rikers Island, on various bureaucratic pretexts and over a period of months, refused to admit her psychiatrist. Justice Carol Berkman declined to intervene on the psychiatrist's behalf, and eventually precluded a psychiatric defense, declaring that adequate notice of such a defense had become impossible. Bloodsaw told Berkman what she thought of the ruling, explained to the McCollums that she had become a liability to Darius, and removed herself from the case.

Darius's next lawyer, Stephen Jackson, accepted a plea, and Justice Berkman scheduled a sentencing hearing. This empowered her to order—as opposed to merely authorizing—a psychiatric examination. A prison psychiatrist, after a cursory evaluation, noted that a neurological disorder called Asperger's syndrome might explain Darius's behavior. Almost simultaneously, Jackson was contacted by members of several Asperger's support groups. Darius, whose arrests had been covered in newspapers for twenty years, had become well-known among Asperger's experts and activists, and his case had been cited in at least one scholarly work. There was a strong consensus in the Asperger's community that Darius suffered from the syndrome, and dismay that his treatment had consisted entirely of jail time. Jackson decided to request an adjournment in court so that Darius could be examined and might receive a counseling-based sentence.

Stooped and silent at his sentencing, in late March of last year, Darius stood at the very edge of the courtroom, just in front of the holding-cell door through which he had been led. In accordance with the law, he faced Justice Berkman, who sat on a high plinth before a ten-foot mural of the Lady of Justice, between half-furled flags on eagle-tipped poles. The justice had black-gray hair and a squinty, repudiative face. She often listened to the lawyers with her chin on her upturned palms and her incredulous mouth open; she often rolled her eyes with unusual vigor and range, her head following, as if drawn by her eyes, until it almost touched her shoulder. Darius looked around only once, for his mother. Mrs. McCollum, anxious and carrying an accumulation of anger at the legal system, forced herself to smile at him. Darius says he wasn't thinking about anything: He knew what was going to happen.

I arrived before Darius and watched a few brusque bail hearings. The distant ceiling diminished the few spectators. Then the clerk called Darius's docket number and the lawyers identified themselves. They had spare tables at the foot of Justice Berkman's plinth. ADA Dougherty—plain, young, resolute—sat alone. Stephen Jackson sat with Alvin Schlesinger, a former colleague of Justice Berkman's who had been recruited by the president of an Asperger's organization. Jackson is tall; every aspect of his appearance had been managed. His manner was measured and grandiloquent: He seemed to take a special pleasure in formality. (When I called him afterward and asked for an interview, he said, "Certainly I would be amenable at some point in time. Would you like to do it telephonically?") Schlesinger, who had retired to the country, seemed patient in a practiced, almost impervious way; after the sentencing he would drive back to Vermont without stopping, drink a double scotch, and write Justice Berkman a letter he would never send.

Jackson rose. "Your Honor," he said, "after the Court agreed to provide a plea to satisfy the indictment, I was inundated with information regarding Darius's possible psychological condition. It is apparent that he may be afflicted with Asperger's syndrome. . . . The Court is aware of the letters that were sent to the Court providing the Court with information regarding the disease, and—"

"I'm sorry, Mr. Jackson," Justice Berkman said, staring hard at various faces in the courtroom, "but perhaps we could bottom-line this . . . having educated myself on the website and with the *DSM* and so forth, Mr. McCollum has some characteristics which are very much inconsistent with Asperger's. He's got a lot of friends. You told me he has a fiancée, and one of the major signs . . . is social dysfunction. Not just, gee, his friends think he's a little strange sometimes but an inability to relate to others. . . ." Mrs. McCollum started to get up and was pulled back down by the people on either side of her.

"In any event," Berkman said, "I don't understand what the point is. . . . So far as I can tell there's no treatment for Asperger's. That is number one. . . . Number two, Asperger's would not disable him from knowing that he's not supposed to form credentials identifying him as an employee of the Transit Authority and go in and take trains or buses or vans or cars or other modes of transportation, which I gather has been his specialty. . . . I don't see any reason to delay this further, because for some reason the press thinks that, oh, Darius is not responsible. Darius *is* responsible. . . . He can stop doing this, if his family and friends would stop telling him, Oh, isn't this amusing. Right?" Mrs. McCollum rose rapidly and was pulled down.

Mr. Schlesinger stood and requested an adjournment so that the defense could have Darius examined and explore treatment options. Many experts felt that Darius had the disorder and to deny treatment was to risk indefinitely perpetuating his past: a limbo in the alternating forms of furtive impersonation and incarceration. Schlesinger had secured a promise from an Asperger's expert at the Yale Child Study Center to examine Darius and recommend a residential treatment facility. Assistant District Attorney Dougherty stood and opposed the request. Given his history of parole and probation violations, Darius was a bad candidate for any treatment program. Stephen Jackson stood and pointed out the circularity: Darius is not a good candidate for treatment because of his condition, and his condition persists because he's not a good candidate for treatment.

Resisting several defense attempts to respond, Justice Berkman stabbed out: "Well, now that I've been accused of presiding over a travesty of justice and condemning Darius to a life sentence, I suppose there is no way of the Court coming out of this looking anything but monstrous. . . . This man is a danger. . . . But in the meantime we've made him a poster boy for the system's lack of compassion for the mentally ill. Well, I have a lot of compassion for the mentally ill. You know, we don't lock them up anymore. We let them have lives, and most of the mentally ill, I hear from the experts . . . lead law-abiding lives. Darius McCollum does not. That's too bad. The law says he has to face the consequences of that, because . . . he has free will, and that's the nature of humanity, and unless he wants to be treated like an animal . . . he has to exert his free will for the good . . . and to say that he is incapable of doing that is to take away his humanity. So all those people out there making faces at me"—Mrs. McCollum was shaking her head exaggeratedly—"thinking of me as the Wicked Witch of the West, are, in fact, the people who are stealing his humanity from him. . . ."

Mrs. McCollum stood up; before she could be pulled down Berkman had sentenced Darius to five years in prison. When the gavel hit, all the released talk overwhelmed her rapid words.

Jackson immediately appealed, on the ground that Justice Berkman's failure to grant an adjournment at sentencing was arbitrary. It's a weak argument: Jackson agreed to a plea and sentencing date and then waited until sentencing to ask for more time; Justice Berkman made no technical mistakes. The DA's office has been disinclined to consider vacating Darius's plea and changing his sentence if he is diagnosed with Asperger's. This option, proposed by Alvin Schlesinger, who as a Supreme Court justice developed a relationship with New York County District Attorney Robert Morgenthau, was theoretically available to the defense as soon as Darius was sentenced. Jackson, inexplicably, has yet to have Darius examined.

Asperger's syndrome, which mainly affects males, is generally considered to be a mild variant of autism, with a prevalence rate several times higher. The *Diagnostic and Statistical Manual of Mental Disorders* requires five symptoms for a diagnosis: "impairment in social interaction," including "failure to develop [appropriate] peer relationships" and a "lack of social or emotional reciprocity"; "restricted repetitive and stereotyped patterns of behavior, interests and activities," including an "encompassing preoccupation with [an area of] interest that is abnormal either in intensity or focus"; "significant impairment in social, occupational or other important areas of functioning"; and "no significant delay in cognitive [4] or language [5] development."

Among the "encompassing preoccupations" in the literature of Asperger's: Abbott and Costello, astrophysics, deep-ocean biology, deep fat fryers, telephone wire insulators, carnivorous dinosaurs, cows, Wagner, nineteenth-century Russian novels, storm drains, steam trains, transit timetables, Zoroastrianism, Zsa Zsa Gabor, and the genealogy of royalty. Entire lives are brought to bear on one tiny piece of the world. Because abstract thought tends to be very difficult for people with Asperger's, they satisfy their obsessions by amassing precisely defined units of information: numbers, terms, codes, dates, titles, materials, names, formulas.

Asperger's precludes normal emotional intuition. Behavioral cues are elusive: Winks and shoulder shrugging and sarcasm are often meaningless. Conversations are one-sided; patients generally deliver long, fact-crowded monologues on their areas of expertise, blind to gestures of boredom or puzzlement. General questions, which can require both speculating abstractly and intuiting a questioner's intent, are often impossible for people with Asperger's to answer. Patients may respond with a far-reaching elaboration of a single related fact or experience.

Conventions of interpersonal behavior, if they are not explicit, remain beyond comprehension, as when a small boy, generally affectionate toward his mother, asks her why, given that he can dress and feed himself, she is still necessary, or when a boy endlessly photographs people while telling them that humans are his favorite animal, or when Darius writes to his parents from prison: "Hello There, People of America lets get down and party on as we say hello and what's going on, cause I know there's something going on . . ." and:

> I am enclosing a reese's peanut butter cup coupon to let you read and see if you can win some money. Just read the directions. . . . I kind of wish that I was a Jeanie so I wouldn't have to be here. "Ha-ha." I've got a stiff neck and itching all over and cold feet and runny nose and watery eyes itchy ears o Mom I'm just in poor shape. There's a rat under my bed and a little green man on my head but there's a true blue inside of you that keeps stopping me to say that I Love You. In here: It's like Death of a Salesman with a happy ending I hope. Well you guys I guess I

will go to bed to get warm so have fun and keep out of trouble.
Give my regards to Broadway . . .

Explicit rules that make sense socially but aren't strictly rational
seem unconvincing and often go unheeded, as when a boy in junior
high asks a female classmate if he can touch her crotch as casually
as if he were asking to borrow an eraser. That explicit and logical
rules exist along a continuum of seriousness is unappreciated, as
when a young man follows a barefoot woman around a supermarket, assiduously trying to conceal her naked feet from employees,
and then stands behind her in the express lane, diligently removing
one of her purchases each time she turns her head until she is no
longer over the ten-item limit.

Speech is oddly formal and often unmarked by accent, as if
verbal local color had been filtered out. Specialized phrases are
applied in a way that is logical but, from the perspective of conven-
tional usage, awkward or bizarre, as when an English boy describes
a hole in his sock as "a temporary loss of knitting."

For people with Asperger's, self-identity has little to do with internal life; information constitutes identity. One boy who was asked
to draw a self-portrait sketched an ocean liner, cracked and sinking beside an iceberg; the *Titanic* was his obsession. Another
self-portrait accurately represented a tsunami-shadowed tract of
California coast; its author was fascinated by plate tectonics. An
autobiographical statement:

I am an intelligent, unsociable, but adaptable person. I would
like to dispel any untrue rumors about me. I am not edible. I cannot fly. I cannot use telekinesis. My brain is not large enough to
destroy the entire world when unfolded. I did not teach my long-
haired guinea pig Chronos to eat everything in sight (that is the
nature of the long-haired guinea pig).

People with Asperger's recognize their difference. One patient said he wished he had a micro-brain on his head to process all the intuitive meaning that surrounded and evaded him. Another patient, studying astronomy, told his therapist that he knew how scientists discovered the stars, and what instruments they used to discover the stars, but not how they discovered the names of the stars. He said he felt like a poor computer simulation of a human being, and he invented algebraic formulas to predict human emotion: frustration (z), talent (x), and lack of opportunity (y) give the equation $x + y = z$.

Darius, explaining that he has never needed to socialize and really only associates with people in transit systems, said to me, "Some people think that I'm different. Okay, fine, I am different, but everybody's different in their own kind of way. Some people just don't know how to directly really react to that." Before Darius's sentencing hearing, Stephen Jackson sent him a pamphlet on Asperger's. It was the first Darius had heard of the disorder. When I asked him about the pamphlet, he said, "I'll put it like this. Out of the twelve things that's on it I think I can identify myself with at least eight or nine. And all you need is five to have, you know, that type of thing."

Asperger's patients choose obsessions the way other people choose interests: Personality accounts for the choice. Sometimes, usually when they're young, patients acquire and discard fixations in swift succession, but eventually a single subject consumes them. They are born to fall down some rabbit hole, from which they never fully emerge.

The Clinton Correctional Facility, where I interviewed Darius, is a leviathan relic from 1845, just south of the Canadian border, with granite walls thirty feet high. In the intake center a guard examined the cassette and batteries in my tape recorder. I was escorted across a lawn to the main prison building. The walls leaned in—thirty feet is claustrophobically high. There were long-barreled guns and searchlights in guard towers. I felt as if I might provoke a terrible reaction by accident. We went through the prison lobby, a leaden door, a corridor, another leaden door, and arrived at the interview room, where the guard left me. Except for a table and chairs, the room was as plain as a cell. I sat waiting in a restless institutional quiet. Two guards brought Darius in. In his jumpsuit he looked lumpy and quiescent. We shook hands—Darius's handshake was bonelessly indifferent—and sat down. The guards left, one whispering to the other, "He's pretty docile."

I made a vague little speech: I was writing an article, etc. Darius nodded politely as I talked but gave no indication that he was interested in my aims or motivations or life. When I finished he asked where I was staying and how much it cost and what train I'd come on and how long it had taken. From the time of the trip he guessed that my train hadn't had an M-10 engine; he wished me luck getting one on the way back. I started asking about his career in transit, and he showed the transporting animation that Detective Mullen had observed. He sketched control panels in the air, he drove trains in mime, he asked for paper and drew the track intersections of subway stations. He often looked away to concentrate on the images he conjured.

Clinton is a maximum-security facility. Darius was there because the Department of Corrections, aware of his impersonation convictions, considered him an escape risk. To keep him safe the DOC had to segregate him from the general population, which meant confining him to his cell for, Darius said, twenty-one hours a day. That morning he had made the guards laugh by wedging a sign in his cell bars that said, "Train Out of Service." He watched TV and read general interest magazines; he studied arrangements of facts in several specialty publications he subscribed to: *Truckers News,*

World of Trains, Truck 'N Trailer; he made lists of various things, like 185 love songs he happened to think of one day; and he wrote a lot of letters requesting information. Unsatisfied by something he saw on TV, he wrote to the Department of Defense, which replied:

> Unfortunately, the term "discretionary warfare" is not cur-
> rently used by the Department of Defense (DoD), so I am
> uncertain what you mean by it. In addition, there are no 12-man
> Special Operations units made up of personnel who are at the
> rank of Colonel or above. There are, however, Special Opera-
> tions units made up of 12 men: the US Army Special Forces A
> Teams. The Specials Forces A team is made up of two officers,
> two operations/intelligence sergeants, two weapons sergeants,
> two communications sergeants, two medics and two engineers —
> all trained in unconventional warfare and cross-trained in each
> other's specialties.

Darius underlined the word "two" every time it appeared.

On May 31 of this year, Darius will have spent 799 days in prison. At his first parole hearing, 912 days into his sentence, the DA's office will present his history of violations. His full sentence comes to 1,825 days. In the interview room of the Clinton Correc-tional Facility, I asked Darius if he thought he would continue to impersonate transit employees and otherwise break the law. He looked at the ceiling and took a long breath. He seemed to have prepared his answer. "Okay," he said, "trains are always going to be my greatest love. It's something that I depend upon because I've been knowing how to do it for twenty-five years. So this is like my home, my best friend, my everything. Everything that I need and want is there. But I don't want to get caught up with that again, and I'm probably going to need a little help. That much I can admit. If I can find—I know there's no such program as Trains Anonymous, but if I can get some kind of counseling it would be really beneficial towards me."

Darius doesn't like prison and complains about its deprivations, but he never expresses despair or outrage at the severity of his punishment. He sees his experience in terms of its daily components, without considering the entirety of his sentence—the abstract unbroken length of time between the present and his release. "I'll get out of here sooner or later," he says. And it doesn't occur to him to imagine an alternative life for himself: He never wonders what he might have been.

———

Darius calls me from prison all the time: He doesn't appreciate the distinction between friendships and sympathetic writer-subject relationships. I take maybe a third of his calls. Unless we talk about trains, the conversations are short — he gives brief factual reports and makes requests. When he asks how I'm doing and I actually talk about my frustrations or joys, his attention instantly migrates. At the first pause he'll ask, "So do you think the Eagles are going to win their division?" or "Did you get my subscription to Billboard *yet?" (I got him a subscription to* Rolling Stone, *but it didn't have enough music business statistics to satisfy him.) Once I told him I thought high-speed trains in Europe were cool and mentioned Acela, Amtrak's version. "Yeah, I drove the prototype," he said. "Now see, with Acela . . ." When he reemerged, I said that looking out the windows of high-speed trains made me dizzy. "You have to look out at an angle," he said, "at an angle."*

Last summer, shortly before his parole hearing, Darius was finally examined by a psychiatrist and diagnosed with Asperger's. The psychiatrist told the parole board that treatment, which is unavailable in state prison, was vital to Darius's rehabilitation. Asperger's experts and activists wrote letters to the parole board. I sent my article, the sentencing transcript, the DSM criteria for Asperger's, and a ten-page letter, in which I said that Darius's criminal history was entirely attributable to his disease, there was no evidence he had ever endangered anyone, and Justice Berkman's sentencing decision was demonstrably arbitrary. The board members did not discuss anything submitted on Darius's behalf before denying his parole request. He was a danger to society, they wrote, and lacked insight into his own behavior. Darius will be released this summer. He is scheduled to enter a life-skills program for people with Asperger's.

THE BODY FARM
MAXIMILLIAN POTTER

On a two-acre patch of Tennessee woods that is surrounded by an eight-foot-high fence topped with razor wire, Murray Marks kneels next to a rotting dead man. The corpse is faceup on a body bag. Much of the skin is gone; what little remains on the skeleton resembles beef jerky. Marks shakes his head in frustration. "This body," he says in his southern whisper of a voice, "should have been taken out of the bag, and the bag laid on top of him. Otherwise the body doesn't decompose properly; it is just going to stew in its own juices."

Marks, a 47-year-old associate professor of anthropology at the University of Tennessee, grabs the bag near the body's torso and pulls the plastic down flat against the ground. A liquid the color and texture of tobacco spit streams out from under the body onto the leaf-covered earth. It is the organic soup of putrefied organs.

"When I find out which of my students put this body here like this," Marks says, "their heads are on the chopping block." He stands up and scans the area within the gates for other bodies that may need his attention. Dozens are scattered about in various states of decay.

A nearby skeleton looks as if it had been scooped up by the hand of God, the bones shaken like dice and rolled across the dirt. A couple of badly decomposed corpses are duct-taped to trees; they are slouched over with what's left of their hands taped behind their backs. Many of the dead still wear the clothes they had on when they died or—like the body from Chattanooga, the one whose skull was shattered by a gunshot blast—when they were murdered.

Two corpses are what Marks describes as "fresh dead." Carefully stepping over body parts and ducking tree limbs, he makes his way to one of them: a naked woman belly-up at the base of a tree. A tuft of gray hair protrudes from her scalp, a scalp that has begun to slide off her skull. Marks figures she was in her early sixties when she died.

"Smell that?" he asks me. I take a deep breath; the pungent odor is something like a mixture of fresh mulch and wet garbage, only worse. In the still heat of the Tennessee summer, the foul stench blankets this wooded bluff behind the University of Tennessee Medical Center.

For a few long, quiet moments, we gaze at the woman. A bird chirps. A plane roars overhead. Tree branches rattle in the wind. A dozen or so flies are inching across the woman; one takes off and lands on Marks's crisp white shirt. Watching the bug, he says the scent of blood draws them. Soon, he adds, flies will swarm the body; they will crawl into every orifice; they will lay eggs, and these larvae will hatch into maggots; the maggots will eat almost everything down to the bone.

Sensing my queasiness, Marks touches my arm and says, "What you need to keep in mind is that this person made the ultimate sacrifice: She or her family decided that this is more important than a traditional burial." By this Marks means donating her remains to the University of Tennessee Anthropology Research Facility, the only outdoor "laboratory" in the world where researchers study human decomposition. Here at the Body Farm, as the facility is known, scientists harvest information about death to help law enforcement catch killers.

One of the central questions in any homicide investigation is How long has the victim been dead? In cop speak, the answer is "time since death," or TSD. Once detectives know the TSD, they can establish a timeline of the victim's final hours and minutes, which can lead to the murderer—or at the very least, to the last person who saw the victim alive. When a body is found within hours of a crime, a medical examiner performs an autopsy, studies the soft tissue and organs, and fairly easily determines the time and cause of death. But when a body is not found until days or weeks or months later and it has begun to decompose or has decomposed entirely—leaving behind bugs and bones—investigators turn to the Body Farmers. Marks and his colleagues have been so effective at helping cops solve otherwise unsolvable homicides that now the FBI sends agents here for a week every year for what amounts to a Death 101 class.

Standing over the dead woman, Marks points to what could be mistaken for varicose veins, and he slips into forensic investigator mode. "Death is a process," he says. "She was pronounced dead, but that body is still doing stuff. That marbling on her legs is something we see happening in the vascular system; it means the environment reached a certain temperature, and knowing that I can determine TSD." The formula, he explains, goes like this: Marbling occurs at about 400 degrees. Divide that number by the average daily temperature, which lately in Tennessee has been in the fifties, and there you have it. The woman has been dead about eight days. In another two weeks, when the body will have been exposed to 1,200 degrees, flesh will give way to bone. "If this were a crime scene," Marks says, "the first question I would be asked is 'Hey, Doc, how long has she been dead?' And from all the research we've done here, I would be able to give an answer."

It was one of the most cold-blooded homicides Mississippi had ever seen. On December 16, 1993, Pike County police got a call from a Michael Rubenstein. The 47-year-old reported that he had just arrived at his cabin in the woods outside the town of Summit and found the bodies of his stepson, 24-year-old Darryl Perry; Perry's

20-year-old wife, Annie Marie; and the couple's 4-year-old daughter, Crystal.

Police and an investigator from the Mississippi Highway Patrol rushed to the scene. They covered their mouths, fought through the stench and flies inside the closed-up cabin, and were horrified by what they saw. Darryl's and Annie Marie's bodies were on the bloodstained linoleum floor. Crystal's corpse was on a mattress atop a blood-soaked bedspread. The family had decomposed to the point of being partially mummified. Their faces were covered with maggots. Three days later, a medical examiner determined that the two adults had been stabbed and the girl had been strangled.

Rubenstein told police that the Perrys had been having marital problems and he had loaned them his cabin as a place to work things out. He said he had driven the Perrys from their home in New Orleans to the cabin in early November. When no one heard from them for a couple of weeks, Annie Marie's mom became concerned and Rubenstein "volunteered" to check on them. Rubenstein, a taxicab driver who was also from New Orleans, said the cabin had been empty when he visited on November 16 and November 27.

Other than the bodies, the killer left no physical evidence. Nevertheless, the highway patrol investigator was troubled by Rubenstein's story. Why, the detective wondered, didn't Rubenstein report the Perrys missing when he had twice checked on them and found them missing?

The investigator discovered that in August 1991, Rubenstein had applied for a $250,000 life insurance policy on Crystal. New York Life had rejected that application because Rubenstein's stepson was not married to Annie Marie; therefore he had no "insurable interest" in the girl. Then, within weeks of the rejection, Darryl and Annie Marie wed, Darryl adopted Crystal, and Rubenstein successfully reapplied to New York Life.

What's more, investigators learned that in 1979, Rubenstein took out a $240,000 insurance policy on a business partner; three months later, that partner was fatally shot in the back during a hunting-trip accident that included Rubenstein and Darryl Perry.

Five years after the homicide, in September 1998, the state police investigator persuaded the DA's office to present the facts to a grand jury. Rubenstein was indicted on three counts of murder. He was facing a death sentence. The prosecution's star witness was Murray Marks's mentor, William M. Bass—the head of UT's anthropology department, a nationally renowned forensic anthropologist, and the Ph.D. behind the Body Farm.

Bass got the call on the Rubenstein case in May 1999, about a year after he retired from UT. For all of his twenty-one years with the university, he was the anthropology department head. Today he is a 73-year-old professor emeritus, still active in forensic anthropology. Matter of fact, on this quiet afternoon, as we sit in the kitchen of the Knoxville home he shares with his wife, Carol, and his beagle, Knox, Bass is waiting for a call from a neighboring county's DA. A murderer whom Bass helped convict is before a judge asking for a new trial; Bass is on standby in the event the court again requires his testimony.

In the meantime, Bass is showing me slides of the crime scene for that case—flashing on the wall of his kitchen the same gruesome images he once showed to a jury. The slide projector clicks, and there's the decomposed headless corpse of an 18-year-old boy in the woods. Click, there's the skull in a shallow creek bed. Click, a close-up of the skull. The kid was shot three times in the head. Near as Bass can recollect, the teen was "done in" for $300. Hunters found the body on a hill, whereas the skull was discovered in the creek at the base of the slope. As the body decayed, the skull came off and rolled down the hill.

"Interesting thing about this case was the maggot activity," Bass says as he rises from the kitchen table and walks over to the scene on the wall. "Maggots don't like sunlight, so they ate all the flesh under the clothing. See that?" He points to the dark stains on the victim's shirt and pants. "But they left the skin here"—he points to the dead boy's arms below his shirtsleeves—"and here." He points to the skin on the legs between the tattered sneaker and cuff of the jeans. "The maggots left an umbrella of flesh."

Bass is an owlish man with square glasses, a tan freckled face, and a buzz cut that he has kept high and tight since his days in the Korean War. He has a warm, gravelly southern drawl. Even though he's talking about a brutal murder, he sounds as if he's reading *Winnie-the-Pooh.*

While Bass is standing in the light of the projector, the image of the decapitated kid washing over him, his wife hobbles into the kitchen. Carol grew up outside Lynchburg, Virginia, on a farm not far from where Bass spent much of his childhood. Now 64 years old, short with silver hair, she requires a cane to get around. Yet she possesses the effervescent personality of a 16-year-old southern debutante. "Lord, please," she says, "make yourself right at home." As she prepares us a lunch of chicken salad sandwiches and iced tea, I ask if the scene on the wall troubles her.

"Oh no," she says. "The only thing that bothers me—a deputy sheriff came here a few months ago with a skull he found that still had a little matter on it. And he put it on my nice tablecloth. They rolled it around. Back and forth. Of course I didn't say anything. But it was one of my favorite tablecloths."

Bass chuckles and shrugs. The raised-eyebrow look on his face seems to say, "Betcha never thought an anthropologist would be doing that."

Anthropology is the study of human beings. Academia breaks the subject into archaeology, which focuses on man's relics; cultural anthropology, which examines, well, our cultures; and physical anthropology, which is concerned with human bones. Forensic anthropology is an extension of physical anthropology.

Bass discovered his passion for this anthropological niche accidentally. After the Korean War, he enrolled at the University of Kentucky, planning on getting his master's in counseling. But at Kentucky, he ended up exhuming a dead woman and changed his plans.

One hot April afternoon in 1955, the professor of an anthropology elective Bass was taking asked him if he would like to go out on a forensic case. A lawyer had hired the prof to exhume a body and identify it. Shortly after the professor opened the muddy coffin, Bass puked, and soon after that he began working toward a master's degree in physical anthropology. "The fact that you could take bones," Bass says, "piece them together as if it were a puzzle and identify a body—that to me was exciting."

The UT campus is across the Tennessee River from the Body Farm. The anthropology department is buried in the bowels of the football stadium—Home of the Volunteers. The white cinder-block offices and classrooms used to be players' dorms. Years ago, however, the Vols had a home built for them exclusively; the anthropologists took what they could get.

The physical appearance of the department didn't change much when Bass took over, but everything else improved quickly. Bass earned his master's from Kentucky, did his doctoral thesis at the University of Pennsylvania, and then taught at two universities—Nebraska, then Kansas. All the while, he worked with authorities on forensic cases. Then, in 1971, UT asked him to run its anthropology department.

By the time he came to UT, Bass was well-known in the forensic community. Soon after he arrived, the Tennessee medical examiner, Jerry Francisco, M.D., appointed him the state forensic anthropologist. With Francisco's support, Bass began going to crime scenes rather than waiting for the cops to bring the remains to him. He didn't want to miss any salient details.

Many of the small towns Bass visited while working for the M.E.'s office didn't have the resources to store more than two bodies at a time. Often, with the evidence gathered, cops began asking Bass if he could take the corpses. It occurred to the professor that the bodies would make excellent teaching aids. Modern skeletons are extremely hard to come by.

Bass asked the UT dean for a place where he could lay the bodies to decompose and was given part of the university's sow barn, out on the agricultural campus, a forty-minute ride from the main campus. Word of the farm spread, and soon unidentified homicide victims and indigents who died at local hospitals were being sent his way. As Bass's forensic work gained publicity, people began bequeathing or otherwise donating bodies to the facility.

Bass was happy with the research he and his students were doing—that is, until 1977. In a dug-up grave in a nearby county, police had found a coffin and a man's body. The body was in good shape, which puzzled police, as the cemetery hadn't been used for more than a hundred years. Authorities wanted to know if this scene was the work of grave robbers or, given the well-preserved corpse, if perhaps a murderer had been trying to hide a recent victim.

At the scene, Bass told police that based on the decomposition, it was a 25-to-28-year-old white male, dead for six months to a year— probably not the work of grave robbers. Bass said he'd be able to give a more specific TSD after a thorough examination of the remains.

Back at UT, Bass discovered his TSD approximation had been off—by more than a hundred years. The corpse was that of a Confederate army colonel, William Shy.

"It was an understandable mistake to make on the site," recalls

Doug Owsley, one of Bass's former graduate students who assisted the professor with the Shy case. "The body was incredibly well preserved because Shy's family had bought the best coffin money could buy, an early version of the modern sealer casket—airtight. It retarded decomposition."

In the wake of this blunder, Bass was more frustrated researcher than humiliated expert. "He learned from it," says Owsley, now a curator with the Smithsonian Institution. "He knew this was all part of the scientific method: to learn from data. But that was when Bass realized just how little data there was on human decomposition and he decided it was time for new research, his own research." He became obsessed with wanting to study the whole postmortem continuum, rather than just glimpsing the snapshots in time that he had been seeing.

In 1980, Bass persuaded the university to give him a new lot of land, the area behind the UT Medical Center, and the contemporary Body Farm was born. Since then, Bass and the researchers from around the world who have used the facility have produced groundbreaking data and technology. Thanks to the Farm, a pair of specialists invented a device that lifts fingerprints off a corpse, the FBI improved a ground-penetrating-radar gizmo that detects buried bodies, and a UT graduate student discovered it's possible to determine TSD by measuring the amount of organic soup that leaks into the soil. Yet the most revolutionary discoveries at the Farm have come from studying the bugs—specifically, the flies. Insect science, or entomology, is what made the difference in the Rubenstein case.

The Rubenstein trial got under way in June 1999, long after the accused had collected and spent all $250,000 of the insurance money. ("What did you spend the money on?" the prosecution asked Rubenstein. "I don't remember," he said. "I just spent it.") Given the overwhelming amount of circumstantial evidence against him,

Rubenstein's credibility was the central issue. Each side based its case on Rubenstein's claim that when he had visited the cabin on November 16 and November 27, he had found it empty. The prosecution claimed the defendant was lying and therefore was the killer; the defense, naturally, maintained the man was truthful and innocent.

Rubenstein's attorneys called to the stand Dr. Lamar Meek, an entomologist at Louisiana State University. Meek testified that all three Perrys died at approximately the same time and had been dead for about two weeks. Meek's TSD was consistent with Rubenstein's story. Bass's expert opinion was that the Perrys had been dead for almost a month when Rubenstein made the call to police. Bass's conclusion was based on an examination of several four-by-six photos of the bodies and a videotape of the crime scene and took into account the temperature in Pike County during the months of November and December.

Bass's testimony convinced all but one of the twelve jurors. Rubenstein walked. But because his trial had ended with a hung jury, he could and did face another trial. It began in January 2000, and this time Bass saw something he had missed in round one.

When the medical examiner took the stand, he showed the jury pictures of 4-year-old Crystal's badly decomposed head. The color slides were projected in the front of the courtroom. The images were much larger than any of the pictures Bass had seen, and from his seat in the gallery Bass now spotted scientific proof that the Perrys had been dead for at least twenty-one days when their bodies were discovered.

There are five major stages of decomp: "fresh"; then "bloat," which occurs when gases trapped in the stomach and intestines cause the abdomen to puff; then comes "decay," when organs putrefy and the elements wear away or eat away soft tissue; Mother Nature then leaves the corpse to "dry"; and finally "skeletal." Temperature and other factors affect the rate of decomposition.

Although researchers have divided the postmortem into these five states, it is more of a fluid slide than a distinct step-by-step process. But at the Body Farm, Bass and his team of anthropologists have worked with forensic entomologists and learned it is possible to time-stamp the decomp continuum by looking at the insects that are on or around a body.

Looking up at the giant color slides of Crystal that Meek was using, Bass saw maggot pupal casings in the girl's hair. He had looked for them in the small photos and the video of the crime scene that he had been given, but he hadn't seen them. Now, however, there they were, plain as day. Thanks in large part to research done at the Body Farm, every forensic scientist knows that for flies to find a body and lay their larvae, the larvae to hatch into maggots, and the maggots to pupate, it takes at least twenty-one days. At least. And considering that the bodies were in a closed-up cabin, it likely took a few days for the flies to even find the bodies. Bass's TSD estimate was as much of a scientific certainty as anyone could ask for.

Bass took the stand, presented the facts in his aw-shucks Pooh Bear way, and the jury delivered a guilty verdict. Rubenstein is now appealing his death sentence.

We as a society are at once fascinated and revolted by death. While some people have protested Bass's facility, other folks made Patricia Cornwell's novel *The Body Farm*, which celebrates the gory yet necessary work done there, a national best-seller.

Bass understands the dichotomy. "We're not a culture of death," he says, sitting in his kitchen. "We try to cover it up. When someone is killed, the police come and put a sheet over him; you can't see the body. And when you see the person in the casket, he doesn't look dead; he's been made to look like what he looked like when he was alive. It's because people don't know much about death."

Bass says he has never been troubled by the cases he has worked because he views each one as a puzzle rather than as a human tragedy. Tapping his psychology background, he suspects it's a defense mechanism. He doesn't think about the victims as people for the same reason that he tells morbid death jokes at crime scenes: Like the rest of us, he doesn't like to confront his own mortality.

But unlike the rest of us, Bass hasn't had much of a choice. Death has been his life, both on and off the farm. One sort of forensic job does bother him: suicide. Every time one comes his way he thinks about his father. When Bass was 4 years old—the same age as Crystal when she was strangled—his dad went to work at his law office, closed the door, and shot himself in the head. "It's something my mother and my family never talked about," Bass says, taking off his glasses and rubbing his eyes. "But now as I'm getting older, as I look at my grandson who's four years old and I think, Why did Dad do that? I think, Something must have had him pretty depressed to give up Mom and me."

Bass has buried two wives. His first wife, to whom he was married for thirty-nine and a half years—and, yes, that half year matters to Bass—died of colon cancer in 1993. His second wife, who was his secretary in the anthropology department for many years, died not long after their third anniversary. She also died of cancer.

How has death changed Bill Bass? Carol would prefer he didn't answer the question. She looks at him from across the kitchen table and shakes her head. "No, I wish you wouldn't, Bill."

"It's all right," Bass says. "What she doesn't want me to say is that I'm no longer a believer. I was raised a devout Baptist. I even taught Sunday school. But now I guess you'd say I'm a nonbeliever." Carol blurts out that if such a revelation were read by his former students, "Well, they would call me up and say, 'What's wrong with Dr. Bass?'"

"What's wrong is, I lost two wives," Bass says, coming as close as the man can to getting snippy. "They died because they did not have the genetic ability to adapt to the cancer. No matter how much praying I did, it didn't make a bit of difference. It wouldn't have mattered if I'd had ten million people out there praying." Bass pauses and strokes Knox, who has coiled up at his master's feet. He falls silent as if making the point that he did indeed have ten million people out there praying. "I think we've got this whole thing backward, to tell you the truth," Bass adds. "I don't think a god created us in his image. I think we created a god in our image."

About a month after our afternoon together, Bass suffered another death in the family: His beagle, Knox, had to be put down. Bass wanted to bury the dog in a "special place." Their backyard was too small, so Bass and one of his three sons who was home visiting laid Knox to rest at the Body Farm.

When Bass retired, his biggest fear was that his anthropology department and research facility would be radically changed. He even worried that the forensic program would be done away with altogether and the facility closed. He had reason to worry: Two forensic anthropologists retired from academia right about the same time he did. One left the University of New Mexico, the other left the University of Arizona; the institutions haven't replaced them with forensic anthropologists.

To ensure that his legacy endures, Bass saw to it that two of his former graduate students and fellow teachers inherited his life's work. Richard Jantz was appointed director of the forensic center, and Murray Marks was named Jantz's number two. Jantz is nearing retirement age himself; before long Marks will likely assume control.

The day after Marks gave me a tour of the farm, we returned. He wanted to remove that body bag from under the dead man and cut down a corpse from a tree, basically tidy up before the FBI class arrived a few weeks later. One body propped up against a tree, he explained, had been an experiment. Last summer a local assistant district attorney came to see Marks and asked him if he could determine a murder victim's TSD. The lawyer gave him pictures of a dead woman. She was partially undressed and tied to a tree. She had been out jogging and was mugged, dragged into the woods, raped, and strangled to death.

Marks couldn't give the prosecutor an answer. According to the information about the scene and the pictures Marks was looking at, it was obvious that vertical corpses decompose much more slowly than horizontal corpses. But Marks couldn't say how much slower, because, well, he'd never researched the rate of decomp for vertical corpses.

"I wanted to speak for this victim," Marks tells me. The regret is thick in his voice. "But looking at those pictures, I was once again reminded how little we know about death." Marks came out here to the farm, taped a body to a tree, and began looking for answers, just the way Bass would have done.

———

By the time I learned that Dr. William Bass's Body Farm existed, a good bit had been written about the place. Yet no one had dealt with the obvious and perhaps most compelling question: What motivated Bass to pursue such a macabre science? My hunch was that Bass's own life story must be at least as interesting as the gruesome homicides he had helped solve. Fortunately, my editor in chief, Art Cooper, trusted my instincts, and Bass turned out to be far more fascinating than I had imagined.

Bass continues to be the busiest retired forensic anthropologist in the field. He's been an expert witness for plaintiffs in a class action suit against the Tri-State Crematory in Noble, Georgia, where instead of cremating hundreds of corpses as they were paid to do, the operators allegedly tossed the cadavers into the woods and sent grieving families home with urns filled with charred sawdust. Meanwhile, Bass has been advising several graduate students, like the one who's perfected a ground-penetrating-radar device that can detect a corpse buried under concrete. And thanks to Bass's cache, the size of the Body Farm itself has doubled. Last fall, the University of Tennessee gave the forensic program of the anthropology department an additional acre and a half of land.

Much to the chagrin of his wife, Carol, during what little downtime Bass has had lately, he's been cowriting a book about his life's work. It will be published in fall 2003. Patricia Cornwell, author of the best-selling crime novel The Body Farm, *is penning the foreword. The working title of Bass's book is* The Real Body Farm.

HOW TWO LIVES MET IN DEATH
JOSHUA HAMMER

APRIL 15, 2002

It was a typical Friday afternoon in the Kiryat Hayovel neighborhood of southern Jerusalem. At the Supersol market, the Sabbath rush was underway; shoppers pushed their carts past shelves stripped bare of bread and stacked with matzos for the weeklong Passover holiday. A line had formed at the delicatessen counter in the back, where Sivan Peretz wrapped chicken breasts and salmon steaks and made small talk with his customers. A middle-aged security guard stood poised inside the supermarket entrance, carefully searching bags. At 1:49 P.M., 17-year-old Rachel Levy—petite, with flowing hair and a girlish gap between her teeth—stepped off the bus from her nearby apartment block and strolled toward the market on a quick trip to buy red pepper and herbs for a fish dinner with her mother and two brothers. At the same moment, another girl— strikingly attractive, with intense hazel eyes—walked toward the store's glass double doors. The teenagers met at the entrance, brushing past each other as the guard reached out to grab the hazel-eyed girl, whose outfit may have aroused suspicion. "Wait!" the guard cried. A split second later, a powerful explosion tore through the supermarket, gutting shelves and sending bodies flying. When the smoke cleared and the screaming stopped, the two teenage girls and the guard lay dead, three more victims of the madness of martyrdom.

Ayat al-Akhras and Rachel Levy never knew each other, but they grew up less than four miles apart. One had spent her life locked within the grim confines of the Dehaishe refugee camp outside Bethlehem, a densely packed slum whose 12,000 residents lived in poverty and frustration. The other dwelled in the shadow of a sleek shopping mall filled with cinemas, cafés, and boutiques. In their different worlds, the girls were typical teenagers. Ayat was deeply politicized by the rage, gunfire, violent death, and fervently anti-Israeli messages that surrounded her. Rachel did her best to shut out the violence and pretend that Israel was a normal country. In another time and another place, they could have been schoolmates, even friends. But the intifada cast them in the role of adversaries and, ultimately, executioner and victim. "When an eighteen-year-old Palestinian girl is induced to blow herself up, and in the process kills a seventeen-year-old Israeli girl," President George W. Bush said as he announced plans to dispatch Colin Powell to the region in an attempt to stop the bloodletting, "the future itself is dying."

For the most part, the world has been accustomed to one kind of suicide bomber—the angry Islamic male driven by visions of paradise who martyrs himself as he kills infidels. Since September 2000, 170 Israelis have been killed by more than 60 Palestinian suicide bombers, prompting a full-scale invasion of the West Bank last week. Now the story of Ayat al-Akhras may signal a new and terrifying phase in the Middle East and perhaps elsewhere: the spread of suicide bombing to all levels of society. There was something about staring into the almost-twin faces of the bomber and her victim last week that moved the seemingly unending tale of strife in the region to a deeper and even more unsettling place: to women and children as weapons as well as casualties of war. Martyrdom—or, depending on your point of view, murder—is becoming mainstream. As Powell's mission goes forward, the world hopes for a resolution, or at least an end to the terrible violence of recent weeks. But the forces that pushed Ayat to become a human bomb will take far longer to defuse.

· · ·

Ayat al-Akhras grew up hearing stories of Israeli aggression and Palestinian flight. Both her mother, Khadra Kattous, and her father, Muhammad al-Akhras, grew up in a tent camp in the Gaza Strip, where their parents had fled from Arab villages near Tel Aviv at the end of the 1948 war. After Israel occupied Gaza in 1967, Muham-mad migrated to the Dehaishe camp near Bethlehem, a maze of cinder-block buildings, refuse-strewn alleyways, and open sewers. Khadra moved there as well, and three years later the couple were married. Muhammad found a job as a supervisor with an Israeli construction firm at the settlement of Betar Ilit, building houses for Jews as they expanded their hold on the territories. He built himself a three-story concrete house in an alley in Dehaishe, and there raised his eleven children, four boys and seven girls, alongside thousands of other families of the Palestinian dispossessed. Earning a steady paycheck, al-Akhras was able to support his large clan with a better life than most. Many of Dehaishe's residents took a dim view of his working for Israelis, but they also recognized that he needed to provide for his family.

When the first intifada erupted in 1987, the camp became a hotbed of militancy. Local youths fought street battles with the occupying army; dozens were killed and injured. The oldest child in the al-Akhras family, Samir, was jailed twice for throwing stones at Israeli soldiers. And Ayat—the brightest of their children, accord-ing to her parents—became infected by politics. An outstanding student in love with the written word, she wanted to become a jour-nalist "to communicate to the world about the Palestinian cause," says her mother. Fiercely opinionated, Ayat dominated conversa-tions at family gatherings: "She would stick to her arguments even if everybody else argued the opposite."

But she had a softer side, too. She covered the walls of her tiny bedroom with posters of pop singers from Iraq and Egypt. Every Ramadan, she traveled with her mother across the Green Line to pray at the Al Aqsa Mosque on the Temple Mount in Jerusalem, virtually the only excursions she made outside the camp. Her life was bounded by her home, her public girls' school, the small local mosque she attended on holidays, and the outdoor market in Bethlehem where she shopped with her mother and sisters. Shortly after she turned 15, she met a slim young man named Shadi Abu Laban, who had put aside his college plans to earn a living working as a tile layer. Ayat and Shadi became inseparable. Last year they got engaged, with a traditional wedding and feast planned for July. Ayat insisted they hold the party in the alley in front of her home—an all-day festival of food, dancing, and music that would be open to everyone in the neighborhood. She planned to enroll at Bethlehem University in September to pursue a journalism degree.

Rachel Levy's childhood was more moneyed, but it wasn't easy. As an infant she moved with her parents from Israel to California's Silicon Valley, where her mother, Avigail, joined the family electronics business and her father, Amos, worked in the furniture trade. A family illness took them back to Israel eight years later. The marriage collapsed, and Avigail moved the kids—Rachel and her brothers, Guy, now 22, and Kobi, 7—to a small apartment in the Ramat Sharett quarter of southern Jerusalem, a series of drab high-rises in the shadow of the Jerusalem shopping mall. Rachel had a tough time making the transition from the United States. She considered Israelis brash; she preferred speaking English. But after a trip back to the United States last summer, she returned convinced that Israel was where she belonged, telling her mother, "I feel at home here."

She finally adapted to the rhythms of teenage life. She fretted about the gap between her teeth and agonized about her weight. Like many teenage girls, she filled her diary with poetry about love and death—including long passages from the Song of Songs and the Book of Psalms. To stay trim, she worked out every day and usually ate the same meal when she went out: a salad, a Diet Pepsi, a lollipop, and a pickle. She listened to the music of Pink Floyd and

Christina Aguilera, liked *Pretty Woman* and *Titanic,* and socialized at the Jerusalem mall. Though the Palestinian uprising had cast a pall over that life—a suicide bomber killed three people in a downtown café where Rachel and her friends hung out—she remained apolitical and unconcerned, caught up in teenage passions. "She wasn't afraid of bombs," says a friend. "'Aren't you afraid to go [out]?' I would ask her. And she said, 'No, why would I be?'"

Across the Green Line in Dehaishe, the second intifada had erupted. After the collapse of peace talks at Camp David and Ariel Sharon's provocative visit to the Temple Mount, Dehaishe had become one of the hotbeds of the uprising that began in September 2000. Ayat al-Akhras was in the middle of it. Masked militants often marched through the neighborhood after the funerals of suicide bombers and guerrillas killed by Israeli troops, firing their automatic rifles in the air. Night after night, Ayat spent hours glued to news reports on Al-Jazeera and Al Manar, the television network of Lebanon's Hizbullah movement. Then the uprising touched her personally: Her brother was shot and wounded by Israeli troops. Three cousins, all members of Hamas, were killed in the Gaza Strip—a place that Ayat and her immediate family, lacking permits, were unable to visit. Ayat's family recoiled at the group's suicide bombings of civilians, but like most people in Dehaishe, her parents say they were strong supporters of the Tanzim guerrillas who killed Jewish settlers and soldiers in the territories; they considered those to be legitimate targets. When Mahmud Mughrabi, a close family friend and a member of Fatah, was shot dead while planting a roadside bomb near a Jewish settlement, the al-Akhras family hung a poster of the militant in their living room. "I made the frame myself," Ayat's mother says with pride.

Like many Palestinian girls her age—even smart, ambitious ones—Ayat was eventually drawn to the cult of martyrdom. For the first year of the intifada, suicide bombings were the exclusive province of Islamic radicals, who accepted only male recruits and motivated them with promises of virgins and paradise. Women could not become suicide bombers, the Hamas and Islamic Jihad leaders maintained, because a woman traveling out of the home without a *makram*—her husband, brother, or father—constituted a breach of Islamic law. The rule was ironclad, though Hamas spiritual leader Sheik Ahmed Yassin did allow that "we will start using women when we have run out of men."

But as the violence intensified, Palestinian nationalism became as strong a motivation for martyrdom as Islamic radicalism. Last winter the secular Al Aqsa Martyrs Brigades embraced suicide bombings as well, believing that such tactics would inflict far more pain on the Israelis than guerrilla warfare would, hastening an end to the occupation. They even started a unit for female recruits. Wafa Idriss, a divorced 26-year-old ambulance worker from a Ramallah refugee camp, became the first female suicide bomber, blowing herself up in central Jerusalem in January and killing an elderly Jewish man. Dareen Abu Ayish, a student at Nablus University who was considered brilliant by her classmates, tried in vain to join Hamas earlier this year. After she was rejected, she joined the Al Aqsa brigades, and detonated herself at a checkpoint near Jerusalem in February, injuring five Israelis.

Many girls in the Dehaishe camp rejoiced that women were now playing a role in throwing off Israeli occupation. Even the youngest children were affected. "Since last Christmas, the girls don't want dolls anymore," says Vivian Khamis, a professor of psychology at Bethlehem University. "All they want are guns and tanks."

Ayat's anger peaked when the Israel Defense Forces rolled into Dehaishe in early March. On the evening of March 8, neighbor Isa Zakari Faraj and his daughter were playing with Legos when he was shot through the window by Israeli troops. Ayat's brother Samir and a cousin tried to carry the mortally wounded man to a nearby hospital, but he died in their arms. "When Ayat saw me and our cousin carrying Isa past the doorway, she screamed out in pain, and I told her to get back inside," says Samir.

Faraj's death had a powerful impact on Ayat. Shortly afterward, her friends believe, she either sought out or was approached by the Al Aqsa brigades' suicide unit. "You send out signals at school or mosque, and those in charge of suicide attacks gather information about the candidates," says a teacher in the camp, explaining that stating admiration for martyrs or a willingness to die for the cause is often enough to alert the operatives. "At that very moment everything becomes secret. [Once recruited,] the would-be martyr might then tell her friends, 'I was just kidding when I made those statements.'" Experts say Ayat's self-discipline and intelligence made her a natural candidate for the brigades. They say she probably needed little psychological preparation for her task, which helps explain why she didn't vary her daily routine in the weeks before her death.

As the appointed hour grew near, though, she made little attempt to conceal her hatred of Israel, or what she saw as Arab passivity. Watching the Arab summit on TV with her parents last month, she seethed at the failure of Arab leaders to rush to the defense of Palestine. Days before her operation, she met in a secret location with at least one accomplice from Al Aqsa, who videotaped her final message and dropped it off with a local TV station in Bethlehem after her attack. Backlit, with her head wrapped in the black-and-white checked kaffiyeh of the Fatah movement, she reads from a prepared statement in a strong monotone: "I say to the Arab leaders, 'Stop sleeping. Stop failing to fulfill your duty. Shame on the Arab armies who are sitting and watching the girls of Palestine fighting while they are asleep.'"

Rachel Levy spent the days before Passover in ebullient spirits. A photography project that she had labored on for weeks—water scenes around Jerusalem—went on display at her high school, winning rave reviews from teachers, classmates, and parents. "She became far more outgoing after that," says her mother. "I think the success of her exhibit gave her a lot of confidence in herself." On the first night of Passover, the family gathered at Avigail's brother's house in the settlement of Pisgat Zeev on the eastern edge of Jerusalem. At 10:30 somebody switched on the television—and the family, horrified, watched the scenes of the devastating suicide attack in Netanya. "Racheli became sad, worried, said she wanted to go home," her mother recalls. "We left. But the next day, Racheli was herself again. She looked radiant."

She spent Thursday night, March 28, at the Jerusalem mall with her older brother and his girlfriend, returning home in the wee hours. After sleeping in, she and her mother drank coffee in the kitchen and discussed the family's Friday-evening meal. "Racheli said she would like a change, fish instead of chicken, but we didn't have all the ingredients," her mother says. "We were missing parsley, *kousbara* [coriander], and red pepper. I told Racheli to go down to the local store to pick up those items, but she insisted on going to the supermarket in Kiryat Hayovel. I said, 'Okay, go, but be quick. It's late.'"

On Thursday night, Ayat's fiancé dropped by her house as usual, spending an hour having tea and talking with her family before returning home. Muhammad al-Akhras remained awake until 4:00 A.M. watching live TV coverage of another suicide operation: A Palestinian gunman had entered the Jewish settlement of Eilot Moreh, killing a family of four and barricading himself inside their house for hours before being shot dead by Israeli troops. His daughter, he said, stayed up through the night as well, apparently studying in her room. Palestinian schools are normally closed on Fridays, but the students in Dehaishe had lost two weeks during the Israeli Army's March incursion, and makeup classes had been scheduled for that morning. At 7:30 A.M., Ayat gathered her books and hustled out the door to class. "She said, 'Please wish me well on my test today,'" her mother remembers. "Then she waved goodbye." At the end of classes that morning, Ayat's closest friend, Shuruq Awwad, was struck by her parting words. "She said, 'I'm going to pray in Al Aqsa; I won't see you anymore.' I asked her, 'Are you going to do something, are you going to do some operations?' But she said, 'No, no.'"

Ayat followed a route along footpaths and through fields, skirting Israeli military checkpoints and crossing unnoticed into Jerusalem. Palestinian sources believe that an accomplice was waiting for her in a car on the other side of the Green Line. There she received her belt of explosives and was driven to a drop-off point near the Supersol market in Kiryat Hayovel. She was so composed before her act that she shooed away two Palestinian women selling herbs and scallions in front of the supermarket. Then she walked purposefully toward the door, where the security guard, fifty-five-year-old Haim Smadar, may have attempted to block her path. At that moment Rachel Levy brushed by Ayat. Ayat pressed the detonator, blowing herself in one direction and Rachel in the other. Their bodies were found on opposite ends of the entrance to the Supersol market.

Avigail Levy knew that something was wrong when she heard sirens near her apartment. She immediately phoned her sister, who switched on the radio and relayed the report of a bomb at the Supersol market. Avigail screamed, "My daughter is there!" and rushed with her son to the scene. Hours later she identified her daughter's remains at the morgue. "Her body was mangled, but her face was perfect, untouched," she said, sitting in her cramped living room last week. Undisturbed since the bombing, the shelves in Rachel's bedroom provide a poignant snapshot of a teenage girl's life: Tommy Girl perfume, Clinique makeup, Victoria's Secret fruit body lotions, stuffed dolls, and tiny blue trolls from her childhood that she'd refused to throw away. A picture taped to the wall was drawn by her adored brother Kobi the day she died, showing a sad person and two flowers. "To Rachel, I love you," reads the childish scrawl. "I wish you were alive. I want you to live." Composed yet in deep mourning for her only daughter, Avigail Levy says she strongly supports Ariel Sharon's massive military occupation of the West Bank. "I don't want revenge," she insists. "But I want the government to make it clear that if another family sends their child to be killed, they will suffer. This is the only way for them to understand—when they feel what we feel."

Muhammad al-Akhras heard about the attack on Palestinian television. He received confirmation that his daughter was the suicide bomber when half a dozen militiamen from the Al Aqsa Martyrs Brigades stood outside his house and fired their guns in the air in salute. Though convention calls for the father of a martyr to express pride in the act, al-Akhras seemed as overwhelmed by grief as Avigail Levy as he sat in his tiny family room a few hours later. "Words cannot express the pain I feel," he mumbled, staring down at a studio photograph of his daughter taken in front of a fake cityscape of lower Manhattan, the Twin Towers above her head. As he spoke, relatives carried out the prostrate body of another daughter, who had fainted from shock a few moments before. In a garage across the alley, a stream of visitors, from local Hamas leaders to the mayor of Bethlehem, dropped by to express their condolences. They sipped strong Arabic coffee and warmed themselves in the freezing rain by huddling around a wood fire burning in a metal drum. Ayat's fiancé seemed as uncomprehending as her father about her suicide attack. "If she had just told me what she was planning, I would have stopped her," he said softly. "May God forgive her for what she has done." Other members of her family insisted that they regarded suicide bombings as morally wrong, but explained that Israeli brutality had left Palestinians no other choice. "Sharon has killed hope in our life," said Ayat's cousin Mutlak Qassas. "Today Ayat went to send him a message with her blood and her body."

Muhammad al-Akhras knew he would have to keep the mourning period short. Dozens of Israeli tanks were already massing at the entry points to Bethlehem, and he was worried the troops would exact retribution on the men of his family. He said that he had received no offers of financial support from either the Palestinian Authority or the Iraqi government, which has paid as much as $25,000 to the families of suicide bombers. He wasn't sure whether he would accept such an offer, though he conceded that he might have no other choice: As the father of a suicide bomber, he was all but certain that he would be fired by his Israeli employers. His sons had already left the camp on their own and found their way to different hiding places. "Nobody should have to experience this kind of loss," al-Akhras said. Yet taped to the windshield of his car was a black-and-white poster of Ayat draped in a flowing kaffiyeh and brandishing a pistol—the same picture that had begun to appear in the alleys of Dehaishe, inspiring new martyrs to the cause.

———

On the afternoon of March 29, 2002, I was hunkered down behind a wall in the freezing rain in Ramallah, covering the siege of Yasser Arafat's compound, when I received word that a teenaged female suicide bomber from Dehaishe refugee camp had blown herself up in a supermarket in southern Jerusalem. Sensing a story, I immediately left the combat zone around Arafat's headquarters—driving through a cordon of tanks and armored personnel carriers—and headed for Bethlehem. I spent the next three days piecing together the parallel lives of Ayat al-Akhras and one of her two victims, 17-year-old Rachel Levy.

There was one vital piece of information I was unable to discover in time for the deadline: How had Ayat been recruited for her fatal mission? In the course of writing a book on Bethlehem during the intifada, I pieced together the whole tale: Her handler was Ahmed Mughrabi, 27, commander of an Al Aqsa Martyrs Brigades cell in Dehaishe, whose younger brother had been a close friend and coworker of Ayat's older brother, Samir. Beginning in early March 2002, Ayat had written four letters to Ahmed Mughrabi offering her-

self as a martyr; three days before her death, the Al Aqsa cell leader had met her in his hideout, interviewed her for several hours, and come away convinced of her commitment. She was the third of a total of six suicide bombers, most of them teenagers, that Mughrabi dispatched to Israel before his capture by Israeli soldiers in Dehaishe in late May 2002. Now incarcerated in Nafha prison in the Negev Desert, he faces a likely prison term of eighteen consecutive life sentences, one for each of his victims. The Mughrabi family and the al-Akhras family, ironically, remain close. Late last year, Ayat's older sister Zainat was engaged to be married to Mohammed Mughrabi, the 21-year-old brother of the man who sent Ayat to her death.

THE ACCUSED
PAIGE WILLIAMS

M ike Garrish took the stand and swore before God and judge and what appeared to be all of Habersham County to tell the whole truth and nothing but. His wife sat anxiously in the courtroom, as did his only remaining sister. His parents, barred from watching the trial because they were on the witness list, waited in a room down the hall.

At the prosecution table sat Jim Hallman, the Georgia Bureau of Investigation agent who had sat Mike down at the kitchen table one November night twenty-two years ago when Mike was 16 and his little sister lay murdered in a bedroom down the hall and said, "You did this, and I'm going to see you go to the electric chair for it."

Behind Hallman, filling the courtroom, were the people of Demorest, population 1,000. All these years they had watched Mike, judged him, refused to let their daughters date him, kept the gossip alive as only a small town can do: *That's the boy who killed his sister.*

Until this day, Mike had never opened his mouth. He knew the danger of talking. The day his sister was killed he opened his mouth and his words were misunderstood, twisted, and for that he had paid. He had resolved to say nothing until his day in court, which he had stopped believing would come. Now that it had, he thought it should feel like deliverance, some sort of turning point toward resolution and freedom, but the slant of the questions and the fear in his wife's eyes told him this might not be the end after all.

"Do you remember talking to Agent Hallman here that day?" asked District Attorney Mike Crawford.

"Yes, sir," Mike said. He was in his late thirties now, thin and balding, with a deep drawl and big serious wary brown eyes.

"And do you remember him asking if you had killed your sister?"

". . . Yes."

"What did you say?"

"I said I did not kill her," Mike said.

"Do you recall ever telling Jim Hallman that 'If I did, I don't remember'?"

"Yes, sir."

"Why did you tell him that?"

"I was mad at him for asking me the question," Mike said. "And it wasn't—the statement was said, 'If I did, I don't remember it.' It was more or less a hateful remark."

"You were a suspect in this case for a long time, were you not?"

"Yes, sir."

"What kind of effect did that have on you?"

Now here was a question—the central question, in fact, of Michael Garrish's life. What kind of effect does it have on you to be called home from work one day when you're 16 years old to find your house and yard full of investigators, medics, crime scene technicians, and neighbors; your 13-year-old sister lying dead in a back bedroom, her blood still wet on the shag carpet; your father, who discovered the body, in tears and shock on the front walk? What kind of effect does it have on you to have the GBI interrogate you at length about your whereabouts until you make the mistake of uttering the seven most poorly chosen words of your life, words that make you a temporary suspect in the eyes of the law but forever guilty in the eyes of the community?

What kind of effect does it have on you when the police stop suspecting you but no one knows that, not even you—because they keep that little tidbit to themselves? What kind of effect does it have when the case stays open and the real killer goes uncaught for more than two decades?

"What kind of effect did that have on you?"

From the stand, Mike said, "It made me angry."

The DA wound it up. "Did you have anything to do with your sister's death?" he asked.

"Absolutely not."

When he finished testifying, Mike stepped off the stand and walked past the judge, lawyers, bailiffs, and townspeople, past agent Hallman, and ultimately out of the courthouse, free.

Mike Garrish had always in fact been free. He just had never *felt* free.

WEDNESDAY, NOVEMBER 1, 1978

He is 16 years old, a tenth grader in Demorest, a good little place to grow up. Everybody knows everybody. Everybody knows everybody's *dog*. The Garrish house (modest one-story brick ranch) is on Hancock Road, a two-laner through the pine barrens of Habersham County, 80 miles northeast of Atlanta. The house seems big to Mike, the woods out back so vast, the walk up the driveway to catch the school bus interminable when in fact it is maybe forty yards at most. The closest neighbors are the Hansards, across the road, and the Pruitts, next door, a couple of acres away. A prison guard and his wife and son live there. The boy, Tony Pruitt, is 14. He rides the school bus with Mike's younger sister, Lisa.

In the Garrish house live father, son, and daughter. They have been through a lot lately. A move from Demorest to LaGrange and back again, a shift in the family structure. They are three where once they were five: father, John; mother, Pat; children Vicky, Mike, and Lisa. But then John and Pat divorced, and Pat stayed in LaGrange. Vicky married and moved to Michigan, leaving John, Mike, and Lisa in the house on Hancock Road.

John fixes Pepsi machines and restaurant fountains. Mike works after school as a doffer at the Chicopee textile mill across town. Lisa takes care of the house and is good at it. She's a tough little kid with a strong sense of self, a unique way of doing things. When the teacher asks for, say, a report on a foreign country, most kids might pick England or Spain, but Lisa never fails to pick some place no one has ever heard of, just to be different.

One Saturday when she was 8, Lisa walked through the back door with fists full of change and her mother asked, "Where did you get all that money?" Lisa had been selling pony rides for a quarter to the neighborhood kids. Now she is 13—actually, two weeks away from 14. When she grows up she wants to be a lawyer, rock star, and horse rancher, all at the same time. She plays clarinet in the band. She is starting to curl her hair and experiment with makeup and jewelry. She is five foot six and weighs 130 pounds. She is mature for her age, and boys notice.

As brother and sister, Mike and Lisa are typical. They aren't the Bradys and they aren't the opposite of the Bradys; they are just two kids in your average hardworking family in a small town in North Georgia.

This day, a Wednesday, begins normally enough. Mike drives to school. He gets out around one o'clock because he has to punch the factory clock at 4:00 P.M. Meanwhile he goes over to Tower Mountain, a hangout spot, and hooks up with some friends. They decide to go to Mike's and smoke a joint. They smoke the joint and the friends leave around 3:30 as Mike gets ready for work. Lisa's school bus drops her off, and Mike is just leaving as Lisa walks down the driveway to the house. She has a sack of last night's Halloween candy in her hand. Here's some candy, she says, get some if you want it. Mike gets a fistful, they say bye.

It is just another ordinary coming and going, but then again it's not: Mike will never see his little sister alive again.

Lisa usually has a snack, does some homework, watches her favorite afternoon television shows, and waits for her father to come home from work. His schedule depends on how many service calls he has and where they are. This afternoon he finishes up early with a call in Helen and arrives around 4:30. In the den he finds the TV on, a half-empty glass of iced tea on the hearth, Lisa's Adidas and socks on the floor by the chair. In the kitchen, he stops to go through the mail on the counter. He calls for Lisa. She doesn't answer. He looks in her bedroom. She isn't there. He goes to the phone to call Mrs. Pruitt next door, see if she's seen Lisa. As he picks up the phone, he glimpses through his bedroom door and sees his daughter lying motionless on the floor.

Lisa is on her back, between the foot of the bed and the dresser, a rivulet of blood at her nose and mouth, down the side of her face. Her right hand is bloody and sliced almost to the bone. She wears a brown plaid shirt with puffed sleeves, tucked into her blue jeans; the bow-tie collar is soaked with blood. On her left wrist is a bracelet, on her finger a ring. In her earlobes are earrings in the shape of Christmas trees. Her feet are bare; her toenail polish is wearing off. The carpet beneath her is saturated with her blood. John Garrish kneels beside his girl, feels for a pulse, and believes he has found one. He calls an ambulance, then the Hansards across the road.

Across town, on the factory floor, Mike is running bolts of fabric off the machines. His supervisor comes over and says someone's here to see you. At the door is his neighbor, Debbie Hansard, who solemnly says, "Your dad needs you at home." Mike turns around and goes to find his supervisor. Jim Hallman and other investigators later will find this strange. Wouldn't you ask what's wrong? Wouldn't you be curious about why a neighbor would drive across town to tell you to get home as fast as you can? If you don't ask, doesn't that suggest you already know what has happened at home? By the time Mike leaves, Debbie Hansard has gone back toward Hancock

Road. Driving home, Mike thinks his father has had a heart attack. When he arrives to find the road and driveway clogged with sheriffs' cruisers and detectives' cars, he knows he is wrong.

Out front he meets Hallman, a young GBI agent who has been on the force for four years and before that was a Douglas County deputy under the legendary Sheriff Earl Lee. Hallman should not have caught this case at all, because when the call came in he was on his way home. For two seconds, he had thought about letting the after-hours agent handle it but then decided to go ahead and handle it. Couple of hours at most, he told himself, not knowing it would turn into twenty-two years.

Hallman questions Mike in the kitchen. The Garrish family doesn't know it, but this is typical. You first eliminate the people closest to the victim. The father, mother, brother, and so forth. Where were you this afternoon, he asked Mike. What did you do? Say you smoked a little pot? With who? What time did you leave for work? Did you see Lisa? What time was that? Did you have a fight? Did she catch you smoking pot? Were you afraid she was going to tell on you? Hallman finds Mike vague and uncooperative. "If something happened to your loved one and we came to you with questions, we'd expect you to be cooperative," Hallman would explain later. "Maybe you'd be cooperative for an entirely different reason. Maybe you've got fifty kilos of cocaine in the trunk of your car, who knows? If you're not cooperative, that raises suspicion. He was scared. There was the marijuana. And he's a kid."

Hallman ratchets it up a bit, tries to provoke Mike with intimidation: *You did this, didn't you? You did this and I'm going to see you go to the electric chair for it.* Mike—terrified, pissed off—says, intending sarcasm: "If I did, I don't remember it."

Now this, to a detective, is a red flag. Mike Garrish is the last to see Lisa Garrish alive; has spent the afternoon using drugs; does not seem overly distraught about his sister's death or interested in answering questions. And now this little gem—*If I did, I don't remember it*. Hallman thinks he may have his man.

Having just been told he's going to the electric chair, Mike is stunned. He staggers outside into the night and sits beneath a peach tree at the edge of the yard. He is crying now in the dark. When his mother and stepfather pull up and get out of their car, the first thing Mike says is, "Mama I didn't kill her." And his mother says indignantly, "Well who says you did?"

What a mess there is in the Garrish house. Because Lisa has a severely sliced hand and what looked like a cut beneath her chin, investigators at first think she has been stabbed to death. It isn't until later, during the autopsy, that they find the bullet holes in her head and chest. She hasn't been stabbed at all; she was shot with a .38-caliber gun—and a .38-caliber gun is soon discovered missing from her father's closet. The crime scene investigators, out of Atlanta, have to turn around and head back to Demorest to reprocess the scene, pull up the carpet and retrieve the slugs from the hardwood floor.

A murder weapon would be helpful, but the cops can't find one. They are back the next day to search the creek and woods for a gun and/or knife. The Garrish family, meantime, makes funeral arrangements. At the visitation, there are hundreds of people—classmates, teachers, neighbors, coworkers, friends, relatives—and Mike believes every last one of them is staring at him. Actually, some are. Everyone knows the police consider him a suspect and want him to take a polygraph (which he will pass). Many wonder at his dry eyes and composure, even consider it a sign of cold-blooded guilt and will someday testify to that. Mike sits alone on a staircase and wishes they all would just go away.

Before they close the casket he takes all he has on him—a dollar bill—and tears it in half. He puts one half in his sister's coffin and the other in his wallet, where it will remain for the rest of his life.

He cannot bear to return to school. His mother and stepfather have decided to move to Michigan to be near his older sister, so Mike decides he'll go with them. On the day he turns in his textbooks and withdraws from school, there appear to be a million kids in the hall, staring, whispering. The crowd seems to part as Mike walks through. It is all he can do to keep his head up and finish what he started.

Mike and the rest of the Garrish family do not know it, but Hallman has stopped suspecting him because his time card at the factory gives him a solid alibi. Whoever did it left no fingerprints, no murder weapon, no witnesses, nothing. Technology is lacking—no DNA or Luminol to pick up trace blood, none of the sophisticated techniques crime scene specialists would be able to use in the decades to come.

But soon Hallman would develop a theory: Lisa was watching television in the den when the killer arrived, probably with the intention of molesting her. That there was no sign of break-in or struggle suggested she knew the attacker. He pulled a knife. She tried to grab it away and it sliced her right hand to the bone. She went to the kitchen to clean up, unaware of the danger she was in. At some point, Lisa must have gone to her father's bedroom for one of the guns she knew he kept in the closet. The killer either beat her to the gun or wrestled it away from her. He shot her once in the back of the head, three times in the chest, left her for dead on the carpet and fled with the weapons.

This happened right at 4:00 P.M.—just as Mike Garrish was punching the clock at work—because at that moment, R. L. Hansard, who lived across the road, heard chilling screams from the direction of the Garrish house. Not sure what he'd heard, he stepped out onto his porch to listen more closely, but then a motorcycle roared to life somewhere and the screams disappeared.

What could Mike Garrish do but go on?

In Michigan it was cold, too damn cold. He stayed for about a month and then came home to Georgia. His father still lived in the house on Hancock Road. His friends were still around. He tried to fit in. He asked a few girls out but they turned him down. One, whose father had known Mike as far back as Cub Scouts said, "You ain't going nowhere with that boy." As District Attorney Mike Crawford would one day put it: "Can you think of anything worse that could happen to you as a young person than to be accused, wrongfully accused, of killing your own sister?"

Mike's life would've been a hell of a lot easier had Hallman told him he was no longer a suspect—better yet if he'd come out with it publicly, like cops sometimes do. Problem was, Hallman was sure but the sheriff wasn't. Despite the time card, despite witnesses who put Mike at work at the time of the murder, Sheriff Bill Pitts made it clear to agents that he believed Mike killed his sister to keep her quiet about his drug use. The Garrishes would not learn this for many years—and would have their theories about why the sheriff clung so strongly to his—but bottom line, the contradiction in speculation left Mike "twisting in the wind for twenty-two years," as he puts it. You might in fact call him a two-time victim. First, he lost his sister. Then he was wrongfully considered her killer. "I was so mad and hurt and angry with Jim Hallman," Mike says now. "He was archenemy number one."

Mike believed it would be impossible to return to school or to work in Demorest, so he commuted to Gainesville to work for Pepsi, loading trucks. His friends graduated from high school, but Mike's formal education ended that Wednesday in November.

He joined the Army, got his high school diploma through Savannah Tech, and began driving trucks. Driving trucks was what he had always wanted to do. Four or five years passed. When he got out of the Army he didn't want to go back to Demorest, so he took off again, to drive semis for a living. He hauled carpet west, produce east, whatever kept him moving.

Still, he couldn't escape. Once, at a local fall festival, Mike heard one woman say to another as he passed: *Don't you recognize him? He's the one who killed his sister.* And in Savannah, for St. Patrick's Day festivities, he turned around in a crowd of 10,000 and found himself face-to-face with none other than Jim Hallman. It was a coincidence, nothing more; but to Mike it felt like the haunting never would end. In his worst nightmare he was being led in handcuffs down a prison hallway and saying, "Why won't you just stop and listen to me? Why won't you believe me?"

He felt frustrated but also hurt that anyone could think him capable of violence, much less murder; guilt that he wasn't there for Lisa at the moment she needed him most; self-loathing that his actions—smoking pot, making that sarcastic and ill-timed crack at Hallman—stole precious time from finding the real killer. He spoke to no one of these feelings, not even his family or friends.

During one visit home he attended a cookout at the home of his old friend Todd Kennedy. Todd's little sister, Johnna, had been Lisa's best friend. Now Johnna was a woman. She had never believed any of the things people said about Mike. She accepted a date with him, and then another, and eventually they married. They had two daughters, Micah and Autumn, whom they tried to protect from the darkest family truth, that a long time ago everyone thought Daddy killed his little sister.

The family rarely talked about Lisa. On the first day of each November, they would call each other for comfort. Pat was the obsessive one. She grieved doubly—for her slain daughter and for her suspected son. Both were victims; neither had been vindicated. She hired psychics, kept notes, went over the facts of the case until her head swam. She talked to Lisa at night before bedtime, and sometimes in dreams Lisa talked to her. Pat continually called investigators and the district attorney and said check this and that. She would not—could not—let it go.

Meanwhile, the GBI transferred Jim Hallman to his native Atlanta to work on the investigation of the infamous missing and murdered children case. He still kept in touch with his old friend, boss, and conscience, Douglas County Sheriff Earl Lee, who above all could not abide crimes against children. "What are you doing about Lisa Garrish," Lee asked Hallman every time they met. "Are you going to let that child's death go unpunished?" In 1993, when Hallman made it back to the Gainesville office, one of his first acts as special agent in charge was to rekindle the case.

Hallman's agents began to reinterview people and chase twenty-year-old leads. In 1998, Hallman summoned Mike Garrish and his parents to the GBI office in Gainesville. It was a strange scene. Everyone was twenty years older and had lived with Lisa's murder in his own way. The last time Mike sat down with Hallman was as a terrified teenager with pot in his bloodstream, and as far as he knew, the electric chair in his future. But Hallman—the law, and Mike's nearly lifelong archenemy—did not chastise him, accuse him, shout at him, or antagonize him in any way. He did something extraordinary, something long overdue. He apologized.

What Hallman's agents had just discovered was this: In the hours after Lisa's killing, bloodhounds from the state prison at nearby Alto tracked a scent from the back door of the Garrish house to the back fence of the Pruitt house next door. The dogs' handlers did not let them enter the Pruitts' property. They dismissed the trail—did not even enter it into the investigative file—perhaps because Tony Pruitt's father was a prison guard and the handlers assumed the dogs had latched onto a familiar scent. To Hallman, though, this was significant, because in the days after the killing he and another agent interviewed the Pruitt family and found reason to suspect the teenage son, Tony.

Tony Pruitt rode the bus with Lisa. He was known among his neighbors and peers to be "weird." He was absorbed by space stories and comic books and was an only child. His mother once asked Mike to tutor Tony in algebra and Mike did, for one afternoon, but then told his mother he would never go back because Tony giggled inappropriately and refused to concentrate, was immature beyond words. Neighbors told agents he liked to set bugs and frogs on fire and engaged in the torture of other small animals.

Strange things certainly had happened around the Garrish house. A cow had its eye gouged out, and the pet cat was hanged by a rope from a tree. The Garrishes would come to believe Tony not only watched their comings and goings but also went into their house when they weren't home. Nobody in Demorest locked doors. An intruder could walk in, get the layout, and even learn that John Garrish kept a couple of handguns and a shotgun in his bedroom closet.

Hallman's agents also discovered that on the day of the killing, Tony Pruitt had called a friend, Chuck Whitmore, to tell him Lisa had "been shot" to death—even investigators did not know this because until late that night they thought she had been stabbed. Whitmore also told police that Pruitt many years later confessed the murder to him while drunk at a party.

Pruitt had other troubles, too. In 1996, he was convicted of child molestation and sentenced to fifty years in prison. In the process of that investigation, Pruitt's wife, Mary Sanders, told the GBI that in the mid-1980s Pruitt confessed Lisa Garrish's murder to her, too, but she had been too afraid to say so until now.

At the GBI office that day, Hallman told Mike they were making a case not against him but against the boy next door.

He didn't apologize for suspecting Mike back in 1978 but for having had to do his job that way. ("I always kind of felt bad about getting on him so heavy at the time, when we first started," Hallman says now. "But I was trying to solve a homicide.") It was merely a tactic, he told Mike, and nothing personal, but he couldn't reveal this in 1978 or as the years passed, he said, because the case was still open and investigators disagreed about the chief suspect.

Hallman: "We can't give him that twenty years back, but at least it's over."

Mike: "I don't hold any grudges because I think he was doing the best he could at the time, the best he knew how. But at the same time I don't think he really knew how hard it was. He has turned out to be one of my biggest heroes because he helped us see it through to the end."

On November 1, 1998—twenty years to the day of Lisa's murder—a grand jury indicted Tony Pruitt in her killing. In November 2000, he stood trial. Surely a conviction would clear Mike Garrish in the eyes of the community. Or would it?

All through those days in court the Garrishes swore they heard Mike's name more than the defendant's, that Mike was the one on trial. The defense was playing its only hand: If the jury suspects one man, it can't very well convict another. Yet on the strength of the Whitmore and Sanders testimonies, and on the new fact about the bloodhounds, a jury on November 29, 2000, convicted Pruitt of Lisa Garrish's murder. He is serving a life sentence in addition to the child molestation sentence.

Does Mike Garrish, now 40, finally feel relief and vindication? Of course. Did the conviction close the door on suspicion? "If it had happened within a year of the murder I think it would have," he says. "Because this drug on for twenty-two years and twenty-eight days there's people out there thinking, 'They pinned that on him just to close the case.'"

It's like the reverse of trust, which, once lost, is hard to regain: Once doubt is introduced, it can be impossible to dislodge. Before meeting Mike Garrish, for instance, I read the Pruitt trial transcript and background materials on the case and found that Garrish's guilt seemed, on paper, to be very possible. A few days later, on my way to interview him in Demorest, I was uncomfortable enough to let family know where I would be and with whom. Spending time with Mike Garrish almost immediately erased the doubt, but I began to understand how others inevitably might have felt in his presence back then, and how those doubts must have affected him for most of his life. "It's one of those Richard Jewel syndromes," he says. "He'll be branded for the rest of his life. No matter what, he is branded. And so am I. Best you can do is not worry about it. Forget about it, pull yourself up, and go on."

New people now live in the old family house on Hancock Road, but the Hansards still live across the street, and the Pruitts are still next door. Except for the new highway nearby and the trailer park in the woods, the place might as well be frozen in time.

When Mike Garrish goes there now, he can't get over how small the house looks. He does not wish to go inside. "I feel more sad than anything because this was such a great little town to grow up in," he says. "This was the kind of town you'd want to raise a family in, and I feel like I can never be a part of it anymore."

His life is in Athens now, with Johnna and their daughters and his sales job at a manufacturing plant. They live in a nice, large home on the edge of town. The air there feels lighter now. Mike can wake up in the morning without a sense of fear and dread. He can finally think of the happy times with Lisa, and the family can speak of her. He no longer hates Jim Hallman. In fact, Mike called him at Christmas to tell him happy holidays.

He got the answering machine.

——

Nothing has happened with Mike Garrish since the article was published. He has pretty much gone on with his life, obviously with some relief that he's been publicly vindicated. He still blames himself for his own misery and says if he hadn't been so stupid all those years ago none of this would have happened, but I think he's been too hard on himself. He was a kid caught in an unfathomable situation.

MAD DOGS AND LAWYERS
EVAN WRIGHT

It was about four o'clock on a Friday afternoon, January 26, 2001, when Esther Birkmaier, a single retiree in her seventies, heard screams outside her front door. Birkmaier lives on the sixth floor of an art deco apartment building in the Pacific Heights area of San Francisco, one of the city's prime neighborhoods, known for its panoramic views of the Golden Gate Bridge. As Birkmaier pressed her eye against the peephole, a woman in the hallway outside yelled, "Help me!" Birkmaier couldn't see much from her limited fish-eye perspective, but what she did see shocked her. There was a blond woman on the floor. A huge dog was attacking her.

Birkmaier phoned 911 and reported "dogs running wild" in her hallway. When she hung up, something began pounding on her door. She panicked, phoned 911 again and this time just screamed into the phone. A man heard the screams and also phoned 911 to report what he thought was a rape. Alec Cardenas, a SWAT-team medic and one of the first cops on the scene, arrived about seven minutes later to find the victim lying facedown on the hall carpet in front of her apartment. She was naked, covered in blood, her upper back punctured with dog bites. Blood was splashed on the walls for about twenty feet down the hall. As Cardenas approached, the woman attempted to push herself up and crawl into her home.

About this time, a middle-aged woman who identified herself as Marjorie Knoller stepped out of Apartment 604. She too was covered in blood. But aside from a cut on her hand and a few scratches on her arms, she was not injured. She told the police she had been walking her dog Bane down the hall when he lunged at the victim, who was entering her apartment carrying a bag of groceries. "I told her to stay still," Knoller said. "If she had, this would have never happened." Knoller told police she had managed to lock Bane and his mate, Hera, in her apartment. She was afraid to go back inside.

Animal control officers found Bane in Knoller's bathroom. The officers inched open the bathroom door and peeked inside. Bane was a massive creature. He weighed 120 pounds and was just under three feet tall, with a brindle coat of black and tan tiger stripes. Most of his weight was centered in his powerful chest, bulging legs, and squat head, his most imposing feature. Bane had defecated all over the bathroom. He was soaked in blood. Even his teeth were red.

The animal control officers carried a tranquilizer gun that shoots darts potent enough to knock out a large dog. They fired three into Bane and waited fifteen minutes, but he remained standing. Two of the officers ended up hooking Bane with "catch" poles and walked him down to their van, where they euthanized him with 25 cc of sodium pentobarbital a short time later.

Five hours later, the victim, Diane Whipple, a popular 33-year-old lacrosse coach at nearby St. Mary's College, died at San Francisco General Hospital. Her larynx had been crushed and her throat punctured. But the cause of death was cardiac arrest; she had lost nearly all of her blood. Whipple had been an all-American lacrosse player at Penn State, then an Olympic track-and-field hopeful—an aspiration she was forced to give up in her mid-twenties to battle cancer. Less than a week before the attack, she had run a marathon.

One police officer initially called her death a "tragic accident," but a morally neutral judgment failed to satisfy the public, whose outrage soon turned on Bane's owners, Marjorie Knoller and her husband, Robert Noel. Outwardly, they seemed exemplary San Franciscans. They were do-gooder attorneys honored by the Bar Association of San Francisco for their work helping the homeless and mentally disabled. They were opera patrons who hobnobbed with some of the city's wealthiest citizens. Both on their third marriage, they had wed twelve years earlier and were seen by friends such as their colleague Herman Franck as being "deeply in love, devoted to each other."

But an investigation into their private lives soon yielded secrets that defied explanation. The couple—she is 46, he's 60—had recently adopted an inmate at California's Pelican Bay State Prison, a 39-year-old man serving a life term for armored-car robbery and attempted murder. Their "son," Paul "Cornfed" Schneider, is one of the most feared leaders of the Aryan Brotherhood prison gang and is currently facing federal trial on an indictment for racketeering and a series of murders he allegedly orchestrated from behind bars.

Schneider, who lived in an 11-by-7½-foot concrete cell, had somehow managed to set up a dog-breeding operation—he called it Dog o' War kennels—outside the prison walls. Schneider's associates raised Presa Canarios, an unusual breed of attack dog from Spain introduced to the United States a decade or so earlier. Bane, the dog that killed Whipple, was Schneider's prize stud dog—Presa puppies sell for as much as $2,200. Prison investigators suspected that the dogs were being raised to protect Aryan Brotherhood criminal enterprises such as meth labs.

The fact that Bane and his mate, Hera, wound up living in Knoller and Noel's Pacific Heights apartment was odd enough. Even stranger was the relationship between Knoller, Noel, and their adopted son. It included pornographic letters that the couple exchanged with Schneider and, it was rumored, photographs of Marjorie Knoller having sex with the dogs. It did not help Knoller's cause that days after the city filed a warrant to search for photos that depicted "sexual acts . . . that involved dogs" in Schneider's cell, she admitted that her nickname for one of the dogs had been "my certified lick therapist."

Nothing in the portrait of the couple that was emerging made sense. Nor did the bizarre statements they made in public. They suggested Whipple might have egged on the attack by wearing a pheromone-laced perfume or by menstruating. When Knoller appeared before a grand jury, she wove an almost moving tale of how she risked her life trying to save Whipple's, then blew whatever sympathy she was gaining by saying that Bane had sniffed Whipple's crotch "like she was a bitch in heat."

Since late January 2002, Knoller has been on trial for second-degree murder and her husband for manslaughter. Because the case has received such extensive coverage in their hometown, the trial is being held in Los Angeles. "Bob and Marjorie were so hated in San Francisco," says Herman Franck. "You half expected to see an angry mob with pitchforks and torches to show up outside the courthouse."

If Knoller and Noel were simply on trial for acting like jerks, this would be an open-and-shut case. But proving that this strange couple had a murderous intent will be difficult for prosecutors. Nor will the trial answer all questions about this case, the story of how the once-prominent San Francisco attorneys wound up adopting an Aryan Brotherhood gang leader and his killer dog reveals as much about individual human folly as it does about the peculiar, corrupting hell of the American penal system. Perhaps it should come as no surprise that their journey into this hell was paved with good intentions.

Originally locked up in 1985 for an armored-car robbery, Paul Schneider has been incarcerated since the early 1990s in the Security Housing Unit of Pelican Bay State Prison, where he is locked in his cell twenty-two and a half hours per day, never allowed outdoors, and permitted contact with the outside world only through letters and strictly monitored visits. Keith Whitley, a former guard who first encountered Schneider in 1987, calls him "the most dangerous man in California." Schneider is deemed such a security risk that when he was moved last fall out of Pelican Bay in preparation for his federal trial, U.S. marshals and the California Highway Patrol blocked traffic on the Oakland Bay Bridge in order to transport him across it in a heavily defended motorcade.

When I first meet Schneider, he appears across the reinforced-glass visitation window at his temporary home in the Sacramento County jail looking amazingly fit despite his chalky complexion. Throughout the interview, a steady clanking sound emanates from deep within the jail—chains sliding, locks tumbling, doors slamming, which together sound like the rumbling of the empty stomach of a mechanical beast. Schneider has thick blond hair combed straight back, a direct, blue-eyed gaze, stands about six feet two and weighs 220 pounds. Muscles, traced with blue veins, bulge beneath his pale skin. His right hand is tattooed with an *A* and a *B,* spare advertisements for his affiliation with the notorious Aryan Brotherhood gang.

Schneider, born in 1962, grew up in Cerritos, California, with two younger sisters, his mother, and his stepfather, a retired Air Force officer who ran an industrial cleaning service. He portrays his childhood as a happy one. "My stepdad used to take me flying in Cessnas," he says. "I worked on pit crews for drag-racing boats."

He says that he always loved dogs. When he was about 16, Schneider found a summer job with a Los Angeles company called Continental K-9, which specialized in lending junkyard-protection dogs to small businesses in the city's crime-ridden industrial zone. He would drop off the dogs at night and pick them up early in the morning. Most of the animals were semi-wild, vicious mutts. "Thieves would cut tendons in the dogs' legs," he says. "That was when I learned how loyal dogs are. They would still try to do their job even when their legs were sliced."

In 1979, after graduating from high school early, Schneider

joined the Air Force and was assigned to a special Strategic Air Command unit in eastern Washington. He worked as a crewman aboard KC-130 aerial refueling tankers, large planes that accompanied heavy bombers to the edge of Soviet airspace. He lived a week at a time in an underground bunker called a "mole hole," and he participated in round-the-clock drills in which crews were told nuclear attack was imminent and were given five minutes to scramble their jets. They were never told whether these drills were actual or make-believe Armageddon until their missions were over. The isolation and intense psychological pressure of his military duty would later prove excellent preparation for Schneider's ability to withstand tortuous conditions within the corrections system.

Schneider's sister Tammy offers a much darker view of her brother's childhood than the idyllic picture he paints. Tammy, 38 and married to a firefighter, lives in a rural community about an hour from where she and Paul grew up. She is an attractive woman with an almost doll-like presence, an impression created by her limited ability to move her hands or arms as a result of brain cancer she has battled for twelve years. According to Tammy, the house where she and her brother grew up was run on a regimen that blended military discipline and sadism. "Our house was a prison, and our stepdad was the warden," she says. He would wake the children up in the middle of the night to make them scrub pots or scour the bathroom floor with toothbrushes. Tammy's first beating occurred when she was eight. A couple of years later, her stepfather began to sexually abuse her. "Paul was very protective of me," she remembers. "He stood up to our stepdad. That man used to beat the shit out of Paul."

Schneider did not last long in the authoritarian world of the military. According to Tammy, he and his wife split up two years after he enlisted, and he was kicked out of the Air Force for writing bad checks. He moved back to Cerritos and became the manager of a local pizza parlor. On one of his nights off, he put on a mask, armed himself with a handgun, and robbed the restaurant. A short while later, he began to notice the big sacks of money carried by armored-car drivers at the Alpha Beta supermarket where Tammy worked as a checkout girl. He developed an irrational personal hatred of the guards. "I couldn't believe how arrogant the guards were," Schneider says. "They'd come into the store, with their little revolvers pointing to the ground, and they'd bump into people without even apologizing. I wanted to show them that they weren't so tough."

Schneider robbed the guards and got away with nearly $100,000. Several weeks later, according to his sister, he showed up at his step-father's house flaunting a new motorcycle. His stepfather, suspecting that Schneider was behind the robbery, tipped off the cops, who began to build a case against Schneider. In 1985, at the age of 23, he was arrested and eventually sent to New Folsom State Prison, in California. By July 1987, he had earned his way into the Aryan Brotherhood by stabbing a guard in the neck.

Schneider thrived in the brutal prison environment, pitting his will against the authorities' every chance he had. In 1990, when he was brought into a courthouse under heavy guard to testify in a case involving another inmate, Schneider pulled a knife he had fashioned from a prison soup ladle and stabbed a defense attorney several times. Like a magician guarding the secret behind a trick, Schneider has never revealed how he smuggled the weapon into the courtroom, though his victim's wounds contained unmistakable clues: They were infected with fecal matter.

After the incident, Schneider penned a declaration explaining why he'd attacked the attorney. The assault stemmed from his desire to humiliate a warden at New Folsom State Prison. "I took [associate warden] Campbell's boasting of his new vaunted security procedures as a challenge," he wrote. As for why he chose his victim, he wrote, "I didn't like his attitude, his smart-aleck remarks, nor his demeanor. So I stabbed him. In retrospect, it was a bad idea."

Schneider picked up a life sentence. Displaying an uncanny ability to harass the system even in defeat, he successfully sued the prison administration for excessively X-raying him every time he was transported before and after the soup ladle–knife smuggling episode and collected $11,666.66.

In the meantime, Schneider was transferred to Pelican Bay State Prison shortly after it opened in 1989. The prison was intended to be the crown jewel of the California Department of Corrections, which operates one of the largest penal systems in the world, a gulag with ninety-eight facilities, more than 300,000 inmates under its jurisdiction, and nearly 50,000 employees.

Pelican Bay rises unexpectedly out of redwood forest a few miles off Highway 101, on the desolate Northern California coast, 360 miles north of San Francisco. Its antiseptic corridors resemble passageways in a large, slumbering spaceship. "When you first go inside Pelican Bay," says Russell Clanton, an attorney who represents several inmates there, "it feels like being inside an enormous sensory deprivation tank." The 3,200 inmates are stored like factory-raised poultry in small concrete cells.

Within a few years of the prison's opening, reports began to leak out suggesting that Pelican Bay's neat façade served mainly to conceal its interior horrors from the outside world. In two early incidents, guards were caught using medical facilities to torture inmates— strapping one man to a gurney and beating him, submerging another in scalding water and flaying him with wire brushes. Eventually, several brutality cases filed on behalf of inmates were rolled into a class action suit. After a two-year trial that ended in 1995, U.S. District Court Judge Thelton Henderson ruled that prisoners at Pelican Bay had been subjected to cruel and unusual punishment. His lengthy opinion detailed "assaults, beatings, and naked cagings in inclement weather" and concluded that "the misuse of force at Pelican Bay is not merely aberrational but inevitable." (Since the ruling, prison authorities say conditions have improved.)

In 1997, Schneider was taking a shower in Pelican Bay when, he claims, a guard popped open an electronic door and allowed a sworn enemy from a rival African American gang called the Black Guerrilla Army to enter the shower area and ambush him. Schneider overpowered his assailant. The guard intervened with a weapon misleadingly named a gas gun. The firearm actually uses a gunpowder charge similar to a twelve-gauge shotgun to fire plastic projectiles the size of Ping-Pong balls. Schneider took multiple shots to the head and was taken to the infirmary with a concussion and lacerations. Afterward, Schneider, a jailhouse lawyer of some renown, sued the prison over the incident. His case, however, was thrown out of court.

Upon his release from the infirmary, he was sent into Pelican Bay's Security Housing Unit. Schneider speaks of living in the extreme confinement of the SHU with a sort of twisted pride. "They put us in the SHU to keep us away from the rape-os and chesters," he says, referring to rapists and child molesters. "I'm proud of that. I don't want to be associated with them."

The role of the Aryan Brotherhood, like other race-based gangs, is a complex one within the hostile prison universe. On the one hand, these gangs enforce segregation. But the gangs are also likely to do business with each other: smuggling drugs, manufacturing weapons, running numbers, and brewing alcohol. The gangs also share (along with many guards) a more or less openly homicidal contempt for sex offenders. Under Schneider's leadership, the Aryan Brotherhood is alleged to have recruited at least three guards in its efforts to identify and attack sex offender inmates. In its case against Schneider, the federal government charges him with masterminding the murder or attempted murder of twenty-four people, including the killing of a cop.

In person, Schneider maintains an unnervingly pleasant, almost bland smile, whether he's discussing killing rapists or reading one of his favorite authors, J. R. R. Tolkien. He says his entire mental and physical effort in the SHU "is structured around not going insane." The last stop for those who lose this battle in the SHU is the prison psychiatric unit. Here, the most critical mental cases can be put on heavy doses of psychotropic drugs, then given "group therapy." In these sessions, individual prisoners are locked in telephone-booth-size boxes with plexiglass-and-barred fronts that prisoners call "man cages," and these are propped upright, arrayed in groups of four or six around a therapist.

"You definitely don't want to lose your marbles in the SHU," Schneider says. "But you can find things that cheer you up—getting a cup of instant coffee, news, or a box of saltines. It's important to keep your day full." He stays in shape by wrapping the law books he keeps in his cell and using them as weights. Sometimes he lays his cellmate, a murderer named Dale Bretches, across his arms and bench-presses him like a barbell.

Several years ago, Schneider and Bretches began producing artwork. Since they were forbidden art supplies by prison authorities, they collected scrap paper and soaked it in toilet water until the ink came off. They made pigments by scraping the colors off ads in magazines. "If you want a lot of red," Schneider says, "you look for a Marlboro ad."

His intricate creations look like a cross between tattoo art and the air-brushed murals that adorned vans in the 1970s. The paintings are frequently chock-full of runes—cryptic symbols found in the works of Tolkien. Schneider often depicts himself in his paintings as a bare-chested Norse god riding on the prows of ships surrounded by noble animals.

Devan Hawkes, a special intelligence officer for the CDC, has spent years investigating Schneider. He believes the runes found in Schneider's work contain "secret codes" that convey instructions to Aryan Brotherhood associates outside prison.

Looking for subjects to draw, Schneider began to pester his sister for pictures of the "white Siegfried and Roy tigers" and for copies of

Field & Stream, which he claims was banned by the prison because it contained photos of guns. Then Schneider came across a magazine that would change his life: *Dog Fancy*. "Looking at dogs made me forget I was in prison," says Schneider. Soon, they inspired him to become a dog owner once more.

After they were arrested last March for the dog-mauling case, Knoller and Noel were so broke they were unable to make bail. They have spent nearly a year living separate but parallel lives in different wings of the San Francisco city jail. When he enters the jail visitation room in his orange jumpsuit, Robert Noel slides into a chair and smiles warmly. Noel is an imposing six feet four. His golden-boy features have aged comfortably beneath his shaggy blond hair and walrus mustache. Though he faces up to three years in prison, he projects confidence and freewheeling good cheer.

After chatting amiably about his once high-powered social life, Noel produces a copy of a painting that Schneider made. It depicts Noel, Knoller, and Schneider at a medieval feast presided over by their "royal dog," Bane. Noel traces his finger across the paper and says dreamily, "There's our family," then points to the big dog in the foreground and says affectionately, "That's the Banester."

Noel's first wife, Karen, whom he divorced in 1986 after nearly twenty-three years of marriage, says, "Robert is mentally ill." She furnishes no proof of her opinion but adds that his three children ceased having contact with him several years ago. Noel's only biological son, his namesake, Robert Jr., who is 31, said of his father, "He's a jackass. I don't like my dad, and I never have."

Noel grew up in a working-class home in Baltimore. His father was a pipe fitter and his mother a beautician. His only brother works in the electrical trades. Robert, the family overachiever, entered the University of Maryland on a Marine Corps scholarship, similar to ROTC. He married his high school sweetheart, Karen, the day after John F. Kennedy was shot. A year later, he entered law school. In 1969, when he was 27, Noel took a job in the Justice Department. When he was 34, in 1980, he moved west to become an assistant U.S. attorney in the Southern District Court of San Diego.

Working for the government began to disillusion him. "Being inside the system gave me a unique perspective on its power to crush the individual," he says. He quit the U.S. attorney's office after a year and joined a prestigious corporate law firm in San Diego. By 1987, he had divorced, moved to San Francisco, briefly married and then divorced a legal secretary, then met and fell in love with Marjorie Knoller—all in the space of about a year. "I would trust my life in Marjorie's hands," he says.

The impression that Marjorie Knoller makes upon entering the visitation room is one of meekness. Her faded, silver-threaded brown hair is pulled back in a ponytail, and her brown, dark-ringed eyes have a worried softness. On March 27, when the police entered the home of friends in Northern California, where she and her husband were eating dinner, and told Marjorie she was under arrest for second-degree murder, she collapsed and had to be carried out on a stretcher. During subsequent court appearances, her physical and mental states deteriorated. Rolled into the courtroom in a wheelchair, she seemed almost cuckoo, babbling to herself and cursing the prosecutors. By the end of the summer, bruises began to appear on her thighs and lower back. Then, where there had been bruises, hardened nodules of subcutaneous fat, shaped like fingernails, burst through the surface of her skin. Doctors diagnosed it as a nervous-vascular disorder and put her on medication, alleviating her symptoms enough for her to sit comfortably and walk unassisted.

Growing up in Brooklyn, Knoller was a straight arrow who dreamed of becoming an FBI agent. "Marjorie didn't go with the crowd," says her mother, Harriet. "She skipped her high school graduation. She told me, 'Mom, I'm not going. All the kids in my class are on drugs.'"

She met Robert Noel when she was 32, a divorced law-school graduate just starting her career at the firm where Noel was already a big shot. They made a lunch date one day and moved in together a week later. By May 1988, they had both resigned their jobs and hung out their own shingle. They moved away from the commercial contract and tax law that had been Noel's area of expertise and took on more pro bono work. Then, in 1994, their life was to change drastically when they were referred to what seemed like an interesting case.

The client was a man named John Cox, a guard at Pelican Bay State Prison who had recently broken ranks with fellow corrections officers by testifying on behalf of inmates who'd been brutalized in the prison. Now Cox was being harassed on the job and wanted to sue the California Department of Corrections. Knoller and Noel leapt at the chance to represent him. Within a few months they abandoned what remained of their commercial law practice to concentrate on representing prison guards in grievances against the CDC.

"The good Lord blessed our family by bringing Bob and Marjorie into our lives," says Monica Bermender, who is represented by Noel and Knoller in an ongoing First Amendment federal court case. "They believed in me and in our family when nobody else would."

Despite their devotion to their cause, Knoller and Noel racked up an uneven, some say abysmal, record. They lost the harassment case for their first client, Cox, and he subsequently hanged himself. Susan Beck, who analyzed their cases against the CDC in an article in *The Recorder*, a Bay Area legal newspaper, concluded that Knoller and Noel often made basic procedural mistakes and developed legal strategies based on unsupported conspiracy theories.

"Noel comes across as someone who is competent, but it appears to me there have been serious problems with his conduct on some cases," says Neal Sanders, an expert in prison law.

The fact was that neither Knoller nor Noel had much experience trying criminal cases. Entering the miasma of the prison universe, they were clearly in over their heads. "Prison is like its own ecosystem, with its own rules," says attorney Russell Clanton. "Life inside the wire is unlike anything most people outside of it can even conceive."

The low point of their legal career came in 1997, when they defended a Pelican Bay guard accused of colluding with the Aryan Brotherhood to set up child molesters for beating and murder. Their defense failed, and not only was the guard found guilty but one of the inmates they called as a witness was subsequently murdered.

"It was devastating for us," says Knoller. "I was in shock."

Schneider was among the witnesses they called in that case and was presumably marked for death like the other inmate. "We sent a letter to the CDC informing them of our concern for Paul's safety," says Knoller.

It was about this time that Schneider's dreams of once again owning dogs began to take root. Ads in the back pages of *Dog Fancy* and *Dog World* featuring an unusually fierce breed of dog captured his interest. Called Presa Canarios, they were often touted as "guardian dogs," as "man stoppers," tough enough to "take out pit bulls." Presas are "holding" or "gripping" dogs that were bred by Spanish cattlemen on the Canary Islands in the sixteenth century to pin down bulls for slaughter. They are what breeders call "lip and ear" dogs: They immobilize much larger animals such as bulls by clamping their jaws over their most vulnerable features—their lips or their ears. American-bred Presas look like pit bulls but are about twice as big, sometimes weighing as much as 160 pounds.

Dog behaviorist and breeder Saul Saltars calls many of the Presa lines sold in America "junk dogs"—Presas mixed with pit bulls, Great Danes, English mastiffs. "Some breeders take liberties with what they call Presas," he says. "You might not know what you're getting, how stable the dog will be."

Schneider began dreaming of ways to purchase his own Presas in 1998. He had $23,000 to invest, given to him by a fellow inmate who had won a medical malpractice suit. Schneider's plan was to use surrogates outside prison to breed Presas. He purchased more than $1,000 worth of dog-breeding manuals. He sent letters to breeders and trainers. Most refused to have anything to do with a prison inmate. Nevertheless, he located a breeder in the Midwest who seemed like a good prospect. According to the CDC investigation, his name was James Harris, and he operated a Presa business, Stygian Kennels. Schneider would arrange to buy Bane from Harris.

According to Tracy Hennings, a Presa breeder familiar with Stygian Kennels (now defunct) and its brood of pups, "Bane was not a pure Presa. He was a questionable mix of at least four different breeds."

But Schneider, conducting his business from inside his 11-by-7½-foot concrete box, was unable to do the sort of on-the-spot research other buyers might have undertaken. He had a source for dogs. All he needed was a place to raise them.

Initially, he wrote to his sister Tammy asking whether she and her husband, Greg Keefer, would raise dogs for him. Tammy recalls her reaction when she received this letter from her brother. "What the hell is an inmate doing with dogs? No way."

"One time Paul got us into some deal where he sent us money from one of his legal settlements to buy TV sets for his buddies in prison," Greg Keefer says. "Next thing, FBI agents came to our door and said we were on someone's hit list because we didn't get him a TV."

"I love Paul," says Tammy. "But the guy's in prison for a reason."

Rebuffed by his family, Schneider found the assistance he needed from another quarter. His cellmate, Dale Bretches, the murderer, was receiving regular visits from a woman in a Christian outreach program who came from a small agricultural town about 190 miles from Pelican Bay, called Hayfork. Bretches asked her whether she knew any other good Christians in Hayfork who could visit his cellie, Schneider, and help him out with a problem.

Janet Coumbs is a Mormon woman in her late forties who lived on a four-acre sheep farm in Hayfork, California, with her 18-year-old daughter, Daisy. She is a somewhat heavyset woman who scraped by on disability checks and by selling "little baby sheep" to local families for slaughter. A friend of hers stopped by her ramshackle house one day and told her about the mission work she did at Pelican Bay, trying to bring Jesus into the life of a murderer named Dale Bretches. "[She] told me I wasn't doing my Christian duty by not going with her to the prison to help other inmates," said Coumbs.

Coumbs made her first visit to Schneider in January 1998. Within a couple of months, Schneider had persuaded Coumbs to lend her farm to his Dog o' War kennels. Every two weeks, she was supposed to send Schneider pictures of the dogs and letters describing their life on the farm. One photo showed Bane cuddling with a cat. This enraged Schneider. "You're making a wuss out of Bane," he wrote. "These are royal dogs, and they need to look majestic."

Several months later, Schneider and Coumbs had a falling-out. According to Schneider, the root of their conflict was romantic. He says, "She kept dropping hints about how she wanted me to convert to Mormonism and marry her." After Schneider says he spurned Coumbs's romantic overtures, she stopped sending letters and visit-

ing him altogether. Coumbs has also told investigators that Schneider threatened her. "Things can happen to you and your home," he
allegedly told her. (Reportedly, Coumbs is now in the witness protection program.)

In late 1999, Schneider turned to Knoller and Noel to help him
retrieve his dogs from Coumbs. Perhaps because of their dismal
performance as attorneys, Schneider had resorted to Knoller and
Noel only after another Bay Area attorney had turned him down.

True to form, the lawyers threw themselves into this new ill-
fated cause. They threatened to sue Coumbs if she didn't turn the
dogs over, and then they spent their own money to hire an animal-
transport service and showed up in person at Coumbs's farm on
March 31, 2000. There were now eight Presas on the farm, four of
them pups sired by Bane.

For the previous year, Bane had been chained to an iron stake.
Noel beams when he recalls seeing the dog for the first time. "Bane
was confident, proud, handsome," he says, adding, "Bane had an
eye for ladies. He sees Marjorie, rolls over on his back, and bam,
that big red arrow popped out. He had a hard-on that big." Noel gestures with his hands, indicating Bane's penis length, then grins.
"Boy, was that dog hung."

Noel and Knoller transported seven of the dogs to homes in
Southern California belonging to relatives of Schneider's prison
buddies. They kept Hera, a female that developed a heart condition, and, after spending $3,000 on her veterinary bills, moved her
into their Pacific Heights apartment. In early September, they
brought Bane to live there as well. Greg Keefer says that before
Knoller and Noel rescued Bane, the dog had been neglected.
"Flies had chewed Bane's ears down to their nubs," Keefer says.

By now, they were writing letters and sending dog pictures to
Schneider several times a week. Their odd relationship with him

was reaching full bloom. Knoller says she first floated the idea of adopting Schneider, explaining this unusual arrangement in practical legal terms. "By adopting Paul," says Knoller, "we now have a say in his medical treatment. If something bad happens to him in the prison, we can sue. We adopted him to give him protection."

Her analysis is legally true—and adult adoption has long been a method employed by gay couples to form family units with legal standing—but it fails to explain the couple's interest in a violent inmate. Knoller suggests that she and Schneider had a lot in common, such as a mutual interest in *The Hobbit* and in runes. "Paul has an inner life he shares with us," Knoller says. "He's special. He's our kid, and we love him."

She seems almost convincing, like a doting mom, but if that's true, what about the rumors of bestial photos and kinky fantasies traded with Schneider? Knoller allows that "threesomes are a pretty standard erotic fantasy." She says, "It's a tradition to write erotic letters to inmates. It helps them." Then she tries a different tack. "Paul was writing a novel, an erotic medieval fantasy. We wrote chapters back and forth. We were all characters in it."

Knoller says that, along the way, "I flashed my breasts in some pictures. Bob might have sent one of these to Paul. There was nothing with dogs."

Noel describes their unusual family unit in noble terms: "We were a part of keeping something in Paul alive. Bane punched a hole through that cement box Paul lives in and gave him a window on the world. We wanted to help keep that window open."

A couple of weeks before Knoller and Noel went up to Janet Coumbs's farm to pick up the dogs, they had hired a local veterinarian named Dr. Donald Martin to examine them. Though he gave the dogs shots and went home, something about Bane troubled the veterinarian. A few days later, he sent Knoller a letter to inform her of his fears about the dog. "I would be professionally amiss if I did not mention the following so you can be prepared," he wrote. "These animals would be a liability in any household."

Knoller says she didn't read the letter until long after receiving it. She and Noel nicknamed the dogs "the Mutleys" and "the kids." They structured their lives around the animals, never leaving them alone for more than an hour. Bane was "the Banester." Several mornings a week, Knoller woke up early and cooked bacon, pork, and hamburger for the dogs, which she fed to them along with their dog food.

Keith Whitley, the former guard who used to socialize with Knoller and Noel, noticed the change in them. "I'd get on the phone with Bob to ask him about a case," he says, "and all he did was talk about how big Bane's balls were." Whitley visited their apartment about a week before the fatal attack: "They used to have this charming flat. The dogs turned it into a piss pot. Bob had to bring the dogs out one at a time when he introduced them to me because he couldn't control them."

Awful things started happening almost immediately after they brought Bane home. Bane got into a fight with a dog at a beach four days after he arrived in San Francisco and nearly snapped Noel's finger clean off. Bane and Hera scared the hell out of people in the building and neighborhood. Henry Putek, an unassuming parakeet owner who also lives on the sixth floor, was pinned against a wall one evening when Bane slipped out of Knoller and Noel's partially open door and charged him. "He stared at me silently," said Putek. "With drool hanging down, stinking and smelly."

Neighborhood residents claimed that Bane and Hera attacked at least three local dogs, nearly killing one of them, a German shepherd. People who lived in the area describe their encounters with the dogs in almost supernatural terms. One neighbor recalls that birds started flying crazily when Bane and Hera walked by. Another resident, Alex de Laszlo, remembered encountering the dogs outside a local coffee shop. "I put my hand on Bane's head," he said. "It held a sensation very different from any dog I had ever petted before. There was incredible tension. There was something strong and dark about this animal."

From the vantage point of his concrete box at Pelican Bay, Schneider had an entirely different perspective. "Everything was going perfect. I was getting photos of Bane. Bob and Marjorie told me everything he was doing." Schneider says Bane was growing up right. "I never wanted to see Bane go looking for fights," he says. "But if he was forced into it, I would want him to represent himself well, and not run away crying."

At this point, Schneider was on the verge of realizing an impossible dream. One of his associates on the outside had secured space in *Dog World* to place an ad for Schneider's Dog o' War kennels. "Life was so good, I felt like I did when I was on the streets," says Schneider. "In some ways, I felt better." He sent a picture of Bane to his sister with the caption "El Supremo Bane. Born to raise hell."

On January 11, 2001, Robert Noel wrote Schneider one of his almost daily letters recounting everything that had transpired that day with "the kids." Nearing the end of the letter, Noel described an encounter between the dogs and a neighbor. "As soon as the [elevator] door opens at six, one of our newer female neighbors, a timorous little mousy blond who weighs less than Hera, is met by the dynamic duo exiting and almost has a coronary."

The "mousy blond" he referred to was Diane Whipple, the St. Mary's College lacrosse coach who died exactly fifteen days later in that same hallway. Whipple had had run-ins with the dogs and had made her feeling about her neighbors clear. She claimed to her girlfriend, Sharon Smith, that one of them had snapped at her two weeks earlier. She told her friend Sarah Miller that Noel "was an asshole. He better do something about those dogs."

On the afternoon of January 26, Whipple arrived home carrying a bag of groceries with some tacos she planned to make for dinner for Smith and herself. Around twenty minutes earlier, at about 3:40, Knoller says she had been working on legal research alone in her apartment (Noel was out of the city on business) when Bane started to whimper. She put him on a leash, walked him on the roof of the building, and came inside to put a bag of Bane's poop in the garbage chute when she noticed Whipple standing about thirty feet away by her door.

"She was staring at Bane," says Knoller. Then, for no obvious reason, Knoller says, Bane dragged her toward Whipple. "I battled him the whole way," Knoller insists. While Knoller struggled with Bane and Hera, who had also come into the hall, for several minutes, she says that Whipple simply stood silently in front of her apartment. Her front door was open, but according to Knoller she didn't bother to go inside, even after Bane jumped up on the wall and stuck his head in her crotch. All she said, according to Knoller, was "Your dog jumped on me."

Knoller says that she finally tried to push Whipple into her apartment for her own good, but Whipple resisted, at which point Bane bit her throat and proceeded to rip her clothes apart. Knoller claims the entire attack lasted a good twenty minutes, during which time, she says, "I put my life on the line. It's only dumb luck he didn't kill me."

Knoller denies that Hera took part in the attack, though Hera was also found with blood on her coat by animal control officers. Later, after Hera was taken into custody by animal control, an employee at the city kennel where she was being kept observed fibers that appeared to be multicolored fabric coming out in the dog's stools, though no one at the time thought—or volunteered—to collect this as evidence. Dog behaviorist Saul Saltars points to the shredding of Whipple's clothing as evidence that one or both of the dogs had been taught to be hostile. "Someone trained that dog to bite rags," says Saltars. "It's a technique to build aggression." While Knoller and Noel claim the dogs weren't trained to be aggressive, police recovered a book from their apartment titled *Manstopper!*, a training manual that teaches owners techniques, such as ragging out, to nurture viciousness in dogs.

Though the grand jury largely rejected Knoller's account of the attack (they found it hard to believe that Whipple would stand motionless for such a long time while Bane rampaged through the hall), until now there has been no concrete suggestion that Knoller fabricated her story. But according to Schneider's sister Tammy, Knoller called her that evening and offered an account of the attack that diverges significantly from what Knoller told the police and the grand jury. "Marjorie said she and her neighbor 'got into it,'" says Tammy. "They had an argument before anything happened with those dogs. Marjorie asked her to shut her door so she could take her dogs out in the hall, and that lady was like, 'No, I'm not shutting my door now. Fuck you!'"

Knoller denies this ever occurred, but if this is true, Knoller's defense—that the attack happened spontaneously—is suspect. From the standpoint of the law, a powerful attack dog might be viewed as a weapon not much different from a gun. In other words, if you were holding a gun, and your neighbor was found shot to death, it's a lot harder to prove the whole thing was accidental if people found out you and your dead neighbor were having an argument right before your gun shot her.

There is one element of Knoller's account of events that afternoon in the hallway that no one disputes:

What was the last thing Diane Whipple said to you?

"'Help me,'" Knoller whispers. Then she pauses. Knoller says, "My husband still talks about Bane like we used to, how much he loves him. I can't think of that dog the same way. All I see is the horror, the horror."

Knoller's adopted son expresses his feeling about the attack dif-

ferently. Schneider's blue eyes peer out impassively from behind
the security glass at the visitation booth, and he says, "For once, I try
to do something good, and look what happens. Ain't that buzzard
luck."

———

*Following their trial in Los Angeles, Marjorie Knoller and her hus-
band Robert Noel were each convicted of manslaughter for their roles
in the mauling death of Diane Whipple, and each is serving the maximum four years. Knoller was also convicted of second-degree murder
in connection with Whipple's death, but this was thrown out in a San
Francisco court by Judge James Warren in July 2003 on the grounds
that there was insufficient evidence of Knoller's intent to commit murder. When Judge Warren offered Knoller the opportunity to apologize
to the friends and loved ones of Diane Whipple in court, Knoller
remained silent.*

*Knoller and Noel's adopted son, Pelican Bay inmate Paul "Corn-
fed" Schneider, has pleaded not guilty to federal racketeering charges
that in his role as an Aryan Brotherhood gang leader he ordered eight
murders from behind bars. As bizarre as the killer dog story might
seem to readers unfamiliar with the California corrections system,
those who've experienced it well know its corrosive influence on all
who come into contact with it, no matter which side of the bars they
are on. The California corrections system remains as former inmate
and author Edward Bunker described it, an animal factory. May
everyone who reads "Mad Dogs and Lawyers" say a prayer for the victim, Diane Whipple, and the people who loved her.*

THE JOURNALIST AND THE TERRORIST
ROBERT SAM ANSON

The reporter who comes to Karachi, Pakistan, is given certain cautions.

Do not take a taxi from the airport; arrange for the hotel to send a car and confirm the driver's identity before getting in.

Do not stay in a room that faces the street.

Do not interview sources over the phone.

Do not discuss subjects such as Islam or the Pakistani nuclear program in the presence of hotel staff.

Do not leave notes or tape recordings in your room.

Do not discard work papers in the wastebasket; flush them down the toilet.

Do not use public transportation or accept rides from strangers.

Do not go into markets, movie theaters, parks, or crowds.

Do not go anywhere without telling a trustworthy someone the destination and expected time of return.

And, above all, do not go alone. Ever.

The Marriott in Karachi satisfies lodging guidelines. Metal detectors flank the entrances, guards with sawed-off shotguns patrol the premises, and the shopping arcade leads directly to the U.S. consulate—which seemed a plus until a car bomb killed twelve people there on June 14. My room, per instruction, is on the Marriott's backside, and offers a fine view of the nearby Sheraton, where a bus containing eleven French nationals was blown up by a suicide bomber in May. It is also where, according to a U.S. official, FBI agents recovered a videotape showing an American journalist having his head cut off. His name was Daniel Pearl, he was 38 years old, a father-to-be, and South Asia bureau chief for *The Wall Street Journal*. He got the same security briefing I did.

By now, the horror that befell Danny Pearl is deeply engraved. A handsome young man, loved by everyone—"Sweetest guy in the world," friends call him—goes to a rendezvous he believes will lead him to a scoop. Instead, terrorists are waiting to snatch him from the street. They issue photographs of Danny in chains, a pistol held to his head, and charge that he is a spy and will be executed unless demands are met. Danny's French wife, Mariane—six months pregnant with their first child—appears on television to appeal for his life. But there is only silence. Then, just when things are at their darkest, the terrorist ringleader, a former British public-school boy named Ahmed Omar Saeed Sheikh, is arrested and says Danny is alive. Hopes soar as Pakistan's president, General Pervez Musharraf, predicts his imminent freedom. But all that is released is the videotape. "My father's Jewish, my mother's Jewish, I'm Jewish," it records Daniel Pearl saying. Then he is butchered.

We've been told that Danny was not only a great reporter, with an eye for the offbeat and the absurd, but a cautious one—not the sort who'd look for trouble. We've heard how he grew up in suburban Los Angeles, went to Stanford, and landed at the *Journal*, which sent him to Atlanta, Washington, London, Paris, and, finally, Bombay, a posting he accepted after confirming that there were venues where Mariane could exercise her passion for salsa dancing. We've had described how he was skeptical in the best sense of the word, questioning things taken for granted, unearthing stories others overlooked.

He was working that way on his last story, an investigation of the connections between the "shoe bomber," Richard C. Reid, and a virulently anti-Semitic Muslim militant, Mubarak Ali Shah Gilani, tracing an unbeaten path that led to who knows where.

The who, what, when, and where have been laid out. Everything except the why. Why did Danny Pearl die? Because he was a Jew? A journalist? An American? Or was he simply in the wrong place at the wrong time?

The why is always the hardest question for a journalist to answer, and it's what brought Danny Pearl to Pakistan. "I want to know why they hate us so much," he said. Why he died trying to find out brought me.

My qualification is having been in a similar circumstance a long time ago—August 1970, in Cambodia, to be precise. I was 25 years old then, covering the war for *Time* and feeling invulnerable, a frequent, sometimes fatal journalist's malady. The short of it is that I drove alone to somewhere I shouldn't have, and wound up in a hole with the barrel of an AK-47 pressed to my forehead. I was presumed dead for several weeks, and the conviction of my fellows back in Phnom Penh—just as it is among many today about Danny Pearl—was that I'd asked for it. The difference is, I came back.

There is a lot else about Danny and the people who picked him up that is dissimilar, but every reporter has got to start somewhere. And the place Danny Pearl began, shortly after 9/11, was with a phone call to a number in Manhattan.

On the line that morning was Mansoor Ijaz, founder and chairman of Crescent Investment Management, LLC, and a U.S.-born-and-bred Pakistani-American with unusual friends and interests. His business partner is Lieutenant General James Abrahamson, former director of Ronald Reagan's Star Wars program; the vice-chairman of his board, R. James Woolsey, director of the Central Intelligence Agency under Bill Clinton. For a time Ijaz was also chums with Clinton and his national security adviser Samuel Berger. This came in handy in April 1997, when, as a private citizen, Ijaz negotiated Sudan's counterterrorism offer to the United States, and again in August 2000, when Ijaz had Pakistan and India on the seeming verge of cooling the Kashmir cauldron. The deal broke down, as did the relationship with the White House. But soon enough Ijaz was back, as tight with George W. and Condie as he'd been with Bill and Sandy.

Danny called on a tip from Indian intelligence, which said Ijaz was wired with leading jihadis. Figuring that a prominent Pakistani-American who came recommended by Indian spooks to get to Muslim militants must have been a gold mine for Danny, I did the same nine months later.

Ijaz confirmed my figuring.

"He said he wanted to try to understand the psychology behind the jihadi groups," Ijaz recalls. "He wanted to try to get into the mind of the people running the show. . . . He wanted me to introduce him to people who could open doors for him."

Danny's religion also came up.

"I said to him at one point, 'I presume from your name that you are Jewish. Is that correct?' He said, 'Yes.' I said, 'Well, you have to understand that this is going to be a huge stumbling block for you. Because [the militants] are going to pick up on that very quickly, and *The Wall Street Journal* is not viewed as the voice of the Muslim people.'"

Danny, who'd reported from Iran and Sudan without difficulty, did not seem concerned, and Ijaz made introductions to three sources: Shaheen Sehbai, editor of *The News*, Pakistan's largest English-language daily; a jihadi activist he declines to name; and — most fatefully — Khalid Khawaja, a Muslim militant and a onetime agent with Pakistan's Inter-Services Intelligence agency (ISI) who counts among his very best friends Osama bin Laden.

In late September 2001, Danny flew to Karachi, a sprawling port city of 15 million that is Pakistan's commercial center. Mariane, who is a freelance journalist and frequently accompanied him on interviews, went too.

"We didn't choose a profession," said Mariane, a strong-minded Buddhist who has been likened to Yoko Ono. "We didn't choose it for ego purposes; we chose it because we wanted to change the world."

They checked into the Pearl Continental, where reservations had been made for them by Ikram Sehgal, proprietor of Pakistan's largest security company. Danny had called him before departing from Bombay to see if it was safe to bring Mariane, who they'd recently learned was pregnant. Sehgal delivered a sobering lecture about security precautions, and offered to provide them with an armed guard free of charge. Danny accepted.

I empathized. Compared with Karachi, Cambodia seemed a walk in the park.

For a time in the early 1990s, violence in Karachi was so endemic that the army took over for the cops. When the troops pulled out, killings started averaging eight per day—and those were merely the ones involving political and criminal gangs. No one bothered to count the shootings, bombings, garrotings, and throat slittings between ethnic and religious groups, much less the toll racked up in quotidian armed robberies, home invasions, and just-for-the-hell-of-it sniper slayings.

Americans were special targets. In March 1995 two U.S. consular personnel on their way to work were mowed down by automatic weapons in an ambush at a busy intersection. Two years later, in November 1997, four employees of an American oil company were shot dead in a carbon-copy replay a few blocks from the Sheraton.

Karachi was somewhat quieter when the Pearls arrived—at least, a local magazine was no longer publishing a foldout, color-coded guide to where one was likeliest to be bumped off. Americans hadn't been murdered in a while (Shia Muslim physicians were the victims du jour), but the U.S. consulate was taking no chances. Its staff members were ferried around in armor-plated Chevy Suburbans driven by U.S. Marines.

Journalists acquainting themselves with Pakistan usually come to Karachi last or don't come, period. I'd resolved to be among the latter category, after Benazir Bhutto advised that Karachi was "so dangerous." I changed my mind after several weeks testing calmer Pakistani waters and convincing myself that former prime ministers don't know anything—typical journalist thinking, when a story's good. Danny, however, came here first. He was after Muslim militants, and Karachi is their Rome. Besides, an old friend from the *Journal* was soon to arrive. Her name was Asra Nomani.

Asra, who'd been at the *Journal* since 1988, was a Dow Jones original. For starters, she was an Indian-born Muslim from Morgantown, West Virginia, where her father helped found the first mosque. And corporate America, Asra wasn't: in January 2000 she took a leave to write a book about Tantra.

She'd been conducting her research from India. Shortly after 9/11, however, Salon.com appointed her its Central Asia correspondent and she later took a house in Karachi, a fact that almost certainly did not go unnoticed by Pakistan's ISI, which keeps tabs on foreign journalists, particularly those from India, who are presumed, ipso facto, spies.

Initially, the Pearls' time in Karachi was unremarkable. They lunched with *News* editor Shaheen Sehbai, who found Danny "very keen to do work" but with "no clue how to go about it," and called on Ikram Sehgal, who arranged several appointments to get Danny grounded. "I liked him," says Sehgal. "He was very inquisitive and intense, you know."

It showed. Hardly had Danny cleared customs than he was quoting Sehgal in a *Journal* assessment of Musharraf's future (bleak, Sehgal judged). Within weeks, Danny had dispensed with his gun-toting chaperon—"this shadow," he said—and was in the capital,

Islamabad, 700 miles to the north, for a several-hour session with Khalid Khawaja.

Khawaja was always good for a provocative quote, which made him a journalist favorite. "America is a very vulnerable country," he'd told CBS in July 2001. "Your White House is the most vulnerable target. It's very simple to just get it." After the U.S. began bombing Afghanistan on October 7, 2001, Asra got a zinger, too: "No American is safe now. . . . This is a lifelong war."

Some dismissed Khawaja as a P.R. man. But when it came to Muslim militancy, he was the real deal, having acquired his credentials during the war against the Soviets in Afghanistan, where, as an air force squadron leader, Khawaja was serving with the ISI, which was distributing CIA-purchased munitions to mujahedeen. The more radically Islamist the fighter, the more weapons he got, including Osama bin Laden, who formed an instant bond with Khawaja. It deepened when Khawaja was forced out of the ISI in 1988 after criticizing military strongman Zia ul-Haq for not doing enough to Islamize Pakistan—equivalent to questioning the piety of the Pope.

But despite his talk of bin Laden's being "a man like an angel," Khawaja was sufficiently broad-minded in his allegiances that he got the Taliban to agree to receive Ijaz and ex-CIA director Woolsey.

Khawaja, in short, was a source to kill for, and Danny charmed him. Describing the reporter to Ijaz as "competent, straightforward," and not given to asking "inappropriate questions," Khawaja agreed to steer Danny to leading jihadis and to be a sounding board during his time in-country.

Danny made another valuable acquaintance in Hamid Mir, editor of Islamabad's Urdu-language *Daily Ausaf* and self-proclaimed "official biographer" of Osama bin Laden. In their last chat, in early November, bin Laden had boasted of possessing chemical and nuclear weapons. But, according to Mir, the real reason for his summons was remarks he'd made on a U.S. TV show, saying that bin Laden couldn't back his beliefs with Islamic teachings. "I watched you on *Larry King*," Osama said. "I want to tell you my position."

When I call on Mir he extracts Danny's business card from his wallet with a flourish.

"This is his memory," he says. "I was aware he's a Jew and that he works for *The Wall Street Journal* . . . but I can say that he was a very good friend of mine."

He fondles the card, which is worn from showings. "Some people accused him that he was a spy, because the kind of assignment he was doing and his way of meeting with people and going after the story. . . . I came on CNN and I said, 'No, he was a journalist . . . like me. We journalists take these kinds of risks.' "

Mir, a Taliban enthusiast, was wary of Danny until they attended an anti-American street demonstration in November. Several hundred were on hand, chanting denunciations of the U.S. and fealty to bin Laden, Danny in the midst of them.

"People were burning the flag of the United States of America . . . and I was real careful that I should not become a victim of that fire," says Mir. "But he was standing right under the flag. I said, 'Danny, you should be careful!' He said, 'I want to see in their eyes why they hate us.' I said, 'At least there is one American journalist who wants to find out the reasons.' "

For all Danny's great contacts, his stories weren't leaping off the *Journal*'s front page. While he was writing about trading in Afghan currency, other correspondents were packing up to cover the war next door. But by late November, seven journalists had been killed there. "It's too dangerous," Danny said at a meal with other reporters before Thanksgiving. "I just got married, my wife is pregnant, I'm just not going to do it."

Quietly, though, Danny was onto something much more compelling than the daily bombing reports: He'd found links between the ISI and a "humanitarian" organization accused of leaking nuclear secrets to bin Laden.

The group—Ummah Tameer-e-Nau (UTN)—was headed by Dr. Bashiruddin Mahmood, former chief of Pakistan's nuclear power program and a key player in the development of its atomic bomb. Mahmood—who'd been forced out of his job in 1998 after U.S. intelligence learned of his affection for Muslim extremists—acknowledged making trips to Afghanistan as well as meeting Taliban supreme leader Mullah Mohammed Omar. But he claimed that all they'd discussed was the building of a flour mill in Afghanistan. As for bin Laden, Mahmood said he knew him only as someone who "was helping in different places, renovating schools, opening orphan houses, and [helping with] rehabilitation of widows."

That's not how the CIA saw it. According to the agency, Mahmood and another nuclear scientist, Chaudry Abdul Majid, met with bin Laden in Kabul a few weeks before 9/11—and not to talk about whole wheat bread. U.S. pressure got the scientists detained in late October, and they admitted having provided bin Laden with detailed information about weapons of mass destruction. But, for what was termed "the best interests of the nation," they were released in mid-December.

All this had been reported. What no one had tumbled to, except for Danny and *Journal* correspondent Steve LeVine, were UTN's connections to top levels of Pakistan's ISI and its military. General Hamid Gul—a former ISI director with pronounced anti-American, radically Islamist views—identified himself as UTN's "honorary patron" and said that he had seen Mahmood during his trip to brief bin Laden. Danny and LeVine also discovered that UTN listed as a director an active-duty brigadier general, and ran down a former ISI colonel who claimed that the agency was not only aware of Mahmood's meeting with bin Laden months before his detention but had encouraged his Afghan trips.

"It could be a big scoop—like your scoop," Danny told Mir. But the *Journal* played the story on page 8 on Christmas Eve and it passed without impact.

A few days later Danny was back in the paper with another exclusive, datelined Bahawalpur, headquarters of Jaish-e-Mohammed (one of the most violent jihadi groups, as well as one of the best connected to the ISI). Jaish had been banned by Musharraf, its bank accounts frozen, and its founder, Maulana Masood Azhar, placed under house arrest. However, Danny later reported that the Jaish office in Bahawalpur was still up and running, as was the Jaish account at the local bank.

If Danny hadn't been on the ISI's radarscope before, he was now. But Danny wasn't letting up; he now had his sights set on the "shoe bomber," Richard C. Reid.

Interest in the British ex-con turned Muslim radical had tailed off since December 22, when he had tried to blow up an American Airlines Paris-to-Miami flight by touching a match to an explosive in his tennis sneakers. But there remained some dangling ends, none more intriguing than who was giving Reid orders.

A story in the January 6 edition of *The Boston Globe* got Danny on the case. It reported that U.S. officials believed Reid to be a follower of Sheikh Mubarak Ali Shah Gilani, a leader of an obscure Muslim militant group named Jamaat ul-Fuqra ("The Impoverished"). Described by the State Department's 1995 report on terrorism as dedicated "to purifying Islam through violence," ul-Fuqra recruited devotees from as far away as the Netherlands and had sent jihadis into battle in Kashmir, Chechnya, Bosnia, and Israel. Since the early 1980s, ul-Fuqra had also operated in the U.S., where, under the name Muslims of America, its largely black membership lived on rural communes in nineteen states, where they were linked to a variety of activities, including—according to authorities—money-laundering, arson, murder, and the 1993 attack on the World Trade Center. Gilani—who was said to have had four wives, two of them African-American—was, for a time, himself based in the States, but now he was mostly to be found in a walled compound in Lahore, Pakistan, where a Pakistani official said that one of his visitors was Richard C. Reid.

The *Globe* quoted a Gilani "spokesman" and "friend" as denying any relationship between the sheikh and Reid, and warning that further such accusations were not advisable. "If you push him . . . he has no option but to declare jihad on America," said Khalid Khawaja. "It will blow like a volcano."

Danny had stayed in regular touch with friend Khawaja and, after seeing the *Globe* piece, asked if he could put him together with Gilani. Out of the question, Khawaja said: Gilani hadn't granted an interview in nearly a decade, and he certainly wasn't going to give one now to an American reporter. "Don't try," he warned. "You will not be able to do it."

Undeterred, Danny asked his "fixer," an Islamabad reporter named Asif Faruqi, for a way in.

Faruqi asked around, and a journalist friend told him about a man named "Arif," who knew another man named "Chaudry Bashir," who could lead them to Gilani. Turned out, Faruqi's friend was mistaken. Arif's real name was Hashim Qadeer, and he was a jihadi wanted by the police. As for Chaudry Bashir, his real name was Ahmed Omar Saeed Sheikh.

Like every reporter in Pakistan, I wanted to meet the fabled Sheikh, who'd been described as well educated, charming, arrogant, and a sociopath. But Sheikh wasn't granting interviews just then; he was in solitary confinement in the Karachi Central Jail, a colonial institution that would do well in a remake of *Midnight Express*. I had to settle for learning about Sheikh, and once I had, it was no mystery why Danny had trusted him. I would have in a heartbeat.

He was born on December 23, 1973, in Wanstead, an East London suburb. His parents had immigrated to the U.K. from a village outside Lahore five years before, and Sheikh was the eldest of their three children. His sister would study medicine at Oxford, his brother law at Cambridge. Sheikh's father, Saeed Ahmed Sheikh, was a successful businessman who generated enough income to send Sheikh to the $12,000-a-year Forest School, where one of his classmates was Nasser Hussain, currently captain of the British cricket team.

In 1987 Saeed Ahmed Sheikh moved the family to Pakistan, and Sheikh, then 13 and on his way to being a burly-chested six feet two inches, was enrolled in Aitchison College, the subcontinent's Eton.

He was a standout in his studies and popular with his classmates. The only problem was that once a month or so there'd be a scrap between an old boy and a new, with Sheikh in the middle, punching for the underdog.

Teachers admired his spunk and protected him from serious discipline. But one day late in his second year, the bully Sheikh took on happened to be the son of a most influential personage. Sheikh broke the boy's nose, then presented himself to the headmaster. "Sir," he said, "the chap was very disagreeable. I tried to control myself as much as possible and I have given him the thrashing of his life."

This time, there was no saving Sheikh from expulsion. "He was a wonderful soul," a teacher laments. "A gentleman of the highest order."

Shipped back to the Forest School, Sheikh passed his A levels in 1991 and was admitted to the London School of Economics. He read math and statistics; made $1,500 a day peddling securities to his father's customers; and, in 1992, the same year he received a certificate of commendation for leaping to the rescue of a woman who'd fallen onto the tracks of the Underground, was a member of the British arm-wrestling team that competed in the world championships in Geneva. "A nice bloke," his economics tutor, George Paynter, remembered him.

The first of several turning points came in November 1992, when, during the Islamic Society's Bosnia Week, Sheikh saw *Destruction of a Nation*, a graphic, 45-minute documentary on Serb atrocities committed against Muslims. "[It] shook my heart," he wrote.

During the next Easter holiday, Sheikh joined a "Caravan of Mercy," taking relief supplies to Bosnia. But in Split, Croatia, he became seriously ill from the cold and was forced to remain behind. While he recuperated, bodies were carted in, one of a 13-year-old Muslim girl who'd been raped and murdered by Serbs. Years later, Sheikh would tremble at the memory.

On his return to London, Sheikh immersed himself in military theory, dropped out of the London School of Economics, and went to Pakistan with an elaborate plan for guerrilla operations in Kashmir, including—novel twist—kidnappings. A four-star general who examined his scheme was not impressed, but the jihadis were. Spotted as a comer, he was dispatched for four months of advanced schooling in the arts of ambush, explosives, surveillance, and disguise.

Again his skills were noticed, and in June 1994 he was invited to join a kidnapping plot in India, where his role would be sweet-talking foreign tourists into captivity. The hostages would then be traded for Maulana Masood Azhar, a Harkut ul-Ansar leader, and others who had been taken prisoner in India.

There were miscues from the start. Sheikh didn't think much of his bosses, and they, in turn, didn't appreciate his kibitzing. They liked even less the six-foot-three-inch Israeli tourist Sheikh brought back to their hideout as a proposed first hostage. "You fool," one of them hissed. "You'll get us all killed. Take him back to his hotel at once and come back in the morning."

Posing as a Hindu named Rohit, Sheikh by and by rounded up three Britishers and an American, and dropped off a ransom note with a "rather nice" receptionist at the BBC. "Tonight she'll be telling the whole world that this big, monstrous, terrorist-looking chap came to her in person," he wrote in his diary. "Tomorrow, I'll ring her up and say, 'Actually, my dear, I'm not like that at all.'"

He seemed equally blithe about his captives, challenging them to games of chess (at which Sheikh was expert) and assuring that he would kidnap only people whom he considered intelligent and wanted to spend time with.

At other moments, Sheikh joked about their prospective behead-ings and rattled on about Jews running the British Cabinet and the truths to be had from reading *Mein Kampf*. He also rhapsodized about the pleasures of martyrdom, saying that holy warriors ejacu-lated at the moment of death, knowing that they had entered heaven.

The bizarre idyll climaxed in late October 1994, when Indian provincial police raided the kidnappers' hideouts. In the ensuing gun battles, two officers and one of the kidnappers were killed, and Sheikh shot in the shoulder.

The ISI paid for a lawyer, but it didn't do any good for Sheikh, who was held without trial for the next five years in a maximum security prison, where, he said, he had been beaten and urinated on. But it didn't prevent Sheikh from smuggling out a note to a favorite Aitchison teacher:

I hope this letter finds you soaring the heights of happiness.

Living in the cold, hard world of criminals and the brutal echelons of state power, a world of self-interest and devious cal-culations . . . I often wander down memory lane, seeing with more experienced (hopefully wiser) eyes all those people who gave me love—glowing, unselfish love. Yes, sir, you encouraged me so many times and you stood up for me when I was a hot-headed youngster. I feel indebted to you, and more than a little wistful.

Sir, if possible, please do jot a quick note telling me how you and your family have fared over the last few years. . . . My parents are in London, busy with the old garment business. Naturally, my case came as quite a shock to them, but Allah has given them the strength to cope. They understand that this is the path I've chosen. They have been tremendously supportive.

Sir, if you could put in the occasional prayer for me that would be wonderful. I'll sign off now. Who knows, perhaps I'll pop round to see you soon.

Yours with affectionate respect . . .

In a P.S., Sheikh added, "If there are some spare copies of the last few *Aitchisonians* [the school magazine], I'd be thrilled to have them."

It didn't look as if Sheikh was going to be "popping round" anywhere but his cell for the foreseeable future. But in late December 1999, Azhar's terrorist outfit—now renamed Harkat ul-Mujahadeen—seized an Indian airliner with 155 passengers and crew aboard; slit the throat of a honeymooning Indian businessman; and demanded the release of Azhar, Sheikh, and another jihadi. After the plane sat six days on the Kandahar tarmac under the watchful eyes of the Taliban, the Indians gave in.

Azhar went to Karachi and, before 10,000 howling supporters, called for the destruction of the U.S. and India. Then, after a few weeks touring under the protection of the ISI, he announced the formation of Jaish-e-Mohammed, the terrorist group Danny would find thriving in Bahawalpur.

Sheikh, for his part, stayed at a Kandahar guesthouse for several days, conferring with Taliban leader Mullah Muhammad Omar and—reports had it—Osama bin Laden, who was said to refer to him as "my special son." When he crossed the Pakistan frontier in early January 2000, an ISI colonel was waiting to conduct him to a safe house in Islamabad. From there he proceeded to London, where he reunited with family.

Relaxing with friends on his return to Lahore, Sheikh showed off his wound ("This is the benefit of speaking good English," he joked), talked about his forthcoming marriage ("My wife has an M.A.," he bragged about his bride-to-be), and confessed to pangs about killing. Poison was his instrument of choice (he demonstrated how he secreted it in his wallet), though, according to a U.S. official, he slit a throat once to make his jihadi bones. As for the moral qualms, Sheikh said he resolved those by recalling images of Kashmir and Bosnia.

He went next to Afghanistan, and reportedly helped devise a secure, encrypted Web-based communications system for Al Qaeda. His future in the network seemed limitless; there was even talk of one day succeeding bin Laden.

But Sheikh kept running afoul of superiors. Azhar was said to have sidelined him from Jaish after getting fed up with his bragging about Indian exploits. Following further spats with two other terrorist groups, Sheikh joined up with Aftab Ansari, an Indian-born gangster.

By August 2001, Sheikh's activities had come to the attention of British intelligence, who asked their Indian counterparts to help apprehend him.

Then came 9/11. Tracing the hijackers' funding, investigators discovered that in the weeks before the Trade Center attack someone using the alias Mustafa Muhammad Ahmad had wired more than $100,000 to hijacking ringleader Mohammed Atta. On October 6, CNN reported that the U.S. had decided that Mustafa Muhammad Ahmad and Sheikh were one and the same. Not much later the U.S. asked Pakistan to extradite him for the 1994 kidnapping.

With recruits picked up from other jihadi groups, Sheikh and Ansari, meanwhile, were mounting their first big operation, the October 1 suicide truck-bomb attack on the Kashmir assembly, which left 38 dead. On December 13 they struck again, with a shooting and grenade assault on the Parliament building in New Delhi. That incident—which India charged was staged at the direction of the ISI—claimed fourteen lives and prompted India to mass half a million troops on the Pakistan border. Sheikh was in the midst of planning yet another operation—a drive-by shoot-up of the American Center in Calcutta on January 22, in which five guards were killed—when Danny Pearl dropped into his lap.

"We had nothing personal against Daniel," Sheikh would later say. "Because of his hyperactivity, he caught our interest."

Danny had been here, there, and everywhere, an American Jewish reporter who lived in India, asking inconvenient questions. But his quest for a big score finally seemed within reach. Come to Room 411 of the Akbar International Hotel in Rawalpindi on January 11, he was told; "Bashir" would be waiting.

They talked for three hours. "It was a great meeting," said Sheikh, who shaved his beard and donned sunglasses for the occasion. "We ordered cold coffee and club sandwiches and had great chitchat."

But chitchat is all it was. Not wanting to seem too eager, Sheikh stressed that Gilani was a busy man; he'd have to weigh the question carefully. "I never asked Daniel to do anything," Sheikh later told his interrogators. "It was always him insisting." At the end of the meeting, Danny said he'd send along some examples of his work, and "Bashir" promised to keep him updated via e-mail.

Danny and Mariane then departed for Peshawar—Dodge City, except with Kalashnikovs instead of six-guns. But, according to Rahimullah Yusufzai, the local stringer for the BBC and *Time*, the only thing that bothered Danny was the difficulty in gathering information.

"He said he would be keen to meet anybody from Taliban or Al Qaeda," Yusufzai recalls. "I said, 'They may be here, but [it] is impossible for you to meet them or me to meet them. They are all wanted and they would like to stay quiet. Especially they won't be meeting an American journalist.'

"I told him, 'If you try too hard, it could be risky.' But he was very focused. He was so persistent in meeting everybody who could have helped him in the story. He was after something and he wanted it."

A *Journal* reporter's need for a replacement computer gave Danny more reason than ever to get it.

The reporter, Moscow correspondent Alan Cullison, had had his smashed in late November, when his car rolled over while crossing the Hindu Kush. On his arrival in Kabul, a shopkeeper offered to sell him a used IBM desktop and a Compaq laptop for $4,000. Too steep, New York said; bargain him down. Cullison did, and paid $1,100 for two machines that—in a billion-to-one shot—turned out to have been recovered from the bombed headquarters of Mohammed Atef, Osama bin Laden's abruptly deceased military strategist.

Cullison couldn't get past the Compaq's encryption scheme, but on the IBM's hard drive he found a treasure trove of Al Qaeda materials—at least 1,750 files, recording four years' worth of terrorist doings.

Fearing lives might be at stake, the *Journal* turned over the material to the Defense Department and the CIA for review. The spooks did their screening, and the first *Journal* report about the documents from the IBM machine appeared December 31. But the Compaq laptop was much harder to crack, and it wasn't until January 16 that the *Journal* was able to publish the results. For Danny, it was worth the wait. On the hard drive was the itinerary of a target-scouting expedition by a terrorist referred to as "brother Abdul Ra'uff." It matched to a T the pre-9/11 travels of Richard C. Reid.

There was more good news the same day, with the arrival of an e-mail from Bashir, using an address that showed Sheikh's sense of humor: Nobadmashi@yahoo.com—Urdu for "no rascality."

He reported that he'd forwarded Danny's articles to Gilani and apologized for not having contacted him sooner. "I was preoccupied with looking after my wife who has been ill," Sheikh said. "[She] is back from the hospital and the whole experience was a real eye-opener. Poor people who fall ill here and have to go to hospital have a really miserable and harassing time. Please pray for her health."

Having tugged at Danny's heartstrings with a phony story about his wife, Sheikh set the hook deeper three days later with an e-mail saying that Gilani was looking forward to a get-together. However, he was currently in Karachi and wouldn't be returning for "a number of days." Bashir gave Danny a choice: Wait for Gilani's return, or send e-mail questions, which he'd relay to Gilani's secretary. "If Karachi is your program," Sheikh said, "you are welcome to meet him there."

Danny chose the Karachi meeting, as Sheikh—who understood reporters—must have known he would. Before catching the Pakistan International Airlines flight south, Danny e-mailed him his plans, along with something that Sheikh didn't know: On January 24, he and Mariane would be leaving Dubai and from there transiting to Bombay.

Friends had been urging Danny to take a break, and though another tour of Pakistan was planned, it wouldn't be for an indefinite while. If Danny was going to get Gilani, he had to get him now.

There was another story he wanted to try to cram in: a piece on Karachi underworld boss Dawood Ibrahim, an Indian-born Muslim terrorist who enjoyed the patronage and protection of the ISI. In mid-January, while waiting for Bashir's next missive, Danny called Ikram Sehgal for leads.

"I hadn't heard from him in weeks," Sehgal recalls, sipping tea in his cluttered office. "I think Danny got more and more confident. This was the biggest thing that hit him. He was suddenly having access and chasing down an area where he had no expertise." He stirs the heat from his cup. "I mean, Danny just didn't have it.

"He asked if I had any contacts with the local Mafia. I said, 'Danny, the Mafia head here doesn't function the way you think Mafias do. This is not something out of *The Godfather*. I know the direction you're going in. Don't do this! Forget it! If you want to know something, come over and we'll talk, not on the telephone.'"

Sehgal's phone rings, as it has constantly since March 17, when militants attacked a church in Islamabad, killing U.S. embassy employee Barbara Green and her 17-year-old daughter, Kristen Wormsley. Sehgal is now providing protection for every Christian church in the country gratis.

"I found him a little naive," Sehgal goes on. "I would tell him, 'Danny, stick by the rules. Anybody you want to meet, meet him in a public place. Don't get into cars. Anyone could pick you up.' He would always say, 'Yes, you're right, Ikram, I ought to do that.' But you always had the feeling that what he was saying was perfunctory."

Bashir checked in again on Sunday, January 20, saying that Gilani would be available that coming Tuesday or Wednesday. Sheikh said he'd forward the phone number of a Gilani *mureed* (follower), who would escort him to the meeting.

"It is sad that you are leaving Pakistan so soon," Sheikh wrote. "I hope you have enjoyed your stay."

The next day, Danny and Mariane learned that their baby would be a boy. They decided to call him Adam, a name that resonates with both Muslim and Jew.

Wednesday, January 23, was going to be busy for Danny. Asra was hosting a farewell dinner party for him that night; he wanted to check out a cyber café to see if it was where a message was sent to Richard Reid instructing him to board the next Paris–Miami flight; he had an appointment to see Randall Bennett, the U.S. consulate's regional security officer, at 2:30, and another to see Jamil Yusuf, head of Karachi's Citizens Police Liaison Committee, at 5:45. And then there was Gilani. Bashir by now had told him that Imtiaz Siddiqi was the *mureed* who'd lead him to Gilani. But Danny had yet to hear from him. Nor did he know that Siddiqi's real name was Mansur Hasnain and that he'd been one of the Indian Airlines hijackers who'd freed Sheikh in 1999.

Danny phoned his fixer in Islamabad.

"Give me a quick reply," he said. "Is it safe to see Gilani?"

Asif assured him it was; Gilani was a public figure.

Danny set off on his rounds. Mariane, who was to have come along, wasn't feeling well and stayed at Asra's.

He had a good session with Bennett at the consulate, but the cyber café was a bust; it didn't have the technology to trace who'd sent the e-mail to Reid. On the way to Yusuf's office, Danny called the Dow Jones bureau to ask the resident correspondent, Saaed Azhari, to set up a final appointment for him the next morning. Azhari, who couldn't fathom why Danny chanced taking cabs everywhere, rather than using a hired car and regular driver, like other correspondents, said there was something Danny ought to know: Ghulam Hasnain, the Karachi *Time* stringer, had gone missing the day before. Guessing was, the ISI had picked him up because of an exposé he had written on Dawood Ibrahim for a Pakistani monthly.

Danny seemed unworried, and a few minutes later he was at the Citizens Police Liaison Committee building, talking to Yusuf, a former businessman who'd become a renowned crime-fighter.

On the afternoon I catch up to him, Yusuf—who played a key role in catching Danny's killers—is bemoaning his trouble in getting warrants for cyber searches. "Judges do not understand Yahoo is not a human being," he says, shaking his head. He then describes his last meeting with a reporter of whom he was very fond.

"He asked me about Gilani, and I said, 'I never heard of him. I don't think a lot of people have heard of him in this country.' Then he told me about this Richard Reid thing. I joked with him: I said, 'Danny, do something else. The guy is caught. He is with the FBI. Why waste time?'

"[When] he was sitting here, he got two phone calls. He said, Yes, he was coming there at seven o'clock, somewhere close by. I did not know what was happening. He did not tell me who he was going to meet. . . .

"I advised him, 'You cannot go and meet strangers.' It's just like me going into New York and trying to meet the Mafia, then complaining to the world I got abducted. You don't do those things.

"He was a very docile person, quiet, humble. Not a person who would go out and take risks in reporting. That is what surprised me. . . . [How] he came and sat here for an hour and then went to that stupid appointment of his without telling us."

Yusuf looks out the window down to where the security car he has had to hire to trail him is waiting.

"Kidnapping a journalist is the easiest thing you can do," he says. "They are hungry for information. . . . Anybody could do it."

Danny's caller was the *mureed* he knew as Siddiqi, saying to meet him at the Village Garden Restaurant, next to the Metropole Hotel, a mile or so away. In the cab on the way over, Danny phoned Mariane, telling her where he was going and to start the party without him. He'd be back around eight.

The hour came and went without any sign of Danny, but initially his absence wasn't cause for concern. Pakistanis are famously sociable—Gilani may have insisted on serving dinner, and the talk may have run on, as interviews with Muslim militants tended to. But midnight passed with no word from Danny, who also wasn't answering his cell phone.

Now truly worried, Asra phoned Danny's boss, foreign editor John Bussey, at the *Journal*'s headquarters in South Brunswick, New Jersey, where it was late afternoon. Bussey told her that he'd alert the State Department.

Asra phoned Khawaja, thinking he would know whether Danny actually had a meeting. But Khawaja said he'd never heard of any meeting with Gilani.

The police arrived shortly thereafter, and Asra phoned Khawaja again, this time with an officer on the line. He asked that Khawaja put them in touch with Gilani as soon as possible. Then Asra read off Bashir and Siddiqi's cell phone numbers. Khawaja didn't recognize either of them.

By the time the flight to Dubai left the next afternoon, the story of Danny Pearl's disappearance was moving over the wires. No one was using the word "kidnapping" yet, but that was the suspicion. It was confirmed early Sunday morning, local time, by e-mails to *The New York Times*, *The Washington Post*, the *Los Angeles Times*, and two Pakistani news organizations. Attached were four photographs of Danny in captivity, one showing a 9-millimeter pistol pointed at his head and a message in English and Urdu announcing the capture of "CIA officer Daniel Pearl who was posing as a journalist for *The Wall Street Journal*."

The note demanded that the U.S. hand over F-16 aircraft, whose delivery to Pakistan had been frozen by 1990 nuclear sanctions; that Pakistanis detained for questioning by the FBI over the 9/11 attacks be given access to lawyers and allowed to see their families; that Pakistani nationals held at Guantánamo Bay, Cuba, be returned to their homeland to stand trial; and that the Taliban's ambassador to Pakistan, now held in Afghanistan, be returned to Pakistan.

Of Danny, the note said, "Unfortunately, he is at present being kept in very inhuman circumstances quite similar in fact to the way that Pakistanis and nationals of other sovereign countries are being kept in Cuba by the American Army. If the Americans keep our countrymen in better conditions we will better the conditions of Mr. Pearl and the other Americans that we capture."

Sent on the account of kidnapperguy@hotmail.com, the message was signed, "The National Movement for the Restoration of Pakistani Sovereignty."

Police had never heard of the group, but the name sounded a gong at the Islamabad bureau of the BBC, which in late October had received a package from the National Youth Movement for the Sovereignty of Pakistan. Inside were an unplayable videocassette and a computer printout announcing the capture of an alleged CIA operative, "one Joshua Weinstein, alias Martin Johnson, an American national and a resident of California." Also enclosed was a photograph of a male Caucasian in his thirties. Flanked by two robed and hooded men aiming AK-47s at his head, he was holding up a Pakistani newspaper showing the date of his abduction—just as Danny would months later.

U.S. embassy officials said at the time that no one named Joshua

Weinstein or Martin Johnson had either come to Pakistan or been reported missing, and that the letter was a hoax. When local police agencies and other Western embassies said the same, the BBC let it drop. But the release of the virtually identical Pearl materials got the BBC checking again with American diplomats. Was the first "kidnapping" truly a hoax? Why so many similarities between the October episode and Pearl's abduction? The response was a studied silence.

Police, meanwhile, were focusing their suspicions on Harkat ul-Mujahedeen, the terrorist group that had hijacked the airliner to free Sheikh and Azhar. With a number of its members killed by U.S. air strikes, Harkat ul-Mujahedeen had the motive, as well as the MO, its predecessor group, Harkat ul-Ansar, being thought responsible for the kidnapping and presumed murder of a group of backpackers in India in 1995.

Trouble was, this didn't have the feel of a jihadi operation. Where were the *allahu ahkbars* in the note? The riffs about Palestine and infidels and Western demons? There wasn't even a mention of "Zionist conspiracy." Instead, the demands read like an ACLU press release. The English was too good, too. Usage, spelling, and grammar were virtually perfect, and the few errors seemed deliberate, as if the writer was trying to hide his education. Jihadis didn't have to feign lack of schooling; most were illiterate.

One investigator, inspired, typed "foreign," "kidnapper," and "suspect" onto Google.com and clicked search. The first listing that popped up was "Omar Saeed Sheikh." No one believed it; couldn't be that easy.

Within days, the elite Criminal Investigation Division determined the true identity of Arif and raided his house—where they found relatives in the midst of a Muslim prayer service for the dead. Arif had been killed fighting the Americans in Afghanistan, they claimed. No one believed that either, and a nationwide manhunt got under way.

The *Journal*, meanwhile, was moving on several fronts. Managing editor Paul Steiger issued a statement that Danny was not now nor ever had been an employee of any agency of the U.S. government, and the CIA broke long-standing policy to say the same. Foreign editor Bussey and correspondent Steve LeVine flew in to shepherd Mariane, whose Buddhist group was chanting a mantra for Danny. A media strategy was devised. Mariane made herself available for interviews, but only to outlets that had Pakistan reach, such as CNN and the BBC. Questions about what story Danny was working on were deflected, lest the truth cause him harm. Finally, a confidential appeal was made to major U.S. media organizations to not disclose that Danny's parents were Israeli. All agreed.

But on January 30, Danny's Jewishness leaked. In a story in *The News*, Kamran Khan, the paper's chief investigative reporter, wrote that "some Pakistani security officials—not familiar with the worth of solid investigative reporting in the international media—are privately searching for answers as to why a Jewish American reporter was exceeding 'his limits' to investigate [a] Pakistani religious group."

"An India-based Jewish reporter serving a largely Jewish media organization should have known the hazards of exposing himself to radical Islamic groups, particularly those who recently got crushed under American military might," Khan quoted "a senior Pakistani official" as saying.

Having let the religious cat out of the bag, Khan—who doubles as a special correspondent for *The Washington Post*—revealed Danny's relationship with Asra Nomani, whom he claimed—falsely—Danny had imported from India to be "his full-time assistant."

"Officials are also guessing, rather loudly, as to why Pearl decided to bring in an Indian journalist," Khan wrote. "They [are] also intrigued as to why an American newspaper reporter based in

[Bombay] would also establish a full-time residence in Karachi by renting a residence."

Khan's revelations stunned colleagues. But there was no wondering about the source of his information: He was well-known for his contacts at the highest levels of the ISI.

The same morning Khan's story appeared, the kidnappers released a second note, changing Danny's supposed spying affiliation from the CIA to the Mossad, the Israeli intelligence service.

The language that followed differed radically from the first note:

U cannot fool us and find us. We are inside seas, oceans, hills, grave yards, every where.

We give u 1 more day if America will not meet our demands we will kill Daniel. Then this cycle will continue and no American journalist could enter Pakistan.

Allah is with us and will protect us.

We had given our demands and if u will not then "we" will act and the Amrikans will get teir part what they deserve. Don't think this will be the end, it is the beginning and it is a real war on Amrikans. Amrikans will get the taste of death and destructions what we had got in Afg and Pak.Inshallah

This did not sound like Sheikh—and it wasn't. A note later found on his computer read, "We have investigated and found that Daniel Pearl does not work for the CIA. Therefore, we are releasing him unconditionally."

Having lured Danny, Sheikh had ceased calling the shots; Danny's fate was now in the hands of more murderous others.

Investigators, however, were still concentrating on Gilani, who turned himself in on January 30, protesting his innocence and tick-ing off the names of more than a dozen senior and retired officials who would vouch for his services to state security.

After interrogating Khawaja—who backed Gilani's story—police began having second thoughts. Ul-Fuqra had never been involved with violence in Pakistan and indeed had become so inactive of late the State Department had dropped it from the terrorist list. Someone had set Gilani up. But who?

In Karachi, a newly arrived contingent of FBI men were tracing the source of the kidnappers' e-mails, while Yusuf's Citizens Police Liaison Committee was manually sorting the connections among 23,500 telephone calls. The effort paid off, with the identification of Fahad Naseem, an employee of a cyber café, as the sender of the e-mails and the linking of his phone calls to two other conspirators.

The police moved just after dark, heading off in unmarked vans to grab Fahad. If Pakistani interrogation methods had their usual brutal efficacy, Fahad would quickly lead them to the second kidnapper, who—likewise persuaded—would lead them to the third, who would rapidly decide that giving up the boss was in his best interest. When they got him, they'd have Danny. It all had to be pulled off by morning prayers at the mosque. After that, everyone in town would know.

Stops one, two, and three yielded the desired results. But they were stymied at four. They had the ringleader's name, his phone number, his uncle's Karachi address—before sunup, they even had his uncle, cousin, and aunt in custody. The aunt placed a call to his cell phone, begging him to surrender. Then the lead officer came on the line. "The game's up, Sheikh," he said. The answer was a click.

For days, nothing more happened. Sheikh appeared to have vanished, and there were no further messages from the kidnappers. Fake messages, though, were cascading in, including one which said that Danny's body could be found in a Karachi cemetery. Three-hundred-plus cemeteries were scoured; no body. But a fresh corpse was found in a vacant lot near the airport. Though the face had been rendered unrecognizable by a bullet, to Randall Bennett, who'd been summoned to the morgue, the victim seemed the right age, skin color, and body type. But something was odd about the mouth; ever so slightly, it seemed puffy.

"Roll back his lips," Bennett asked. He let out a breath at the sight of metal. Danny had smiled often during their meeting; Bennett knew he didn't wear braces.

On his way to visit George W. Bush, General Musharraf—who was now blaming India for the abduction—assured the world that all would be well. The case had been cracked; Danny's release was expected any minute.

February 14, Sheikh made a liar out of him.

According to the police, he'd been captured in a daring raid in Lahore two days before. The truth was that he'd been turned over by Brigadier Ejaz Shah, home secretary of Punjab and formerly a hard-line officer of the ISI. Sheikh had turned himself over to Shah February 5, and for a week it had been hidden from the police. "Whatever I have done, right or wrong, I have my reasons, and I confess," Sheikh said when he was brought before a magistrate. "As far as I understand, Daniel Pearl is dead."

Police interrogated him for a week, a silent ISI man always present, but got little else. "You are my Pakistani and Muslim brothers," he said. "You can't be as cruel as Hindu policemen were with me in India."

Then, one day, the lead investigator—the officer who'd said, "The game's up, Sheikh"—visited his cell. They discussed the Koran, and the investigator said, "Show me in the Koran where it says you can lie."

"Give me half an hour," said Sheikh. He said his prayers and made his ablutions, and then he told them nearly everything.

He'd learned that Danny had been killed, he said, when he called Siddiqi from Lahore, February 5, and ordered, "Shift the patient to the doctor"—a prearranged code for Danny to be released. Siddiqi replied, "Dad has expired. We have done the scan and completed the X rays and postmortem"—meaning that Danny had been videotaped and buried. As he understood it, Sheikh said, Danny had been shot while trying to escape. Where the videotape was or what was on it, he said he didn't know.

The sole subject he refused to discuss was the week he had spent with his ISI handlers.

"I know people in the government and they know me and my work" was all he'd say.

A week later the videotape was recovered in a classic sting. A man (authorities won't reveal his identity) called a Karachi journalist (nor his) and said he had a tape of what had happened to Danny Pearl, and would sell it to the movies for $100,000. The journalist told the U.S. consulate, which instructed him to tell the man to bring it to the lobby of the Karachi Sheraton at four o'clock, where a movie producer would meet him. An FBI agent played the role to perfection.

They watched the tape on Bennett's living room VCR—over and over, to make sure of its authenticity. But that was Danny, all right, shirt off, unconscious, on his back. A three-inch wound could be seen in his left side. A hand and part of a forearm came into the frame, holding a large butcher knife. The person wielding it seemed expert.

The rest you probably know by now. Mariane appeared on *Larry King* and signed a book deal and had her baby. People wept at memorial services for Danny in New York, Washington, Los Angeles, London, and Jerusalem. As of this writing, Sheikh and three codefendants were still on trial. Everyone in Pakistan expects all of them to be convicted and sentenced to die by hanging.

You no doubt are aware, too, that Danny's dismembered body was found in a shallow grave in the garden of a nursery outside Karachi in mid-May. The terrorists who led police to it said that Danny was picked up by a taxi outside the Village Garden, taken to a nearby location, put into a van there, and driven around Karachi for hours. He was very calm, they said, and did not resist. When at last they came to their final destination, he asked, "Where is the man I wanted to meet?"

His killing moved people who are normally very tough about such things. The lead investigator wept when he told Mariane Danny was dead, and for the first time in years working hazard posts, Randy Bennett let the grotesque get to him. He was coming back to the consulate after endlessly watching the videotape, and a Pakistani was standing in the street covered in the blood of a goat whose throat he'd just slit. Bennett saw a large butcher knife in his hand, then the man shot him an "I hate Americans" look. He slammed on the brakes, got out, and went up to him jaw to jaw. "You got a problem with me?" he said.

I never did answer the why of everything. Sheikh said that the reason was to strike a blow at Musharraf, while Musharraf himself said it was because Danny was "overly inquisitive." And more than a few knowledgeable Pakistanis think the ISI was involved. When asked by *Vanity Fair* whether it shares that view, *The Wall Street Journal* issued a two-word written answer: "No comment."

One why I was able to answer: Why did Danny risk everything for a story?

I didn't need to go to Karachi to find out; I could remember.

———

There have been a number of developments in the Pearl case since a Pakistani court sentenced Omar Saeed Sheikh to death last July, and handed down 25-year prison terms to three codefendants. (Sheikh and his confederates will be presenting their appeals sometime in 2003.)

Four other men—all of whom were charged as participants in the plot and were said to have guarded Danny during captivity—were arrested shortly after the discovery of Danny's body last spring and currently are awaiting trial.

Meanwhile, police continue to investigate five Yemeni Al Qaeda operatives who were arrested in a raid in Karachi this past September as being involved in Danny's murder. Among them is Ramzi Binalshibh, who is suspected by the United States of being a coordinator of the 9/11 terrorist attacks; and Umar al-Gharib, a brother of the suspected mastermind of the 2000 bombing of the USS Cole in Yemen.

The most recent and by far biggest break in the case was the capture in early March of Khalid Sheikh Mohammed, the Al Qaeda operations chief who planned the attack on the World Trade Center. Mohammed is suspected of being present when Danny's throat was cut, and may even have wielded the murder weapon.

THE TERRIBLE BOY
TOM JUNOD

There is nothing on this earth so terrible as a terrible boy. A terrible boy has learned the specifics of cruelty without learning the generality of mercy. A terrible boy worships what is worst in himself and despises what is best. A terrible boy is alienated by his own sense of enmity and seeks connection through the certainties of slaughter. A terrible boy makes even ants his enemies, for he wishes above all to make his enemies ants—and to entertain himself by squashing them both. When a terrible boy closes his hand, he finds a fist; when he opens it, he finds a rock. So terrible are terrible boys that armies the world over have discovered the utility of using them to do their bidding. So terrible are terrible boys that aboriginal tribes used to dispatch them on impossible and solitary missions, hoping they would come back tempered by quest and grown into men. We, who demand something softer from our civilization, have no such uses for terrible boys and no such rituals. Instead, we call them bullies and by new and coming consensus seek to outlaw them.

Was Jonathan Miller a terrible boy? Was he mean enough, hard enough, heartless enough? Did he *hate* enough? Maybe not. Probably not. Unlike many a terrible boy, he had his sympathies. He loved animals. He loved his family and his friends. He loved the downtrodden and was known to stand up for them when the terrible boys came calling. He was a Boy Scout, for God's sake. He just didn't want to go to school, and, more particularly, he didn't want to go to school in Cherokee County, Georgia. He was from New York, you see. He'd lived happily near Kingston, just upstate from New York City, where he was born. When his father, who worked for a large computer company, transferred to Woodstock, on what used to be the outer edge of Atlanta, he asked to stay in New York with his grandparents. When his parents refused his request, he took on the trappings of the terrible, hoping somehow to achieve by negative means what he couldn't by positive—hoping to force his parents' hand by getting kicked out of the seventh grade.

What did he do? Oh, the usual, his parents say—kid stuff. He shot spitballs. He mouthed off to teachers, often profanely. He farted in a kid's face when he was at the blackboard. He flicked at a kid's ears with a sharp snap of his fingers. He slapped a gym ball out of a girl's grasp. He took up residence in the principal's office, then sampled both forms of suspension, "in school" and "at home." Thirty-odd times, Robin and Alan Miller were called with regard to their son's behavior, but never did they concede that he was a terrible boy, and though he came damn close to getting kicked out of E. T. Booth Middle School, Jonathan seemed to calm down when he moved on to Etowah High, except on the school bus. He didn't like riding the bus, for his brother had a car, and so he adopted the same strategy with regard to the bus that he had once employed with regard to middle school: He pursued the possibility of forced exile. He sat in the back and raised hell, causing the rest of the riders—who were generally students at E. T. Booth rather than Etowah and a year or so younger than Jonathan—to cringe when he got on. Indeed, for the purposes of achieving a triumphant suspension, he carried in his pockets mustard and ketchup packets he obtained from the school cafeteria, and on November 2, 1998, he may—or may not—have thrown one at the head of a boy sitting a few rows in front of him, an eighth grader named Joshua Belluardo.

It was not, in and of itself, the offense—even in light of what was to happen—of a terrible boy. First of all, the boy who was sitting next to Jonathan swears to this day that whatever was thrown at Josh was thrown by someone else. Second, Josh didn't like Jonathan any more than Jonathan liked Josh. They lived one house away from each other on a cul-de-sac called Shallow Cove, and though they were friendly enough when Jonathan first moved in—Josh Belluardo being in Jonathan's recollection the first boy he met when he moved to Georgia—they quickly accepted the terms of mutual estrangement. They were just very different, and out of difference grew dislike. Josh was established in the neighborhood; Jon was new. Josh was quiet, while Jonathan had, in the words of his mother, "a mouth on him." Josh was athletic; Jon preferred those activities in which he could keep to himself—camping, swimming. For reasons only they could know, they had been edging toward a fight for years, and on this day, when Josh accused Jonathan of throwing the mustard packet, Jonathan challenged him to fight, and Josh answered by inviting him to fight in his yard. When the bus stopped at the corner of Shallow Cove and Driftwood Drive, Josh got off first and cut across a neighbor's lawn on the way to his house. Jonathan, following behind him, closed his right hand and found a fist. He took five or six accelerating steps to close the gap between them. Then, with gathered momentum—and without a word of warning—he smote Josh Belluardo in the back of his head and became in that one terrible instant a terrible boy. No, he became more than that: For the purposes of the school, for the purposes of the state, and for the purposes of the media he became a bully, and as a bully, he became, barely one month past his fifteenth birthday, a man who committed murder.

This is a story about cruelty and mercy. It is a story about the mercy *available* to the cruel, and how it—or its absence—shapes not only the lives of American boys, terrible and otherwise, but American boyhood itself. We in America today are deciding not to extend mercy to boys in their common cruelty, and as a result, a boy perceived as cruel—Jonathan Miller—is, in the eyes of the law, no longer a boy at all. When I was a boy, we were at the mercy of the cruel, for the cruel were only at the mercy of, well, themselves. There was no stopping them if they didn't want to be stopped. Our freedoms were genuine, but they were achieved at terrible cost: the cost of terrible boys. This is a story, then, about what we disallow when we try to disallow terrible boys. It is a story not just of one terrible boy but of two, and of the mercies lost when we assume that terrible boys must be terrible forever.

Jonathan Miller is one of this story's terrible boys. I am the other. For a brief time, I was a terrible boy. I was a terrible boy to a boy named, for the purposes of this story, Timmy Titimski. I wasn't terrible to anyone else; I wasn't big enough or strong enough or powerful enough or scary enough. I didn't even know that I was a terrible boy until Timmy Titimski sat in front of me in the fifth grade. I was smart, I was studious, I was *obedient* in a particularly Catholic way. When Timmy Titimski sat in front of me, though, I was transformed. It wasn't simply that he was smaller than I was, or that I was bigger, stronger, more powerful—scarier—than he was. It was that he made me *feel* bigger, stronger, more powerful—scarier. He was new, if I remember correctly. He was scant on friends, so I had him all to myself. He asked me one day what my favorite song was. He volunteered that his own favorite was "Snoopy vs. the Red Baron," and I remember still the distaste he aroused. Timmy Titimski? Timmy Titimski was just a *baby*, and from that observation— that information—I deduced what it was that Timmy Titimski did . . . what it was I could make him do. Timmy Titimski was a baby, and so I could make him do what babies do. I could make him cry.

It took me a while to test my thesis. For most of the year, I kept it to myself, as my own little secret, until one day a spitball fight broke out in my class. We had a lot of spitball fights in the fifth grade. Our teacher had died of a heart attack before Christmas, and so we were often stewarded by substitutes. Fifth grade was one frenzied cross

fire, but on this day, when I saw Timmy Titimski standing against
the blackboard, the chaos dimmed and clarity took over. The
crowded classroom consisted suddenly of me and him, and so what
I did was stand in front of him and methodically paint his face with
spitballs. He didn't fight back or raise a straw of his own. He just
stood there, as if counting on the extent of my mercy, and what he
faced instead was the compass of my cruelty. He did nothing to stop
me, and for some reason his lack of resistance stoked not pity in me
but rage. I just kept going, framing the blackboard behind his head
with threads of spit—my spit—that in time ran like black tears. He
didn't cry, though, not at first. A teacher was returning to our class
after lunch, and to protect me—yes, me—and my terrible endeavor,
a group of boys closed around me—us—in a semicircle. Thus insulated, I was emboldened and inspired, and when I found a wad of
tinfoil, I twisted a piece between my fingers and with a mighty puff
of breath shot the silver spur at an imagined bull's-eye at the center
of Timmy Titimski's forehead. The shot hit its target, and the tinfoil
bounced off the little red mark it had imprinted in Timmy Titimski's skin. It must have hurt a little; he must have felt something of a
nip, but that didn't explain what happened next. No, as I think of it
now, he was not so much a baby as he was an innocent, with as little
resistance to true cruelty as an American Indian had to smallpox.
He simply had no immunity to what I was all about, and when he
saw what I was all about—when he saw the face of the terrible boy
before him—well, he didn't merely cry, and I didn't merely make
him cry. I hit a gusher.

What began that day lasted at least a year, or maybe as long as a
year and a half—well into sixth grade. I had never known that I was
a predator, but now I had found my prey. I was a bully in the truest
sense of the word, which is to say the modern sense of the word,
which is to say the sense of the word as now defined by activists and
experts whose studies have helped frame the debate about the justice deserved by Jonathan Miller. I selected a victim based on what

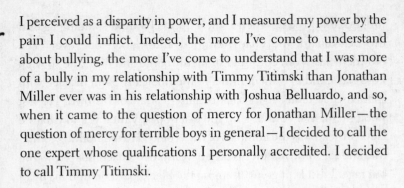

I perceived as a disparity in power, and I measured my power by the pain I could inflict. Indeed, the more I've come to understand about bullying, the more I've come to understand that I was more of a bully in my relationship with Timmy Titimski than Jonathan Miller ever was in his relationship with Joshua Belluardo, and so, when it came to the question of mercy for Jonathan Miller—the question of mercy for terrible boys in general—I decided to call the one expert whose qualifications I personally accredited. I decided to call Timmy Titimski.

You remember them, of course. You remember the bullies; you remember the terrible boys. If you were unlucky, you remember your own personal terrible boy, the one designed for you like a bullet with your name on it. How could you forget him? He *made* you. He helped form you, and for all his cruelties, he helped you grow up by standing like a sentry on the road to adulthood. Once you made it past him, you were home free.

What you don't remember is a school like Etowah High, in the town of Woodstock, in the county of Cherokee, in the state of Georgia. Etowah is where Jonathan Miller went to school. It is where Josh Belluardo—as a student at E. T. Booth Middle School—*would* have gone to school if Jonathan's punch hadn't killed him. Etowah is a large school in what used to be a rural community, turned now, like the rest of America, into a shopping opportunity. Occupying the center of what might be termed a sprawling educational complex, it is flanked by, and shares school buses with, both E. T. Booth Middle School and Chapman Intermediate School. Because it is riven with some of America's trembly little fault lines—between the people who have lived there for a long time, the people who have recently moved there, and the people just passing through— Etowah is institutional in feel and corporate in intent. It is a school that prides itself on giving its students choices, and so it is a school where many students choose to remain insulated by nothing but their own anonymity. It is, in other words, absolutely average, a school not unlike, say, Columbine, outside of Denver. Its homogeneity accentuates disparity, and disparity presents the terrible boys their opportunities to be terrible. It is at schools like Etowah — not to mention Columbine—where bullying mutated from individual incidents to a social and political issue, because it is at schools like Etowah where the nature of bullying is said by activists and legislators to have changed. It is at schools like Etowah where bullies went from being objects of dread and nostalgia to objects of necessary quarantine, because it is at Etowah High School where bullying, in fact, turned into a fatal exercise, not just in the case of Jonathan Miller, but before him, in the case of Brian Head.

You remember Brian Head, and if you don't, you remember someone just like him. If the bully was eternal, so was he; he was the kid the bullies picked on. At E. T. Booth and then at Etowah, he was not only a victim, his victimization was accepted as part of the natural order. He was overweight, and he wore thick glasses. He was quiet, clumsy, and kindhearted. He attended special-education classes and hurried home. His father, Bill Head, thought that Brian loved being home simply because he loved his family, loved the outdoors, and loved his life. He did not suspect what he would find out later—that "Brian loved being home because school was such a nightmare." In the fall of 1993, when Brian came home from school bloodied, his father accepted a teacher's explanation—that Brian was a boy, and boys got into fights—and did not suspect that Brian had gotten bloodied because Brian was considered prey at Etowah. And of course Bill did not suspect that one morning Brian would secret his father's gun in his book bag and take it to economics class. How could he suspect something like that? Brian was not a terrible boy; he was intent on taking a stand *against* the terrible boys. He was in class when one of the terrible boys—a "well-known bully," in Bill Head's words—slapped a kid in the face. Brian came to the kid's defense, as perhaps he had hoped someone would come one day to his. "Hey, pick on someone your own size," is what Bill Head says his son said to the terrible boy. The terrible boy complied and slapped Brian. Brian responded by taking the gun out of his book bag. As his classmates scattered and fled, Brian pointed the gun at the terrible boy and pulled the trigger. The gun did not go off, no bullet was chambered. Brian pointed the gun at his head. "I'm sick of it," he said and once again pulled the trigger. This time, a bullet was chambered. This time, the gun went off, and Brian Head, 15 years old, fell to the floor, dying.

He was the first at Etowah—first at a school where there would be a second—and he was also the first nationally. After Brian came the deluge. After Brian Head brought his gun to school at Etowah, boys brought their guns to school in Paducah, Kentucky; in Jonesboro, Arkansas; in Springfield, Oregon; in Pearl, Mississippi; in Littleton, Colorado; and in Conyers, Georgia. They all succeeded where Brian failed—their guns all had chambered rounds—and they are all remembered as the very essence of terrible boys. What Bill Head discerned in what most citizens saw as random slaughter, however, was a pattern that started with a constant. "There is no doubt in my mind that bullying and peer abuse are at the heart of most schoolyard tragedies," he says. "Schools have failed to protect the children in their care. A kid comes home bloodied, they say he got into a fight. It doesn't matter if he started it or not. It doesn't matter if he was getting picked on. The victim is just as guilty as the perpetrator. No wonder kids take guns to school."

After Brian's death, Bill started a foundation called Kids Hope and poured his savings into a video aimed, essentially, at teaching schoolchildren the mechanics of mercy. He also urged schools to begin making sure "seven-year-olds receive the same basic protections as seventy-year-olds," and to winnow the merciful from the cruel by treating "fights" as instances of *battery*, as instances of *assault* . . . as outright attacks. Although he would never have as much effect as Brian himself—for it was Brian who spoke most eloquently and whose effect was indelible—he was, like Brian, at the head of what would become a groundswell, of what would become, indeed, a movement. As schoolyards became venues of slaughter, the role of the bully became the one issue that generated anything approaching consensus. The issues of handgun availability and the influence of violence on television and in the movies polarized liberals and conservatives along predictable lines. Bullies, though— well, bullies were bad. An antibullying movement flourished because there could be no probullying movement, and by its terms, we can no longer afford to consider bullying an inevitable if unfortunate fact of childhood. What do bullies do? They hurt children. They cause lasting and in some cases fatal damage. They must be stopped, and it is quite simply our moral obligation to stop them, even though they are of course children themselves.

"I used to be able to light up a cigarette in a department store or at the end of a dinner party," says Cindi Seddon of Bully B'ware, an organization at the forefront of antibullying education. "Now the first is against the law, and the second is stigmatized. That's what I would like to see happen with bullying." Based outside Vancouver, Canada, and started by Seddon and her partners in response to the spate of schoolyard shootings and suicides, Bully B'ware has distributed its videotapes and teaching tools to schools across North America and has helped implement antibullying programs. Central to the Bully B'ware mission are two observations that Bully B'ware has itself helped turn into gospel: one, that the bullies who roam the halls of schools like Etowah and Columbine are not the same as the bullies you remember—that the bullies who used to stop at intimidation now don't stop at all; and, two, that bullying is linked to criminality, as both a precursor and an actual manifestation. The Bully B'ware website cites a statistic holding that by age 24, "60 percent of all people identified as childhood bullies have at least one criminal conviction," and in conversation Cindi Seddon notes that jails are filled with criminals who got started as bullies.

Are such statistics reliable? Well, Jonathan Miller was identified as a childhood bully and at age 18 does, in fact, have at least one criminal conviction. The question, though, is whether he was convicted as a murderer because he was identified as a childhood bully. The question is whether he was convicted as an adult because he went to Etowah High School, which was haunted by the death of Brian Head. The question is whether he was convicted as a criminal because the death of Brian Head—along with the deaths of far too many others—had forced our culture to change its mind about bullying and to view it as an act that was in and of itself criminal. The question is whether he was sentenced to life in prison because he stood as indisputable proof of the newly advanced thesis that bullying kills.

It is March 29, 2002, when Bill Head tells me, in a restaurant in Cherokee County, Georgia, not so far from where his son, Brian, and then Josh Belluardo fell dead, what he thinks he knows about Jonathan Miller. "The boy was already a career criminal by the time he murdered Josh," he says. "It was no accidental thing. He used to take an extra lap in the school bus just so he could terrorize kids." He is a big man, thick and dense—so big, in fact, that he never had to deal with bullies when he went to school, because bullies never wanted to deal with him. He wears a broad-brimmed brown hat and sports a thick red beard, and squeezed between the beard and the hat are small and steady blue eyes that are clearly the eyes of a man who has never hurt another soul by intention in his entire life. There is an inkling in him of the man Brian Head might have become if he had survived the trials of his adolescence, and toward the end of the interview, I ask him the date of Brian's death.

"March 28, 1994," he says, and seems startled when he says it—no, *rattled*. In the deep sigh that follows his answer, tears storm his eyes. "So, eight years ago yesterday," he says. "You picked a good day for your interview." Suddenly, the interview is over, for when we stand up to leave, the tears are still shining in the shadow of his hat, and I don't have the heart to ask him the one question I had left to ask. His son was dead. The only solace left to him was that he was able to list Brian among the merciful, among the legions of those beset by the cruel, but from what I knew of adolescence, I knew that sometimes all that separates the cruel from the merciful is one irrevocable moment. In class that day, there were two such moments for Brian Head. In the first, the gun didn't go off. In the second, it did, and what I wanted to ask Bill Head was if he ever allowed himself to wonder what fate would have befallen his family had a bullet been chambered in Brian's gun when he pointed it at the boy who slapped him . . . if he ever allowed himself to think that his son was just one irrevocable moment from being remembered not as one of the victims of the terrible boys but as a terrible boy himself.

On November 2, 1998, Jonathan Miller and Joshua Belluardo each had their irrevocable moment. That's all it was, really; think how long it takes to throw a punch. Because the moment was irrevocable, however, people asked how long Jonathan had had that punch in him and started focusing not on the irrevocable moment but rather on the irrevocable life.

Here is the irrevocable moment. Two boys, Josh and Jonathan, neighbors but not friends, two grades apart in school and fifteen months apart in age, get on Cherokee County school bus number 155, which serves both E. T. Booth Middle School and Etowah High School. Josh sits in what may be roughly defined as the middle of the bus. Jonathan sits in the back with his friend James

Nachtsheim. They are supposed to go camping that night near a local lake, and they start discussing their plans. Or, rather, they start discussing their plans until their general urge to make trouble—to mess around on the school bus—distracts them. They begin throwing packets of ketchup and mustard at some of the other boys, and the other boys start throwing packets of ketchup and mustard at them. Out of the fracas, one of the packets hits Josh in the back of his head. Later, some of the kids will say that Jonathan threw it; James Nachtsheim will say he didn't. It doesn't really matter. This is their moment, the moment they've been heading for ever since the Miller family moved to Shallow Cove, one house away from the Belluardos. Josh turns around and glares at Jonathan, Jonathan responds by asking him to fight, right there on the school bus. Josh accepts his challenge but specifies that the fight will take place not on the bus but on his front lawn, after they get off. "All right, *bitch*," Jonathan says. "All right, *faggot*." "Are you gonna kick his ass, Jon?" one of the kids asks. "Yeah, I'm gonna kick his ass," Jonathan answers. "How you gonna kick his ass, Jon?" the kid asks. "I don't know," Jonathan says, and later, at the trial, one kid will say that Jonathan articulated the idea: "Maybe I'll hit him from behind."

Bus number 155 turns into the Port Victoria subdivision and stops at Shallow Cove. Josh gets off the bus and heads for his front lawn. Jonathan follows, with James Nachtsheim following behind him. Jonathan rushes up behind Josh and hits him in the back of his head before he ever reaches his front lawn. Josh slumps to his knees, Jonathan takes another swing and hits his face, Joshua falls to his neighbor's grass, and Jonathan kicks him in the side. The fight, in Jonathan's mind, is over, and he may or may not stand over Josh, raising his fists in exultation. Then it really is over: Jonathan and James leave Josh behind and go to Jonathan's house to prepare their camping gear. They don't mention the "fight"—or what prosecutors will later call "the assault"; the Belluardos, "the attack"; and the Millers, "the incident" or "the accident"—to Jonathan's father when they say hello to him, and then, as is their custom, they head for the woods in back of the Millers' house. Someone standing on Shallow Cove sees them and calls Jonathan's name. Jonathan hears the anger in the voice, sees the outlines of the storm gathering where Josh fell, and runs. He hides with James in a culvert in the woods, then sneaks off to a friend's house. By now, he knows he is in trouble, but he can't imagine what kind; he can't imagine that his trouble is irrevocable, because he can't imagine that his *moment* was irrevocable: "I didn't think I hit him that hard," he will say later. Certainly, he can't imagine that his first punch opened a microscopic tear in Josh's vertebral artery, and so by the time he threw his second punch, blood was flooding Josh's brain, and so by the time he kicked Josh in the side, Josh was, for all intents and purposes, already dead. He can't imagine Josh turning purple on the grass, or Josh's sister, Katie, crying over him and begging her brother to live, or Josh's mother, a bus driver for the Cherokee County schools, hearing about what was happening to her son by radio dispatch. And no, he can't imagine that with one punch he has destroyed not only Josh's life but also his own, as well as the lives of two families. He's a kid, after all, so he can't imagine moments in terms of their irrevocability, or punches in terms of consequences that are as freakish as they are unforeseen. He just knows he is in trouble, and when his friend drives him home, past the ambulances and police cars and fire trucks, he slumps in the car. He wants to tell his father what happened—what he did—but it is too late: A policeman sees him and arrests him. He is charged with aggravated assault and aggravated battery, and when Josh is taken off life support two days later, he is charged, as an adult, with felony murder. He is 15, and Josh was—the most terrible word a parent can hear—13.

Jonathan's irrevocable life began that night, on television, and the next morning, in the newspapers. The packet of mustard, the challenge, the insults, the attempts at bravado, the first punch, the second punch, the kick in the side, the bus driver's recitation of

Jonathan's victory dance: Everything was there in the news stories, but what might have been adolescent ephemera was now judged by the stain of permanence. Jonathan had been in trouble a lot, it was reported, when he went to E. T. Booth. Jonathan's parents could have curbed his behavior, it was reported, but chose not to. Jonathan terrorized Joshua unmercifully, it was reported, until one day Josh couldn't take it anymore. Jonathan didn't like gay people. Jonathan said, like, gay people deserved to die, or something. Joshua didn't just die at the bus stop; he died at the hands of the "bus-stop bully." Joshua didn't die as the consequence of a punch; he died as a consequence of bullying. Bullying was bad. Bullies were bad. Jonathan was bad. The death of Josh Belluardo became the murder of Josh Belluardo, and the murder of Josh Belluardo entered its endless afterlife as an object lesson in what one antibullying website calls "the number one social concern in America today." Joshua entered heaven as an angelic victim, and Jonathan, although certainly not the first well-known bully in Cherokee County—although not even the first well-known bully involved in a fatality at Etowah High School—entered his earthly career as the first bully in Cherokee County intended to be the last.

Indeed, both Cherokee County and the state of Georgia changed laws and policies as a direct result of Josh's irrevocable death and Jonathan's irrevocable life. In early 1999, Cherokee County instituted "three strike" antibullying programs in all of its schools, whereby bullies would be expelled or assigned to alternative schooling after their third offense, whether verbal or physical. At the same time, the county hired a police chief for its entire school system, and the police chief not only installed armed officers in all the middle and high schools under his supervision but also subtly criminalized the daily scrimmage of the schoolyard. A threat was no longer a threat; specific enough, it counted as simple battery. A shove was no longer a shove; forceful enough, it counted as simple assault. The change in the state began in Cherokee, when a reporter called state representative Chuck Scheid and asked, "What are you going to do about bullying?" In January, Scheid responded by drafting what was known informally as the Josh Belluardo bill and pushing it through Georgia's state legislative session. The bill basically called upon the rest of the counties in Georgia to adopt antibullying policies, and when Jonathan Miller went on trial at the end of April, Representative Scheid visited the courtroom to meet the Belluardos and extend his condolences. He did not speak to the Millers, for he believed what he had heard from trial judge Michael Roach—that the trial of Jonathan Miller on felony murder charges was the tragic result of the Millers' refusal to discipline their son.

The trial of Jonathan Miller, terrible boy, began on April 26, 1999, six days after two terrible boys carried out their slaughter at Columbine. Jonathan's lawyers asked for a continuance, but Judge Roach denied the motion, and the trial began, with both the defense and the prosecution conceding something up front.

The defense conceded that Jonathan killed Joshua and asked the jury to convict Jonathan of involuntary manslaughter. The prosecution conceded that Jonathan never intended to kill Joshua, because, under Georgia's felony murder statute, it did not have to prove that Jonathan intended to kill Joshua. Under Georgia's felony murder statute, all it needed to prove was that Jonathan intended to commit the felonies leading up to Joshua's unintended death— felony battery and felony assault—and so all it needed to prove was that Jonathan was a terrible boy. "Ladies and gentlemen, the defense is preying on your desire and the desire of all people to believe that children are innocent, that fifteen-year-olds couldn't mean to hurt each other," the prosecutor, Rachelle Carnesale, said in her summation. "We know better than that. We know that children every day do horrible things to other children." Then: "The victim wasn't the aggressor. The victim was being bullied on the bus and stood up to the bully." Then: "You need to think about what you are telling the children of this community through your verdict . . . It's time for Mr. Miller to reap the whirlwind."

The jury was out for five hours. Jonathan was found guilty of the charges of felony battery and felony assault, which meant that he was also guilty of felony murder. In accordance with Georgia's sentencing guidelines, Judge Michael Roach sentenced him to life in prison.

I was living in Atlanta when Jonathan killed Josh. I remember reading the story on November 3, and I remember a chill passing through me, because, let me tell you, nothing serves as a better madeleine to a bully's memories than a story of a bully killing a kid at a bus stop. Although I had never gone so far as to hit Timmy Titimski in the back of the head, I had certainly terrorized him, as Jonathan was said to have terrorized Josh, but I had gotten away with it and Jonathan hadn't. What gave me the chill, I guess, was the sudden realization of bullying's irrevocable consequences—the sudden realization that it might be an activity people can't get away with, or shouldn't get away with, or never get away with. What I never doubted, though, was that Jonathan and I were of the same ilk. What I never doubted was the basic characterization of Jonathan Miller as a bully and as a terrible boy.

Four years later, the chill still hadn't gone away. It stayed with me exactly as the memories of torturing Timmy Titimski stayed with me, and I began doing some research into the case as a way of deciding if a boy like Jonathan could ever be forgiven. What I found at first didn't surprise me: a website that portrays bullying as a gay rights issue—because of the abuse suffered by gay teens—portraying Josh Belluardo as the "non-gay victim" of gay bashing; people who still lived in the Port Victoria subdivision portraying Jonathan not only as a bully but as a threat to overall peace and security. In the afterlife of the tragedy, Joshua continued rising as an angel to the precise degree that Jonathan continued mutating into an all-purpose bogeyman, and when I talked to one Port Victoria resident about real estate on Shallow Cove, this is what she told me: "What happened to Josh changed a lot of lives, not just the lives of the Millers and the Belluardos. I think most of the houses in that cul-de-sac have turned over a couple of times. People just left, and you know why? I think it's because they know that however long that boy goes to jail, one day he's going to get out. They know he's coming back, and they don't want to be around."

I was surprised, then, when I met Jonathan's parents, Robin and Alan Miller, and they told me that at the time of the "accident," Jonathan was two inches shorter and nearly twenty pounds lighter than Josh Belluardo. Of course, I was not surprised that the Millers tried their best to present Jonathan as a harmless innocent—hell, they were his parents and had a reputation for defending their son at any cost—but what they told me checked out, and the surprises kept coming. Josh, as it turned out, was not weak. He was not helpless. He was more athletic than Jonathan. He was more popular than Jonathan. He had the reputation as someone who could handle himself; indeed, in some quarters, he had the reputation as something of a bully himself. He was never terrorized by Jonathan because he never allowed himself to be terrorized, and so when I asked Jonathan's friend James Nachtsheim what he expected to happen when Jonathan punched Josh, I was surprised when he said that he expected Josh to turn around and "kick Jonathan's ass." When I went to E. T. Booth Middle School and talked to Pat Patterson, the counselor who runs the school's antibullying program and who knew both Josh and Jonathan, I was surprised to hear him say that the boys' relationship "didn't follow the classic guidelines" of bully and bullied, because "a bully usually recognizes a victim, and that wasn't Josh. Josh was a stand-up kid, and he didn't allow Jonathan to push him around." When I had my interview with Bill Head, I was surprised when he said that after he was quoted calling

Josh another victim of bullying, the Belluardos called and asked him to please stop using Josh's name in his crusade. And when I went to the Belluardos' lawyer and asked to speak to his clients, I was surprised by the explanation the lawyer offered for their refusal: They did not want to speak on the subject of bullying. They do not believe that Josh was bullied. They believe that he was viciously attacked. "And quite frankly," the lawyer said, "they believe that if Jonathan had given Josh a fair fight, Josh would have kicked his ass."

He was not a bully, then. Jonathan Miller, the bus-stop bully, was not a bully—or at least not a bully at the bus stop, and above all not a bully to the boy he was said to have killed as a result of bullying. But if he was not a bully, what was he, and why did people insist on making bullying the basis of his crime? If he was not a bully, how did he suffer the terrible cruelty of being judged a bully for life? And if he was not a bully, well, then was he still a terrible boy?

Here's a story about Jonathan Miller and his parents—a story that Jonathan's parents, Robin and Alan Miller, tell about their son and themselves. Jonathan was in high school at the time: Etowah. He had made it out of middle school. He had made it out of E. T. Booth despite the suspensions, despite the referrals, despite a principal who, according to the Millers, tried to crush his spirit. Here was a boy whose name was decided after his parents watched *Jonathan Livingston Seagull*. Here was a boy who, in Robin's words, "always flew where he wasn't supposed to go," and all the administration at E. T. Booth wanted to do was put him on Ritalin. They convened what Robin calls "the Ritalin meeting" when Jonathan was in eighth grade. Robin stormed out, and after that it just got worse for Jonathan. "They suspended Jonathan three days for farting," she says, " 'Serial farting,' they called it. I mean, *c'mon . . .*" The Millers were lucky that Jonathan wanted to go to school at all after what he went through at E. T. Booth, but at Etowah the assistant principal was creative and amenable to Robin's input. When she called Robin to say that Jonathan was about to be suspended for being continually late to science class, Robin remembers saying, "Don't suspend him. It's gotten so he *likes* suspensions. Give him something he really dislikes." So one day, when Jonathan got out of the class before science class, she was waiting out in the hall for him. "In front of all his friends, I said, 'If you can't make it to class on your own, your mother is going to have to help you.' He said, 'Mom, I can't believe you're doing this.' I said, 'I can't believe you're late for science class.' And you know what? He was never late again."

Do you see? After Josh's death, angry mobs gathered on Atlanta's talk-radio shows and called Robin an unfit mother. Does an unfit mother escort her son to science class? Alan could not help himself: As he drove to his lawyer's office, he used to turn on the radio and listen to complete strangers call for his castration. Does a father who takes his two sons camping and volunteers for the Boy Scouts deserve to be castrated? They were both involved in the life of their son Jonathan. They both made sure they were always *home* for their son Jonathan. The only thing they wouldn't do for their son Jonathan was give up on him. They couldn't give up on him. He was a kid. He was a knucklehead. He was mouthy and reckless. But he wasn't violent, he wasn't mean—he was never a lost cause. Do you know what he did after he found out that he had killed Josh? He screamed for a half hour. He pounded his head against the concrete floor of the jail. He had to be put on suicide watch.

But it's no use, is it? No matter what they say about Jonathan— that he *wasn't*, that he *isn't*—he was and he is. They were and they are. They are marked. Their son killed Joshua Belluardo, and they have nothing left but his cause. Alan Miller is eminently reasonable in his son's cause, almost businesslike; he is a bespectacled man with a pinkish face and longish silver hair and the softness of Tennessee in his voice. Robin Miller is passionately volatile in her son's cause; she's from upstate New York, with her mass of corkscrewed hair tied tightly back, a slight space between her front teeth, a small white scar jabbing her upper lip, and her broad forehead creased with care. They are speaking from the living room of their house, where they are surrounded by pictures of their nieces and nephews, and of their son Jeremy, and of their son Jonathan, which are all at least four years old. Their house is an hour and a half outside of Atlanta. It is a hardscrabble little house in a hardscrabble little neighborhood of the kind that used to ring the mill in hardscrabble Southern towns. They left Shallow Cove not long before the Belluardos did. The Belluardos sued them and are now in the process of suing Cherokee County School District for allowing Jonathan on the bus in the first place. The Millers' insurance company paid the claim, but the suit—and the fees of their lawyers—has bankrupted them. They have lost everything and are fully aware that their cause is sabotaged by the awful fact that they haven't lost enough. Their loss is consummate. The Belluardos' loss is infinite. It's permanent and irrevocable, and now when Robin says, "I'd just love to feel Jonathan's face again," she quickly adds, "I feel guilty saying that. Because Mrs. Belluardo would love to feel Josh's face again. I wrote her a note once, but how can you tell someone, 'I'm sorry my son killed your son'?"

And so they've stopped trying to match loss for loss. They've stopped trying to convince anyone that the scales will ever be equal. In the terrible zero-sum game of life and death, they are the winners: Their son is alive. And now they want him back. They understand that he committed a crime. They agree that he should do time in jail. They do not believe that he was a bully or that the crime he committed was murder. "We still have hope that Jonathan can make something of himself," Alan Miller says. "The Belluardos will never be satisfied with Jonathan's punishment until they get their son back. That's not going to happen. But we can get our son back and give him another chance."

It's a reasonable request and a reasonable position to take. But it's not all they want. It can't be. Like the Belluardos, they want what they cannot have; they want to revoke the irrevocable. They want their boy not to be considered terrible, and now, at the end of the interview, Robin stands up and makes the plea she is consigned to make until Jonathan comes home and the Millers are able to disappear. "I just want people to know we're not bad people," Robin says. "That Jonathan is not a bad person. I used to be really proud of him—his kind heart. But now it's like I'm always saying, We really are good people, we really are good people. . . ."

The terrible boy does not look so terrible behind the glass. He looks tired. He always looks tired behind the glass because he always *is* tired. No, to be more specific, *sleepy*; he is always sleepy behind the glass. The glass is the glass that separates prisoners from visitors. Behind it sits Jonathan Miller, talking by means of a black phone. He is 18 years old. Since November 2, 1998, he has grown five inches and put on nearly sixty pounds. He has spent nearly a quarter of his life in jail, among terrible boys and terrible men. He has grown up behind the glass—he has, in his mother's words, been raised by the state—and he has not only spent the last four years without touching a tree or stepping on grass, he has spent the last four years forgetting what trees and grass feel like.

He is shy, slow-moving, slightly gawky. His face is long, his hair short and combed forward. He has fledgling sideburns and pinkish skin stained with jailhouse acne. He's wearing eyeglasses with a stylish horizontal inclination—the kind of eyeglasses kids his age wear out in the world. His hands are soft and white, uncontaminated by effort. He has a soft, sleepy voice accented not by affect but by occasional complaint—a burbling institutional monotone, cued to react rather than make pronouncements. Although he no longer tries to speak over people—although he's finally learned to keep his big mouth shut, or, at the very least, to speak *under* people, at prison volume—he still likes to talk, and as he does, his right eye starts opening like a flower whose bloom is prodded by trick photography. He's struggling to rouse himself and as he does, the partition between the boy raised by Alan and Robin Miller and the man raised by the state of Georgia becomes more and more apparent. He does not look like a terrible boy, but in his prison jumpsuit— whose horizontal white-and-orange stripes are, in this jail, the designation of a murderer—he has been outfitted with the trappings of a terrible man.

He is still in a county jail. Pending his appeal to the Georgia Supreme Court, he is not yet in the state prison system, but jail is jail, and behind him the turquoise pod of steel and stone looms like a cathedral. Over the last four years, he has moved from one jail to another; he is happy with this one because it allows him to keep a radio in his cell. "What kind of music do you listen to, Jonathan?"

"Well, I like to tell all my macho friends that I listen to rap, but really I like to listen to love songs. Whitney Houston is my favorite."

"Who did you hang around with at Etowah?"

"I didn't really belong to a group. I had a lot of friends, but they were mostly older. In school, I was sort of a loner, going from group to group—two days with these guys, three days with these girls."

"What about Josh?"

"Josh and I were friends at first. Then he turned against me. I guess he thought I was the weakest link or something."

"Were you guys enemies?"

"Well, it wasn't all me. They make him out to be an angel. They make him out to be all good and me all bad. Okay, if they say I'm bad, I must be bad, but I'm good, too. I didn't even want to fight that day. All he had to say was, 'I don't want to fight you,' and none of this would have happened. But he gave me this look and said, 'Fight me at my house,' and I said, 'I'm tired of this.'"

"Why did you hit him in the back of the head? Were you scared?"

"I ain't been afraid of nobody my whole life. I've never been afraid of getting beat up. Maybe I did it because I knew he'd never face me—like, Hey, I'm *here*. It was no big deal; the whole thing lasted ten seconds. I didn't want to fight. I wanted to go camping."

"Did you hit him with your right hand or your left?"

"Right."

"Did you hit him with a roundhouse punch or a straight one?"

"It wasn't no roundhouse. It was a boxing punch. I didn't think I hit him that hard because I didn't break my knuckles or nothing, but I guess I hit him harder than I thought I did, because I was sort of going downhill."

"What was your reaction when you started becoming known as a bully?"

"I got scared. I was like, What? Because people were talking about me in the newspapers, and I didn't even know who they were. I was like, Everybody says I'm bad, so I must be bad, but I'm not all bad. Like in jail, they call me Killer Miller. I told them to stop—I'm no killer—but then I thought, The Belluardos say I'm a killer, the DA says I'm a killer, the judge says I'm a killer, the jury says I'm a killer, why should I get in a fight when people in jail call me a killer? Now I just tell them, When I win my appeal, you can't call me killer no more. Because I know I'm not a killer. I know I didn't mean to kill that boy. But I don't care what anyone thinks of me except the judges who are hearing my case and the Belluardo family. They're the only ones I care about."

It is early afternoon. His right eye is open now, in full bloom, but at five o'clock when they come around and give him his pills, it will start closing again. As a murderer, decked in white-and-orange stripes—as Killer Miller—he's locked down in his cell twenty-one hours a day. As a murderer, he shares his cell with no one, and to make the time pass, the jail affords him what it affords everyone else he's met in the turquoise cathedral: pharmacological intervention. Zoloft, Prozac, Placidyl, Elavil: In the interest of tractability, he's taken them all at one time or another, but now he's just on Elavil, and he sleeps sixteen hours a day. The time passes. By the time his eyes open, they're ready to close again, and in that way, in blank, dreamless sleep, the terrible boy grows up behind the glass.

He remembers. Timmy Titimski remembers the bully—*his* bully, the one designed especially for him, like a bullet with his name on it. I remember him, too, of course. How can I forget? He was crucial. He helped form me, as I suppose I helped form him. He exists as a signal event in my conscience. Hell, he is my conscience. There was nothing else to stop me back then except its slow drip. Today, if I lived in Cherokee County, Georgia, or in any of the other counties across the nation that have adopted three-strikes laws or zero tolerance policies in response to bullying, I would not have had to stop myself. I would have *been* stopped. I would have been suspended, expelled, possibly sent for a spell to a juvenile detention center. Instead, I grew up. I had the freedom to develop a sense of regret— the great sustaining mercy of guilt. I even had the luxury of figuring out why I did what I did to him. It was the matter of tears: I couldn't control my own, so I figured out a way to control his. I was a kid who cried whenever my father yelled at me. My tears were a source of great shame, so when I found a boy whose tears I could turn on and off like a faucet—well, it gave me what shrinks would call a necessary sense of mastery. As the bully stands sentry on his victim's road to manhood, so does the victim stand on the bully's road to self-knowledge, and in time, my shame over my tears has been succeeded by my shame over what I did to him. I am grateful for the time and freedom I was afforded, but I'm sure he isn't; I'm sure he wasn't. I'm sure he prayed for something to stop me because he knew that my own leisurely prerogative wasn't enough. I'm sure he would be grateful for any laws or policies that would keep his children from going through what he went through. And so, one day, I called him. I told myself that I was calling him to see what he thought about Jonathan Miller, and to see if he thought the difference the antibullying movement would have made in his life justifies its existence. But, really, I was calling out of some terrible curiosity. To see if I could speak his name without threat. To see if I had, through some kind of perverse nostalgia, exaggerated what I did to him. To see if he remembers.

He remembers. I knew it before I even spoke to him. I knew it when a little girl answered the phone, her voice like a babbling brook and said, "Daddy, there's a phone call for you"—because I knew he was a father, and so had something to protect. I had never called him anything but Timmy—his name seemed to exist to be spoken in the diminutive—but when he came on the phone, I heard myself saying, "Timothy?" He had a deep voice, deeper than mine. He didn't sound like a Timmy anymore.

"Yes?" he said.

"This is Tom Junod."

He sighed. As if he had been waiting. His voice fashioned itself around a squint of enmity. It consigned me to something, and not just the past. It was poised, and it was patient, and it did not budge. "Tom, how did you get my number?"

I told him that I had gone to a reunion. His name and number were in the commemorative booklet.

"Well, I don't want to waste your time—I don't want to participate in your project, Tom. I don't want to participate in this *conversation*—"

"Can I ask you why?"

He sighed again. He took a breath, preamble to the last words he would ever speak to me. "Tom, I've had to put a lot of things behind me in my life. You're one of them. Please lose my number."

And that was all. It was over. I said, "Okay," but by that time the line was dead. I was preparing to apologize, but I'm sure he knew I was going to ask for forgiveness, and that forgiveness wasn't his to dispense. We had our time long ago, and it was irrevocable. I couldn't get away with it any more than Jonathan Miller could get away with what he had done to Josh Belluardo. Hell, what I had done to Timmy Titimski was *worse* than what Jonathan had done to Josh because it wasn't in error. It was pointed, concerted, extended— a campaign. I did what I wanted to do. I had that freedom back then. It was a terrible freedom, and yet I prefer it to its opposite, for I can't help asking if we can suppress bullying without suppressing the immense and mysterious and ultimately beautiful vagaries of childhood. I can't help asking if we can criminalize bullying without criminalizing childhood itself. I can't help wondering if it's not by our attempt to criminalize childhood that Jonathan Miller paid a man's price for a boy's punch, and if the world he now occupies— where the action of Elavil supplants the action of guilt—mirrors our own, where the dictates of conscience are supplanted by the dictates of law and policy. I ask for mercy for Jonathan Miller. But then again, I'm nothing but a goddamned bully. I ask for mercy for Jonathan as a way of asking for mercy for myself. I ask for mercy for Jonathan Miller as a way of keeping alive the hope of all terrible boys, that they do not become terrible men.

———

On May 2, 2002, the Georgia Supreme Court heard Jonathan Miller's appeal, in—of all things—an auditorium full of high school students in Griffin, Georgia. The venue was chosen as an experiment in education, but the appeal turned into an opportunity for the judges to lecture the students on the evils of bullying, even though neither Jonathan's counsel nor even the Cherokee County district attorney used the word in their arguments. Not surprisingly, the Georgia Supreme Court affirmed Jonathan's conviction on all counts, including the decision to try him as an adult for a crime that seems to me the very essence of a juvenile offense. I mean, if coldcocking—and unintentionally killing—a kid at a bus stop isn't a crime that should be judged in a juvenile court, then what is?

THE BULLY OF TOULON
ROBERT KURSON

On March 22, 2002, sheriff's deputy Adam Streicher was the only cop on duty in Toulon, Illinois, a town of 1,400 that briefly pokes up between cornfields, the municipal equivalent of a prairie dog. Toulon is located 160 miles southwest of Chicago and it feels even farther. Most folks farm the land or work for the town. The lone grocery store has wood floors and hand-drawn signs. A flashing yellow light slows traffic on Main Street.

Deputy Streicher, 23, had dreamed of becoming a cop since childhood, when he admired Ponch, the hero of the TV series *CHiPs*. He had grown up in nearby Annawan, so he knew the rhythms and mores of rural Illinois. As a Stark County deputy, he would be responsible for covering the county's three main towns— Bradford, Wyoming, and Toulon—in an area considerably larger than Chicago. Often he was the only law enforcement officer on duty in the entire county. Streicher had been on the force just three months, but he handled his rounds with confidence.

On a Friday night like this one, an ambitious deputy might nab some beer-chugging teenagers or issue a "Settle down, folks" to a bickering couple. But Streicher didn't intend to sit. He nosed around the Stark County deputy's office—there was usually something if you looked—and found a five-month-old warrant for the arrest of a local man. It seemed routine enough—the man had failed to pay some court fees and had missed his court date. Dressed in starched brown pants and brown shirt, with a Stark County silver badge covering his left breast, Streicher found the squad car keys and began the four-block ride to the man's house.

In Toulon, people mind their business. But anyone who had known Streicher's plan would have spoken up; they would have warned him, Don't do this. But Streicher did not know what Toulon knew.

The deputy turned right on Main Street, left on Miller, and right on Thomas. It took him a minute to arrive at the house of the man named in the warrant. Carrying the document, Streicher walked to the front door and knocked.

Nobody in Toulon pretends that the place is Mayberry. It once was, maybe, in the 1950s, when the town supported an active Main Street, four car dealers, four new farm implement dealers, and three doctors; when the city constable was a one-armed geezer who patrolled on foot and shook business doors to check the locks; when America valued its farmers. That's history now. In Toulon, as in many small towns, young people worry about opportunity. The talented nurture an appetite for the larger world. Empty storefronts embarrass Main Street.

Still, Toulon has its advantages, and they are the kind that don't defer to eras. Everyone knows each other here, not just by name but by hopes, dreams, victories, and disappointments. A newcomer who buys the Williams house will live in Toulon a decade before residents stop referring to it as the Williams place. Gossip—the small town's nectar—is reliably ladled in the town's two coffee shops, ladies at one table, men at another.

But Toulon's biggest advantage is in its biology. The town exists as a living, unified being; no part moves without implication for the other parts, no person lives without affecting other lives. When someone in Toulon gets sick, much of the town rushes to her bedside or comforts her children or takes over her household chores. When someone in Toulon dies, the town converges for fund-raisers, selling candles or car washes or whatever it takes to make the system whole again. In this way, by merging into a single, 1,400-person organism, Toulon survives.

Residents aren't naive enough to believe that bad things can't happen in Toulon. But what they never imagined was that certain kinds of bad things—maybe the worst things—could happen in a place like Toulon because it is small, because everyone knows each other, because the people are so close.

Deputy Streicher waited for an answer at the man's door. The house and property stood out from its tidy neighbors; logs, tires, and appliances lay around the modest carport, forming a meniscus of junk that crawled along the edges of the house. A small yellow tractor sat parked near the front door. A wooden swing on a faded red metal stand stood sentry on the tiny patch of yard.

(The following events of the evening of March 22, 2002, as described here, are drawn from law enforcement allegations and court records including a thirty-count indictment, as well as *Chicago* magazine interviews with witnesses and other sources.)

A 60-year-old man with Einstein salt-and-pepper hair, a disorganized gray beard, and frozen eyes answered the door. He stood perhaps five feet nine. His name was Curtis Thompson, and he was a former coal miner who had lived in the area all his life. Apparently, Deputy Streicher announced the purpose of his visit—to serve an arrest warrant. A brief conversation ensued. Shortly thereafter, law enforcement officials and the indictment allege, Thompson located his sawed-off shotgun and pointed it at the deputy. Before Streicher had much of a chance to react, Thompson pulled the trigger, hitting the deputy in the left shoulder, upper chest, and neck. Streicher fell to Thompson's porch, his face dusted with gunpowder, shotgun wadding stuck to his shirt collar, his upper left side blown away. He likely died before he hit the cement.

Streicher lay on the porch in a pool of blood. Then, the indictment alleges, Curt Thompson took the officer's 9-millimeter pistol and, along with the shotgun, jumped into the deputy's squad car, flipped on the flashing lights, and proceeded down Thomas Street, a glaring, enraged monument to a small town's recent history.

For thirty years, some of the people of Toulon had worried that it could come to this. Curt Thompson was a terrifying bully. He selected his enemies for committing offenses few could fathom, then punished them through methodical stalking—sometimes for years—that derailed their lives and infused them with fear. "He was the meanest person I ever met," says a man who knew Thompson. "He wanted people to be afraid of him, and spent years making threats."

People filed numerous complaints against Thompson. Mayors, city councils, prosecutors, and law enforcement seemed powerless to stop him. (State's attorney James Owens, Stark County sheriff Lonny Dennison, and Toulon's lone police officer, Bob Taylor, would not comment for this story.)

A handful of Toulon residents claim that Thompson was misunderstood. They attest to his intelligence, work ethic, kind wife, and instinct to help those in need. Some even mention his sense of humor. "There was quite a bit good about him," says Mary Jane Swank, whose husband is Thompson's cousin. "There was nothing Curt wouldn't do for you." Few, however, express complete surprise at how things turned out for Thompson and Toulon.

The shock came when Thompson began to terrorize people. Then Toulon's strength—its smallness—became its biggest liability. Residents who otherwise massed to help neighbors now advised one another to "just ignore" Thompson. Police counseled citizens to "just stay away from him." In the town's two coffee shops, headquarters for Toulon's get-involved impulse, the mantra on Thompson became "You know how Curt is. Just leave him be."

Several decades ago, the town of Skidmore, Missouri, suffered under the rage of its own bully. Ken McElroy, a hulking, 47-year-old farmer with long black sideburns, manufactured feuds and then stalked his foes. For years, McElroy defied authorities. One day in 1981, a posse of thirty or forty followed the bully to his truck and, in broad daylight, shot him dead. When authorities asked for witnesses, no one came forward. The case remains open. By midnight on March 22, 2002, some in Toulon would be wondering if the same fate shouldn't have befallen Curt Thompson.

The details of Thompson's life are sketchy. Acquaintances say he grew up on a farm near Toulon, the youngest of several children. His father died when Curt was six years old, leaving the family to struggle for the basics.

"Curt had to go work on farms when he was in grade school," says Barry Taylor (no relation to Bob Taylor), who knew Thompson when they were children. "It's a rotten childhood when you have to work in grade school."

"His mother was good in ways," recalls Mary Jane Swank. "She could be stubborn; things had to be her way. She didn't want anyone to touch any of her stuff, and she raised her kids like that. If she got mad at someone, she'd hold that against them forever. But she was smart, and she was a beautiful writer."

Taylor recalls Thompson as bright, serious, and an excellent high school football player for Toulon High School (now Stark County High). He tells that Thompson had to quit school at 16 to work full-time. "He had no choice. He had to eat."

Thompson married a girl from his high school class, a woman

Taylor describes as "fun and nice and pleasant," and to whom he is still married. He went to work on various farms, then took a job in an Illinois coal mine. Without exception, those who knew him describe him as a capable and hard worker able to do almost any odd job or farm task. Somewhere along the line, however, Thompson began to get very angry.

At the Stark County courthouse in Toulon, where Abraham Lincoln spoke in 1858, records of legal proceedings are still entered by hand in hefty leather diaries. Under the letter *T*, going back more than thirty years, are myriad cases against Curt Thompson.

Some appear harmless enough: a dispute with an employer; traffic citations; failure to keep a dog's vaccination records current; violation of a litter ordinance. But others seem bonded by a common theme — vendetta.

For decades, Thompson maintained grudges against various Toulon residents. Anyone who had taken him to court, or who he perceived had complained about him or violated his sense of territory, made his enemies list, and it was a list often written in indelible ink. As town talk had it, those who angered Thompson might expect to live in constant fear.

"Fear" does not mean in Toulon what it means in Chicago. In Toulon, where most residents live a few blocks from each other and pass on the street several times a day, having an enemy virtually assures a meeting with him in public. When that enemy is Curt Thompson, an intelligent man with time on his hands who dedicated thought and energy to creating fear, it could ruin your life.

Thompson's modus operandi, at least in recent years, was predictable and intimidating. According to many, he would drive his pickup truck past the home of his foe, slow to a crawl, and glare. He might follow his enemy down the rural roads that led out of Toulon, or block him with his truck at intersections. Always, he would glare.

"He was a bully," says Jim Pearson, who worked as a Stark County deputy from 1982 to 1987, and who now works as a Peoria County sheriff's lieutenant. "The glaring, the following, the threatening—he even did it to elderly people."

"Everyone knew about his temper," says one of Thompson's neighbors, who asked that his name be withheld. "He held a grudge. If someone bothered him, he'd bother them back, and he'd stay at it. I told Curt, 'I don't hold grudges.' He said, 'Well, I do.'"

Early on, Toulon evolved a defense against Thompson that seemed to run counter to its instinct to unify against threats. Whereas the town would mobilize to save a school or care for a sick child, it largely decided to ignore Thompson, to maintain a safe distance, to cross to the other side of the street.

"People talked about Thompson being crazy," says Art Mott, who has lived in Toulon for ten years. "The thinking was to stay away from him."

"It was a small-town mentality," says another Toulon resident. "People thought: Nothing major is going to happen; he's just crazy; ignore him; he's been harassing people for years, so just ignore him."

No one remembers any formative incident in Thompson's life that might explain the roots of his temper. Rather, it appears that his encyclopedia of grudges grew out of his particular notions about territory. "He wouldn't have a problem with a stranger on the street," says one person who knew Thompson. "But if your wash blew onto his lawn, he'd have a big problem with that. Personal space was a big issue with him."

Unlike most bullies, Thompson targeted more than the weak. Sheriffs, politicians, even black belts in karate qualified for vendetta if they managed to wrong Thompson.

In 1984, Toulon's mayor, Rick Collins, followed up on a citizen's complaint against one of Thompson's dogs. "That started Curt's grudge against me," says Collins, now a commercial pilot for a major airline. The next year, he and Thompson attended a retirement party for a bus driver at a restaurant just outside Toulon.

"I nodded across the table, a friendly hello," Collins says. "He glared. Later, as I was leaving, Curt came up behind me, threatening me with all kinds of profanities. I ignored it. He struck me a couple blows to the head, then pushed me down a small flight of stairs. I hit the bottom on my hands and knees, but just got up and kept going. Had I gone after him, the only way the confrontation would have ended would have been death or jail." Neither the Toulon city policeman nor the Stark County sheriff, Collins says, was interested in pursuing the matter, claiming it to be outside their jurisdictions.

In 1980, Thompson had a run-in with Kenneth Richardson, then the Toulon city policeman. Thompson and Richardson owned adjoining properties. While working outside, Thompson and Richardson began to argue about the property line. A struggle ensued, during which Richardson managed to get atop Thompson and hold him down.

"I had gone to take a bottle of pop to my husband," recalls Sandra Richardson, Kenneth's wife. "When Curt saw me, he yelled to his son, 'She's going to hit me with that bottle! Get her or I'll get you!'" She alleged in a lawsuit that Thompson's son, a football player, ran and tackled her and broke her wrist in six places.

The Richardsons filed two lawsuits. The first, by Kenneth, claimed that Thompson had punched him, and had been "verbally abusive, hostile, and obscene" for weeks before the incident. The second was filed by Sandra against Thompson's son, Curtis Jr.

"After that," Sandra says, "Curt would set at the stop sign at the end of our driveway and glare."

. . .

One law enforcement official who seemed willing to confront Thompson was Kenneth "Buck" Dison, the Stark County sheriff from 1970 to 1982. For nearly thirty years—well into Dison's old age and retirement—Thompson maintained a feud with the sheriff.

No one knows for certain the origins of the dispute. Court records show that Dison arrested Thompson in 1971 after Thompson allegedly threatened a man at a Toulon feed store. It didn't take long, according to many, for the feud to blaze.

"Curt would come after Dad every time he saw him," says Kathy Ptasnik, Dison's daughter. "He backed up his truck and glared into the house when my parents were socializing. He'd follow Dad and flip him the finger. Dad was afraid of Curt having revenge. He told us never to walk past his house." Even among her siblings, Ptasnik says, the instinct was to turn away from Thompson. "My brother and I begged Dad to ignore him," she says.

"Dison didn't take any shit," says Collins, the former mayor. "He wasn't afraid to stand up to Curt." Others say Dison gave as good as he got. "After Buck had retired, I saw him flip Curt the bird when Curt was just minding his own business," says a friend of Thompson's who asked to remain anonymous.

In 1987, Thompson pulled his pickup in front of Dison's car on a rural road, blocking the former sheriff. Thompson got out of his truck and approached Dison's car. The two men argued and, Dison claimed, Thompson threatened him (Dison was 68 years old at the time; Thompson was 46). Thompson was charged with reckless driving and disorderly conduct.

At trial in the plain white courthouse on Main Street, Thompson testified that Dison had been harassing his family. He stopped the former sheriff, he said, to warn him against bothering his family. "I told him, 'You fucking old man, you pull it again, and I'm coming after you.'" When asked if he always stopped those he was angry with on a public road, Thompson testified, "It depends on where they are."

The jury convicted Thompson on both charges. He was fined $150 and sentenced to 21 days in jail. The disorderly conduct verdict, however, was reversed by the Third District appellate court, which reasoned that the trial judge had improperly excluded testimony about the long-running feud between Dison and Thompson and his family.

Seven years later, in 1994, Dison claimed that Thompson approached his car in the parking lot of the local grocery and threatened him. This time, Thompson was charged with aggravated assault and disorderly conduct. At trial, he denied leaving his truck, but acknowledged the gist of the remarks. "I told him to go on in the store or I'd bury his ass," Thompson told the court. In arguments before the judge, prosecutor James Owens called Thompson "a street thug" and "a schoolyard bully who never left the schoolyard." Thompson was convicted of disorderly conduct, but not the more serious charge of aggravated assault. He was sentenced to a year of probation, $111 in court costs, and 100 hours of community service.

"Up until the end of Dad's life, Curt harassed him," Ptasnik says. "Dad was an old man in very poor health. He used a walker! And Curt would still pull up beside him and give him that glare. [Dad] was so upset that nothing could be done about Curt, but not just for himself. He was convinced Curt could kill someone."

The Richardson "pop bottle" cases lay dormant for four years before being dismissed for lack of pursuit by the plaintiffs. "I think they dropped it because the judge was retiring," Sandra says. "No one was interested in pursuing it."

The idea of "not pursuing it" became central to Toulon's approach to dealing with Thompson. A few, like the Richardsons, filed charges and took Thompson to court. Many more opted to ignore him.

"People would come in and complain," says Pearson, the former deputy. "They would tell me about the intimidation. But almost no one would file charges. They just put up with him for the most part. The thinking was to ignore him, and hopefully things would get better."

"I think people rationalized that the problem wasn't severe enough to justify the effort required to resolve it," says Jim Nowlan, editor of the *Stark County News*, a weekly newspaper. "I might have been guilty of it myself."

Nowlan and others in Toulon tell of hearing several years ago that the Toulon City Council did not intend to enforce a litter ordinance against Thompson. "That infuriated me," Nowlan says. "I thought the whole town should go over there at once and confront Thompson. I thought we should be united. But my passion cooled and I ultimately forgot about it, and that was probably pretty typical."

Some suggest, too, that law enforcement was afraid of Thompson.

"The various police from the town and county over the years, not all of them, but some, have been fearful of Thompson," Nowlan says. "Not in terms of the old-fashioned fistfight, but for fear of an extremely violent reaction."

Pearson has another take. "We were in a tough situation," he says of law enforcement. "It's not against the law to drive your car down a public road or an alley and glare at someone. When [Thompson] did something more serious and someone was willing to file charges, action was taken by the police. But most people chose just to ignore him."

And the few in Toulon who were willing to file charges were the people Thompson was on his way to see after he allegedly killed Deputy Streicher.

Jim and Janet Giesenhagen were perfectly Toulon. His mother, Ardelle, lived across the alley on a homestead bought by her great-

great-grandfather in 1829. Jim co-owned a local television/heating/
air-conditioning business, earned a black belt in karate, attended
church every Sunday, led a Boy Scout troop. Janet worked long
hours at a Peoria grocery store, about an hour away, then went
home to play with their daughter, Ashley, and surf the Internet.
Ashley played soccer and piano, and remained a daddy's girl. Most
Friday nights the family went out for supper, often for pizza at
Happy Joe's in Kewanee. Their future plans were simple: Save
money for retirement, take a trip to Disney World.

In 1986, the Giesenhagens told police that Thompson's Labrador
retriever had bitten 6-year-old Shawn Henderson, Janet's son from a
previous marriage, who lived with them. Stark County authorities
filed charges, and the case went to trial. The jury found in favor of
Thompson. The Giesenhagens were now on Thompson's list.

Ardelle Giesenhagen, Jim's mother, and others say Thompson
began to stalk the Giesenhagen family, and kept it up for years. "Day
after day, around eight in the morning, Curt would drive down the
alley behind Jim's house, just circling very slow, three or four times,
almost not moving, and glaring," recalls Joe Tracy, Jim's best friend.
"He knew that was about the time Ashley went to school. And it
didn't quit. Jim made complaints. Nothing was ever done."

Jim began driving Ashley the few blocks to school. In his car, day
or night, he zigzagged rather than take the shortest route, always
careful to avoid passing near Thompson's house. Though Jim held
a black belt in karate, he rarely, if ever, confronted Thompson; he
knew that the man owned guns, and believed that a challenge
might short-circuit Thompson's temper.

Ardelle Giesenhagen, then in her sixties, was not so patient.
After Thompson extended his vendetta to her and her husband,
and began to circle her house and glare at her, she told him, "Curt,
you're not God! I'm not scared of you. You could shoot me today
and it wouldn't worry me because I know where I'm going. But I
don't know if you're going anyplace but down below." Thompson

just glared at her. Another time, when he parked in the alley and glowered while Ardelle gardened, she shook her finger at him and said, "Curt, what do you think you're doin'? Move it!" Thompson only snickered and drove off.

Perhaps the moment that most frightened Ardelle occurred just after her husband died, in 1999. She, Jim, Janet, and Ashley were in her backyard playing with Ardelle's cats. "Curt drove his truck down the alley and told Jim and Janet he was going to kill them," Ardelle recalls. "Someone called the police. Bob Taylor came. Curt said he'd get him, too. Taylor did nothing. He didn't arrest him. Nothing."

About five years ago, shortly after Joe Tracy went to work for Jim Giesenhagen, he too began to have problems with Thompson. "I had no connection to Curt, no dealings with him," Tracy says. "My only offense was that I was friends with Jim."

Sometimes Thompson would block Tracy on Main Street with his truck or follow him out of town or try to run him off the road as he walked to the grocery store. Every day, Tracy says, Thompson circled his house, glaring. When he told Thompson, "Curt, why don't you just leave us alone? We're not bothering you." Thompson replied, "Yes, you are bothering me. You're harassing me all the time," and Tracy could only shake his head.

In 1999, Tracy filed a criminal complaint claiming that Thompson had followed him for two miles into the country, then jumped out of his truck at an intersection and waved a hammer threateningly. Jim and Janet Giesenhagen gave statements about Thompson's behavior in connection with that case. Thompson was convicted of simple assault, and in August 2000, he was ordered to pay $116 in court costs, $25 per month in probation fees for twenty-four months, and a $100 public defender's fee. He was also ordered to stay away from Joe Tracy and his family, and from Jim Giesenhagen and his family—an order Tracy says Thompson violated repeatedly.

"Jim didn't know what to do," Tracy says. "He went to the law, he made lots of calls, and they didn't do anything."

Finally, Jim set up a video camera on the back of his garage and pointed it toward the alley. Thompson drove by and glared. Often Jim and Tracy believed that this was clear evidence of violation of the court order prohibiting contact with the Giesenhagens. Jim delivered the tapes to the state's attorney. Tracy says they never heard back.

More than a year after the conviction in the hammer-waving case, Thompson had paid just $18 of the required fees and costs. Judge Scott Shore issued a summons for him to appear before the court for nonpayment. Thompson did not appear. On October 15, 2001, Shore issued a warrant for Thompson's arrest. It was this warrant that Deputy Streicher had tried to serve the night he was shot, more than five months after it had been issued.

On that Friday night last March, while Deputy Streicher lay on Curt Thompson's porch, Thompson streaked in the squad car toward the Giesenhagen house. Inside, the family was enjoying a quiet evening together. Janet was on the couch. Jim and Ashley had gone to the basement, probably to fetch a vaporizer to soothe Janet's asthma.

Court documents allege that, armed with Streicher's service revolver and his own sawed-off shotgun, Thompson pulled into the driveway of the house, smashing the rear end of a parked Mercury SUV and driving it through wooden fence posts and into a pole flying the American flag. Thompson jumped out of the vehicle with the shotgun. He climbed the four wooden steps that led to the side door of the house, leaving the squad car lights flashing in the driveway. Then, the indictment alleges, Thompson broke down the door to the house and burst in, carrying his sawed-off shotgun. At close range, he fired at Janet, hitting her in the arms and the chest, leaving her left forearm dangling by a thread of skin as she collapsed to the floor. Then, authorities say, he likely moved to the basement, where he fired the shotgun and struck Jim Giesenhagen in the face, the buckshot obliterating his tongue and the floor of his mouth. Jim fell dead. Thompson did not harm Ashley, who probably witnessed her father's killing. Finished, Thompson left the house.

Ashley called her grandmother, Ardelle. Toulon does not have 911 service; the town voted it down twice, thinking it too expensive, at $2.85 a month, to adopt. Ashley told Ardelle, "Grandma, come quick! Curt Thompson just killed my daddy and hurt my mommy." Ardelle, who did not know whether Thompson was still inside the Giesenhagen home, threw on her shoes and coat and ran across the alley.

When Ardelle stepped inside, she saw Janet on the floor, one hand to her chest, the other nearly detached from her arm. "Grandma, he's down there," Ashley said. Ardelle looked down the stairs and saw Jim lying in a pool of blood, a hole in his head. She could tell that he was dead, but wondered what had happened to his beard.

Ardelle called the sheriff's office. Janet asked for a pillow, which Ardelle retrieved for her. "My back hurts," Janet said. Ardelle placed the pillow behind Janet's back then covered her with a blanket.

As Ardelle waited for an ambulance, she went to Ashley's bedroom. Just a few weeks earlier, after Thompson had driven by Ardelle's house and glared, Ashley had locked the windows and said, "You know what, Grandma? We need to pray for Curt. He doesn't have anybody to love him." Now Ashley's socks were soaked in blood. "Let's kneel and pray for Mommy because I think she might make it," Ardelle told her granddaughter. Then she noticed that Ashley had started to pack a suitcase of clothes because she knew she wouldn't be staying home that night.

. . .

Lights still flashing, Thompson drove the now-damaged squad car west to the intersection of Commercial and Franklin Streets. There, he spotted a pickup truck being driven by his young neighbor Jason Rice, with whom he purportedly had been feuding. According to the indictment, Thompson rammed the pickup. Rice, believing he had been struck by a deputy, approached the squad car to offer help. Thompson pointed the shotgun. Rice ran from the scene.

At the Giesenhagen house, Ardelle still waited for an ambulance as Janet clung to life. It had been, by her estimation, several minutes since she had called the sheriff's office. She called again. "I need help now!" she told the dispatcher. "Where is the ambulance?" Ardelle says the dispatcher told her, "You have to call it yourself." Incredulous, Ardelle found the number to the local ambulance, located just blocks away, and called. Ardelle believes "at least" fifteen or twenty minutes passed from the time she first called the dispatcher until the ambulance arrived.

By now, calls for help had been broadcast to officers in two other Stark County towns—Wyoming (six miles away) and Bradford (fifteen miles away). Sources say that the Toulon city policeman, Bob Taylor, was not on duty, but he raced to the scene upon learning what was happening.

Thompson was now pointed south on Franklin Street. Backup law enforcement was still minutes away. One witness says that Thompson approached another house, this one belonging to Joe Tracy, Jim Giesenhagen's best friend.

As Thompson drove past Tracy's house, Tracy's telephone rang furiously inside. By now, friends and family had heard word that Thompson had done something terrible, and they were desperate to warn Tracy. The phone kept ringing. Tracy and his wife had eaten dinner at the Barn House in Kewanee that night, and had stopped to talk to Joe's stepdaughter. Their house was empty.

By about 8:15 P.M., squad cars from Wyoming and Bradford, along with Bob Taylor in the Toulon city police car, had converged, sirens blaring. Thompson turned east on Thomas Street, then south on Miller Street, lights still flashing. He was within a block of his own house, where the slain deputy still lay.

The Bradford policeman, driving north on Miller, came head-to-head with the stolen squad car. Thompson stopped. The Wyoming and Toulon cars, which had gone first to Thompson's house, now came racing around the corner onto Miller and stopped behind the stolen vehicle. Thompson was surrounded.

The police aimed their weapons at Thompson. Still seated in the deputy's car, the indictment alleges, Thompson reached for a shotgun and fired through the windshield at the officers. The officers returned fire. Then nothing moved. The only sounds in Toulon that moment were the officers' heaving breaths and the whine of distant sirens racing to save the town.

Then more shots rang out, so many and for so long that some, describing it afterward, would liken it to the grand finale of a fireworks display. Then, another, longer silence, this one crushing in its implication—it was time for the officers to approach the stolen vehicle.

The police moved in, their lives thrust up against the crescendo of a thirty-year rage. Nothing moved inside the squad car. They stepped closer. Toulon's lone traffic light, blinking a block away on Main Street, lit the scene in uncertain yellow. Thompson had been shot in the face. He appeared unconscious. Police dragged him from the car, handcuffed him, and continued to point their service revolvers at him. A medevac helicopter landed on the nearby high school football field and airlifted Thompson to a Peoria hospital.

Janet Giesenhagen was rushed to the same football field, where a helicopter awaited. She was pronounced dead on the field. That night, 10-year-old Ashley took her suitcase and slept at her grandmother's house.

. . .

Thompson was placed on life support at OSF St. Francis Medical Center in Peoria. His condition improved over the course of the next week. On April 1, ten days after the murders in Toulon, he was transferred to the Peoria County Jail, and placed in a cell by himself. A few days later, he appeared in court in Toulon and demanded to represent himself, saying his court-appointed attorneys in previous cases had not been "worth throwing back." He finally consented to a public defender—Matthew Maloney, an attorney certified to handle capital cases, from Princeton, Illinois, northeast of Toulon.

There are people in Toulon—and they do not make themselves loud or visible—who knew another side to Curt Thompson. They speak of a farm boy who lost his father at an early age, who had to work for room and board in grade school, who was bright and well-read and married a lovely woman to whom he stayed married and with whom he produced three children. They know that Thompson will be remembered in Toulon as a monster. They say they will remember more than that.

"Curt was probably born a hundred years too late," says one of Thompson's neighbors. "He butchered his own meat. He lived frugally and was a very intelligent person. He knew the biology of livestock and was well-read in politics and life events. He was very capable. I would have hired the man in an instant if not for his temper."

"If you needed anything, Curt and his wife would come," recalls Mary Jane Swank. "When I came home from the hospital, they fixed us a complete meal, and I mean complete: chicken, pork chops, corn, potatoes, everything. Just a few days before [the shootings], Curt brought us some meat he'd butchered.

"I knew he had problems with people. But if anyone treated him fair, he'd treat you fair back. Curt had so much to give—that's the part that hurts me a lot. If he was treated decent . . . you know how small towns are—they have to pick at somebody and never let up."

"I felt bad for him sometimes," says a friend of Thompson's. "He never drove a fancy truck. A lot of his life was spent not having more than minimum finances. He always had two big black Lab dogs— salivated all over, but very nice, never growled or snapped. He'd bring the dogs along sometimes. About ten years ago, I noticed that he had only one of the dogs. He told me he had to put the other dog to sleep because it had heartworms. I asked if heartworms couldn't be treated. He said, 'Yeah, you can treat it, but I did not have enough money.' You should have seen his face. I thought he was going to cry. To me, it showed that he had a heart like anyone else."

Shortly after Jim and Janet Giesenhagen died, Toulon united to throw several fund-raisers for Ashley. In a candle sale, citizens collected $3,500 for her future education. It had been the kind of gesture instinctive to the town since before Lincoln's speech on the courthouse lawn.

When asked about Thompson, many in Toulon do not want to talk. They are polite about it, all of them. And they are consistent in their reasoning.

"I don't want to think about it," one resident says. "I wish this would all just go away."

A month after the murders, Curt Thompson was taken to the Stark County courthouse to enter pleas in the thirty-count indictment against him. Under heavy guard and wearing an old-fashioned gray-and-white-striped prisoner's jumpsuit, he walked deliberately into the courtroom, making eye contact with no one. Ashley Giesenhagen, seated in the back of the room, began sobbing at the sight of Thompson.

As the prosecutor read the indictment, questions wafted out the open courtroom window, through Toulon's two coffee shops, past Casey's gas station, and into the fields that frame Stark County. Why hadn't the sheriff's dispatcher called an ambulance immediately? Why had a rookie deputy tried on his own to serve a five-month-old warrant on a Friday night to a man known to be violent? Why hadn't law enforcement prosecuted Thompson if he had violated court protective orders? Had police been afraid of Thompson? Had the state's attorney done enough to stop him?

And, most important: Had the beauty of small-town life—that shoulder-to-shoulder proximity to everything and everyone—become its ugly undoing?

Thompson, through his lawyer, pleaded not guilty to all charges. The proceedings lasted about thirty minutes. After he was unshackled from a table, Thompson walked toward the door as he had entered—slowly and without expression. Just before leaving, he turned briefly toward the public who had packed the courtroom, and stared.

———

When word reached Chicago in early 2002 of a triple murder in Toulon, a tiny farming community of 1,400 in rural Illinois, I presumed it to be the usual small-town crime of passion, the kind none of the residents could have imagined a day earlier. Instead, a sheriff's deputy and a husband and wife lay shotgunned to death in an eruption of violence nearly everyone had expected for decades.

It was the decades part of the story that grabbed me. Since Abraham Lincoln had spoken on its courthouse steps, Toulon had survived by caring for its own. Its citizens reacted to—even anticipated—news of sick or bankrupt or suffering neighbors like antibodies in the bloodstream, converging as a whole to attack the problem and heal its kind. The more I learned about the town's history, the deeper I came to understand the place as a self-contained biological entity.

That biology got sick when Curt Thompson came to town. A man with a complex and painful past, Thompson began in the 1970s to feud with town residents, mayors, and police staff, weaving creative terror into vendettas and then nursing them for years. Many who looked into his glaring eyes believed him capable of great violence, even murder. Because Thompson lived among them, too few in Toulon were willing to confront him or to pursue serious legal remedies against him. Many instead chose to avoid him, and in this way the organism that had protected Toulon for so long short-circuited like cells in a cancer-stricken body. Thompson remained a free man for decades. In March 2002, he was charged with a triple murder people both couldn't believe and fully expected.

When I arrived to investigate the story, Thompson was in custody and finally separated from the town he had bullied. He faced the death penalty if convicted. Still, few were willing to speak of him. In a town that still holds candle sales for its needy and food drives for its hungry, many explained that they still feared Thompson, prison cell or not.

THE LAST RIDE OF
JESSE JAMES HOLLYWOOD
JESSE KATZ

The boy in the video is named Jesse James Hollywood. That is what his birth certificate says. He is close to 20 but could pass for 15. His hair is short and blond. His eyes are blue. He is nearly as small—five feet five, 140 pounds—as most of his friends were in junior high school.

Jesse James Hollywood is drinking a Heineken. He is smoking weed from a long yellow bong. He is wearing baggy jeans, a baby blue Dodgers cap turned backward, and a T-shirt manufactured by Serial Killer Inc. The shirt has a black-and-white movie frame on the chest, a scene from *Heat*, the 1995 LA crime saga. It shows Robert De Niro and Val Kilmer making their getaway from a downtown bank heist. The caption is a single word: MONEY.

The music thumping on the stereo is Mac Dre, an Oakland rapper. He once got five years for conspiring to rob a bank. "Life's a Bitch" is the title of the song. When Jesse James Hollywood speaks, he mimics the cadences of the hood, an act that is alternately reverential and derisive. He is pretending to be a Crip—a meticulous study—yet the fakery is spiked with contempt. "One time I was walking down the street, cuz," he says, mugging for the camera. "Some nigga hit me up, cuz. I'm like, 'What up, cuz?' Nigga straight ran my ass over. That's why I'm a little fucked up right now, cuz." When he decides the shtick has grown old, Jesse James Hollywood says, "Get the camera away from me, cuz. Before I have to bust yo' lip, cuz."

The party is in Jesse James Hollywood's home, a three-bed, two-bath staple of 1950s suburbia that he bought on his own. There is a big-screen TV in the living room, along with a wave-shaped bubble lamp and a vase of artificial flowers; the kitchen has a built-in microwave and a double-door refrigerator; a gas barbecue grill sits on the patio. The house is in West Hills, at the far edge of the San Fernando Valley. It is among the whitest corners of Los Angeles — an affluent, educated, conservative bedroom community, once part of Canoga Park until home owners decided that a name change would enhance their neighborhood's image. The pride of West Hills is its youth baseball complex, a collection of mini-stadiums with padded outfield fences and electronic scoreboards, Marathon Sod and crushed-brick base paths. As a child Jesse James Hollywood played on those diamonds. He was an All-Star pitcher and third baseman. His dad was a coach. His mom brought snacks. At least three of his guests here — all drinking beer, smoking dope, taking turns with the camera — played in the same league, some years on the same team. One of them is Ryan Hoyt, a lefty first baseman. He aims the lens into the face of another ex–Little League friend.

"You been drinking tonight?" Ryan asks, in a mock interrogation.

"Fuck the police!" his subject howls.

Ryan follows him with the camera, then breaks into the theme from the TV show COPS: "Bad boys, bad boys, whatcha gonna do?" he sings. "Whatcha gonna do when they come for you?"

The tape is more than an uncensored testament to cocky, middle-class, Valley Boy indulgence. It is evidence in a murder. By this time in his life, Jesse James Hollywood was the boss of a thuggish little drug ring. He trafficked in vacuum-sealed bricks of British Columbian marijuana, a potent strain known as B.C. Bud. His clownish friends were his marketing staff, breaking the pounds into ounces that went for $300 on the street. The arrangement served them all, funding their nightly binges and paying for Jesse James Hollywood's mortgage, except for one problem: His cartel had a habit of smoking more than it sold. Ryan was the worst. His consumption had reduced him from dope dealer to indentured servant. He arrived at Jesse James Hollywood's house every day to clean, garden, paint, and pick up after an ill-mannered pit bull named Chump, yet even after months of menial chores he was unable to erase his pot-smoking debt. At the time of the video he was in for $1,200, and Jesse James Hollywood was not about to let him forget.

"Now how much money you got in your bank?" Jesse James Hollywood asks, cornering Ryan in the kitchen.

"Stop recording," Ryan says.

"How much? How much can you get from the bank?"

"Enough to pay you some money."

"What's gonna be there tomorrow, Hoyt? I'm serious, man. I can see it's gonna be like nothing."

"It's not gonna be nothing."

"What's it gonna be then? Just tell me."

The video was shot in early 2000. Six months later the party would be over, the tape seized by homicide detectives. A drug dispute had gone haywire, and Jesse James Hollywood and his crew were now implicated in the kidnapping and execution of a 15-year-old boy, the younger brother of one of their own henchmen. As a bunch, they might best be described as slackers with an edge, children of relative privilege yet barely functional as adults. They came from nice homes but broken families. They attended the finest schools without opening their eyes. When they lost their way, it had more to do with abundance—too much freedom, too much money, too much time—than with deprivation. Their violence was committed while numb, not in a rage. Part of that was surely the drugs, which turned their world into a full-scale PlayStation, no more real than the lives taken and restored on-screen. But there seemed to be something else going on in West Hills, a malaise born of entitlement, of parents who found it easier to grant independence than to set limits. How does a community without gangs breed an entire team of gangsta disciples? To what extent does living in a "good" area allow a false sense of security, even laziness, to creep into the work of raising kids?

To settle his debt Ryan agreed to be the triggerman. He was found guilty in November and sentenced to die. Three cohorts were accused of abducting the victim and digging his grave. They are being held without bail, awaiting trial. The final defendant is the ringleader himself, the one with the unforgettable name. He is nowhere to be found.

Of all the West Hills stoners selling Jesse James Hollywood's pot, the one least in awe of him, the one most capable of doing him damage, was a neighbor named Benjamin Markowitz. He was in the same baseball league as a child but a couple years older— bigger and badder and just a bit nuttier.

By the time he was 15 Ben had slashed tires, stolen a car, cracked open a boy's forehead with brass knuckles, and done eight months in a juvenile probation camp. His nickname was Bugsy. He had covered himself in tattoos including the insignia of the Peckerwoods, a San Fernando Valley gang with white supremacist leanings—never mind that he was Jewish. His father, who makes aerospace parts in a family-run machine shop, tried everything he could think of to turn Ben around, from psychotherapy to Ritalin to martial arts. He tussled with Ben. He dragged him to work. He paid a tae kwon do instructor to take him in as a ward. "I didn't know what the hell to do," says Jeff Markowitz, who divorced Ben's mother when their son was 4 and assumed custody when he was 12. "Ben was an urban legend in our town."

Remarriage had introduced a stepmother, Susan, and a half brother, Nicholas, seven years younger than Ben. If the Markowitzes had tried to blur those lines of separation in the beginning, they took to drawing them more sharply as Ben careened through adolescence. Susan was especially doting with Nick, hoping to insulate him from his older brother. "My whole life, I was trying to keep Nick from seeing or knowing the truth about Ben's trouble," she says. "It was a lot of work keeping them apart." In the end it was also futile. Nick came to idolize Ben, and Ben somehow managed to keep dragging the family into his craziness, like the time he showed up drunk, with a shaved head, at Nick's bar mitzvah and demanded to drive his brother home in a low-rider Impala.

It would be trite to say that West Hills was too small for both Ben Markowitz and Jesse James Hollywood, but that might not be far from the truth. They lived only a dozen blocks from each other and attended the same prestigious high school, El Camino Real, winner of the state academic decathlon for five of the last ten years. Ben got expelled for hitting a girl who threw a milk carton his way. Jesse got expelled for spewing obscenities at an administrator who objected to the tank top he was wearing. Ben never finished school, but Jesse went on to graduate from Calabasas High in 1998. Compared with Ben—and every other member of his crew, for that matter—Jesse was the model of success, ambitious and status conscious. With five to ten dealers each netting him about $500 to $1,000 a month, Jesse was living on maybe $50,000 a year, tax free—enough for a thick bankroll in his pocket, a girl on his arm, and an endless supply of weed for his friends. He used to show up for school in a tricked-out silver '95 Honda Accord DX coupe, the '57 Chevy of the *Fast and the Furious* generation. Loaded with hydraulic switches, fluorescent lights, $2,000 Niche Gefell rims, and a sound system capable of rattling windows, the car drew envious stares in the student parking lot, even from kids who had no interest in the dope business. By 19 Jesse owned a $205,000 home on Cohasset Street, just a few blocks from his parents'. "He was slinging some spliff," acknowledges his father, Jack Hollywood, employing a Rasta-flavored lexicon somewhat at odds with the image of a Little League coach. "But it wasn't even that much of a bad rhythm. There was no trouble until this Ben Markowitz guy came around."

Like most of the dealers in Jesse's circle, Ben was often careless about money, losing product—or using it—and falling into debt. Unlike them he was a genuine hoodlum, refusing to take orders and damning the consequences. "Ben was a fly in the ointment," says Ken Reinstadler, a Santa Barbara County sheriff's lieutenant, who would later oversee the murder investigation. "Jesse James Hollywood is a wanna-be bad boy. Ben is one tough hombre." During the first half of 2000, the two were locked in a tit-for-tat feud, at once childish and menacing. Ben would get messages on his voice mail: "I thought we were homies. Why don't you come kick it? Let's straighten this thing out." Jesse would also get messages on his voice mail: "I know where you live, too, buddy, so you make the first move." One night in February Jesse and his girlfriend went to a restaurant in Woodland Hills where Ben's girlfriend worked. They ate and drank up a tab of $50, then left a note: "Take this off Ben's debt." Ben upped the ante, threatening to expose a $35,000 insurance scam that involved the customized Honda. Jesse had chopped up the car, sold the parts, then reported it stolen. "This is what Ben's been doing forever—latching onto people, terrorizing them," says Jack Hollywood. "My son was scared to death. He was going to move out and try to get away from the whole situation."

The pissing match came to a head on August 6, 2000, a Sunday. Jesse had packed up his house and put everything in storage. Sometime during the previous day or two, Ben had come over and busted a couple of windows with a metal pipe. Jesse piled his crew into a cargo van, lent to him by a friend of his father's to help with the move. In the driver's seat was Jesse Rugge, a speedy center fielder from their baseball years. After his parents divorced, he split his time between his father's house in Santa Barbara and his mother's in West Hills. A high school dropout, he had a shaved head and a body covered with tattoos—scorpions on both arms, a skull on his right leg, and a simulation of ripped skin, with exposed muscle, on his left—all courtesy of a brother-in-law who works at a parlor called Iron Cross. In the back was William Skidmore, probably the best hitter and fielder of them all. He was living in Simi Valley but grew up in West Hills, halfway between the Rugges and the Hollywoods. The others sometimes called him *vato loco*, a crazy dude—his mother is Latina—and he once told police, after being arrested on a minor drug charge, that his gang name was Capone. But his affiliations, oddly, were Asian; he had the logo of a Filipino gang, Satanas, tattooed across his stomach and chest. Ryan Hoyt stayed behind, ordered to sweep up the broken glass.

They had been planning to go up to Santa Barbara for Old Spanish Days, a Mardi Gras–style festival. But everyone inside the van agreed that Ben's latest incursion could not go ignored. They talked of hunting him down, or maybe just swinging by the Markowitz home and shattering a few panes as payback. As they cruised the quiet, pine-shrouded streets of West Hills, the last thing they expected was to stumble upon Nick Markowitz, wandering past Taxco Trails Park at about 1:00 P.M. Nick was hardly the ruffian that Ben was—he had appeared in Shakespeare plays at school, volunteered as a peer counselor, and once signed a journal entry "Rabbi Nick"—but he was still having his troubles. He was regularly popping Valium and smoking dope. He had already been caught at school with a bit of weed and arrested. On Saturday night he had gone with friends to City Walk and come home looking zonked. This morning, rather than face a confrontation with his parents, Nick had sneaked out while his mom was making breakfast. "He was just picking everything apart," his father says, "the life that he was deciding to choose or not to choose."

The van pulled up to the curb and Jesse's crew jumped out. They pummeled Nick, kicking and hitting, then dragged him inside. As they did, Pauline Ann Mahoney came driving by on her way home from church. Before the van peeled out she got close enough to read the license plate. "All right, boys," she said to the three children in her Cadillac, "this is the number." They chanted it together until Mahoney could get home and dial 911. "These guys were beating the crap out of this kid," she told the emergency operator. "Four versus one. All white." Two Los Angeles police officers were advised, but a series of missteps ended any chance of catching up. The 911 staff, it turned out, had coded the incident as an assault rather than a kidnapping in progress—even after a second witness made a similar call. Thinking the matter was less serious, an officer talked to Mahoney via cell phone but never took a direct statement. They also failed to reach the registered owner of the van, partly because they had misread his address. "This was not the LAPD at its best," says Xavier Hermosillo, a member of the department's Board of Rights, which investigated the lapse. The officers received written reprimands; two emergency dispatchers ended up with three-day suspensions.

It would be the first in a succession of opportunities to halt the crime, opportunities killed by an apathy that seemed to grip everyone who came in contact with Nick. Over the next sixty hours, at least two dozen people would meet him—or learn of his plight—and none would intercede. Jeff and Susan Markowitz would later sue them all, alleging that each could have, and should have, done something to save their son. To be fair, it was not always clear that Nick was a hostage. His captors acted haphazardly, sometimes leaving him unguarded. He went along with their instructions rather good-naturedly, believing that his cooperation would best serve his brother. At times he even romanticized the odyssey. "Don't worry," he said on the rare occasion that anyone expressed concern. "It's just another story to tell my grandkids."

With Nick in the van, Fiesta was pretty much out of the question, but Jesse James Hollywood and his crew drove up to Santa Barbara anyway, not knowing what else to do. On the way, Nick's pager began to beep. His parents had given it to him the previous week, on the condition that he respond immediately when called. Now his mother was punching in their number, over and over. Jesse took it away. "If you run, I'll break your teeth," he said to Nick. Jesse rummaged through Nick's pockets and pulled out several plastic bags of weed and Valium. He let Nick fire up and drop a pill. He also snatched a small address book from him. He ripped out the page with Ben's number and tossed the rest out the window. For all his bluster, Jesse would not call Ben that day, or ever again.

When they got to Santa Barbara, they needed a place to stash Nick. That task fell to Jesse Rugge, the crew's northern connection. He steered them to the home of a friend in the Hidden Valley neighborhood, a guy he often partied with named Ricky Hoeflinger. They herded Nick into Ricky's bedroom, bound his wrists with duct tape, and blindfolded him with a sock. Ricky had a friend over, and he asked what was going on. "Hollywood is tripping out," Rugge explained. It was loud enough for Jesse James Hollywood to overhear. "Keep your fucking mouth shut," he snapped at Rugge. Then he whispered to Ricky's friend, "You don't say shit." Ricky and his friend took off, leaving the kidnappers and their captive alone in his house. "I didn't want to know what was going on," Ricky says. "I didn't want any involvement."

Two guys in the crew also wanted out. One was Will Skidmore; the other was Brian Affronti, whom they had picked up after grabbing Nick. Not wanting to rouse Jesse's suspicions, Brian made up a story about having a date that night back in the Valley. "That way it wouldn't seem like I was just trying to get out of something," he says. Jesse agreed to let them take the van, a concession that ended their role in the crime but not their liability. As one of the abductors, Will was legally responsible for Nick's fate, even if he had no idea what would later happen to him; a plea bargain is being negotiated. Brian, only tacitly involved, was given a grant of immunity, one of ten that prosecutors would hand out in order to piece together events.

Jesse eventually took off, too, though his phone card was used later that night to call Ricky's house, presumably to check on Nick. Freed of his duct tape, Nick was relaxed, maybe even a little tickled to be hanging with his brother's older crowd. He and Rugge took bong hits, sipped Tanqueray gin, and played a James Bond 007 video game, Nick's favorite. His computer screen name was remag—*gamer* spelled backward. "He was the best," says Jeff Markowitz, trying to envision his son at ease. "I'm sure he was beating the pants off every one of those guys."

At the end of the night, Rugge took Nick to his father's place, about a mile away. Barron Rugge manages a biological science greenhouse at UC Santa Barbara. His wife is active in her church, playing guitar and singing hymns on a Christian radio program. They both saw Nick but never questioned why he was spending the night in their home.

The next day, Monday, August 7, brought a new parade of witnesses. Two of them were girls, Natasha Adams-Young, 17, and Kelly Carpenter, 16. They had been hanging out that summer with a 17-year-old boy named Graham Pressley, who was dealing dope for the crew in Santa Barbara. Now they were all at Rugge's house, along with Nick, watching TV, smoking pot, grabbing food from the fridge. "Like everyone was really friendly and the atmosphere wasn't tense at all," Natasha says. "It was mostly light and like fun." She took an interest in Nick. He lied, telling her he was 17, too. After a while they all jumped in Natasha's car and drove to her house. She had learned by then that Nick was not in Santa Barbara by choice. "He told me that it was okay because he was doing it for his brother, and that as long as his brother was okay, he was okay," Natasha says. "He was going along with it." He had a scrape on his arm from the beating, and she brought him rubbing alcohol and ointment. Rugge took off a little bit later, leaving Nick alone with

Natasha, Kelly, and Graham—the only time that none of the original kidnappers was present.

It could be argued that the kidnapping had in fact ended. By every indication, Nick was free to leave. "Frankly, in hindsight, all of us wish and hope he had done something different and just walked away," says Santa Barbara County senior deputy district attorney Ron Zonen, who is prosecuting each of the defendants. He contends, however, that in Nick's mind he was still a hostage. "Being passive," Zonen says, "does not amount to consent."

When Natasha drove everyone back to Rugge's house later that day, essentially returning Nick to his captors, Jesse James Hollywood was waiting. He had introduced yet another person into the mix—a petite party girl named Michele Lasher, who was baring midriff and sitting in his lap. She lived with her parents in a gated community in Calabasas and taught children's gymnastics in Woodland Hills. She also had JESSE JAMES tattooed just above her butt. During the investigation police would have doubts about whether Jesse and Michele were actually there that day; they were never spotted in Santa Barbara again. But Natasha and Kelly were adamant. How could they be so sure? Neither could stop talking about Michele's boob job, reportedly paid for by Jesse. "Very lovely," says Kelly, "but a little unreal."

On Tuesday, August 8—his third day in Santa Barbara—Nick was still at the Rugges'. Of all the people who had seen him, only Natasha seemed to sense that something was wrong or that someone should speak up. She went to her mother, a criminal defense attorney. Natasha left out the names and addresses but explained that she knew of a boy who might be in trouble. Her mother urged her to call the police. Before sounding the alarm, Natasha wanted to be sure that Nick was really in danger. She went to see Graham and asked him to go for a walk in the park. Graham told her not to worry, that Nick would be fine. But he also told her to keep quiet or else they might all end up dead—"because Jesse Hollywood was quote-unquote crazy." Natasha then went to see Rugge. "He looked me in the eye and he swore to me that he was going to take Nick home," she says. Rugge told Nick the same thing, suggesting that he might give him some cash for a bus or a train that evening, but he wanted some assurance: "All I can say is there better not be a policeman coming at my door the next day."

To celebrate Nick's imminent release his keepers decided to rent a motel room and have a pool party. Needing a ride, Graham called his mother, a real estate appraiser. She was on her way to a 5:30 P.M. yoga class but agreed to swing by and pick everyone up. When they got in the car, Graham introduced Nick: "He is staying with Jesse for a few days." Christina Pressley turned to the backseat to get a good look. She was worried about her son's choice of friends, enough so that she had taken Rugge out to lunch a few months earlier, "because he had tattoos on him and my husband and I were concerned about the influence, because our son was coming out of his own rough time." She knew that Graham smoked pot—though she had yet to learn that he was selling it—and she was in the habit of checking for warning signs. "Nice to meet you," she said. "Nice to meet you, too, Mrs. Pressley," Nick said. "Thanks for the ride."

She dropped them off near the Lemon Tree Inn, a mid-range motel on State Street, a good ways up from the tourist strip. For several hours they smoked dope and drank rum and Cokes. Nick even went swimming. The question of escape came up again. "I'm going home," Nick insisted. "Why would I complicate it?"

For three days the Markowitzes had been in a panic, driving the streets of West Hills, tacking up homemade posters, tracking down every friend they could think of. On the third day they formally reported Nick missing to the LAPD. They remembered how, just six months earlier, he had gotten lost riding his bike and had called them in desperation. "He was so relieved to have made it home," his mother says. "He didn't even know where he was around our own neighborhood." She used to sleep on the side of the bed closest to the door so that she could get to Nick's room faster in the event of an earthquake. Now she switched to the side of the bed closest to the window.

Jesse James Hollywood was also worried, afraid to hold on to Nick and afraid to let Nick go. On that same Tuesday, about the time the others were planning their trip to the Lemon Tree, Jesse went to visit his lawyer. Stephen Hogg had been a friend of the Hollywood family for nearly twenty years. He had already represented Jesse on two previous criminal charges, resisting arrest and being a minor in possession of alcohol. While smoking a cigarette on the back patio of Hogg's Simi Valley home, Jesse revealed that some friends were holding a boy hostage. When prosecutors tried to question Hogg about their conversation, he initially refused, citing attorney-client privilege. A judge later ordered him to testify.

"What do I do?" Jesse asked.

"You got to go to the police," Hogg told him.

"I can't."

"Jesse, you have got to."

Jesse asked what kind of trouble his friends might be in.

"If they ask for ransom," Hogg said, "they can get life."

Jesse bolted from the backyard.

Hogg grew worried and began paging him. Jesse never called back. Within an hour, though, Jack Hollywood called Hogg. He was in Big Sur with his estranged wife, Laurie, spending a few days at the Ventana Inn & Spa. Hogg explained the problem. "Get ahold of Jesse," his father said, "and sit on him for me."

Jack Hollywood also asked Hogg to track down John Roberts, another longtime family friend. Roberts was a 68-year-old retired wise guy with a checkered past in Chicago. He also happened to be the owner of the cargo van that had been used in Nick's abduction. "I'm going to go out and find where the child is, and I'm going to do

my Chicago act in front of these twenty-year-old boys," he concluded after speaking with Hogg. He would give the victim some
money to keep his mouth shut. "That's old-fashioned 1950s—you
know what I'm trying to say?—it's old-fashioned gangster talk."
Hogg continued to page Jesse. Before he checked out of the Ventana, Jack Hollywood made a flurry of calls: to Jesse's pager, to
Jesse's cell phone, to Jesse's girlfriend, to Roberts, to Hogg again.
The one call that none of them made was to the police.

Jesse had heard enough. He went to see Ryan Hoyt and asked
him if he wanted to erase his debt. "He said there was a mess that
needed to be cleaned up," Ryan says. "He said I needed to go take
care of somebody." Ryan is tall and lanky, with dark, slicked-back
hair, a heavy brow, and droopy, slightly flushed cheeks. He was the
gang's whipping boy—"the quote-unquote lame guy," his attorney
says—a high school dropout who tried to join the navy but failed
the drug test. His mother has battled mental illness and alcoholism
most of her life. His father, a construction worker, allegedly beat
her. His older sister is a heroin addict. She once dated Ben
Markowitz. His younger brother is doing twelve years for armed
robbery. As a teenager Ryan went searching for a family and found
it among the Hollywoods. He baby-sat Jesse's younger brother. He
helped Jesse's mom clean house. When Jesse bought his own place,
Ryan was there every day, getting high, trying to please. He claims
that his debt to Jesse was down to $200 by the time of the abduc-
tion. If a week were to go by without payment, though, Jesse would
add another $100 in interest to the tab. "That's pretty brutal, I
know," Ryan says. But falling from Jesse's favor was an option Ryan
could not afford. "Imagine how he would treat me if I had told him
to just—excuse my language—fuck off."

Ryan's twenty-first birthday was two days away. To be given the
opportunity to clear his debt before that milestone was a better present than he could have hoped for. Not only would he be free of
Jesse's taunting, but he would be moving up in the hierarchy, hav-

ing been entrusted with an assignment far weightier than beer cans and dog poop. "This could be the change in his lifestyle he was looking for," says Zonen, the prosecutor. "This had a certain feel to it that pleased him."

Jesse gave Ryan a duffel bag. Inside was an assault pistol known as a TEC-DC9, a model whose role in rampages, including the Columbine shooting, has led to numerous lawsuits and legislation. This one had been modified into a fully automatic machine gun capable of spraying twelve rounds a second. About 8:30 P.M. Jesse's phone card was used to make a call to the Lemon Tree. With Ryan on his way, "the thing with Nick is being taken care of," Jesse explained to another friend. His final task involved Michele. She was turning 20 this day. Jesse took her to the Outback Steakhouse in Northridge. It would keep her happy and help with his alibi. Dinner came to $108.98. He put it on his American Express card.

A couple hours later, up at the Lemon Tree, the party was coming to an end. "I'm sorry, ladies, I don't mean to be rude, but you have to leave," Rugge announced shortly before 11:00 P.M. "Someone is going to come and pick up Nick." On the way there, Ryan got lost and had to call for directions. When he arrived, Nick was alone with Rugge and Graham. Up to that point Graham's role had been minimal; Ryan had never even met him before. Now he guided Ryan out Highway 154, up through the San Marcos Pass, to West Camino Cielo, a single-lane road that winds along the crest of the Santa Ynez Mountains. It is a fifteen-mile drive, spectacular by day, precarious at night. They pulled over and began hiking through the brush. After a hundred yards or so they came upon a boulder with a large gap in its center, known to Santa Barbara teenagers as Lizard's Mouth. Graham began digging with a shovel. He would later tell police that Ryan was aiming the TEC-DC9 at him, saying, "You'll dig if you know what's good for you." Ryan denies ever threatening Graham: "I didn't have to." The ground was dense and rocky. The grave was only a foot or two deep.

They drove back to the Lemon Tree and picked up Rugge and Nick. It was sometime after midnight, the early hours of August 9. They retraced the route to Lizard's Mouth. Graham stayed in the car while Ryan and Rugge marched Nick up to the boulder. When Nick saw the gun, did he at last understand what was happening — or did he think they were merely trying to scare him? When they duct-taped his mouth, and his hands behind him, did he tell them that it was unnecessary, that he was still going along with their game? Detectives would later ask Ryan about that moment, if it haunted him, if he woke up at night thinking about someone saying "please"? Ryan sighed. "You don't even want to know that one," he said.

Ryan whacked Nick's head with a shovel, then pushed him into the grave. He aimed the gun and, with a single squeeze of the trigger, sprayed nine bullets — a fusillade that stopped only because the weapon jammed. The shots hit Nick in the stomach, chest, neck, and chin. Most of them ripped through his insides and out his back. Ryan slipped the gun under Nick's legs. They tried covering him with dirt, but the hole was too shallow. They piled branches on top. Rugge vomited. Ryan, for the moment at least, seemed pleased with his handiwork. "That's the first time I ever did anybody," he said, back in the car. "I didn't know he would go that quick."

In the days that followed, everyone in Jesse James Hollywood's crew lied — to their parents, to their friends, to each other, to themselves.

They dropped off Graham at the Lemon Tree and told him to check out in the morning. His curfew was normally 11:00 P.M., but his mother had fallen asleep, not realizing that he had been out all night until he called, at 6:00 A.M., asking for a ride home. "I asked him why he looked so pale — was he all right?" Christina Pressley says. "He said he didn't feel very well and that he didn't sleep much. He was clearly sick or shaken or something was very wrong." When he got home, Graham called Natasha and told her that he had given Nick a ride back to the San Fernando Valley. Natasha was relieved and told her mom that everything had turned out okay.

Ryan drove down to West Hills. Jesse gave him $400. Ryan went shopping for new clothes at the 118 Board Shop, a skate- and snowboard store in Granada Hills. Most days for him were a blur of brew and weed, but the next, August 10, was even foggier. "Mass consumption," says Ryan, who was drinking, smoking, snorting lines, and popping muscle relaxants. "It was my birthday, my twenty-first birthday." Most of the crew partied that night at the home of Casey Sheehan, another West Hills baseball alumnus who had once sold dope for Jesse. In his stupor Ryan confessed. "He didn't show me that much emotion as far as, you know, like he had a lot of guilt on his conscience or anything like that, so I was still in disbelief about what had happened, what he had said to me," Casey says. It was Casey's car that Ryan had driven to Santa Barbara, and Casey was concerned enough to confront Jesse, who was also celebrating that night. "Just don't worry about it," Jesse told him.

The party might have gone on indefinitely had the killers only been more prudent in their disposal of the victim. Lizard's Mouth may have seemed remote at two in the morning after a night of bong hits, but the grave was right in the middle of a trail—surrounded by graffiti, broken beer bottles, and the remnants of bonfires. That Saturday, August 12, three days after Nick's murder, a group of hikers discovered the spot, alerted by the smell and the swarm of flies. They thought a dead animal was under the branches. When they saw a bloodied pant leg, they called the police. The summer heat had done terrible things to Nick's body. His eyes and nose and wounds were filled with larvae. It took Santa Barbara County homicide detectives two days to identify him; a badly decomposed fingerprint matched the arrest record from the time Nick was busted with pot.

On Monday, August 14, detectives drove down to West Hills. They pulled up to the Markowitz home at 6:30 A.M. Susan was in bed. Jeff peeked out the window and told her that men in black suits were at the door. She knew Nick was dead.

The next day, August 15, the story was in the papers. It was accompanied by a photo of Nick at his bar mitzvah, in a white tuxedo and black bow tie. Natasha looked at the *Santa Barbara News-Press* that morning and saw him, the sweet, funny, gangly boy she had worried about the week before. She collapsed in tears. She called Jesse Rugge. "It's not what you think," Rugge told her. She headed to his house. He was not wearing a shirt. "I could see his heart beating through his chest," Natasha says. She went to her mom's law office and talked to an attorney, who arranged for a grant of immunity. By 4:00 P.M. she was sitting with detectives, spilling the entire story, this time with names and addresses.

Jesse Rugge was arrested early on the morning of the sixteenth, followed by Graham Pressley, Will Skidmore, and by the end of the day, Ryan Hoyt. They talked, implicating themselves and each other. From jail Ryan called his mother, Victoria Hoyt, a conversation that authorities recorded and later played at his trial. With her voice wavering between a growl and a whimper she pressured Ryan into talking to detectives without an attorney, never pausing to think that he might be guilty.

"Ryan, Ryan, you are innocent, you are so innocent," she said. "You are guilty by association."

"I know," he said.

"Who did this? You tell them right now!"

"I don't know."

"Where is Jesse? Where the fuck is he?"

"I don't know."

"Then find him! Spill your fucking guts and get out now! Do it for me, do it for your family, do it for yourself. Tell them what you know. Ryan, you tell them now! You fucking asshole. Don't defend anybody. This is your life."

Then she recited the Lord's Prayer.

After hanging up, Ryan called a guard and said he wanted to speak to somebody about the crime. He was brought to an interview room equipped with a hidden camera and a microphone. He was wearing an orange jailhouse jumpsuit, slumped in a chair, rubbing his forehead. Two detectives arrived and asked him what he wanted to talk about. "If I talk, does it get said in court that I said it?" Ryan asked.

He would later claim to remember none of what he said, but jurors would get to see and hear him for themselves. He began to recount the story of the murder, hoping to minimize his involvement at every possible juncture. "What Ben owed Jesse didn't, in my opinion—I'm going to say this off the record—in my opinion, didn't justify this kid's death," Ryan said. He made it clear that he had nothing to do with the kidnapping. He was also offended by reports that he had dug Nick's grave. "I feel like I've been shit on, excuse my language." When he was told that the other defendants were ratting him out, saying he had put the duct tape on Nick, Ryan was indignant. "Really?" he said. "I love this one."

There was one matter he wanted to set straight: "The only thing I did was kill him."

While the rest were blurting out confessions, proving themselves to be as detached from their own interests as they were from Nick's, Jesse James Hollywood was demonstrating a slyness that would confound just about everyone.

That is not to say that Jesse was discreet. He had always had a flamboyance about him, a compulsion to live out the mythology of the dope man—the pimp, the playa, the mac daddy—to a degree that exceeded the fantasies of most suburban kids. Jesse's favorite alias, Sean Michaels, is the name of an African American porn star who sells replicas of his genitalia on the Internet for $69. When

Jesse's ghetto-fabulous "Hollywood Honda" ended up in the fall 1999 edition of *Lowrider Euro*, under the headline RIDING OFF INTO THE SUNSET WITH JESSE JAMES' WILD RIDE, it was only because he had mailed photos of it to the magazine's editor. "I never thought that I would take it to this level," Jesse says in the article, referring to his investment in the car. "I guess I got addicted to it." But if Jesse was obsessed with projecting an image that few five-foot-five, 140-pound white boys can command, he at least understood the game he was playing better than any of the lost souls in his crew.

In the days after the murder he began collecting on old debts. Brian Affronti, one of the boys who had driven the van back from Santa Barbara, owed him $4,000. He was also storing a shotgun for Jesse, wrapped in a sleeping bag. Brian was not home when Jesse came for the money but had told him where it was hidden—and instructed him to pick up the sleeping bag while he was at it. "That way it wouldn't look odd to my parents," Brian says. Now driving a leased Lincoln LS, Jesse headed to Palm Springs, where Michele was attending a modeling convention. He drained $24,000 from his bank account, and they took off for Las Vegas. Jesse checked them into the Bellagio, a place that could not possibly have more security cameras. This time he paid cash.

The day Nick's body was identified in the newspapers, Jack Hollywood was stunned. Ever since he learned of the abduction, he had been pressing Jesse for answers but getting no response. He paged his son. Jesse finally called back to say that he was on his way to Colorado, where the family had lived for a few years in the mid-1990s. His father called Richard Dispenza, a 48-year-old assistant football coach at Woodland Park High School in Colorado Springs. Dispenza was Jesse's godfather. "I think my kid is in some kind of trouble, and I'm not sure, you know, how involved he is or what's going on, but the last I heard he was headed that way," Jack Hollywood told him. On the day of the arrests Jesse and Michele stayed with Dispenza. Then Michele caught a flight back to LA, and Dispenza checked Jesse into a Ramada Inn. When Santa Barbara County detectives interviewed Dispenza the next day, Jesse was still at the motel. Dispenza had just been named his school's Teacher of the Year. He was the founder of an antismoking group called Tobacco-Free Teens. If he had wanted to, he could have ended the manhunt right then. But he lied. A judge later sentenced him to three years' probation and 480 hours of community service for harboring a fugitive.

Jesse left the motel on August 20. He had abandoned the Lincoln at Dispenza's house, along with a twelve-gauge shotgun and an AR-15 assault rifle. He walked to the home of Chas Saulsbury, a friend from his early teens whom he had not spoken to in years. Jesse told Chas's mom that he had been pickpocketed in Vegas. Chas agreed to give Jesse a ride back there. Jesse paid for everything out of a plastic bag full of $100 bills. In Vegas he convinced Chas to take him all the way to LA, and during the drive he told Chas the whole story, saying they had snatched Nick to get back at Ben. "But, pretty much, like he said, they made a mistake grabbing him, and once they had him they kind of were just a little bit scared to let him go," Chas says. Only after consulting with his attorney did Jesse decide to cut his losses. "He talked to his lawyer to find out the implications of the kidnapping and whatnot, and at that point, from what he told me, the lawyer says that he was in enough trouble already and they should get rid of the kid."

By the time they reached West Hills, Chas was spooked. Jesse wanted to visit John Roberts. "Old John," as he is known to the Hollywoods, was watching a baseball game—one that he had made a little wager on—when he noticed Jesse standing at the screen door. "I got up and went to the door and grabbed him, pulled him into the house and shut the door, and it was a very emotional meeting, both of us," he says. Roberts had already taken it upon himself to have the van washed and wiped with solvent, hoping to erase any evidence of Jesse's role in the abduction. But when Jesse asked for a fake ID, Roberts says he balked. "I knew people that used to do it, I knew people in Chicago that do it, but I couldn't do it and I couldn't give him any money and he could not stay at my house." A week later Santa Barbara County sheriff's investigators showed up to serve a search warrant and thought they heard voices inside. When nobody came out, they called in a SWAT team. Roberts finally emerged, saying he had been asleep. Officers still bombarded the house with tear gas but found no sign of Jesse.

That was a year and a half ago.

Today Jesse James Hollywood is on the FBI's Most Wanted List. The bureau's website features eight color photos of him. Agents even took the unusual step of hosting an Internet chat, hoping to generate tips. He has been profiled three times on *Unsolved Mysteries*, and four times on *America's Most Wanted*. The reward for his capture stands at $50,000, of which $30,000 is being offered by the Markowitzes; if he surrenders voluntarily, they have pledged to put their share in a college fund for his 12-year-old brother. Yet for all of Jesse James Hollywood's splashiness, his posturing, his arrogance, and his youth, there has not been another verified sighting—no leads, no arrests.

Jesse, in fact, is just about the only person tied to the case who has shown any initiative or moxie. Nearly everyone else who played a role in the crime or watched it unfold was hobbled by a kind of nonchalance, impassively going along with things—from the killers to the witnesses to, sadly, the victim himself. Most of them were stoned, which is not that unusual; half of all U.S. high school seniors have at some time smoked pot. This group's pot smoking, however, was not merely excessive. Whether cause or effect, a stultifying moral indifference infected their partying; they stumbled through the ordeal with the vacancy of their video games, bereft of judgment or consequence. Even Natasha—the story's heroine, to the extent that one exists—deluded herself into thinking that things were not how they appeared. "It didn't really seem real," she says in perfect teenspeak. The parents who wandered in and out of the picture also missed signals. So many of them saw only what they wanted to see, never asking the inconvenient questions that might expose the lie.

Jesse's situation was different. He enjoyed not only a level of drive and talent that eluded the others but also a degree of support from his parents—especially his father—that set him apart. Far from being removed, much less disapproving, Jack Hollywood was Jesse's role model. "It's just that the father is much more sophisticated, savvy, low-profile, and seemingly has much better judgment than his son," says Bruce Correll, chief deputy of the Santa Barbara County sheriff's department. For the past two decades, according to authorities, Jesse's dad has been a large-scale San Fernando Valley marijuana trafficker—a pleasant, unassuming wholesaler who uses his love for baseball as cover. "Jack Hollywood is a mobster," Zonen, the prosecutor, has said in court, contending that Jesse was successful "because he went into the family business." Ben Markowitz has testified that Jesse got dope from his father. John Roberts also has testified that he and Jesse's father "were involved together at one time, some time ago. But may I say, never in conjunction, never in conjunction with Jesse, ever." During a search of Jack Hollywood's residence, officers seized tax documents, check stubs, and mortgage statements, along with several small bags of marijuana and a cardboard box containing $7,600 in cash, but have yet to file charges. "They don't charge me with anything," Jack Hollywood says, "so how can I prove I'm innocent?"

Unlike Jesse, who flouted the taboos of the suburbs, his dad knew how to blend into West Hills. At one point he opened a baseball-card shop. At another he ran a car-wholesaling business, advertising in Jesse's Little League yearbooks. His passion for the sport puts a new twist on the old Yogi Berra quip, a saying featured on the West Hills baseball website: "Little League baseball is a very good thing because it keeps the parents off the street." The case against Jack

Hollywood has yet to be proved, but prosecutors and detectives believe it will eventually explain everything about Jesse—why he was able to manipulate his cohorts so effectively and, more important, how he has managed to survive so long on the lam. They believe that his father knows where Jesse is hiding and is using his own underworld connections to keep him there. In the beginning Jesse did what most novice fugitives do, visiting familiar people and places, flashing cash, discussing the crime. Once he returned to West Hills, though, he vanished.

"That's Jack Hollywood's personality taking control," Chief Deputy Correll says. "If he had not taken control, Jesse would be in jail right now."

In the time that Jesse James Hollywood has been missing, Jeff and Susan Markowitz have transformed their home into a shrine. The relics of Nick's life are everywhere: baby handprints, stuffed animals, the decoration from his first birthday cake—and his second and third and fourth and fifth—a karate robe, the cast from a broken right foot, an ornamental egg filled with soil from his grave. Susan has tried to console herself by writing poems, their titles blunt and raw: "Denial," "Fading," "Drifting," "What Day Is This?" The screensaver on her computer is a picture of Nick's marble headstone. Her e-mail address is aching4nick.

Evidence of Ben's life is scarcer. Four months after the murder he was arrested on a pair of armed robbery warrants. The cases were weak—one victim was a druggie; the other, a reputed prostitute, accompanied him to a strip joint and a cheap motel—but Ben still drew a sixteen-month prison term. Susan could not forgive his lack of repentance. "He's rubbing his brother's name in the dirt," she says.

When Susan talks, she seems to be floating. She wants to die.

Inside, she says, she already has. Twice she has been hospitalized, after overdosing on a combination of sleeping pills and champagne. Instead of finding peace she managed only to rack up $20,000 in medical bills. She made it through the first trial by taking Nick's leather jacket to court, clutching it as his final hours were relived. She has vowed to stay alive long enough to see that all of his accused killers are brought to justice—and that includes Jesse James Hollywood, if and when he is captured. She does not know how long that will be. But she knows it will fulfill her last obligation as a mother.

———

That name. It was almost too good to be true. I would hesitate to call it a predictor of destiny. On the other hand, when you christen your son Jesse James Hollywood, the chances of him growing up to be a cer-tified public accountant seem rather slim. In reporting this story, one of my first missions was to visit the Los Angeles county registrar-recorder's office. I wanted to view his birth certificate. I had to know whether that whole trifurcated business—a name so much greater than the sum of its parts—was genuine, not a nickname, a gang name, a stage name, or some other self-mythologizing moniker. To be fair, the Hollywood part was unavoidable; it is the family appella-tion. The Jesse part (and here I must admit to some bias) is a perfectly fine Old Testament echo. But to deliberately sandwich them around James—to brand a newborn with such a theatrically infamous iden-tity—now that made me wonder: What the hell were his parents thinking?

Although this article was ostensibly about a group of bored middle-class young people in the San Fernando Valley and their murderous exploits, it was at its heart about parents. Parents who offered too lit-tle guidance or the wrong kind of guidance, floating in and out of their children's lives like ghosts. It would be foolish to say that Jesse

James Hollywood would have followed the straight and narrow if his folks had just called him Mortimer. But there is no question that bearing all three of those names made him an especially attractive subject for a *Los Angeles Magazine* crime story. We put him on the cover of our February 2002 issue. "WANTED," the headline read, "JESSE JAMES HOLLYWOOD." *True to his name, he remains on the run.*

MY UNDERTAKER, MY PIMP

JAY KIRK

For a year I worked in an office where I spoke to dying people on the telephone every day. The office was that of a funeral-consumer watchdog, which meant that we kept an eye on the funeral industry and helped the imminently bereaved and imminently deceased to make affordable funeral plans. Above my desk I kept an index card with a Faulkner quotation, "Between grief and nothing I will take grief." On a particularly bad day I scratched out the last word and changed it to "nothing."

Because I am a person who has obsessively meditated on his own death since the age of 5, my friends and family thought it uncanny, if not alarming, that I had taken the job. When I was 6 my parents were worried enough that my father, a minister, took me to funerals, thinking (reasonably) that my trouble was all in my mind and that a swift dose of reality might cure me. What my father did not understand was that no matter how assuringly he winked at me over the bowed heads, death is ultimately a problem of the imagination. The funerals only gave mine dark fodder.

As did, inevitably, the job that put me on the phone with death every day. When I found myself flirting with a terminally ill 22-year-old girl, I knew it was time to "move on." On my last day, my coworkers gave me a cardboard coffin, which they had all signed, like a giant crematable birthday card. I absconded with two numbers: the girl's (I wanted to meet her in person—to sleep with a dying girl, I think—and from our conversations it seemed mutual, but it never happened, I never called, and then she died) and that of an Oregon undertaker who, after some controversy with his mortuary board, had fled the state and opened a brothel. The man's name is Mack Moore, and the brothel, in Beatty, Nevada, is called Angel's Ladies. Because this man had made what I saw as the happy leap from Thanatos to Eros, I knew that I had to seek him out. He was older than I expected—71—but when he shook my hand, in the driveway of his Las Vegas mansion, what struck me were the lustrous strawberry-blond curls that fell like a halo around his ears.

The eponymous Angel, Mack's wife, helped Mack and me pack my trunk with whorehouse provisions—laundry detergent, toilet paper, tubs of mayonnaise, hot cocoa—before we set out on the 120-mile drive to Beatty. Angel stayed behind to tidy up, since the police had returned their confiscated belongings just a week earlier and the house was still a disaster. I was soon to hear much about the night that Angel had been held hostage in her living room while the cops looked for evidence of illegal "outcalls."

The elderly pimp shuttles back and forth between his Vegas mansion and the desert brothel a few times a week. The lonesomeness of the drive is total and exhilarating: a haunting landscape of gray-green sagebrush broken here and there by a streak of martian red, a rumpled mountain range, a demonic cactus. In almost two hours the only blips of civilization are the town of Amargosa Valley (Mack points out and curses the Cherry Patch 2 bordello, a rival), a New Age temple, and the south entrance to the Nevada Test Site.

Beatty, in Nye County, is the last town to survive from among the many that popped up during the 1904 Rhyolite gold rush. Now Rhyolite, once the fourth largest city in Nevada, is a ghost town, and Beatty is the place where you had better stop to buy gas. The Bullfrog Mine, the major employer until central banks across Europe released large parts of their gold reserves into the market, shut down in 1998 and is now down to a skeleton crew doing mop-up; Beatty's population has dwindled severely as a result. The economy is sporadic, and stability is as fleeting as it was for the nomadic Shoshone, who summered on the oasis. Other jobs are scarce to nonexistent. Even the Nevada Test Site, despite being literally just over the hill, provides only a handful of jobs to the few willing to commute—the nearest gates are 103 miles north and 54 miles south. The Yucca Mountain Project, a planned federal graveyard for 77,000 tons of high-level radioactive decay, offers possible hope for the future, but it's less than certain, and even if it flies, it won't guarantee jobs for Beatty. For now, the town survives on tourism: Death Valley hikers, truckers, gamblers, and men visiting Angel's Ladies.

The prostitutes settled this area with the miners. Only the former remain in business. The only other trace of the miners are the wild burros that roam the town like dust-shrouded ghosts. Mack says that if some people get their way and Angel's is closed, the town will suffer badly, and it's probably true. The Beatty Chamber of Commerce is one of the brothel's greatest boosters.

Mack wears thick-soled Adidas tennis shoes with ankle socks and a powder-blue cardigan, and as he rambles on in his puttering unpunctuated way, every so often his eyes get flirty, like he's going to share something extremely funny or something deep and meaningful, but each time he tries to address the sex-death continuum, or answer my timid, oblique questions to that end, he veers into the sententious whey of condolence cards.

The first time I called he answered from his shower and let me know, over vigorous lathering, that his brothel had been suspended because of a sting coming out of a conspiracy involving the sheriff, a rival brothel owner, a former madam, and maybe even the assistant DA; that he was going to sue the shit out of Nye County for violating his civil rights; that he took Viagra; that he and his wife were swingers; and that when I came to visit he would put me up in the Fantasy Bungalow. Most of the drive he talked about which swinging magazines are best for meeting other swingers and how since Angel was so much younger and prettier than he, she got more dates than he did, but by the way he told me this, I was led to believe that it was probably the other way around, that he was the Lothario, something later confirmed unenthusiastically by the girls who make up Angel's staff. Despite his candor about his sex life, the circumstances surrounding his abrupt exit from the funeral trade remain hazy. There is ample stuff for nightmares, if you believe all the accusations: The matter of a missing corpse. Bodies buried in the wrong graves. Bodies exhumed on the sly. Bodies cremated in parties of two. Between 1992 and 1994 alone, eighteen complaints were filed against Moore with the Oregon Cemetery and Mortuary Board. But, thanks to the state's confidentiality laws, the board's investigative records are sealed, and I'm left without a full grasp of the mystery behind the man with whom I'm now zooming into the heart of nowhere.

Mack started out selling headstones to put himself through Bible college, but when Oregon cemeteries colluded to require that markers be purchased directly from them, driving out the independent monument dealers, he was nearly put out of business. Fighting mad, Mack became a spectacle, getting dragged out of more than one cemetery in handcuffs for barging in with wheelbarrow and spade to plant a rebel headstone. Fourteen years, three trials, and three appeals after he filed a lawsuit against the cemeteries in 1969, the exclusive installation requirement was ruled a violation of the Sherman Anti-Trust Act; Mack took over four of the defendants' cemeteries—financially weakened by the judgment—built more funeral homes, and began his necropolitan reign over Lane County. He promptly made new enemies of rival funeral directors, who bristled at his aggressive salesmanship—full-page color ads of caskets, coupons, raffles, cut-rate burials—ploys, they felt, more suitable for selling box springs. One Christmas he advertised a special "Holiday Memorial Service," promising a special appearance by Santa Claus, who, "in person, will tell how he remembers his wife who died of cancer."

Soon after Angel was hired as a janitor (she quickly worked her way up to hairdresser, and, according to Mack, did a lovely job with the women's hair), her youngest son was killed in a motorbike accident. Mack embalmed the boy. Not a year later, Angel's husband died. Mack did that funeral, too. Mack's wife and business partner, Eva, grew suspicious of his relationship with his widowed employee, but he denied any hanky-panky: "I never got involved with any woman that I'd served as a funeral director. But it was not because I didn't have the chance." After Eva divorced Mack and they divided the properties—making them, in essence, competitors—he tacked an addition onto one of his parlors, rechristened it Celestial Funeral Home and Wedding Chapel, and invited the entire town to his and Angel's wedding. Because of her tragic losses, Mack says, Angel made an excellent funeral professional. It is the same compassion for human frailty, Mack says, that's made her such a damn good prostitute—but that's rushing ahead.

The odd rivalry with Eva came to a head, gruesomely, in late August 1993, when a man died who had prearranged for his funeral at Chapel of Memories (owned by Eva) but who had bought a cemetery plot at Springfield Memorial Gardens (owned by Mack). His body was taken to Eva's. The man's stepson went to Mack's, understandably confused. Mack, with mattress-salesman finesse, persuaded the stepson that since his father was going to be buried at Mack's cemetery *anyway*, it might be easier, less *grief*, not to mention cheaper, because, well, Mack was prepared to give him a great deal, if he just let Mack do the burial *and* the funeral. All he'd have to do is sign the transfer and Mack would go over to Eva's and get his stepdaddy. The stepson was persuaded. Unfortunately for Mack, Eva had dumped the body in the casket, wearing nothing but diapers, covered in its own postmortem foulness. "We worked on that damn casket for hours trying to get the damn stink out," Mack says. Some time during the mayhem, no doubt perturbed, probably thinking that his wife had done this to him on purpose—"she did dirty"—Mack took color photos of the soiled dead man and showed them to the stepson, suggesting he file a complaint against Eva. The stepson was not pleased, and the family took both Moores to court for $7 million. Eva was eventually dropped from the suit, and Mack settled for $21,000. By this point, however, the mortuary board was fed up and proposed suspending Mack's license for illegally soliciting bodies from a rival funeral home. This was, after all, not the first time.

Then Angel's eldest son, Jesse, died from drug abuse. The boy and his father had allegedly argued about who had the worse kidneys; it's not clear that the father won by dying first, since Jesse died just a week short of his thirtieth birthday. For Angel, it was a world-ending blow.

Given their troubles, leaving was an easy decision. In October 1995, Mack sold to a corporate funeral home, and by March 1996 he and Angel had moved to Vegas. Then they bought the brothel, and Angel, vanquished by grief, registered as a legal prostitute.

Mack has since found new loopholes to finger, and the Nevada Brothel Owners Association has castigated him for jeopardizing an industry that likes to keep as low a profile as the funeral trade. The director of the association, George Flint, says that Mack has "turned what is a fairly halfway respected industry into a kind of farce." Angel's Ladies was busted in the spring of 1999 after sending their blondest girl, Cindi, to a motel when a cop, posing as a trick, called for room service. (Prostitution is only legal in Nevada *inside* a licensed brothel.) It took three calls for the cop to persuade the madam, Wanda Towns, but Wanda and her husband, Clint, who works as a security guard at Angel's Ladies and who drove Cindi to the motel, were arrested and convicted with Cindi for attempting to solicit an illegal outcall. Mack argues that Cindi was just going to "dance" for the man, that it was just an "escort" date, a distinction not made by the Nye County brothel ordinance. A month later the county sheriff's office simultaneously raided the brothel and the Moores' Vegas home. Evidence showed a history of outcalls, and the county commissioners shut down the brothel for two weeks, but an appeals judge later ruled entrapment, reversed the convictions, and ordered the Moores' belongings returned. Still, a gross misdemeanor charge of conspiracy to engage in illegal prostitution looms over the Townses and Cindi, pending a possible settlement with the county. But with Mack blaming everyone for being part of a conspiracy and threatening to sue the county for violating his civil rights (holding Angel hostage, depriving Clint, who has asbestosis, of his oxygen, refusing to return important personal documents), and the county dredging up new pandering charges (trafficking girls to Vegas), the fight will likely drag on until both sides run out of steam. On the other hand, if Mack makes good on his threat to sue the county and wins, he may expand his business. There's a vacant building across from the Burro Inn and Casino that he's thinking about buying and turning into a funeral parlor.

Mack walks the line of the law as deftly as he walks the line between grief and lust. How very blurry that line is in a free-market culture that survives on the myopic propaganda of manufactured need, in which need is predicated on fear of loss, fear of not having; in which images of grief are routinely brought into focus as images of desire. Between grief and nothing, nothing sells better than grief. Except maybe pussy.

We pull around the side of the brothel, a compound of linked trailers painted antacid pink. Electric angels dance over the front porch of the double-wide. "That's Shanda," Mack says before we get out of the car. "She is a bubbling-over girl. So is Cindi. Those two girls will kill you off." Shanda, in a bowler and a pajama top unbuttoned to the navel, is ankle deep in cats; she ministers to one with an eye-dropper. Thirty or forty surround her like pigeons. She drops the kitten and greets me with a chipper Texan drawl. Two litters of the feral cats were born this week; their eyes are weepy and shuttered. Shanda helps Mack and me unload my car. We can't help but toe mewling cats out of our path to the brothel.

Dinner is already on the table, waiting (Mack called from twenty miles back to let them know to set an extra plate for me). Wanda takes off an oven mitt to greet me and then runs to the kitchen for a last-minute dish. Mack sits at the head of the table; at the other end sits Clint Towns, who watches the news, an oxygen tube strapped under his nose. Cindi is a jittery blond in a red leather jacket. Diane tells me that if I want a good story then I should ask her about the time she and her daughter got lost in the Sahara and her daughter ran out of Kool-Aid and they were saved by a mysterious being.

On the counter is a row of egg timers, each with a girl's name. Angel's has a license for five girls but employs eight, so they work in shifts. Angel, out of compassion and pity, has been known to take on men that the other girls refuse, and for less money. The dining room doubles as the madam's office, with phones, a copier, and a status board on the wall. The board says in green Magic Marker that Coco, Cajun, Dizyre, and Mia are "off property." A joke traffic sign by the door says, "Parking for L♥vers Only, All Others Will Be Towed." On the wall between the TV room and dining room is an authentic Old West wood placard:

> Why Walk Around Half Dead When
> We Can Bury You
> For Only $22.00
> We Use Choice Pine Coffins (Select
> Pine from Mexico)

Our New Burial Coach — Finest in the
Arizona Territory
TOMBSTONE UNDERTAKERS

Mack lets me know that they pray before meals. He takes my hand, and I take Shanda's, to my left. During his prayer, Mack caresses my hand with his thumb, not in a kinky way but in the same way my mother does during her blessing over Thanksgiving dinner, describing the same rosette with her thumb. Unlike most Nevada whorehouses, Angel's Ladies does not have a bar. Mack does not drink or smoke or gamble. He and Angel are born-again, and Angel's is the closest thing anyone is going to get to a Christian brothel. They like to say that they "live the example." Why not? The ancients lived happily for millennia with the paradox of temple prostitution. A timer goes off and we are presently joined by Nikki, wearing a peignoir, looking freshly showered. Wanda asks if her "guy" doesn't want to join us, and she murmurs that no, he does not. The other women look her over and then pass the casserole.

Because we are allegedly across the street from Area 51, I broach the subject of UFOs. Instant hit. Everyone at the table, except Mack, has had a sighting. Twice since she's been here, Wanda has seen lights above the ridge over Area 51. The second time was with a trick. He'd just buzzed and she was opening the front door. It was a brilliant yellow flare, almost gold. Clint, who worked for the government, has seen stuff, too. Diane has had the most sightings. She is writing a book, she says, called *The Hooker and the Aliens*. Mack gets irritated with the bunkum and pulls the dessert, a pan of chocolate-frosted cake, his way. He cuts two bricks and serves me one. He takes a bite and then asks, sternly, "You like yella cake?" I say that yeah, I like yella cake. "Me too," he says. Then there's a buzz and the girls scurry. Mack excuses himself.

The girls keep out of sight till called to the front parlor for the lineup. Peeking around the corner, I can't see much more than the visitor's shoes on the pink carpet. When we overhear the trick tell Mack that on his way over tonight he saw eight cop cars outside the Exchange Club, one of the three casino hotels in town, Wanda looks shaken. Mack sits on the couch, ankle crossed over his knee, wooing the man in his warm, unforced voice, telling him what a fine selection of ladies he has to choose from, how this place is different from other brothels: The others will rush you, the others are just in it for the money, the others aren't Christian, but here there's free pop and free coffee and seventy-seven acres to take a moonlight stroll or take a girl for a skinny-dip in the natural spring-fed pool. Hell, one former girl, Jennifer—"she had these great big natural titties"—ended up *marrying* a trick; that's right, dreams do come true. Hell, Mack had the honor of giving her away at the chapel in Reno, and after you've gruntled yourself with sex every which way you ever wanted, if you're hungry, why, feel free to join us for supper, there's still some on the table now.

During the lineup, Wanda clears dishes and I flick crumbs, lulled by the mechanical sips of Clint's oxygen. Wanda joins me with a cup of tea. She wears green satin pajamas. She is not a glamorous or gaudy madam. The Townses went to the Beatty Community Church until the pastor, Reverend Jeff Taguchi—also the owner of the one-hour Photostop and, ironically, a county commissioner on the brothel licensing board—exhorted the couple one Sunday after their arrests to "go forth and sin no more." Wanda holds her husband's hand on the table. She is terrified that Clint, who's dying of the same thing that Shanda claims is taking the kittens, could go to jail. They're holding their breath till the trial; it's been postponed twice already. She never sent a girl on an outcall before that night, she says. They only did it because the detective lied and said he was in a wheelchair. Her son, actually both her children, are wheelchair bound. She gets up and brings me a picture: a kid with long greasy hair, in a wheelchair. Diane enters the room, naked but for a black gauzy body stocking that smooshes her nipples. She drops $600 on the table and says the guy wants two and a half hours. While Wanda "books" the cash, Diane tells me that if I want, later, she'll let me read a chapter from her book. Then Wanda sets a timer, and Diane leaves.

After a trick chooses which girl he wants from the lineup, the price negotiation is done privately in the girl's room. (Each girl's room is supposed to have a panic button.) Wanda listens in over an intercom hidden in the spice cabinet. Each woman is an independent contractor who sets her own price, generally $200 to $400 an hour; 45 percent goes to the house. Each sex act is negotiated and priced separately—done piecework, à la carte. Or, as Lora Shaner, a former madam, puts it in her book, *Madam: Chronicles of a Nevada Cathouse*, "You want to play with my tits? That's an extra fifty. Suck my nipples? Seventy-five more. Nibble my toes? Forty bucks. . . ." Funeral expenses, as mandated by the Federal Trade Commission funeral rule, are similarly itemized.

Mack has given me a key to the Fantasy Bungalow, a dismal trailer set a hundred yards behind the main compound. Mack accused his last madam of burning down the first Fantasy Bungalow. Its charred remains are scattered at the bottom of the hill. The one where I get to sleep is perched on cement blocks, snuggled against a steep crag that bears a giant white A, like an aleph of shame. To get there I rely largely on instinct, stepping over cats tensed like fists in the dark. A few stars make an effort in the sky.

The decor of the Fantasy Bungalow is meant to be homey, as the Angel's Ladies website put it recently, for "playing house or something different!" Angel oversaw the decorating, just as she did for their Oregon funeral parlors. The curtains are quaint and the wallpaper quainter. Mirrors in the bungalow apprise me of my whereabouts at all times, including one that surely registers my expression when I open the refrigerator and find, alone on the second shelf, a jumbo-sized box of chilled latex gloves. The video library is sparse: *Hung and Hard*, *Bang'Er 17 Times*, and *SEASLUTS*, Volume 2. In the back, past a beaded curtain, is my bedroom, furnished with more mirrors, and a vanity, where I leave my car keys by a Virgen de Guadalupe candle with a hornet entombed in the wax. Two lurid lamps with red bulbs clinch the mood. I try to call my wife, but I'm beyond cellular range. Mindful of a story that Shaner tells about a moll who once forced a trick to his knees at knifepoint to persuade him to accept Jesus as his personal savior, I look everywhere but find no panic button, only an unplugged Radio Shack intercom, and beneath the nightstand a five-quart stainless-steel bowl with a dozen Liquid Tight Hygienic Disposal System Safe-T-Bags. To my dismay, the smoke detector is missing its battery.

I pick up *Bang'Er 17 Times*, left in the VCR, in medias res, while I fix myself a cup of Lemon Zinger from the complimentary tea sampler. The actors look lonely and bored, insincere, like the professional mourners in Greece who wail and writhe and tear out their hair for a fee; it's easy to sift out the truly bereaved from the faker, like pointing out the professional laugher in the studio audience, just as it's easy to tell that this porn actress is only miming lust. There is no precipice behind her eyes; she is too sober, she looks up at the camera, her audience, hungry only for ratings; she is a busker, a drone. Although the video is a bit proctologic for my tastes, I watch while listening to snippets of tape of Mack in the car.

ME: You know how some authors put sex and death together in literature. Why do you think that is?

MACK: Well, I think probably because death is so devastating in our emotions, and sex is so exciting in our emotions. It's two highs. Or you might call one *extreme* low and the other high. If you want to get a newspaper, see, the most things that's written in the newspaper is what gets the headlines, is death-murder or, uh, Clinton got his dick sucked by that girl.

Having finished the movie, now filled with a lonely, hollow pubescent guilt, I go outside. I stand in the blowing dark. Looking down at the brothel, I wonder which of the five whores will share their master's bed tonight while his bereaved wife sleeps alone 120 miles away. Mostly, I'm disappointed that this man, who panders to those most human conundrums, grief and lust—the very antipodes of the carnal spectrum—a man who possesses a meat-and-potatoes soul if ever there was one, finds the subject of sex and death to be just that, meat and potatoes. When I go to bed I read the grief self-help book I brought. I couldn't help but notice that the death and dying section is coterminous with the human sexuality section at my Barnes & Noble. This book recommends getting a puppy.

In the morning, after I shower with the heart-shaped soap that I found on the back of the toilet, Shanda cooks me eggs. She is wearing her bowler, and her slippered toes peekaboo like miniature marshmallows. Diane sits at the table smoking and flipping through cookie recipes. It's going to be a slow day. Almost everyone in the industry refers to prostitutes as girls. But, as it happens, Shanda just became a grandma and Diane has two kids in college. Mack would have you think that Angel's ladies are the demimonde, but the women I've met are worn and mournful. They have the wan charm of (I imagine) the whores of ancient Rome, the *bustuariae*, sexual servants of the gods of the dead, who made their assignations in cemetery groves. Angel herself, just a few years younger than Mack, is the most weathered. I have yet to spend any time with Angel, but I have gotten to know her, a little, from the photo album in the parlor of her and Mack copulating. It is a plain album, the sort in which you would expect to find vacation photos. A number of pictures include another man having sex with Angel while Mack, pouchy and removed, looks on. In one snapshot, her contorted face looks carved out of grief, but it could be the strain of ecstasy turning her inside out. When Mack comes in with his newspaper, Shanda runs off to dress for a Halloween Fantasy Fetish Ball in Vegas. There are Halloween parties everywhere in Nevada this weekend. Mack will not participate. He is staying in to put the finishing touches on a forty-page missive of gripes, ammunition for his lawyer. Since Mack has work to do, he can't join me at the Burro Races, the high-light of Beatty Days, this weekend's celebration of Nevada's anniversary of statehood (Halloween 1864), but he encourages me to go anyway, saying he's heard that they're "sort of funny." I ask Diane if she wants to go, but Mack answers for her. Of course she can't. Someone has to be here when the fornicators ring the bell.

High noon finds a crowd around the burro pit, an arena the size of a ballfield, behind the Burro Inn and Casino. Stranded in the center is a rusty oil drum. There are aisles of pickups and spectators roost-ing on car hoods. We are under a bleak hill painted with a giant white B. Back in the fifties, when Beatty was the closest town to the aboveground nuclear tests, residents gathered at this same spot behind the Burro Inn, née Atomic Club, in the early morning with lawn chairs and coolers to watch the apocalyptic fireballs light up over the hills. Fortunately, Beatty lies upwind of the Nevada Test Site, and residents have been spared the tragedy that has befallen many downwinders, though, according to the Department of Energy, which tests the town for radionuclides weekly—as often as the girls at Angel's Ladies are tested for sexually transmitted dis-eases—the town runs a little hot. In the semi-shade of the announcer's box, a tin-roofed platform on stilts, are three docile burros tied to the fence. The animals are cute, almost toy-sized, except for their distractingly big genitalia.

Since the species originated in North Africa, the burro adapted quickly to Nevada's desert climate and made the perfect pack ani-mal for the nomadic prospector. The beasts were thought to be preternaturally "tuned" to precious metals. In fact, the prospector who filed the first claim in Rhyolite was allegedly led to the gold by his own pack of ungulate dowsers.

I grab a spot close to the fence, between a perambulator and a collegiate-looking guy with a camera. There must be two hundred people now, maybe more. A burro wails, just as mournful as Eeyore. There are a number of leathery-armed folk wearing visors that span the visor spectrum from monogrammed cotton to blue sparkle plastic, but more wear cowboy hats. A scruffy-looking guy dressed in suspenders and a sand-dusted crushed hat climbs up onto a tin box and hollers the rules:

All gear must be unpacked and placed neatly on the ground before starting fire or mixing batter.
No sweets or other foods are to be used to assist in leading burros.
Pancake must be cooked on both sides. Hold pancake between thumb and forefinger for judge's approval before it is offered to the burro.

Originally, before harassing wild burros was outlawed, the contestants first had to catch one, which they then led, over the course of three days, about forty miles, not without some violence upon the contestants' persons. Today, the burros are tame, and the three "prospectors" are students at Beatty High School.

The arena turns to dust the instant the announcer blasts a pistol, and the jockeys launch forward in slow motion. Five minutes into this race nobody has yet inveigled their animal to the oil drum. A rangy kid with baggy shorts and white socks hiked up to his kneecaps—his name is Jeff—gets about a foot before his burro ceases to be persuaded and stops cold. Todd, who looks like the school quarterback, leads by a nose. Dottie, with red streaks in her hair, is first to round the drum, do-si-do. Before Todd even crosses the drum's lengthening shadow, Dottie has hitched her burro near where a judge sits at one of the three equidistant stations and begun unloading the waiting gear (shovel, matches, kindling, skillet) from its scrawny back. Todd clears the barrel but loses speed on the lee side of the drum. Poor Jeff might as well be trying to persuade a dog to evolve. Just as Todd starts to pack his gear, Dottie's burro sets back out for the second loop around the drum and then back to her station, where she begins to prepare a firepit. Just a fetlock behind, Todd digs a hole the size of a pet's grave, cracks wood over his knee, and starts striking matches. He contends with wind more than Dottie, given that his judge doesn't block the wind as well as Dottie's judge, deliberately or not, hard to say. Jeff's judge sits pensively, the shovel and gear unclaimed at her feet. Dot's judge yells "flame!" but recants when the smoke ends up just being dust kicked up by the burro. Todd takes the lead tenuously; he shelters a weak flame with his hands. Dottie has fire in the hole and it's a good fire, better than Todd's.

Dottie warms the skillet while Todd still struggles, blowing. She pours batter. Oops. There's a problem. The judges huddle. Dottie forgot to oil her pan. For a second it's unclear if this means disqualification, but they let it slide. The crowd is seized with suspense as Dottie lifts the now nicely browned flapjack to the burro's muzzle. It takes a sniff. Oddly purses its lips. Then, to the shock of all, the burro bolts backward with a violent capriole. It hates pancakes. The infuriated burro storms across the pen, dragging behind it the terrified girl who is unfortunately connected to the dreaded griddlecake. Todd patiently oils his pan, pours batter, and proffers the lightly browned flapjack to his burro, who blithely opens its mouth and accepts communion.

Later that afternoon, after Mack's nap, he and I take a drive in his RAV4 out to Rhyolite. We wind upward to the ghost town, wrapped around the slagged remains of the Bullfrog Hills, past half-dismantled mills, to a sweeping view of the tailings pond, a 340-acre lake of slurry laced with cyanide that reflects the setting sun bluish-greenly. Rhyolite is nothing but ruins. Devoured facades. The wind actually whistles in a creepy minor key. Ancient street signs poke comically out of the sagebrush. Just past the once opulent bank, a three-story concrete husk, Mack turns the RAV onto a rutted path, and we bump roughly down Gold Lane, toward the trepanned mountainside. Up close it looks like the burrows of some stygian sparrowlike dirt-hill-dwelling people.

Trundling along here, I find Mack easy company. In this ghost town, speaking about cycles of boom and bust, I ask how well his business rode the New Economy, and it takes us, not as circuitously as you might wish, to the heart of Angel's grief-lust nexus. Which should have been a good thing. I had been struggling over how to approach the subject. It seemed so obvious, yet delicate, and I was momentarily elated to have an inroad into what I expected would prove to be the key to understanding this central paradox. But the subject bores him. He points out a shack where miners slept. The whores back then kept "cribs," little huts much like the ancient Roman prostitutes' *cellae*, grim mausoleums with the names of each woman etched over the entrance. By my third day with Mack, talking about funeral parlors and sex parlors, sometimes in the same breath, it's hard not to become confused, so that the tenor of my thoughts is macabre-erotic to the point that I half consciously think of these fallen angels, in turn, as ghosts, necrophilic whores, floozily dressed zombies . . .

Eleven A.M., Sunday morning, the Beatty Community Church is packed. The church is on a hill, exposed to the raw wind that hasn't let up since yesterday. (The Fantasy Bungalow creaked like a dinghy all night.) The walls are decorated with Sunday-school handiwork, and the windows are pink-and-blue stained glass. Rev-

erend Taguchi, a brawny Japanese American with longish hair and
a goatee, mounts the pulpit. Service starts with three hymns back-to-
back (all in F major). I sit out "Blessed Be the Name of the Lord"
but, to mark time, sing along with "All Hail, King Jesus."

After "Unto Thee, O Lord," everybody gets up to greet and min-
gle. I am touched, if uneasy, when most come over to shake my
hand, all except a strung-out-looking guy who stands in his pew,
nodding forlornly. Tucked in his coat is a pit bull puppy.

After the service the guy with the pit bull comes over while I'm
waiting for Reverend Taguchi. He sits beside me in the pew and
asks my name. His is Walter. For a second it doesn't look like it's
going to go any further between us and then he starts to cry. Finally
he manages to ask if we can go outside. He needs to talk privately.
Why not? I follow Walter out to the parking lot. It is blustery. In fact,
at that moment I see my first and only tumbleweed. It is a bantam,
disappointing little thing that bounces across the parking lot and
then wheels out of sight. Walter wants to know if I'm going to Vegas;
he needs a ride. But I'm not going back to Vegas for three more
days. Walter seems like an imperiled enough character that I briefly
consider making a detour for him, but I've already spent an afternoon watching the burro races, a detour that led me to no conclusions except that I do not believe a burro would put up with a sport
like that if he were conscious of his own mortality. I ask Walt if he
worked at the gold mine, and he says that he's on "disability," he's
only lived here six months, that he's from Philadelphia, which I
ignore, since I live in Philadelphia and I don't feel like having anything in common at the moment. Walt starts to cry again when the
dog laps his thumb; a meniscus gently swells at the rim of his left
nostril. His brow quivers. He really needs to go to Vegas. There's this
model, he says. This is the sad old story, I think, until he says Hob-
bytown USA, and I gather that it's a model airplane he's pining after.

After a potluck lunch Reverend Taguchi invites me over to his
house, a block away, a peeling wind-rattled home with chimes dan-

gling on the porch. As a county commissioner who vice-chairs the brothel licensing board, Taguchi, despite his moral qualms, cannot say much about Mack's case, except that he thinks Beatty will survive just fine without Angel's if the brothel goes under, so we talk about whether or not Beatty will turn into a ghost town now that the mine's gone. He thinks not. I ask him again how dependent Beatty is on the revenue of Angel's, and he brushes it off. He cannot abide the suggestion that his town is in any way dependent on the sinful lucre of merchandised sex. There are plenty of other economic options, he says. Like the Yucca Mountain Project? As for the $38 million that the DOE will have given the county by the time the final site recommendation gets approved by President Bush in 2002, his official position, he grins, as a commissioner, is "neutral." He's more eager to talk about the county getting money from Mercedes, BMW, Chevy, and Ford, who all do heat testing in the summertime in Death Valley. "They can actually go from below sea level to 10,000 feet in a two-hour period. The *extremes*." When the reverend walks me out the door we find Walt on the porch. He's still looking for a ride to Hobbytown USA. By the way that Reverend Taguchi kindly sends him on his way, I get the impression that this is an ongoing thing and by refusing I'm not supposed to feel bad, but I can't help feeling like I should help Walt escape this place, maybe even take him back to Philadelphia, if that's where he's really from. Walt is the saddest thing I've seen since I got here; sadder than the burros, sadder than the bored whores flipping through cookie recipes. He is clearly bereaved—of what, I know not. But I can help him no more than the aging pimp can help me. When it comes to grief and lust we are all tumbleweeds.

I end up going to Vegas alone. Halloween morning, I meet Mack for the last time at his gated stucco mansion in northwest Vegas. He answers the door wearing a pink shirt and looking five years younger than the last time I saw him. He's just gone to his "beautician," he says. His cherubic curls look freshly gilt. Elvis croons in the background. Angel is off somewhere sorting through their returned possessions, which choke the hallway along with chaotic piles of court records, unopened mail, and boxes. Mack says that everything hasn't been returned by the cops, including some pictures of Angel's dead boys. When he goes in search of something he wants me to see, I poke around. In every nook and cranny is an Elvis doll, an Elvis telephone, or a tiny Elvis under a bell jar. I'm on my knees looking at a video in an evidence bag when Angel emerges, hovering over me.

Her face pale, her mouth drawn, she looks convalescent. She takes me for a tour of her Elvis collection, down the hallway, where pictures of her boys hang on the wall beside portraits of Elvis, to a back room, where all four walls are covered floor to ceiling with plates from the King's Franklin Mint collection. There is not enough cake in the world to fill all the plates.

Then for no real reason—other than that I was just nosing around their video collection—Angel starts to tell me about the night that the cops searched her house and kept her hostage in the living room. Her voice quavers, and she clutches the bagged video in her hands the way a woman about to be mugged would clutch her purse. She was alone. Mack was in Beatty. When she thought she would lose it (they wouldn't let her get her "pressure" pills), she got up and put a video in the VCR. It was a tape her son Jesse had made two months before he died. He wanted it played at the funeral, she says, "mainly to apologize to anybody that he had ever done any wrong thing to." Her eyes jump when a bird flies past the window; after a long moment, while she struggles not to cry, she says that her son told her on the tape, "If you think that you're alone, you're not. He said, It's going to be all right, Mom. It's Our Father in Heaven." I am, I think, convinced when she tells me that the cop guarding her was moved to tears, too.

Mack bustles into the room and, with a pained expression, shows me an official inventory from the police; typed at the top it reads, "Swinging File has been removed from this evidence bag and placed in evidence bag marked employee/record files. Report #: 00-0578." This list of potential lovers, Mack lets me know, has not been returned. It makes him mad enough to launch into a hot tirade about suing the bastards. This is a great loss to him. He wants that list back and he cannot quite believe that it is gone. I can see it in his eyes. It is a dire, horrible loss.

For the rest of the day, waiting for my midnight flight, ominously moody because I have to fly, I nap in my room at the Imperial Palace to minimize exposure to the Strip and thereby avoid the migrainous hell's bells and numismatic crepitations of the slots. When the sun goes down I meekly venture out for something to eat. Although it's Halloween, hardly anyone on the street is in costume. I see the pope hailing a cab. Then I see a hooker in a black velvet cape and a silvery metallic top. I don't know if she's a real hooker or not—it doesn't matter. I stand still until it is all thoroughly convincing. The smell of chlorine from the fountain. The unpared fingernails of the Mexican kid who hands me a flyer for an escort service. The couple that passes and the man who says to his wife: "It beats a sharp stick in the eye!" These details come to life. My life, like the night, seems never-ending.

——

I was surprised to have the notion brought to my attention—via the happy inclusion of my writing in this very anthology—that I'd written a piece about crime. Mack Moore was a crook, there's no doubt, and some breaking of the law had inarguably transpired the night he sent the forlorn Cindi on her fateful date at the Stagecoach Hotel, though to this day he insists he did no wrong. What I really wanted to write about was God's crime against humanity for sticking us with too much grief (and I guess too much lust), and Mack seemed like an apt object lesson. The desert pimp, as I saw him, was a sort of self-destructive Job.

Since my visit to Angel's Ladies, the Nye County commissioners dropped their charges—or rather, let the issue slip into limbo—while Mack continues to make idle threats about "suing the sonofabitches" for entrapment. In a way, I have to say I'm glad he got off. Partly because of my stubborn belief that consensual crimes are not crimes—prostitution, as far as I know, does not fund terrorism—and in this case, the cops had clearly set up Mack.

The saddest outcome is that Clint Towns died en route for treatment in New Mexico and that his wife, Wanda, who is no longer the madam at Angel's Ladies, is devastated. There's some more grief for you. Mack blames the Nye County sheriff's office for Clint's precipitous end, since he'd been detained for six hours without his oxygen tank. The other shocker, I guess, is that Mack put Angel's Ranch on the market. He hasn't found the right buyer yet, so if you happen to be looking for a thirdhand brothel, there's a tip. The land is rich, perfect for growing tomatoes and watermelons, and there's a natural-fed spring out back by the Fantasy Bungalow, perfect for a midnight skinny-dip.

THE ENRON WARS
MARIE BRENNER

It was at first inconceivable to Jan Avery that her position at the Enron Corporation could make her a valuable witness in the largest bankruptcy case in American history. On the morning of January 25, when former Enron vice-chairman Cliff Baxter was found dead in his Mercedes with a suicide note and a bullet wound in his head, Avery was home sifting through proxy statements and SEC filings she had kept in storage. Like Baxter, she had been interviewed by lawyers and investigators who were convinced that her testimony could illuminate what had led to Enron's collapse. Shortly before his death, Baxter told colleagues that he had become a pivotal figure in the scandal, and that he stood between Ken Lay and Jeff Skilling (former CEOs of Enron) going to jail. Avery was apprehensive as well. For eight years she had consulted on the myriad complex structures that fueled the Enron delusion. "The pattern began very early," she said, "much earlier than anyone has reported. It started in the gray area of what was acceptable in accounting principles and, in my opinion, later turned into a clear case of fraud."

The mystery of Enron presented itself to Avery in 1993, during her earliest days in the company's tax department. Trained as an accountant—what Enron called a "middle person"—she placed confidentiality at a premium. Avery had a special expertise in oil-and-gas tax procedures, used to compute state and federal taxes. From her days as a young woman going to night school, she had been taken by the simple beauty of accounting, balancing credits and debits. She had even run her own marketing company, jockeying to buy and move gas on the newly deregulated pipelines that crisscrossed Texas and New Mexico. In an Enron that would soon fill up with young MBAs in polo shirts and khakis, Avery was an anomaly. She dressed in blazers and suits and always kept flowers in her office. Her paternal grandmother had been born on a plantation in Alabama, and good breeding showed on Avery's face, but the family had lost everything, so a determination was there as well. In the wild, optimistic days of Enron's romance with the opening energy markets, Jan Avery was a perfect hire. The Soviet Union had fallen, and the idea of privatizing electricity, natural gas, and other commodities was sweeping the world. Like FedEx, Enron seemed poised to be in the vanguard of the newest frontier of American business.

Avery's first assignment, in 1993, seemed routine. She was to compute a schedule of amended state tax returns for Enron Oil, a former subsidiary of the company. Enron Oil had shown a loss on its books, her boss told her, and Avery was supposed to calculate the carryback on the company records. She had worked at such major accounting firms as Arthur Young, Arthur Andersen, and Touche Ross, so she knew what to expect: a thick file with a schedule of tax depreciations. It was standard stuff—years of book-value depletion for oil and gas, company officers' life insurance, liabilities of all kinds. She waited for the file to be delivered, but it didn't appear. "Where is the file?" she asked her colleagues, and they gave vague answers, as if they hadn't understood what she was talking about. Days passed, and still no file arrived. Finally, she says, she was given a thin manila folder containing three sheets, on one of which was a number: $142 million. This was no routine loss; it was a staggering amount for a young company. Avery assumed it was a mistake; she scoured the storage room next to her cubicle and continued to ask her coworkers, "Where are the books for Enron Oil? How am I supposed to justify a $142 million loss for state-tax purposes?" No one could answer her.

"It made no sense to me," she said. "You do not have an entire file of financials disappear." Enron Oil had gone out of business; there had to be officers you could track down. Since she had no data, she refused to sign off on the $142 million figure. "I questioned it and questioned it. I went to the financial office. Finally I wrote a research report, trying to come up with some kind of basis, but it was impossible to do the research without the facts," she said.

Soon after that Avery's boss walked into her office and said, "Here is your answer. We had a little problem." He paused and said, "Rogue traders." That was the first Avery heard of a bizarre case that had disappeared without much notice. For a moment she thought he was joking. She wondered if certain files were kept in his office so that Enron could claim that they were protected under attorney-client privilege and could not be subpoenaed. Finally he let Avery see the Enron Oil file, but it yielded no data to clarify what had really gone on. "This was the clear beginning for me, when I realized that they were trying to hide all the losses," she later said.

Jan Avery had arrived early in the Enron Corporation's drama of willful blindness, during an attempt to perfume a disaster Kenneth Lay, Enron's architect, had inherited in 1985 when he merged his company, Houston Natural Gas, with InterNorth, an Omaha-based concern. In December 1993, Arthur Andersen would become the in-house auditors. Enron Oil was an overture to thousands of off-the-books partnerships which would subsequently dizzy readers trying to figure out what the Enron debacle was really about. It was a harbinger of the future Enron pattern of hiding losses, no matter what. Avery's initial confusion over accounting discrepancies and

missing documents only presaged the bafflement of the battalion of
bankruptcy lawyers who would be assigned to unravel the morass,
of the thousands of Enron employees who would find that their
401(k) plans were nearly worthless, and of all the congressmen—71
in the Senate and 187 in the House—who had received campaign
contributions from Enron. The taint of the energy giant would
soon permeate the White House and the president's men as George
W. Bush and Dick Cheney, close friends and associates of Ken and
Linda Lay for years, stonewalled requests from the General Accounting Office for documents, issued new terrorist warnings, and gave
lengthy interviews to *The Washington Post* in which Bush talked
about being choked with emotion in the days after September 11.
To many these actions appeared to be a full-out legal defense and
public relations campaign, a smoke screen to keep the political
leaders' web of Enron connections from scrutiny. They overwhelmed the footage on the nightly news shows of former Enron
employees in T-shirts dragging ficus trees from their offices down
the steps of the two gleaming corporate skyscrapers on Houston's
Smith Street.

Avery had been hired to work on tax collages, researching case
law and the tax code and briefing executives on Enron's interests in
deals. "We take an aggressive position on losses," she was told, but
that policy sounded benign. The enigma of the Enron Oil loss confounded her because it seemed to be constructed to cover up a
criminal fiasco. In October 1985 the heads of a trading operation—
soon to be renamed Enron Oil—based in Valhalla, New York, had
set up a scam: Using two sets of financial books, they ran hundreds
of millions of dollars of phony trades through four sham Cayman
Island partnerships. Masterminded by Louis Borget and Thomas
Mastroeni, the president and vice president, the trades glided into
the Enron Corporation's machinery, and in the swirl of the start-up
the bogus trading operation continued smoothly for two years. One
former executive remembered the day Enron got an urgent phone

call from the Treasury Department questioning the enormousness
of one Enron Oil trade.

In fact, the future Ken Lay business model started with Enron Oil,
a flourishing petroleum-marketing operation with twenty-eight
employees and offices in New York, London, and Singapore. Enron
Oil seemed to be the one bright spot in the sea of debt incurred in
the Houston Natural Gas and InterNorth merger. On the books, it
looked like a success story, earning $50 million over the two and a
half years before its collapse. Months before federal prosecutors targeted the crime, an in-house Enron auditor began to keep a meticulous and lengthy file on the episode. Later, there was talk in the
company that the auditor was so frustrated that he took fifty cartons
of evidence and spirited them away in his attic.

Borget and Mastroeni pleaded guilty to conspiracy to defraud
and to filing false tax returns, and Borget went to prison. The minor
scandal hardly registered a blip in the financial press. Ken Lay told
The New York Times that the loss was "an expensive embarrassment." The Enron board quickly voted to disband Enron Oil, and
the loss almost tanked the new company. Enron had to liquidate
assets, including a portion of a new power business, to cover it.

There remained, however, a larger question: How much of a loss
had the company actually sustained? Enron gave the *Times* a figure
of $85 million. Avery's file with no backup data said $142 million.
No explanation for the loss ever appeared in subsequent annual
reports, according to London's *Financial Times*. Avery became
obsessed with trying to solve that first accounting puzzle. "It was
clear to me, even then, that the management wanted as few people
as possible to have any access to the records. It was the beginning of
management's attempt to hide records from the SEC and the shareholders."

Studying SEC documents, Avery discovered that in an 8-K filing

for 1987 the loss showed up as $85 million. This number appeared
to her to have been computed using a standard that would become
applicable only the following year. "This was a huge discrepancy,"
she later said. I asked Avery to explain what the numbers meant.
She faxed several pages photocopied from 8-K's and Enron financials, and wrote, "It appears that management convinced Arthur
Andersen to sign off on showing the loss and provides the first hint
of Enron's ability to persuade Andersen to see things in Enron's best
light."

Jan Avery and I met in early January for the first of many conversations. Like most people I interviewed during weeks of traveling
back and forth between New York and Houston, she radiated anxiety about being seen with a reporter. A divorcée with a daughter
who is a college freshman, Avery was concerned that she would be
recognized in River Oaks by friends in the oil and gas business. In
her years at Enron, she had participated in a heady world of ego and
manipulation, dealing with an array of Cayman Island partnerships
charted on whiteboards in conference rooms, jimmying utilities
contracts during the California brownouts, bundling energy for
Safeway stores, and creating a nationwide energy program for Citi-
group. She supervised teams building power plants in Nicaragua
and spent nine months in Europe, traveling often to the United
Arab Emirates, where she was closing the $3 billion creation of the
Dolphin pipeline.

For days I remained at the St. Regis Hotel in Houston as frightened Enron managers, lawyers, deal originators, and vice presidents—
most of them women—came through the lobby, past the holiday
gingerbread house that seemed frozen in the air-conditioning. It
was the women of Enron, I soon discovered, who had detected the
web of intrigue, predicted the fall, written futile letters to board members, tipped financial analysts, and tried to avert the final collapse.

. . .

Cynthia Harkness, an Enron lawyer, still at the company, described the moment when chief financial officer Andrew Fastow introduced her to a concept of monetization in which future revenue is booked immediately. The lawyer was baffled by the nerve behind Fastow's logic. She told him, "Andy, it seems to me that if you do a ten-year deal, and suck all the earnings out in one year, you will then have to keep the profit coming through years 4, 5, 6, and all the way to 10, by doing more of these deals. . . . How are you going to do that if the market changes? Book more deals?" It looked to Harkness like a pyramid scheme, but she knew that the accounting department had signed off on it. She recalled Fastow looking at her and saying, "Yes, you have to keep doing more of these deals each year."

It was Harkness's first week in Enron's global finance group, and she had yet to parse the world within the world that was Enron. Harkness had come to Houston from a large French investment bank, and she asked her new colleagues about partnerships called LJM, which were controlled by Fastow. (The name came from the initials for Fastow's wife and children.) "Isn't there a conflict here?" she asked. "Their answer always was 'This has been approved by the board.' They said, 'It's dicey, but it has been carefully scrubbed. They have put in extra hoops and procedures to make sure they're all right.'"

The language of the culture was borrowed from ornithology, with partnerships called Osprey, Raptor, and Condor as created vehicles to hide debts and losses. A special fiefdom was arranged for Fastow, with names taken from George Lucas films: JEDI, Chewco. It was a sign of status to have earned a life-size furry Chewbacca head as a token of having worked on the Chewco deal. "At first we believed there was nothing wrong with this," Shirley Hudler, the manager of the JEDI I partnership, said as friends of Fastow's walked away with huge profits.

Hudler, like Harkness, worked with Fastow and understood the mechanism of the partnership deals. "They would say, 'Okay, we need to get these assets off the books. We can either put it in Osprey or, if Osprey is full right now, we can sell it to LJM, which can hold it. And *then* we can move it.'" Years before that, the future whistle-blower Sherron Watkins would sit in meetings and say openly, "This is a circle jerk." Hudler said, "There was so much pressure on us to make earnings, and the Arthur Andersen staff we worked with would never challenge these structures. We could always bully them into getting what we wanted. We made them push the enve-lope. If they had questions, they would call Chicago—their head-quarters. I don't think they were doing their job." (Arthur Andersen lays the entire blame for Enron's difficulties on Enron's board and management.)

Enron, many of the women said, was a hotbed of hormones, a testosterone culture. A vice president openly displayed a "hottie board," on which he ranked the sexual allure of Enron women. There was occasional violence. One trader, learning that his annual bonus was a mere $500,000, was said to have thrown his plasma screen across the trading floor. Another, fearing he would be a victim of an upcoming performance review, slammed his boss up against a wall, accusing him of lying about the trader's perform-ance. "Forget you saw that," the man's boss told the woman who later described the event. "He's having a bad day."

Arriving at the St. Regis Hotel on a Sunday morning, Avery wore a black pantsuit and high-heeled boots and carried a slim folder of documents, as if she were on her way to a deposition. She had driven from her house near West University, a neighborhood for-merly inhabited by Rice University professors which had been taken over by the young Enron crowd. Many of the brick cottages had been expanded into mini-mansions, and SUVs and Porsches circled the area. At former chief financial officer Andrew Fastow's house, a guard stood in the winter fog. There was an atmosphere of impending catastrophe in the city.

I had first noticed Avery a month earlier at an Enron hearing in federal court. She was seated directly behind me in the press section, scribbling in a black ledger. She wore a vivid purple suit and had the put-together look of a woman who knew her way around Neiman Marcus. It was impossible not to notice her in the press seats, because she did not join in the easy conversation of the reporters seated around her. She had an aura of vulnerability underneath her good looks, a sadness around the edges. I guessed she might work for a law firm, but before I could speak to her she had vanished. Later, Avery told me she was actually trying to look like a reporter. It was her first time inside federal court, and before the hearing she had sat in the empty courtroom and watched a flotilla of lawyers wheel in seven carts of documents. To calm herself, she started counting the attorneys arriving in Judge Lee Rosenthal's court; she stopped at thirty. Fearing that she would be caught in the background by one of the camera crews outside, she left during a break.

Avery had come to court to watch William Lerach in action. Lerach and his firm, Milberg Weiss Bershad Hynes & Lerach, were vying for a share of the billions of dollars in potential awards claimed by the hundreds of corporate creditors and pension funds that had seen their investments in Enron become worthless. The University of California retirement system alone had lost $145 million; Florida claimed $335 million. The total loss to state pension funds was $2.9 billion. Lerach's assistant worked the press row, passing out an oversize color chart. It was the first time I had ever seen a lawyer employ a public relations intern at a routine hearing. The chart appeared to show the astonishing profits made by twenty-nine Enron officials who had sold off $1.1 billion of company shares.

This was early in December, and the narrative of Enron as corporate Antichrist had yet to grip the networks. There was no mob of shouting bankrupt employees outside the courthouse, no Jesse Jackson, no CNN tent in front of the chrome Enron headquarters, no Linda Lay dragging NBC across an emerald lawn and declaring that the Lay family was impoverished. Lerach was attempting to freeze the assets of the twenty-nine officials, but he was also selling his story, attempting to launch a fusillade into the national media.

"This is fraud at the top," Lerach declared in a booming voice with the thick sound of his native Pittsburgh. "Enron's goal . . . was to keep these debts off the balance sheet so the rating agencies would not be able to see them." Lerach's task was to convince Judge Rosenthal that a group of Houston's finest citizens, whom she saw socially in River Oaks, had morphed into this decade's Robert Vesco and Marc Rich, global money launderers, and might be attempting to evade prosecution. "We know that the other night [Andrew Fastow] pre-cleared customs in Houston . . . and had booked passage to Tel Aviv on three separate flights! . . . Skilling has been in Brazil for the last couple of weeks! . . . One top executive named McMahon, the treasurer, was known for going around the company after he met with Skilling, Lay, and Fastow, and they directed him to do some bogus deal and say, 'Well, we've all got to go drink the Kool-Aid.'" Lerach tossed out unfamiliar terms like grenades—"costless collars," "derivative trades."

Lerach, the scourge of the tort reform anti-lawsuit lobby in Washington for his championing of class action suits, from tobacco cases to those involving nursing homes, has a passion for theatrics, and his unruly hair looks as if he had stuck his finger into an electrical outlet. Standing in front of a chart of what he called "the Mike Milken model"—a reference to the Drexel Burnham Lambert architect of junk-bond finance in the eighties, who ultimately went to jail for securities fraud—Lerach pounded on the board with his black marker and then drew an immense daisy. "[Milken] was here in the middle . . . so what Milken used to do is trade the bonds around. . . . It goes around and around in a big circle . . . it creates the phony appearance of a market." Then Lerach threw out more sinister phrases—"dark swaps," "massive insider trading."

Judge Rosenthal studied Lerach coolly, as if she were trying to come to terms with a new set of variables for the Ken Lay who had chaired a campaign for the local United Way, who went to dinners at the White House, and who threw out the first baseball at Enron Field. Lerach, who once directed a civil case against Milken and others that collected damages of almost a billion dollars, appeared hardwired with moral outrage as he told the court, "A member of Enron's tax group who structured many of these transactions has told us he was told his job was to keep Fastow out of jail!" At that moment, I turned in my seat and saw the woman in purple behind me blanch. Later, I would learn that the remark had been made to her as a joke by Fastow's friend Jordan Mintz, an Enron senior attorney who in February would testify before the House of Representatives that he had attempted to warn Jeff Skilling in May 2001 that his off-the-books partnerships were questionable. "I am keeping all my papers in a salt dome," Mintz had told a friend.

Lerach, who calls himself a private attorney general, is a connoisseur of criminal schmutz. He and his partner Mel Weiss run a thriving class action firm which employs about two hundred lawyers from San Diego to New York and twelve private investigators. They target savings banks, drug companies, and offshore scams. Their specialty is securities fraud, a form of plaintiff law that has been stymied by the 1995 tort reform act, which was pushed through Congress by a group led primarily by Chris Dodd, senator from Connecticut, with the financial backing of the powerful insurance lobby. Tort reform advocates insist that it lessens the ambulance chasing that used to clog the legal system; trial lawyers rail that it punishes victims and allows large corporations to get away with outrageous financial manipulations. The act put a stop to virtual automatic discovery of legal documents in class action cases; because of that, lawyers like Lerach say, the standard of proof for legal pleadings has become onerous, and the investigations needed to file airtight complaints have become unduly expensive.

William Lerach is one of the foremost practitioners of aggressive research, and his investigators scour the world for witnesses and class members, an activity that is questionable under the new law, which prohibits lawyers from trolling for victims. Lerach is also criticized for his public displays. Last fall he chose an unusual strategy to win the Enron case. He decided to feed the media openly and ignore the barrage of legal moralists who would take him to task for it. He reasoned correctly that the bigger the story became, the sooner Enron whistle-blowers and witnesses would come out of hiding. Under tort reform, plaintiff firms must compete for the ultimate stake of being the assigned class leader. "I see it as a $3 billion case," Lerach told a partner, meaning the aggregate of all the claims. The class leader could reportedly earn between 10 and 30 percent of that.

By the time I saw Lerach in court, he was competing with law firms representing Florida and Illinois. Outside in the hall that day, he held forth with fiery indignation. "This is nothing but a Ponzi scheme! There it all was: *You have to drink the Kool-Aid!*" Within weeks Lerach's accusations proved to be accurate and made the leads of national news stories. His strategy—called "Leraching" by his detractors—had worked perfectly. According to one of his partners, "After that hearing we went back to the Four Seasons and for two days did not leave the room, there were so many Enron former employees who wanted to talk to us." (In February, Milberg Weiss won the class-leader position.)

In the early days of the scandal, Houston reverberated with the social and legal conflicts arising out of all the possible Enron prosecutions. Judge Rosenthal's husband, Gary, is an attorney who used to work at Vinson & Elkins, Enron's lawyers, and the *Houston Press* would later report that Ken Lay had once lobbied unsuccessfully to get Lee Rosenthal a circuit judgeship. Within weeks, Judge Rosenthal recused herself from the case, as did the entire Houston U.S. Attorney's Office. By the time I arrived in the city, fear verging on panic was spreading through the River Oaks set. As a South Texas native, I had a modest acquaintance with the folkways of Houston, but Enron had turned the village of oil into an almost unrecognizable society. One truism remained: The city has never been neutral about the poetry of money. The collapse of Enron had caused the cave dwellers to begin to reconsider their friendships with Ken and Linda Lay. Lay had ascended into an orbit so rarefied in Houston that his very presence at parties could change the atmosphere. He would stand in one place, as a king might, and allow himself to be greeted with fulsome praise. He brought a new persona to Houston, appearing to be a kindly naïf, in contrast to Oscar Wyatt, the former head of Coastal Corporation, the energy company. Houston has long tolerated the foibles of Wyatt, who revels in his flamboyant reputation for buying oil from Saddam Hussein.

By early December the easy hyperbole of Texans swearing eternal loyalty to friends who are potential felons was sounding thin. Ken Lay and chief officers Jeff Skilling, who had left the company abruptly in August, and Andrew Fastow, who had been fired by October, were at ground zero in the Texas endgame, victims of the "tall poppy" syndrome, the phrase Australian Enron traders used for unspeakable hubris.

On my first night in town, at a grand dinner in the Huntingdon, a luxurious River Oaks high-rise, several floors away from the Lays' 13,000-square-foot, $7 million spread, Ken Lay's friends were speaking in code about the loss of his fortune. "Ken went to see Fayez to ask him for help," one said. "Fayez told him no way." In the Houston big-money world, this haiku spoke volumes. Fayez Sarofim, the secretive Egyptian money manager with multiple mansions, Rolls-Royces, and wives—one of whom died after collapsing mysteriously on Mount Kilimanjaro two years ago—could have delayed Lay's fate with a single call, but he dismissed him peremptorily. "I wouldn't dream of recommending Enron," he said. His remark circulated quickly through the Tudor mansions of River Oaks and Shadyside, many of whose owners are Sarofim clients. That same week Lay appeared pink-cheeked and cheerful to have lunch at the Coronado Club, implying in the casual tone he had learned to use that he was in communication with the president and Laura. But, as Lay's intimates could tell you, their friend was out selling. It was known that Ken's fervent phone calls to "the Oval" were not being returned.

"Hi, I'm Jan Avery, the president of Southwest Reserves and their only employee. I am a WMBE—a woman in a minority business enterprise—trying to move MM BTUs from the Permian Basin to the California border." That's how Jan Avery would cajole representatives from the pipeline companies who worked the booths at gas trade shows and energy conventions in New Mexico and Oklahoma. It was 1990. Avery had invested $250 to start her one-woman corporation, taking advantage of a new regulation which gave women and minorities special advantages. She had the legs of a model and did not play down her good looks, but she was also adept at fending off advances at a time when a subtext of sexual favors permeated the wildcatter atmosphere. Avery was struggling with a vicious divorce. She had run away from a grueling marriage to a rich lawyer from Arkansas and was living with her 7-year-old daughter, Kay, short for Katherine, in a small rented house in Santa Fe. The only telephone was in the hallway, and all day long she would make calls on it, pretending she was in an office, trying to get people to buy her brokered gas.

When Jan Avery talks about her history, she tends to skip over difficult periods. She grew up in Leeds, Alabama, outside Birmingham. Her father was a sheet-metal worker, the son of an heiress whose only remaining legacy was her insistence on fine linens, good manners, and a full-time housekeeper. She taught her granddaughter to appreciate finery and to excel in school. After attending a junior college, Jan worked as a receptionist for a forklift company. She also helped out with the books and became so intrigued with accounting that she enrolled in night school. In 1974 she married her first husband, Gary Kirsch, and soon followed him to Houston, where at 29 she got a job at Arthur Andersen. In the office she met Bob Avery, who worked near her in the tax department. Her marriage broke up, but she and Kirsch remained friends. Avery moved to Tulsa, and Jan followed, getting a job at Arthur Young, just when oil was moving toward $60 a barrel. There she had her first view of the sea of criminality surrounding the wildcatter crowd. When she came to believe that one of her clients was defrauding investors, she and Arthur Young walked away from the account.

Avery and Jan went out for three years before they married. Avery's wealthy father owned an oil field machinery company. The couple moved to the Avery family plantation in Eudora, Arkansas, but when the marriage crumbled, Jan took her baby daughter and fled. She struggled over custody issues while trying to maintain a relationship with Avery. "I loved him," she said, "and I wanted Kay to have a father." When Kay was 5, Jan moved to Santa Fe, where she worked part-time as an accountant and sold gas on the phone in the hall. A neighbor recalls that Jan said she was terrified of Avery.

Through cold-calling Jan met the chairman of Gas Mark in Houston, and he agreed to back her on her first deal to move gas on

Enron's pipeline to Southern California. Then the market changed, and only big players could stay in the business. Jan became clinically depressed and for a time followed a doctor's advice and took lithium, a fact she confided to Bob Avery. That year Kay went to see her father and his new wife and children over spring vacation, and Avery, a part-time district attorney, filed a motion for custody. According to Jan, he refused to allow his daughter to return home, using the fact that Jan had once fled as a way to convince the court that she was an unfit mother.

Jan finally had to agree to an onerous custody situation; she could visit Kay four weekends a year and have her for summer vacations and alternating holidays. They were allowed to talk on the phone once a week for fifteen minutes. Jan always spoke to her daughter as if she were an adult. "I am going to fight for you, but it is going to be very expensive," she told her. "You know how much I love you, and I will do everything in my power to get you back." (Robert Avery rejects Jan's version of events.)

Avery moved to Houston in order to be closer to her daughter. Through friends at Arthur Andersen, she started working part-time at Enron. She became married to her job, spending long hours working on the tax aspects of the multiplying partnerships—there would be about 3,000 by the time the company imploded. She was often sharp with her colleagues, quick to assert herself: "I am the only person who can work on that deal. I know how they work," she would say. Her bonuses depended on the earnings value of the deals she structured. The more money I make, she thought, the sooner I can afford the legal fees to fight for Kay.

When Jan Avery arrived at Enron, she already possessed an understanding of the arrogance of the company's culture. Of all the energy companies she knew, only Enron didn't deal with businesses owned by women. "I could never get them to give me the time of day," she told me. "And they controlled the best pipelines." By 1993, Ken Lay had established his system of rivalries. Forrest

Hoglund ran the oil and gas division, Stan Horton was in place at the staid and traditional pipeline company, Jeff Skilling had arrived to set up a trading operation, and Rich Kinder, the chief operating officer, kept a brake on the financials, discouraging Lay's grandiose schemes with a droll Texas remark, "Let's not drink our own whiskey, Ken." From time to time Kinder would lose his temper. "Goddamn it, how can we be doing all this?" He was uncomfortable with the rapid expansion, and Lay would say teasingly, "I'll die with a lot of friends, and Rich will have all the money."

And then there was Rebecca Mark, a young banker who in 1982 moved to what would become, in 1985, Enron's treasury department. With her blond hair and gold earrings, she looked like a Texas sun queen. Her mentor at the time was John Wing, a West Point graduate and canny negotiator, whom she reported to. She and Wing went to work opening power plants, but her division was partially sold to help cover the debt incurred by the rogue-trading scandal. In 1988 she took time off, bundled up her toddler twin boys, and entered Harvard Business School. She negotiated the contracts for a power plant for Enron outside Boston, and after she earned her MBA she returned to the company full-time. Soon she was setting up power plants and pipelines in England, India, and the Philippines. Mark would ultimately spar with Jeff Skilling, who had been a Baker Scholar at Harvard Business School and a consultant at McKinsey & Company before joining Enron. "Jeff may have been the single best student I ever had, and he did not suffer fools," said Chip Bupp, a professor of Skilling's at Harvard. Bupp likened Skilling's personality to the icy capability of Robert McNamara, President Kennedy's secretary of defense.

Skilling thrived on confrontation and had a perfect command of the minutiae of deals. In interviews he could stun financial writers with his grasp of details, but that same superiority made corporate meetings enervating for his colleagues. His vision was messianic. Skilling kept a sign on his desk: I.R.I.S., which stood for "First they Ignore you, then Ridicule you, then Imitate you, and then Steal your idea." From the beginning, colleagues say, Skilling's pattern was to scapegoat others without leaving a trail that could lead back to him. In meetings that Ken Lay chaired, Skilling was often silent, letting Lay believe that he was completely in control. But at other times Skilling could be very volatile. He was divorced, and his office was a shrine to his children; on long plane rides with colleagues he might spend hours talking about them. He would often blurt out astonishing remarks in public—he once, famously, called a stock analyst an asshole during a conference call—and the public relations staff worried each time he gave an interview.

Andrew Fastow, a Skilling protégé, was recruited early on in Skilling's first fiefdom, Enron Capital & Trade. As Skilling consolidated his power, he and Fastow allegedly designed the partnerships that were constructed to hide losses and maximize profits. Testifying before Congress, tax lawyer Jordan Mintz recalled sending a memo and leaving messages for Skilling asking him to sign off on crucial legal documents. Skilling testified that he had no memory of that. Last December, *The New York Times* had Skilling saying that the partnerships were Fastow's idea. Bupp, who remained close to Skilling, is now confounded. "I can't believe he did not know what was going on, yet I can't believe Jeff would lie . . . [The partnerships are] a clear black-and-white conflict of interest. Holy smokes!"

One day in 1995, Jan Avery sat in a conference room and watched Andrew Fastow, standing in front of a whiteboard, grapple with how to deal with a coming loss on the books of his group's investment in an MTBE fuel-additive plant outside Houston. Fastow and Skilling had gambled on the toxic additive used in gasoline, but as a result of a steady attack from the media and environmentalists, the market for MTBE had virtually disappeared. Fastow exuded anxiety, Avery remembered, raising his voice, barking orders. "We have to be able to come up with something! We have to construct a structure where the loss could be camouflaged." Most of Enron's now notorious partnerships were still in the future, but Fastow had already seen the possibilities they offered. There were already roughly three hundred in place. "Losses were never allowed at Enron, even then," Avery said. "You did not recognize losses." She remembered that the meeting stretched on for much of the day, and Fastow became increasingly agitated. Avery recalled thinking, This has gone too far.

"We sat there and bounced it around," she said, while Fastow frantically drew circles representing subsidiary corporations all over the board—partnerships within partnerships—to suggest how to move the loss. Fastow also asked them for ideas on how to maintain the value. "That was our language for hiding a loss. We called it 'maintaining value,'" Avery said. "I knew that this was something that was ultimately going to drag the company down, because you could not maintain this level of loss. It was hundreds of millions of dollars, never acknowledged on the books." Isn't that fraud? I asked. "It was still within the realm of accounting rules, but they were way out in the gray zone. It became criminal when they continued it to such a degree that it put all the shareholders at risk." Did anyone raise an objection? "All the time. We called it house-of-cards accounting and would openly discuss how crazy it was. In meetings, we were always told the same thing: 'You have to be able to come up with a solution.' There was no alternative."

Fastow's wife, Lea Weingarten, was in the room; she too worked at Enron, which was not unusual in the culture. Fastow had met Weingarten, the daughter of one of Houston's prominent Jewish families, when they were at Tufts. The Weingartens' fortune had come from a chain of grocery stores. Around town the couple was thought of as a study in opposites; Lea Weingarten was low-key, with the casual style of old money Texas.

Enron was hermetic and pulsing with sexuality. Ken Lay had married his secretary; Jeff Skilling had left his wife and taken up with Rebecca Carter, whom he promoted to company secretary and who earned more than $600,000 last year.

People who know Kenneth Lay well insist that his destruction can be understood by looking at his longtime attraction to ruthless, brainy alter egos such as Jeff Skilling and Andrew Fastow, who could act out Lay's ambitions while he played Mr. Congeniality. The aura of fraud permeated Enron from its inception in 1985, when the legacy and corporate style of Michael Milken were imprinted on Lay and his company. It was Michael Milken and Drexel Burnham that helped raise the $2.3 billion needed for the InterNorth–Houston Natural Gas merger. A little-known fact is that Enron stock was one ingredient of the scandal that brought down Michael Milken and Dennis Levine. Tipped off by a banker at Lazard Frères, Levine and his group of insider traders profiteered on the merger, as James B. Stewart has reported in *Den of Thieves*. They later went to prison.

Lay thrived in a culture of rivalries. He was a man of parts, a winner of awards and member of committees, generous with young associates, serving them himself when they traveled with him on one of the many Enron planes. "All these planes give my CEOs something to aspire to," Lay said to an ABC news reporter just months before Enron crashed. Inside the company, Lay overlooked, even encouraged, all the vicious infighting that went on. Lay came from a modest background, had a cheerful salesman's facade, and wore a Mr. Magoo mask of disconnection. He was a Gatsby of the pipelines, a minister's son from Missouri fueled with the desire for grandiose status. He earned a Ph.D. in economics at the University of Houston, was a navy officer, and clocked time in Washington as an undersecretary in the Department of the Interior.

He was attracted to Houston by the hope of staggering returns in the oil and gas world.

When Lay became allied with Milken in 1985, the junk bond king's reputation as the genius of inventive financial structures was at its peak. Not long before Drexel Burnham chief executive Frederick Joseph denounced the press for its "outrageous" allegations linking Milken to insider trading and the unsavory affairs of arbitrageur Ivan Boesky, Lay arrived in Beverly Hills in search of the financing he needed to realize his dream. The steady drumbeat of allegations in 1986 concerning Milken's honesty would have alarmed a more prudent CEO. In a 1987 interview, Milken went as far as to defend his business practices by boasting that he was helping Enron increase the size of its debt offering by an additional $225 million. Lay never cut his ties with Milken, and would later talk about him as a visionary who had been unfairly prosecuted. After Milken got out of jail, Lay invited him to speak at an Enron conference, despite a vocal protest from lawyers inside the company. "Ken always thought Mike was an out-of-the-box thinker who deserved sympathy," an Enron executive said.

In one magazine spread, Lay was portrayed as the wizard of energy, his body a glowing electric power line. As for the Kool-Aid, it was the elixir of money. Young traders just out of school were tantalized with promises of $500,000 in bonuses within a year. The Enron car of choice was a silver Porsche; the parking garage in Houston was full of them. Vice presidents and managers preparing to make a budget presentation in front of Lay, Skilling, and Fastow were told, "Here is your number." The numbers—always larger than what was feasible to demand on a contract—would have to be reached or, the vice president and managers knew, they could be "re-deployed," Enron language for being switched to another department, often before being forced out in a vicious biannual performance review. These performance reviews, referred to as "rank and yanks," were a variation on the old English Star Chamber. Your picture was displayed, and your colleagues blasted your job performance, knowing that their own advancement depended on your demise. Originators of deals might find that their numbers had been tampered with so that in the performance review their deal structures no longer made sense. "Because of the complexity of the math, it could take you weeks to figure out what had been changed, and by that time your deal was shot down or you were fired," one former associate recalled. Skilling would be very blunt with vice presidents who questioned these methods: *Change your assumptions. You can always refinance! You can always get the deal done!* In addition, the public relations staff had to keep Lay's competing division heads from getting too many cover stories in *Fortune* and *Forbes.* "Ken didn't like it," one told me. "He wanted the coverage for himself."

By the mid-nineties, Fastow was the whiz kid of Enron's financial structuring, always ready with sophisticated accounting arcana such as the "costless collar"—a complex financial instrument which allowed an investor to sell a stock in partnership with a bank at a guaranteed trigger price and yet not have it reported to the SEC. Jan Avery, for one, grew more and more alarmed at the accounting tricks required to support Skilling's and Fastow's bookkeeping. She used the term "feeding the monster" to describe the process.

As the Enron tentacles spread, it became increasingly difficult for Fastow and Skilling to disguise their ambitions. The deal structures became more and more byzantine. At the broadband division, which trafficked in the fiber-optic cable used in high-speed Internet connections, trades called "Barney deals"—meaning "I love you, you love me"—were constructed. Enron would sometimes swap control of its fiber lines with those of another company, only to undo the transaction a few days later, so as to create the appearance of volume. Other maneuvers pushed hundreds of millions of dollars of trading equity around in a circle, a practice employed by such companies as Qwest, Cisco, and Global Crossing, which was headed by Gary Winnick, who had trained at Drexel Burnham. When Global Crossing went bankrupt in January, Winnick was able to walk away with a reported $735 million. At the broadband group, Fastow used the lawyer Kristina Mordaunt, who represented the group in its dealings with the separate partnership of LJM2, which was run by Fastow. In March 2000, Mordaunt was invited into a Fastow venture called Southampton Place. She put down $5,800. She heard a few weeks later that the deal was winding down. Opening her bank statement the next month, she saw a deposit of $1 million. Another friend of Fastow's, managing director of Enron Global Finance Michael Kopper, would make more than $10 million from a $125,000 investment in Chewco, according to the report released by Enron directors in February.

"There is someone you should talk to," Alex Conn told Milberg Weiss partner David Walton in a surprise telephone call. Conn, an Austin software entrepreneur, had met Jan Avery when he negotiated with Enron, and he was impressed by her. Several weeks after Enron collapsed, he reached out to the people at Milberg Weiss to let them know what a valuable witness she could be. It was November 2001, and Walton, a Milberg forensic accountant, arranged a conference call with Paul Howes, who is the Milberg partner in charge of day-to-day operations for the Enron investigation. Howes has thick blond hair, a former athlete's build, and the empathic conversational style of the Southwest; in his years as a Washington-based assistant U.S. attorney, he radiated such useful kindness that he could get drug lords to confess. After his conversation with Avery, in which she talked about her experience at Enron International, which ran the company's projects overseas, Howes got on a plane to Houston. From then on, in his research reports Avery was referred to only as "confidential witness." He had yet to determine whether her information would check out.

By 1996, Avery had been transferred to Enron International and was therefore in the middle of the drama that would define the fall of Enron. It involved assets versus trading, and a rivalry between Rebecca Mark and Jeff Skilling, which led to the demise of Enron International, frequently referred to as "the purge." The war was fought over "paper gas," as the executives at Enron International called Skilling's ruthless consolidation of his power on the trading side. Skilling's traders occupied three floors in the Enron headquarters, and the trading room had more plasma screens than any other office in America. The atmosphere, according to one former Enron manager, was "the Royalton Hotel meets the Death Star." At the height of Skilling's power, the company was moving toward a peak moment, when the partnership structures would enable price-earnings ratios of 60, and the stock would surge in 2000 to $90.

Avery entered Enron International on the tax side and soon began working eighteen-hour days. She kept a picture in her office of Kay, now 11 with long blond hair, but when people asked her, "Who is that?," Avery would reply only, "My daughter." She rarely talked about her private life, but during the last weeks of each summer, as Kay got ready to return to her father, Avery was clearly under strain. Kay would lie in bed, crying, "Please let me stay." By 1999, Avery was earning more than most vice presidents, almost $300,000 a year with her bonus. She was angry that Enron refused to give her the title, and was convinced that, at 49, she was a victim of ageism. She took on an onerous amount of work in order to blot out her anger over her custody problems. Exploring the foreign-tax implications for Enron dealmakers negotiating for pipelines and power plants in Brazil, Bolivia, Peru, Eastern Europe, and Africa, Avery had to learn the tax code for each country. By then "the Skilling atmosphere," as it is often called, had begun to permeate the department. Avery recalled, "We were told constantly, 'Keep the debt off the balance sheets.'" This was done not only through off-the-books partnerships but also through loopholes in the tax laws of the foreign countries. Tax meetings would go on for hours, but Avery rarely complained.

Sent to Rio, she stayed for months in Copacabana, mastering the Brazilian tax code in order to facilitate negotiations for a pipeline between Brazil and Bolivia. She also began an affair with a member of the Enron team and for the first time in years felt it was possible to have an emotional life. She then went to Bolivia and Peru, spent weeks in Warsaw, returned to Houston, and flew to Africa, attempting to explain to Kay why it was often nine or ten hours later where she was calling from.

During this period, she was searching for lawyers in the counties around Eudora, Arkansas, hoping to find a talented attorney who would take on the Avery family. She knew she could not defend her travel schedule in a courtroom; she was on constant call, and, as she confided to her friends, the strain was becoming unbearable. How could she put an 11-year-old through the hell of an ugly custody battle?

In 1997 she was invited to the Enron International executive retreat in Beaver Creek, Colorado. At lunch during a ski break, she was joined at an outdoor table by Rebecca Mark, who was there with her 12-year-old twins. Mark was also divorced, and they talked about the constant emotional pull exerted on single working mothers. That day Avery resolved that she would try to become a deal originator in order to make more creative use of her time. At the bar, she sought out Mark's co-CEO, Joseph Sutton, a former brigadier general who resembled Burt Lancaster. Taking power and American investments around the world had made Mark and Sutton well-known in developing countries, but also, at times, the targets of scathing criticism for supporting the alleged imperial exploitation of local workers. In India they were accused of pushing through a $2 billion energy plant at Dabhol with bribes and threats, and of manhandling laborers. The Indian press is notorious for libel, and Enron officials vigorously denied the charges, which were never proved. Sutton was intrigued when Avery told him she had once set up her own pipeline marketing business, and he suggested that she write a letter to Mark.

I went to Houston determined to meet Rebecca Mark. For the last decade Mark had been a template of female achievement for the business press—named twice to *Fortune*'s list of the 50 top women CEOs. Her style had become famous—the size 6 Armani skirts, the stiletto heels. As the head of Enron International, she had early on taken part, with John Wing, in negotiating the billion-dollar power plant in England called Teesside, and had structured the deals for the Indian facility at Dabhol and the Brazilian pipeline. She and Henry Kissinger dealt with the Chinese premier, Israeli prime minister Ariel Sharon took her calls, Indian taxi drivers in Delhi would ask Enron executives, "Do you know the famous Miss Mark?" Back in Houston, she would work the phone late into the night in her flannel pajamas as her twins complained, "Mother, get off the phone!" She was an absence in the Houston social firmament; her ambitions were global, at the greatest remove from the Houston Country Club. As with Jan Avery, her job was her life, and her attractiveness and her ability to draw crowds in such places as Brazil and Vietnam helped to establish Ken Lay's political bona fides and extend the Enron brand.

The day I went to see her, her houseman was hanging Christmas boughs on the front gates of her mansion. Mark lives palatially behind a high wall in River Oaks. As I walked toward the house, two large dogs came bounding up to me, followed by a tall blond with a distinct Texas-rich-girl look, a bouncing mane of hair, and the skintight pale-blue stonewashed jeans that Houston and Hollywood power women pair with a $1,000 blazer and a white Gap T-shirt. Estimates of Mark's personal fortune vary wildly, from $30 million to $80 million. She married for the second time two years ago to Michael Jusbasche, who was born in Bolivia and owns a chemical company.

Like Ken Lay, Mark came from a small town in Missouri, one of four children in a farm family with deep fundamentalist beliefs. Her conversational style has been polished in Texas, and she is a master of "hillbillying," the trick of playing up one's humble origins. "Sometimes it was so cold in our farmhouse that frost was on the quilt," Mark told me as we sat in her vast drawing room with a grand piano in it and looked out on the garden. Within Enron International, Mark presented herself with the same down-home attitude, along with a rapier-sharp skill in marshaling rigorous arguments for deals. She was a booster of talent, particularly in women, and she created an atmosphere that felt familial. She would throw Christmas parties for as many as nine hundred people at her house, with carolers, clowns, and rides for the children. As a CEO operating under terrible tension, she told me, she taught herself to conceal her anger behind a midwestern-sorority-girl smile, particularly as she felt the Enron culture turning increasingly ruthless. She had a trick: When other executives excoriated her in meetings for not producing enough profits, she would not fight back but would simply tell herself that she was the smartest person in the room. "I was looking at them but it wasn't real," she said. "It was like an out-of-body experience."

At the time I met Mark, she was angry about an ongoing attack on her abilities in the business press. Moreover, she was bound by a confidentiality agreement and had been named as one of the twenty-nine officials who are potential defendants in the class action cases against Enron. As she told me later, "I am prepared for two stories: the 'I had sex with everyone in the universe' story and 'Rebecca's assets stink.' If they have a reason to try to destroy me, it will be over the quality of my business and what they will make up about my love life. The sole reason will be to put less credibility on the side of the asset business I built up."

There appear to be few people in Houston who do not hold strong opinions about Mark's investments. One economist who knows her well described her as "a bundle of energy . . . but she and John Wing figured out a way to take a juicy bite of the apple with their power plant development, and the credulous banks went along with them . . . loaning 95 percent financing on the basis of pro formas that no fool would believe. . . . The poor Indian and Chinese residential electricity consumers would have been spending half their disposable annual income on electricity." A prominent money manager who shorted Enron stock in 2000 said, "Almost everything that Mark touched at Enron was catastrophic in terms of investment return. The company had to either recognize the losses or cover them up. To Skilling's detriment, he chose to cover them up." When I asked Mark about this, she said, "None of the money managers have ever read the contracts backing up these businesses. The companies we created around the world are not bankrupt."

Some insiders theorized that Mark's "special relationship" with Ken Lay may have given her carte blanche to operate with no checks and balances. It was commonly thought that Rebecca Mark and Jeff Skilling had had an affair; they were both divorced, had children the same ages, and often went to school sporting events together. Mark's detractors suggest that she also had relationships with several members of her development team. Mark has become used to hearing this type of sexual branding, and believes it is a classic attempt to diminish her tenacity and achievement. "These were people outside the international arena who did not know how we worked," she said. "I used to make jokes about this in speeches and say, 'I had no idea I was so staggeringly attractive.' And how in the world would I ever have time, when I have passports so thick they look like volumes of the Bible."

For years, Mark operated under the protection of Ken Lay and Rich Kinder. She represented the assets-based side of Enron, which went back to the early days of the company, when Lay realized that gas could be traded as a commodity. By then the government had forced the utilities to accept the notion of unregulated power. Mark's great skill as a CEO was always in presentation, her colleagues say, not in operation, which was routinely handled by other executives. Mark was able to persuade the Indian government to change its policies and reverse its course on the power plant at Dabhol, and she negotiated ironclad agreements protecting the assets in the event the government should change. She understood that her ability to survive at the highest level required her to project certitude, a sense that she was comfortable in her own skin.

In the early days of Enron International, Mark was told repeatedly, "You eat what you kill," and initially she and her team worked without bonuses. However, she was able to come up with a lucrative contract-value-percentage arrangement that ultimately earned her close to $80 million in stock options and reportedly enraged Jeff Skilling. "I think they gave us this deal because they were convinced we couldn't get anything done," she said. She and Joe Sutton operated on sheer nerve. Sutton would tell her, "Act like we've already won," as they went into meetings with foreign leaders.

A former executive at Shell Oil described Mark in Bolivia, determined to sell the government on the idea of giving Enron the contract to assist in building a billion-dollar pipeline between Brazil and Bolivia, a project so politically problematic that even industry leaders such as Shell and Mobil wouldn't touch it. Mark sailed into one presentation and spoke for hours without notes to three hundred officials, dazzling them with her command of the area's problems and stimulating them with her assurances of what Enron could bring to the table. She was less successful in dealing with complexities in the Middle East. The Enron team arrived in Qatar to set up a three-country development deal for the richest supply of natural gas in the world. "No one tells us how to negotiate—we are Enron," Mark allegedly said to one diplomat representing the emir. Moreover, the Enron bids were couched in very aggressive language. "They told us they were doing us a public relations favor, letting our negotiation be a model for good relations with Israel," the diplomat said, startled at the team's lack of understanding of the region. In fact, Mark later told me, she had inherited this deal from another division of the company and found herself locked in a negotiating struggle with two governments. "We walked into a mess, and the Qataris were angry," she said. "But we felt we could not leave a billion dollars on the ground." Two years later the emir was said to be offended by the low price Enron bid for the gas. Ken Lay tried to smooth out the difficulties and renegotiate. "Not if you send in the same group," the emir said sternly, according to an official who was in the room.

In 1998, Jan Avery was in Nicaragua as a project developer, supervising the building of a $75 million barge power plant, one of Enron International's last enterprises. The night before the final approvals, she was on a conference call with Skilling's aide Rick Buy and the Enron International executive who was presenting the Nicaraguan barge plant to the board. "They were screaming at each other," Avery recalled. "It was clear how Skilling and his group were out to put a stop to all assets being developed. They were trying to make us lower the assessments, although the numbers had already been presented." By then Skilling had turned against Mark, telling her in meetings, according to one of her associates, that her assets were a disaster, the worst investments Enron had ever made.

Nine months after Avery moved to Managua, she developed a persistent cough. The working conditions were filthy, she recalled, and the air was full of smoke and pollution. The barge project had caused a political firestorm. The president of Nicaragua was demanding a payment of $2 million to allow the company to finish the work, and a warrant was put out by the Nicaraguan government for the arrest of Enron executives. "You have a spot on your lung," her doctor told her. "You have to go home immediately." In Houston she was diagnosed with a rare bacterial disease. She spent the next five months in the hospital, and several times her blood pressure climbed so high that she was close to death.

At the top of Enron International, the pressure on Rebecca Mark was increasing. She confided to friends that Skilling's approach was like Chinese water torture, a subtle, continual bombardment of what she was doing. He was attempting to consolidate his power, moving Enron into a future where it was asset-light, as he said. He was still an icon of the business magazines, celebrated for his Gas Bank innovation, which moved Enron into a new world where it created a market in gas. His elliptical phrases, such as "vertical integration," became koans of the dot-com era. One day Mark sat him down and asked him how his business worked. She was curious, she told colleagues, about broadband and the emerging energy markets. "I wanted a sense of comparison," she said. "Are we that bad? Or are they that good?" Mark was operating in a closed system. Enron International had separate accounting and was in a different building. At the height of this internal war, Rich Kinder, who for years had kept a brake on the company's exponential expansion, was passed over for CEO. Later, Ken Lay reportedly ran into Rich

Kinder's wife and told her that none of Enron's problems would have happened if Kinder were still at the company. After Kinder left Enron, he started a new energy company, Kinder Morgan, which is traded publicly; he is said to be a billionaire.

One day Rebecca Mark confronted Lay in a meeting. "You are being snookered, Ken," she told her old friend. "These are profits from the sale of assets. These are not trading profits." Their conversation was about their European business, and Lay's response, Mark told someone close to her, was to look at her kindly, condescendingly, as if to indicate that her lack of vision made her a dinosaur. Her assets, at best, could return 14 percent, but she was planning for the long run with equity investments, a strategy designed to hold an investment for decades, and the company had veered inexorably toward the culture of traders, where profits now soared to close to 30 percent every year.

It became clear, Mark told a few intimate friends, that Skilling was trying to shove her out. She began to negotiate a partnership agreement with Shell to sell half of Enron International's assets, which would have brought $3.2 billion of equity to the company. They negotiated for several months, a Shell executive remembered. Inside Enron International, it was generally assumed that Mark's position as a CEO of the new company would ensure her prestige, but the Shell executive said that the fluctuating stock price made the deal impossible to close. Mark was made a vice-chairman—a position known as "the ejector seat"—and allowed to take a bold gamble and explore treating water as a commodity in the international markets. The board approved the $2.3 billion purchase of an English water company called Wessex Water, which would become the backbone of Enron's global water company, Azurix, and which looked to be a great source of profit, but which turned into a disaster when Britain changed its water rates. Soon the whole water business changed, and Azurix was losing so much money that it was affecting the price of Enron's stock. When asked to respond, Mark said, "It wasn't a disaster. We couldn't survive as a public company because we didn't have earnings sufficient to support the growth of the stock."

As Skilling moved against Mark, Cliff Baxter found himself in an increasingly untenable position. He was a lieutenant with a conflict, whose responsibility it was to enforce the new Skilling culture, and his loyalty, many believe, was what would ultimately drive him to suicide. By 1997, Skilling had consolidated his power and had assembled his own team, which included Fastow and Baxter. The group was known as "the beautiful people" or "the seven dwarfs." One day the accounting staff at Enron International learned that Skilling's team had reaudited Mark's assets and was planning to sabotage her in front of the board. She arrived at the meeting to hear Skilling say, "These assets are a disaster. Not just Azurix—everything. They are returning 3 percent, not 14 percent." Mark tried to remain calm and responded, "I take issue with these numbers. My analysis is there for anyone to see." According to an associate of Mark's, however, Lay conveyed a few days later that it made no difference to him what her analysis said about the assets; he wanted no debate about getting rid of all of them, because he wanted the cash for the trading operation. In August 2000, Mark was asked to leave the company she had helped start. She immediately sold all of her Enron stock.

For Jan Avery, Enron had become incomprehensible; nothing she had experienced since Nicaragua had prepared her for the internal chaos she found. Sent to Abu Dhabi in October 1999, Avery watched Skilling torpedo nine months of negotiations on the $3 billion Dolphin pipeline. The projected pipeline would link the United Arab Emirates with Qatar in a deal so innovative that Conoco, Amoco, and British Petroleum were all vying for it. The pipeline business had once been the very basis of Enron's financial strength, and this deal—which required Enron to invest $300 million—was projected to return tenfold profits to the company.

In Abu Dhabi, Avery supervised a ten-person team through months of due diligence and negotiations. The Dolphin pipeline became a symbol of the Middle East's emergence into the twenty-first century and a staple in the European press. Surrounded by computer models and sheikhs in robes, Avery was oblivious to what was going on in Houston. Skilling was directing his attention to broadband, to which he had pledged $3 billion. Three days before the press conference announcing the successful acquisition of the Dolphin contract, Avery received an agitated phone call from Joe Sutton, who was now sitting in the ejector seat as vice-chair. "Stop the press conference," he told her. "This cannot go through. Skilling has put a stop to it." But it was too late. The Dolphin pipeline had been announced throughout Europe and the Middle East. Nevertheless, within months Skilling had walked away from the deal. "I don't want any assets," he announced.

In Houston, Avery went to Broadband Services, and during her interview there she was asked to take a look at the projected trading models. It would be her job to help determine the pricing for the broadband swaps—trades that would later provide the basis of Bill Lerach's invective in court, when he would compare them to Michael Milken's fraudulent operations.

Avery studied the models and told the head of the division, "There is no way that these can work." She then walked away from the job and was moved to the international group, where she worked on a deal to create a trading hub for liquid gas in Malaysia. Skilling's purge had now infected the entire company, and there were waves of firings. While in Kuala Lumpur to negotiate with the local oil and gas company, Avery learned of the "ethnic cleansing" being used to close down her division. "Don't worry, they are keeping the best people and re-deploying them," she was told.

She was next assigned to Enron Energy Services (EES), the playground of Lou Pai, who had set up a division to trade energy in California. The move meant changing buildings and giving up her large office for a trading desk. Enron Energy Services sold "bundled energy" to customers such as Starwood Hotels, JC Penney, Quaker Oats, and Owens-Illinois, the glass company. The "bundle" was a promise of future service—meaning air-conditioning replaced, lightbulbs changed, wiring fixed. In her first weeks, Avery approached a commodity analyst who was proposing a price that would absolutely guarantee a loss to Enron. "We can't do this," Avery told him. "How can you be selling something that is a negative?" The commodity analyst replied belligerently, "Just do it. We sell negatives all the time."

That was during last year's California brownouts, and Avery made a startling discovery. Enron had sold contracts to retail customers, including the University of California and the Simon Property Group, which owned malls in San Francisco. As the cost of power soared, Enron returned the power to the utilities, employing a loophole the Enron salesmen had cleverly provided. The resulting cost to the state of California by one estimate was close to $500 million, but within Enron there was no acknowledgment of the larger meaning. Avery remembers that the press releases were still rosy. No mention was made of Enron's reduction of a buying price from $1,500 per megawatt to $10. "This was disguised as normal business procedure," Avery said. "What it meant was that all their contracts were under water."

"Margaret, this is insane," Avery said to Margaret Ceconi, who sat next to her at the trading desk. Like Avery, Ceconi was new to the department, having been hired from GE Capital with the promise of annual bonuses as high as $1 million. Ceconi was voluble and freewheeling, a person who would throw pool parties and invite several boyfriends only to describe their reactions with bursts of laughter the next day at work. "We have to find some new men for *you*, Jan!" she told Avery, and soon they were spending time together. "This place is going down," Ceconi said to Avery, "and we have to get off the ship." They talked about financial analysts they could tip off, finally settling on Carol Coale at Prudential, who for months had been cautioning that Enron was not sound.

One day in the summer of 2001, Skilling arrived at the EES floor and jumped on a desk. By then the new-business developers were frequently logging on to thomsonFN.com, which tracks insider trading. "Why are you selling your stock, Jeff?" someone shouted at him. According to Ceconi, Skilling, after citing a list of dubious reasons for unloading his shares, reassured the developers that "life was good" and that they should keep buying Enron stock. After that, Ceconi said to Avery, "You and I are going to write a letter to the board, Jan." Avery was wary. Two weeks before Skilling's abrupt departure, both women lost their jobs. It was early August, shortly before Kay Avery, finally in her mother's custody, was to leave for Baylor University. Without a job, Jan could no longer afford the $20,000-a-year tuition.

"You don't know me," said Margaret Ceconi in a phone call to Carol Coale, "but I'm a friend who wants to tell you what's really going on at Enron." Ceconi, who didn't reveal her identity at first, began writing to Coale from an e-mail account with the address Enron-truth. "We are sending you a lengthy letter that we have sent to the Enron board," Ceconi wrote. The letter, like Sherron Watkins's now famous warning to Ken Lay, spelled out $500 million in false profits Enron had claimed in the last year. Unlike

Watkins's straightforward, cogent criticism, Ceconi's letter began with a litany of complaints about the company. More reasoned analysis of the financials was buried on subsequent pages.

The SEC opened its inquiry into Enron's accounting on October 22. Ken Lay continued to tout his company's stock in a conference call the following day. On October 24, Carol Coale, fed up with Enron's rosy predictions, downgraded the stock to a "sell." The company filed for bankruptcy six weeks later. Ceconi's letter was given to Apache Oil, an Enron competitor. It ultimately found its way to the congressional committees working on the investigation into Enron. The day Ceconi's letter was published in the *Houston Chronicle*, sixty-five news organizations contacted her. She was on *Good Morning America*, being interviewed by Diane Sawyer, at the same time Linda Lay was telling NBC's Lisa Myers, "Other than the home we live in, everything we own is for sale."

"Good God, it's a Rorschach test," Paul Howes said to Jan Avery during one session in Houston as he studied a diagram of an Enron partnership. It was the first time the lawyer had ever seen the circles and boxes that would soon confound even the most sophisticated economists. "It is simple to understand," Avery told him. "The more circles and boxes, the bigger the bonuses, and the more the customer is confused." Howes had weighed Avery's unhappiness over her treatment by Enron with her expertise on the financials and had decided to use her as a consultant. He was working on the Enron case with a team of investigators and Frank Karam, a partner from the New York office, as well as with Lynn Hodges, whose California firm, L. R. Hodges & Associates, specializes in "witness development."

In January, Howes and his team were fielding more than a hundred calls and e-mails a day. "This is the most exhausting case I have ever done," Hodges told me. "All I am doing at the moment is reacting." She had received that morning an e-mail with a photo-graph of a shredding company truck parked outside the Enron building. One Saturday, Howes spent eight hours in a hotel room with an auditor from Enron International, another "confidential wit-ness." He and a second auditor told Howes that Robert Jaedicke—then dean of the Graduate Business School at Stanford and the head of the Enron audit committee—visited the internal audit staff in March 1989. "How do you view your role as an independent director?," Jaedicke was asked. "I'm here to support management. I'm here to support Ken Lay," he replied. The two auditors took this remark as an indication of where Jaedicke's loyalties lay. Later, they told Howes, Enron International developers in pursuit of bonuses put through projects rife with engineering problems, which later became budget nightmares. They had been disgusted to be out-sourced to Arthur Andersen. "Jeff Skilling ran a casino for a busi-ness side and a day care center for junior auditors," one said.

In early February, Howes told me he had finally tracked down Herb Perry, the auditor who fifteen years earlier had gathered an inves-tigative file on the rogue trading operation at Enron Oil that had so mystified Jan Avery in her first months on the job. Avery had told Howes about the missing file, and Howes finally persuaded Perry, who had just retired, to see him. The day before Sherron Watkins testified in Congress, Howes flew to New Orleans and drove for an hour to a house near the water. A 10-year-old sheltie came out to greet him, and Howes, who is passionate about dogs, played with her before he said hello to Perry and his wife. "Well, if our dog likes you, you must be all right," Perry's wife said.

The men drove to a nearby café and shared a shrimp po'boy sandwich. To an investigator, Perry's background was impeccable. Before going to Enron in June 1986, he had spent seventeen years at Shell on internal audits and fraud investigation. His specialty was white-collar crime. He found Enron's accounting department in disarray, he later told me; the new corporation was still trying to integrate InterNorth and Houston Natural Gas. The board had six members from each, and the group was fraught with tension, because the Houston executives had profited in the merger, and the InterNorth members had not. Ken Lay and Rich Kinder, who had been together at Florida Gas, were running the new company, with Kinder as general counsel.

On January 23, 1987, Perry says, his boss, David Woytek, the vice president of audit, got a call from a security officer at Apple Bank on 42nd Street in New York. "Hey, something interesting happened. You should know about it. There are unusual cash transactions from the Isle of Guernsey coming into my bank from Enron in $100,000 increments!" the officer said. The approvals of the transactions, he went on, were not coming from authorized corporate treasurers but from two executives in Valhalla, New York, named Louis Borget and Thomas Mastroeni. "Borget and Mastroeni appear to be writing checks to themselves," the bank officer said.

Woytek called Rich Kinder and then spoke to an aide of Enron's John Harding. The news of the suspected fraud rocked the audit staff. Enron Oil appeared to be a great source of profit for Enron, and Harding had personally appeared before the board, one auditor told me, describing in detail the connections to the Saudi royals and Kuwait that had enabled his executives to make such vast trading profits. All the midwesterners at Enron, including Ken Lay, understood pipelines and their rich, dependable cash flow, but Harding's description of the potential bonanza to be made in trading money thrilled them. "They swallowed it hook, line, and sinker," the auditor said. Lay was told that the amount at issue in Valhalla was no more than $2 to $4 million, a relatively small amount since Enron Oil was reporting profits of more than $30 million a year—one-third of the earnings of the company at that time. "Lay told us, 'Just go up there and get the money back,'" Perry said. By then the audit department had gotten statements from Apple Bank and suspected that Borget and Mastroeni were keeping double books. Perry, who went with Woytek to Valhalla, was sternly warned, "Whatever you do, do not upset Borget."

Before Perry left Houston, he made a to-do list of nineteen items, which included "locking the system down, getting a warrant to track the Western Union teletypes, because that was how the deals were confirmed in those days."

Arriving in New York, Perry and Woytek discovered that the trading operation was controlled completely by Borget and Mastroeni. To go there, you had to be picked up in a limo, Perry recalled. "I don't want the competition to get close to my staff," Borget told him to explain the quirky privacy procedures. The Houston employees were not allowed to interview anyone on the staff. One member of the Houston team was an Arthur Andersen partner and an expert in oil and gas trading. "Everything is proper," Borget told Perry. "We've just had an audit done."

Perry and Woytek sat in an octagonal trading room with John Beard, another Enron auditor, trying to unravel the fraud. Two days later a call came from Houston; Perry remembers distinctly that the caller was Rich Kinder. "I am hearing one side of it," he said. "Woytek was just beside himself. He carried on with Kinder, getting quite aggressive. He was saying, 'I can't believe you are going to ask us to do this.' Kinder told Woytek, 'Get out of the building and come back to Houston. You are off the case.'" The reason? "They were all scared," one auditor told me, "that the traders would get upset and they would lose the income." He is not sure whether the call came from Kinder or John Seidl, the president of Enron, but he said that Perry's memory is "sharp" and he kept perfect notes.

Perry remembered Kinder saying, "We are turning the investigation over to Arthur Andersen." Soon a flotilla of Arthur Andersen auditors arrived from Houston; among them was the young Jeffrey McMahon, who in 2002 would replace Andrew Fastow as Enron's chief financial officer.

The Houston auditors appeared before the audit committee in April 1987 and reported on what the Enron staff and Arthur Andersen had found in Valhalla. The two groups were in complete agreement. Woytek had managed to retrieve the millions that Borget and Mastroeni had misappropriated, but one auditor recalls Woytek telling Lay and the committee that they had to get rid of the two men. They were adamant; they should have been gone in February, they said. Borget had told the auditors that he was keeping the money in a personal account but that it would soon come back to Enron. One auditor said, "If the Apple Bank had not called, this money might never have been recovered."

I asked the auditor to read me the minutes from the April 29, 1987, meeting. "Dr. Jaedicke called upon management for a matter that involved Enron Oil Corporation that was investigated by the company and subsequently investigated by Arthur Andersen. . . . After a full discussion, management ['This was Ken Lay,' the auditor said] recommended the person involved be kept on the payroll but relieved of financial responsibility, and a new chief financial officer of Enron Oil Corp. be appointed. The committee agreed with reservations. . . . Mr. Orloff [the future general counsel, who is now at Bracewell & Patterson] reported on possible legal consequences. He stated that all legal work for Enron Oil Corp. would now be done in Houston by an attorney reporting to him."

Fifteen years later, the auditor is still upset. "And when they say 'management,' I can remember Ken Lay sitting there saying, 'I have made the decision!' . . . What can I say? He was the CEO, and he felt that they could put controls in place and that he needed those earnings. That was his call. . . . We all knew those people were crooks! We told him that."

. . .

He became solemn as he read out the names of the people gathered in the room, several of them now familiar players in the Enron drama, who would maintain their silence and remain aligned with Kenneth Lay right up until the corporation collapsed. Robert Jaedicke, the distinguished accounting professor, would appear before the congressional subcommittee this year. Herbert Winokur Jr., a Harvard overseer, would also testify as the chief of the finance committee who in the wake of the scandal finally ordered an investigation. Arthur Belfer's family would lose about $2 billion in Enron stock. Steve Goddard of Arthur Andersen would be relieved of his management responsibilities.

At least two people in the room that day questioned Lay's judgment. One was Ronald Roskens, then the president of the University of Nebraska, who would leave the board two years later to join the government. The other was Carolyn Kee, from Arthur Andersen. "When we walked out of the room, Carolyn Kee turned to me and said, 'I am just sick about this,'" one auditor remembered. Kee was concerned about the lack of internal controls and would spend months dealing with the fallout from future shareholder suits and the SEC inquiry. Within three years she left Enron and is now in private practice in Arkansas.

For the Enron auditors, the April board meeting was prophetic. "It was obvious to us and to Arthur Andersen that [Borget and Mastroeni] had opened fraudulent bank accounts, and we felt that they were going to continue to manipulate transactions," one auditor told me. "Lay read the report and he read his budget, and estimated how much they made and if they were fired what he could lose. . . . My conclusion was that this is a guy who puts earnings before scruples, rather than reacting to the dishonesty right in front of him."

. . .

Does that establish a pattern of fraud? I asked Herb Perry, a question I had often asked Jan Avery. "It is certainly the indicator that there is significant collusion between the executives at Enron and the senior people at Arthur Andersen. They were willing to tolerate improprieties."

Lay's designated watchdog was delayed in getting to Valhalla in 1987, and soon Borget and Mastroeni had spun out of control. They bet long on oil as the prices dropped and shorted when the prices rose. Borget called Houston and said, "There is going to be a huge loss. About a billion dollars."

I asked one auditor what it was like around Enron when that staggering figure was revealed. "Bad," he said. "We were all concerned because we thought that someone would be made a scapegoat." According to the auditor, the in-house lawyer Gary Orloff asked for the files. "They came to us and said, 'We want all of your files. We want everything. . . .' Kinder was the chief operating officer and . . . Orloff seemed to be protecting Lay in this thing." When Jan Avery went to work at Enron, she could hardly have known that the files on Enron Oil she tried so hard to find had vanished six years earlier.

By the autumn of 1987, federal prosecutors in New York working under then U.S. attorney Rudolph Giuliani had detected the crime. The prosecutor who ran the case, James Comey, now has Giuliani's former job. Lay's inability to operate within the strict rules of corporate propriety had left his company close to collapse. What had started as "an expensive embarrassment" had become herculean. Lay had had to dispatch an Enron team, led by Mike Muckleroy, from Enron Oil Trade & Transportation, to unwind many of the deals. Muckleroy was able to reduce the loss to $185 million, a figure closer to the number Jan Avery first saw.

In September 1993, the year Jan Avery went to work for Enron, Perry learned that Arthur Andersen would be taking over all of Enron's auditing functions at the end of that year. The company said it was a cost-saving measure, but Perry believes that the real significance of the change was that internal investigation of offshore partnerships and off-balance-sheet partnerships were no longer pursued. The new Arthur Andersen model, Perry was told, would be used as an exemplar for the rest of the industry. Perry remained on assignment for Enron Oil & Gas, a subsidiary of Enron which had gone public and had a separate accounting staff.

On February 8, a week before Howes went to New Orleans, Jeff Skilling appeared before the House Energy and Commerce Oversight Subcommittee, one of a dozen government panels investigating the Enron debacle. Executives still working at the corporate headquarters in Houston watched him on television. One of them recalls hearing Andrew Fastow on any number of occasions mention his conversations with Skilling about the off-the-books partnerships Skilling was now telling congressmen he knew very little about. Earlier that day, Skilling had sat with cold eyes and an odd smirk on his face and told the committee, "I was not aware of any financing arrangements designed to conceal liabilities or inflate profitability. . . . I did not believe that the company was in any imminent financial peril." At that, several financial officers screamed at the set, "Bullshit!" One kept saying during Skilling's testimony, "Now Jeff will say, 'I don't recall,'" and twenty-seven times Skilling did not disappoint him. These Enron executives, who had cheered Skilling when he was named CEO, now studied him on the screen with contempt.

Congressman Ed Markey of Massachusetts, who had been the chairman of the House Telecommunications and Finance Subcommittee that investigated Michael Milken in the 1980s, said of Jeff Skilling, "He testified like he was a guest on *I've Got a Secret*. He was treating Congress like he had treated his shareholders."

. . .

In Louisiana, Herb Perry spent Valentine's Day in his La-Z-Boy armchair watching Sherron Watkins testify before Congress. After the criminal investigation of Borget and Mastroeni began, Perry had turned over a copy of his Valhalla file to his boss, David Woytek. What happened to Perry's fifty cartons of documents about Enron's dealings over the years? "I shredded those," he said. "I did not want to carry them around, and I certainly did not want to be dragged into legal issues with Arthur Andersen." Watching Watkins in front of the committee, Perry was at first impressed with her stolid manner and muted outrage, but he began to revise his opinion as Watkins mused about Ken Lay's personal culpability. Watkins described a moment where she had tried to explain the cascade of partnership accounting fantasies to Lay. "He did not seem to understand," she said. Sitting with his wife and his dog, Perry laughed out loud. "I said a lot of language I can't repeat," he told me. He said he was mystified that an intelligent woman could have made such an assertion without fully understanding the history of the company. I asked Perry what he thought when Watkins asserted, "Mr. Lay was duped." He laughed. "Ken Lay duped? Well, I guess now you know better, don't you?"

———

There she was, in the courtroom in Houston, the mysterious woman in a purple suit, nervous and in disguise. I was drawn to her immediately. She seemed to know something about a case that had just entered the American language and would rage in the news for the months ahead. In fact Jan Avery did have a secret—a big one. She would help to illuminate a vast web of corporate crime. Avery, now in hot demand to scour the books for lawyers pursuing white-collar crime, first heard about the auditors who had spirited away the files from Enron's dark history. The rogue traders of the 1980s were an important clue that Ken Lay had decades of secrets to be found.

Now Enron has become its own adjective to describe an era of fraud and concealment. Enron taught America hard lessons—that numbers could not be trusted and the finest accountants manipulate facts. It was a business story that the public understood easily—bad guys in private jets, living in mansions in Houston hiding the truth from employees whose savings were tied up in a virtual company that evaporated overnight. The term "Ponzi scheme" was used by the lawyers to describe what had happened in Enron, but the trick seemed closer to three-card monte. Cards pushed this way and that, a crowd gambling and fooled by its own delusions.

And what of the players? As this book goes to press, Andrew Fastow, indicted for his role at the company, braced for a possible new indictment. Jeffrey Skilling, holed up in his River Oaks mansion, had become the Greta Garbo of the town. Ken Lay, the fallen Alpha yet to do the perp walk, was a pariah in Houston, but as pink-cheeked and smiling as ever, worked the tables at local restaurants gladhanding anyone who would greet him. Christmas of 2002 found him far from the Bush White House as in palmier times, but at his sister's condo near Galveston. He was, as ever, obsessed with image, hinting of onerous margin calls. He dropped hints in the business news that he was a pitiful figure, down to his last $6 million, and how could he ever afford to keep up his string of vacation homes and staff? I wondered reading this if Lay's trick was picked up by studying the career of the late Clark Clifford, the adviser to presidents who became ensnared in a messy banking scandal. At the height of the BCCI caper, friends of Clifford worked the phones: "We are taking baskets of food to poor Clark." The Lays as well played it for all it was worth; Linda Lay, who once told NBC from her multimillion-dollar penthouse how low the family had fallen, now could be found at a thrift shop boutique she ran to sell off the family's silver trays.

By the winter of 2002, Arthur Andersen was prosecuted by the government in an unwieldy case that left many unsatisfied, but lawyers widened their net and targeted law firms and banks that had participated in the Enron mirage. Traveling from Florida nursing homes to South Texas ranches, the class action lawyer Paul Howes continued to work massive hours talking to potential witnesses. "An eighty-year-old is willing to get on an airplane and sit for a deposition because he said, 'They lied to me and they lied to the market and we have to do something about that,'" he said.

This was a story that as well ennobled its women, who were the first in the company to sense that something was wrong. The gifted Houston writer Mimi Swartz, whose book Power Failure: The Inside Story of the Collapse of Enron, written with whistle-blower Sherron Watkins, offered a sweeping history of the case, paraphrased Jung: "Whatever you deny will come back to you as fate." And in true American fashion, Watkins became a national heroine and made the cover of Time. The last time I was in Houston, the lawyers were all reading an American classic, Theodore Dreiser's The Financier. Lay appeared to them as large and elusive as Dreiser's hero who rises, falls, and rises again.

DIRTY LITTLE SECRET
DOUG MOST

Ever taken a shot to the gut? Maybe a soccer ball caught you flush or a bad spill off a bike knocked the wind out of you. Suddenly, you're on the ground, curled up like a fetus, wheezing for air. Scary, isn't it? Especially that split second when the dizziness hits and you really start to panic.

This is a story about one crushing blow delivered by a man from Newton, and the people he's left doubled over in pain—from his fiancée to his parents and kid brother to his professors and Air Force buddies. They all thought they knew him. No, scratch that: They did know him. He was the kid built like a fire hydrant, with the neat brown hair and clean-shaven face, the one who played the piano, sang a cappella, swam like a dolphin, volunteered with kids, and could set up a website faster than you could butter your toast. They did know him. They just didn't know all of him.

First Lieutenant Sean Galliher of the 517th Airlift Squadron was a military man. But he didn't die in battle. For reasons only he knew, his end came alone; he was too ashamed to face his accusers. There was no picture of him on the evening news in full military uniform because his last breath didn't come in the cockpit of his C-130 Hercules. Death for this young man from an idyllic Boston suburb came in a cramped one-bedroom apartment in Anchorage, Alaska, his morning newspaper still outside his door and two orange cats roaming around his living room. It came with him not in his uniform but in his civvies—black turtleneck, blue jeans, and white socks. It came with his limp body hanging from his bedroom door, a black computer cable wrapped and knotted tightly around his neck.

The two e-mails land in my in-box minutes apart, sent by a non-profit group called WiredPatrol, a sort of neighborhood watchdog for the Internet. "I'm very happy to help you out," the first one starts. "Here are a couple sites you might find of interest." The links to three strangely titled websites are listed, but before I can click away, the second message lands. "I'd suggest, when you're finished, that you clean the computer you used by deleting all cookies, temporary Internet files, and history. You don't want anyone else who may access your computer to view these sites." Detailed instructions explain how to permanently spike the links. Not just trash them, but erase them as if they were never here. It looks complicated. But that's for later. It's the first e-mail that should explain what led investigators, on a brisk Alaskan night, to raid Galliher's apartment—and to his suicide two days later.

A few years back, a website was launched showing pictures of kids. Naked kids. It wouldn't crop up in an ordinary Yahoo search: You had to know where to hunt for it deep in the folds of the Internet. Yet in its first three months, the site recorded 256,000 hits— almost 3,000 a day, with 4.2 million images downloaded, or 50,000 images a day. Only when investigators were able to trace its origin and arrest six people was it shut down. Who looks? Typically, either loners who tell no one what they're doing or those who seek to hook up with secret communities that validate urges society never will. Beyond that, there is no "typical" pedophile, no profile, only trends. An increasing number of young men in their twenties are being arrested for it; one in every four pedophiles was molested himself as a child.

Just looking at these pictures isn't a crime. The crime is clicking "download" to move an image to your hard drive—that's possession of child porn—or attaching one to an e-mail and sending it, which is distribution. But until you've seen child pornography—cops call it KP, for kiddie porn—it's impossible to imagine it. Adjectives are worthless. You see it and feel dirty. That bitter taste will surface, the one that fills your mouth just before you vomit. These aren't borderline adults staring out of the computer screen, teenagers made up to look 18. These are kids, a few boys, mostly girls, no hips, no breasts, no curves. One of them is just standing there, nude, a few bales of hay behind her, as if she's about to tend the stable, a big smile radiating from her face. Another is lying on a bed, nude, looking back over her shoulder at the camera. A third is on her knees, nude, beside a man's legs—also nude. Some of them are being raped. It looks consensual, but they can't be older than 12 or 13. There's one picture called "Me and My Girls," which looks like any vacation snapshot of a smiling father and his two daughters standing knee deep in a beautiful, secluded pond—except they're all nude, the bearded guy with the basketball belly and the reed-thin girls on either side of him.

This is what officials say they found on Galliher's computer—and what they were about to arrest him for having. His hard drive had been wiped clean when investigators got it, but they were able to recall some of the images that had been stored. Why he did it is not nearly as important to investigators as how he got these pictures, and that's what is now at the heart of an international investigation that began one night last November. Police in a small city in western Germany, suspicious that a 40-year-old man was distributing child porn, barged in on him while he was sitting in front of his computer, online in his private chat room with ten other people. Straight out of a script from *Law & Order*, he turned rat, having been convicted once before of spreading child porn. He confessed that he had launched the chat room, which he called the Round Table, to exchange child porn over the Internet, and that a dozen people from around the world were participating, each using passwords and sophisticated encryption tools to hide from the web police. In order to remain a part of the group, members had to occasionally provide the others with child pornography photos. He didn't care how they got them, or whether the photos were of kids actually being molested or harmless snapshots that had been altered. He was simply building an archive, though as Detective Superintendent Mick Deats at the National Hi-Tech Crime Unit in London, which arrested two men in the Round Table case, says: "Every image represents a child being abused. They're creating a demand for new images and creating more victims."

The German man gave police the nicknames used by the others in the Round Table. He didn't know their real names, or that there was a nurse, an artist, a network administrator for a publishing house, or a U.S. Air Force pilot among them. But he knew enough to spark a worldwide probe, called Operation Artus, that would ultimately lead investigators to a gated apartment complex near an Alaskan Air Force base.

"Mr. Galliher was leading a double life with this," says Steve Skrocki, an assistant U.S. attorney in Anchorage, who says the evidence proves that Galliher was an active member of the Round Table. "While this is extremely unfortunate, and tragic to his family and friends, the investigation results are quite clear. We were left with no doubt in our minds that he was involved in the collection and distribution of child pornography. No doubt."

If only it were that simple. Because for those who knew Sean Galliher, there is so much doubt.

Sean Parrish Galliher was born on February 18, 1977, at the Boston Hospital for Women to Michelle Susan LaBrecque Galliher, a 24-year-old secretary, and Parrish McLaren Galliher, a 23-year-old research technician. They were living on Commonwealth Avenue in Allston when their first child arrived, and he arrived quickly, almost nine months to the day from their wedding at St. James Church in Stratford, Connecticut. Four years after Sean's birth, his brother, Eric, was born, and two and a half years after that, in August 1983, the Gallihers divorced, blaming "an irretrievable breakdown" of their seven-year marriage, according to court records. Michelle LaBrecque is now a lawyer who practices in South Natick; Parrish Galliher, an executive with Millennium Pharmaceuticals. Both have since remarried. Both declined to comment for this story.

Suddenly faced at 30 with having to single-handedly raise two boys aged 6 and 2, Michelle threw herself into her career. In 1987, four years after becoming a single mother, and twelve years after she had graduated magna cum laude from Boston University, she earned the same honors from Boston College Law School and went into family law practice, an area with which she was by now intimately familiar. She worked with battered wives and single mothers struggling with questions about child support, visitation rights, and custody agreements. She also took on troubling cases, representing the parents of a comatose woman who gave birth to a premature baby after allegedly being raped in a nursing home, for example.

LaBrecque's own children thrived, taking up photography and learning their way around computers. Sean played the piano and trombone and started singing in choral groups and swimming competitively. By the winter of 1992, he was a sophomore, swimming the 100-meter freestyle for Newton North. "He had a big, broad smile," remembers Jim Marini, the principal at Newton North back then and now associate superintendent for secondary schools. "He was involved in a lot of school activities—Mr. High School USA." When the swim season began, the team had a problem: too few divers. Meets are won by combining each team's fastest swim times with the best dives, so a weakness in diving can crush a team's hopes. Jonathan Taqqu, who was also on the swim team, remembers what happened as the need for divers grew. "Sean tried diving," he says. "There was a need for the team, and he did it. It was indicative of his mentality."

The two of them spent a lot of time in the water together—as teammates at Newton North and as lifeguards at the little municipal beach on Crystal Lake. He was a lifeguard there and a swim instructor, and he and Taqqu used their computer skills to set up a Crystal Lake website. "I remember we'd all sit around on a couch in the lifeguard room, and we just had great laughs," Taqqu says.

It was also in high school that Galliher and Britt-Anya Bursell became friends. By the time they finished college, they would be engaged. They made no mention of each other under their high school yearbook pictures, however. Under his coat-and-tie photo, Galliher thanked "Mom and the best friends in the world" and quoted one of Stephen King's darkest tomes, *The Stand*, a book about the destruction of the world's population. It was a curious choice for such a cheerful kid, but it's Bursell's words from Shakespeare that now look eerie: "We know what we are, but know not what we may be." From high school, Bursell went to UMass, while Galliher headed off to Syracuse to study mechanical engineering. And pursue a new dream.

Juggling the demands of the Reserve Officer Training Corps with a mechanical engineering workload requires maturity and discipline few 18-year-olds possess, but the leadership skills Galliher sprouted in high school blossomed in college. His major called for a brutal mix of courses, from calculus to thermodynamics to aerospace engineering, but he also found time for a technical writing course, for swing and ballroom dance classes, and to teach local swim teams.

"Sean was a very good student. He worked for the department doing some computer consulting," remembers Eric Spina, who chaired Syracuse's mechanical, aerospace, and manufacturing engineering department in the late 1990s and is now associate dean of the engineering college. "A stand-up kid—bright, intelligent, well-spoken. He seemed to be a leader among the students."

It was no different outside of class. As the ROTC officers began reviewing their cadets for grades, leadership, and fitness, Galliher stood out. "He was one of our sharp young cadets," says Colonel Mark D. Perodeau, commander and professor of aerospace studies for Syracuse's Air Force ROTC unit. Galliher was selected for pilot training, as sure a sign as any of how impressed the Air Force was with his potential, given that only 500 out of 2,000 cadets commissioned each year nationwide are chosen for it.

By joining the military, Galliher was committing not only to a four-year stint after graduating, but also to a lifestyle of conformity and rules, from how to make your bed, store your shoes, and fold your shirt to how to salute an officer. The so-called Air Force Core Values are more than a set of rules: They're a way of life that leaves no room for misinterpretation. "Integrity first," the code says. "It's the inner voice, the source of self-control, the basis for the trust imperative in today's military." One line, in particular, speaks to the behavior cadets must show: "It's doing the right thing when nobody's looking."

Galliher graduated cum laude in 1999 and shipped off to Texas for pilot training at Laughlin Air Force Base, where he was like a kid at an amusement park. "Our first major milestone is on June 30," he wrote on a website he ran for his fellow pilots, "when the Air Force tells us what kind of aircraft system we will be flying. Between now and then, formation flight training is the rule of the day. It is probably one of the most challenging skills to learn." He posted pictures of the planes they'd be flying, describing some as "AWESOME," and explained the training in detail: how they'd learn to fly level in bad weather and as little as three feet apart. "The days are long and packed with simulator rides, academic classes, and flights out and around southern Texas, which for those of you in the North, had its first 110-degree day two weeks ago," he wrote. He was tapped to fly a large four-propeller, tactical cargo plane called the C-130 Hercules, used to drop troops and equipment into war zones or, if necessary, land on isolated dirt strips. And he got his squadron assignment.

Last November, Sean Galliher, a stocky five foot nine, 170 pounds, arrived for duty at Elmendorf Air Force Base, a huge installation with 64,000 people. It was by no means the most desirable pick of the lot, surrounded as it is by mountains and vast tundra, but to someone who lived for the outdoors, it was hardly a consolation prize. With no living quarters on the base for single officers—Galliher's fiancée was back in Massachusetts—he found a place ten minutes away at the Highlands Apartments complex. He set up his new home in apartment J108, including the computer that would allow him to stay in touch with family and friends back home. "He seemed to be well liked in his squadron," Major John Kennedy at Elmendorf says now. "I was never aware of any problems he had."

Detective Lieutenant John J. McLean rolls his chair up to his Compaq laptop. Time to go hunting. A big-bellied Irish redhead, McLean is a cop whose beat is patrolling cyberspace, and in his dingy second-floor office in downtown Medford, filled with metal desks and file cabinets, the fruits of his efforts are stacked along the walls like stuffed deer heads. A dozen computers line the shelves, all seized as evidence. His laptop beeps loudly, and he taps in a few secret codes before he goes into an Internet relay chat channel, or IRC. These are the back alleys of the Web, where users break out into private rooms on all sorts of subjects—often sex. Experts say the IRC is the most dangerous place on the Internet because it's where kids go to explore and predators go to hunt, and the two inevitably cross paths like Little Red Riding Hood and the Big Bad Wolf. What draws adults to kids and sex is still something of a mystery— some call it a disease, others a fetish. But officials are usually less concerned with the why than the how: how the pictures and movies get here and whether the children shown were molested.

"In my experience," says one investigator on Galliher's case, "motive is different with every suspect. But one thing in common is the gratification they get from the images."

McLean, who spearheads a regional computer crime unit for northeastern Massachusetts, points out the chat rooms for teen sex, cybersex, preteens, and family sex, before he enters a room called "Cute Asians," using his undercover name. He begins to peek at the servers of people inside to see the images they've got. The smart ones here have masked their identities—not just their names, but also their service providers, so cops can't track them down so easily. "There's a perceived level of anonymity online," McLean says. "You're not 100 percent anonymous, but you can be close."

He's been inside the "Cute Asians" room barely a minute when he strikes up a dialogue with another user.

"Hi," he writes.

"How are you?" comes the response.

"'Kay. Skipped school. Sick." McLean wants to sound like a teenager. "Are you from Boston, too?" he writes.

"No, sorry."

"Where?"

"Australia."

Probably a lie, but who knows. The dialogue dies—anyone who's savvy reveals nothing online—and McLean moves on. It's taken police years to catch up with the cyberworld techies, but now that they have, he says, they have to become more proactive, go out and find the porn and shut it down. Since the early 1990s, pedophiles, child molesters, and sexual deviants have increasingly turned to the computer to find porn. They use film-free digital cameras, CD-ROMs, and cutting-edge digital CD reproduction equipment. That's what Operation Artus involved, and, like many child pornography cases, its roots were in western Europe.

.   .   .

It took five months for the case to unfold, but when it did it happened in a blink. On the evening of March 19, agents in the United States and around the world, from England to Canada, France to Switzerland, Spain to Japan, fanned out with search warrants. Because child porn is international contraband, with the Internet serving as the cargo ship that carries it across the oceans, Interpol led the probe. Forty-six suspects were targeted in eleven countries, including eight in the United States, in New York, Pennsylvania, Ohio, Tennessee, Nevada, Oregon, and Alaska. When the raid was over, 12 computers, 600 CDs, floppy disks, and external drives, 200 videos, one digital camcorder, a book on how to seduce children, and thousands of images of children being sexually abused had been seized. Twelve people were arrested immediately as the warrants were being served.

When they got to Galliher, Skrocki, the assistant U.S. attorney, says, "We asked him if there was anything he wanted to say." He said nothing, and a few hours later, Anchorage police and the U.S. Attorney's Office were carting away his computer. He was never arrested. "The analysis of his computer left no doubt," Skrocki says, refusing to elaborate on what specifically was found.

Why would a young man engaged to be married, a highly touted Air Force pilot with an engineering degree, spend his spare time camped in front of his computer sending and receiving pictures of kids having sex? Skrocki answers after a long pause. "The investigation revealed no evidence of hacking or of a third person collecting images." Courts have sealed details of the closed case because of the broader ongoing porn investigation, but Skrocki says in Galliher's case, as in most child porn cases in his district, investigators did not find an explanation for "why he made this turn."

"Was he troubled?" Skrocki adds. "Yes, he was."

No one knew just how troubled.

. . .

Word of the investigation spread quickly through the Air Force base with Galliher's apartment complex, and early in the afternoon of March 22, George Crowley, a friend of Galliher's, went over to the Highlands office. Crowley urged Debbie Wilder, the property manager, to go into Galliher's apartment because he hadn't been returning calls. At 2:19 P.M., Wilder found Galliher's body hanging from the bedroom door, a small blue chair tipped over in front of him, the computer cable over his black turtleneck stretched from his neck lengthwise around the door twice and then around both doorknobs three times. An Ace bandage covered his left wrist, and smears of blood were on the toilet, in the sink, and on the floor. He had tried to cut his wrist.

For investigators, the suicide was more frustrating than an acquittal would have been, because death leaves lingering questions. "It's tragic," says Michael Fleming, a spokesman for U.S. Customs. "None of us in Customs has a sense of relief or satisfaction or anything less than concern for his family."

The reaction of suicide after being charged with child porn is not unusual, says Parry Aftab of WiredPatrol, which uncovers 600 child porn websites each week, some depicting children as young as two, which it reports to authorities. "In the old days, people would plead guilty just to avoid the stigma." A 1998 case called Operation Wonderland, the largest child porn case to date, saw four suicides in the days after arrests were made in twelve countries.

"The allegation is taboo," says Michael Netherland, assistant director of the CyberSmuggling Center for U.S. Customs. "These people operate in the shadows. And when this comes to light, it's very stressful and they see suicide as the only way out."

Since Wonderland, the laws regarding child pornography have changed to eliminate the possibility that police might arrest someone who has only a few images on his computer and might not actually be trafficking in kiddie porn. That's why, Aftab says, she has little doubt that Galliher was doing what authorities suspected when they raided his apartment and took his computer. "There is no way they would have taken on someone in the military unless they were sure he could have been convicted," she says. But she's quick to add: "You're innocent until proven guilty, and this young man is still innocent and maybe really is innocent. I hope this boy wasn't innocent, but it's so sad that he thought there was no choice."

When the news got back to Newton, it was talked about only in whispers. No one cared that the Customs CyberSmuggling Center, which since 1992 has arrested more than 1,200 people for child porn–related charges, has never lost a case. They were burying a soldier, a hero who'd come home, and his funeral had all the trimmings—flags, military uniforms, and a flyover by a C-130. The eulogies were warm, recalling Galliher's love of community, the water, his family, and his fiancée. He was remembered for what he did, not what he was accused of doing. But for some, the questions hurt.

"There is definitely a frustration that our fond memories are tainted now," Jonathan Taqqu says a few weeks after the funeral. "But the fond memories are what I'll remember."

Jim Marini, the ex-principal at Newton North, doesn't see the sense in trying to understand a dark side he never saw. He talks about the thousands of students he's come to know over the years, who have passed through the halls of his school, graduated, and disappeared. "You never know what happens to people in life," he says. As for Galliher, he says, "It didn't fit for me, to the point where we don't talk about that. What is that all about? I can say with all honesty, it's about what a great kid he was."

And Sean Galliher was a great kid, as far as Marini knows. He may just not have known all of him.

Sadly, there is no final twist to this story. There was no discovery that it was all a horrible mistake, there was no announcement that Sean was never really involved in this international child porn ring, there was no statement from his family. I was drawn to this story because it just didn't make sense, and even to my frustration, it still doesn't. Psychologists will tell you there has to be some scar, some wound, deep down in the soul, to drive someone to this kind of activity. But sometimes, as the D.C. sniper shootings showed us, experts are wrong. Maybe this really was nothing more than one man satisfying his urges that no one knew he had, and his unbearable shame at getting caught.

SLAVES OF THE BROTHEL
SEBASTIAN JUNGER

The plan called for a "soft entry," which meant that the police officers would ask to come in, rather than break down the door. It was 1:45 on the morning of July 6, 2001, and a convoy of white-painted U.N. police vehicles were gunning through Priština's deserted streets on their way to raid the infamous Miami Beach Club. The convoy passed a dead dog and a row of overflowing garbage bins and the destroyed post office and groups of tough-looking young men who turned to stare at the SUVs as they went by.

The owner of the Miami Beach, Milam Maraj, was suspected of trafficking in women and forcing them into prostitution. What to all outward appearances was a regular strip club was, in fact, a brothel, and the girls who worked there—teenagers from the former Soviet Union—were in all likelihood being held in conditions amounting to virtual slavery. Several months earlier, Maraj had been crippled by a bullet to the knee because he was willing to testify against a local strongman named Sabit Geci, who was also involved in trafficking and prostitution. Geci was sentenced to six years in prison—the first major victory against organized crime in Kosovo—but it cost Maraj his knee. Now he had to walk with crutches and carry a gun for protection and was suspected by the U.N. of engaging in the same kind of crimes that had put his archrival in jail.

The convoy of SUVs ground up the dark, pitted streets of Jablanica Hill and came to a stop a hundred yards from the bar. The raid went down fast. A team of heavily armed U.S. soldiers stood guard

on the perimeter while half a dozen police officers rushed the front
door and flattened the two bouncers up against the wall. From
there they moved into the dimly lit bar and screamed for more light
as they pushed the men to one side of the room and the women to
the other. Maraj hobbled out on his crutches and played host with
as charming a smile as he could muster. "Please, do your jobs," he
invited, sweeping one hand toward the girls, who were already sitting at a table, waiting to be questioned by the police. "There is no
problem. You will see."

And in fact he was right. An hour later the police left, empty-
handed. Of the dozen or so girls found at the club that night, not
one had a forged visa, not one had entered the country illegally, not
one admitted having been trafficked, beaten up, raped, or threatened. They just flirted with the police officers and then waved
goodbye prettily when the officers trooped back out the door. The
incident was all too typical of the failure to combat forced prostitution, which has spiraled out of control, becoming one of Europe's
major problems.

Most of the prostitutes in Kosovo have been trafficked illegally from
the poorest parts of the ruined Soviet state. They are lured by the
promise of a good job, usually in Italy or Germany, their passports
are confiscated, and they generally wind up sold to Albanian pimps,
who force them to work in brothels to pay off their "debt," i.e., what
it cost the pimp to buy them. Not surprisingly, the system is set up so
that that is virtually impossible, and the women essentially become
trapped in the dark, violent world of the Albanian Mafia. A moder-
ately attractive young woman goes for around $1,000. Tall ones are
worth more, and very beautiful ones are worth more. Moldovan
women are preferred because they are particularly desperate—the
living wage in their country is calculated at $100 a month, and the
average income is a quarter of that—and they are remarkably beau-

tiful. Moldova seems to have beautiful women the way Sierra Leone has diamonds—peculiar national treasures that haven't done either country much good.

The problem with investigating human trafficking in Europe is that the women themselves often deny needing help. They are too scared, manipulated, or desperate for money to dare admit anything to the police. The only way around the problem is undercover work, but the U.N. mandate in Kosovo until very recently did not include such intelligence gathering. Journalists, however, have never been bound by such rules. One weekday night in the pouring rain, photographer Teun Voeten and I drove out of Priština toward the Macedonian border, where there are dozens of brothels tucked away in the smaller towns. We were with two Albanian translators, Erol and Valon, who spoke Serbian and whose appearance let them pass for anything—Serb or Albanian, Kosovo or Macedonian. Our idea was to walk into a brothel, pretend to be American servicemen in Kosovo, and buy an hour or two with one of the women. In the privacy of a motel room, out of sight of the Albanian Mafia, which runs the brothels—in fact, some would say, runs the whole country—we could interview the woman with a tape recorder and get the real story of how she got there.

The highway was two narrow lanes of ruined pavement. Convoys of trucks blasted past us in the oncoming lane, and U.N. tanks and armored trucks slowed traffic heading south, toward Macedonia, to a crawl. Albanian rebels had seized a large part of the mountainous border between the two countries, and the U.N. peacekeepers were building up their presence in case they had to intervene on short notice. Off in the distance we could see the diffuse yellow glow of Camp Bondsteel reflecting off the cloud cover. Bondsteel is an enormous American base built close to a nasty little industrial town called Ferizaj. As a result, Ferizaj has an inordinate number of brothels, and at a gas station outside of town, with the rain drumming down and the trucks roaring past, the pump attendant advised us to check out one called the Apaci. It had the best girls in town, he said, so that was where all the American officers went. We thanked him and drove around the ghastly apartment blocks and ruined factories of Ferizaj until we found a low concrete building covered in camouflage netting. It had a photograph of an Apache attack helicopter on the door. We parked by some railroad tracks and walked in.

There are very good reasons why something amounting to slavery has been allowed to thrive in the middle of Europe. Not only is the Albanian Mafia notoriously violent—Kosovo has one of the highest murder rates in Europe—but it has attempted to infiltrate and buy off both the local police force and the government. "Those who have money here have power," as one United Nations police officer says. "And the Mafia has money." Undercover work in the brothels is dangerous, and attempting a police action that the Mafia doesn't get tipped off to is extremely difficult. Furthermore, the Mafia is deeply intertwined with the Kosovo Liberation Army (KLA), which fought the Serb Army and then started an insurrection in Macedonia, and it has access to plenty of weapons. Last year a German relief worker made the mistake of talking to some trafficked women about the possibility of escape, and that night someone attempted to throw a grenade into his hotel room. It was tossed into Room 69, which was empty; the relief worker was staying in Room 96.

No one paid us much attention when we walked in. There was a group of tough-looking Albanians in one corner, talking very seriously among themselves, and an American officer in uniform in another corner with his back to the wall. He was sitting with two Albanian translators and a blond in a very short skirt who was feigning interest in whatever he was saying. Between her bad English and the music, she couldn't have understood much. We sat up front by the stage and made sure that the bartender couldn't get a clear

view of Teun, who had a small, low-light camera in his pocket. He
carefully took it out and put it under his hat.

There were eight or ten girls ranged at the table in front of us,
drinking soda and smoking cigarettes and barely talking. Some had
hair dyed jet black, and the rest had hair bleached so blond it almost
looked blue. Occasionally I'd catch one of them looking at us, but
then I'd realize she was looking right through us and was too bored
even to make eye contact. They sat with their legs crossed, waiting
for their next shift on the stage, occasionally getting up without
much enthusiasm to go talk to the table of Albanian men. They were
pretty, but not extraordinarily so. A couple looked to be straight out
of the Romanian peasantry—big, strong girls with rough faces and
too much makeup—but one stood out from the rest. She was petite
and had platinum-blond hair pulled back tight across her skull and
dark glossy lipstick and one of those heartbreaking Slavic faces—
high cheekbones, dark eyes, a slightly Asian cast—that you remember for years. She sat off by herself, oblivious to everyone around
her, and when the DJ put on an Algerian song called "Aicha," she
stubbed out her cigarette and got up to dance.

There was something different about her—she was distant from
the other girls, almost disdainful. I thought that maybe she would
speak more openly than the others. "Her," I said to Erol before
she'd even finished her dance. Erol waved the bartender over, a
young guy with his hair bound improbably into a topknot, and
negotiated the deal: We were to wait until closing time and then go
out to our car and follow the security guys to a motel. The girls
would already be there. Erol would go up alone at a cost of about
$150. If he wanted to take her home with him he had to put down a
deposit of her full price—$2,000—and if she escaped he would for-
feit all of it.

After she finished her dance the bartender sent her over to our
table. She was young—in her late teens, maybe—and unnervingly
self-possessed. She sat there playing with her hair and smoking ciga-

rettes and said that it was her first night at the Apaci and she was not happy to be there. She also said that her name was Niki and that she was from a small town in Moldova. (In order to protect her, I have changed her name.)

"Where did you work before here?" I asked.

"Banja Luka."

Banja Luka was the capital of Serb Bosnia, the site of some of the worst ethnic cleansing in the war.

"What did you think of Banja Luka?"

"If I could drop a bomb on Banja Luka," she said, "I would do it tomorrow."

It was around two in the morning when the lights went up. A hard, ugly rain was coming down outside, and the place had cleared out except for us and the thugs and the girls, who had been herded into the corner. The thugs who ran them were putting on their leather jackets. We were getting ready to go when a heavyset man—later thought by U.N. investigators to be Bashkim Beqiri—walked in the door. Beqiri was a local boxing champion who ran a strip bar called Europe 2000. One hand jammed in his pocket, he planted himself before an Apaci security guy and started yelling. The security guy didn't say much, and his buddies stood around, shifting from foot to foot while the girls looked away and Beqiri hollered. I asked Erol what was going on.

"That man wants his money," Erol whispered back. "He says he wants [$2,000] right now or he's going to kill the girl."

We couldn't tell which woman he was talking about. Beqiri turned and walked out the door, saying he would be back the next day. The security guys held a quick council and then herded the women outside into the pouring rain to a couple of late-model BMWs parked next to the railroad tracks. They looked dumb and well-muscled, and they squeezed themselves into a couple more cars and motioned for us to follow. We trailed them in our car through the dark streets of Ferizaj to a place called the Muhaxheri Motel, off a side street at the center of town.

The Muhaxheri was a slapdash five-story modern building with a cheap plastic sign outside and no one at the front desk. The thugs got out of their cars and looked around and then pulled the women out and shoved them toward the door. A police car drove by slowly but didn't stop. One of the men motioned to Erol, who got out of our car and nodded to us and disappeared into the motel. Another carload of men pulled up and went into the Muhaxheri and came out ten minutes later and drove off. We waited an hour like that, the rain coming down, an occasional car pulling up and then driving away, and Erol never emerged from the motel.

War has been good for the Albanian Mafia. In February and March 1998, Serb military and paramilitary forces carried out a series of massacres in the Drenica region of central Kosovo that quickly grew into a massive campaign of ethnic cleansing. By the time NATO intervened a year later, as many as 10,000 ethnic Albanians had been killed and an estimated 800,000 driven across the country's borders. A massive NATO bombing campaign finally forced the Serbs to concede defeat, and they withdrew on June 10, 1999. Within hours, approximately 43,000 NATO troops poured into Kosovo to impose order, but it wasn't fast enough. Groups of young Albanian toughs were already patrolling the streets of Priština and other large towns, establishing control in a society that had been completely sundered by the Serb occupation. Already in a position of power because they had helped fund and arm the KLA, the Mafia bought off local officials, infiltrated the police force, and killed anyone they couldn't intimidate.

Kosovo was, and still is, the perfect place to base a criminal network—chaotic, violent, and ringed by porous borders. Local and international authorities can't hope to control the trafficking routes. To the north are Serb gangsters who work closely with the Russian Mafia and are only too happy to overlook old ethnic hatreds in the interest of business. To the east are Bulgarian *moutri* — "thick-necks," mostly graduates of wrestling schools — who work for security firms that double as racketeering outfits. Criminal clans in Albania proper, given free rein by a corrupt, bankrupt, and utterly impotent government, have taken over the port town of Vlorë and use 500-horse-power inflatable rafts called *scafi* to run illegal immigrants and drugs across the Adriatic into Italy. An estimated 10 percent of the population of Vlorë are in business with the local Mafia, and two-thirds of the cars on the streets have been stolen from Western Europe.

Worldwide, the effect has been disastrous. The Balkan drug trade, which moves more than 70 percent of the heroin destined for Europe, is valued at an estimated $400 billion a year. By early 2001 the Albanian Mafia had muscled its competition out of the way and all but taken over London's crime-ridden red-light district, Soho. Albanian organized crime has established alliances with the Italian Mafia and with criminal gangs in Turkey. In February 2001 an Albanian insurrection started in Macedonia, and the Mafia quickly moved in to help arm and pay for the guerrilla movement that went from several hundred to several thousand men in a matter of months. In some cases, Mafia bosses simply became local rebel commanders and funded their military operations through criminal enterprises that could operate much more effectively under the cover of war.

The Organization for Security and Cooperation in Europe (OSCE) — part of the temporary governing body in Kosovo — estimates that around 200,000 women each year are trafficked from Eastern Europe and Central Asia, most of them as prostitutes. The value of their services has been estimated at between $7 and $12 billion. Even before the Kosovo war, human trafficking in Europe — much of it through the Balkans — was worth as much as

$4 billion a year. Bulgaria alone loses 10,000 women a year to the traffickers. Moldova—a country so poor that a quarter of the population has emigrated in search of work—reportedly supplies two-thirds of the prostitutes working in Kosovo. Romania is a distant runner-up, followed by Ukraine, Bulgaria, Albania, and Russia.

Prostitution became a mainstay of the criminal economy within months of NATO intervention in Kosovo. With 43,000 men stationed on military bases, and spending by international reconstruction groups making up 5 to 10 percent of Kosovo's economy, the problem was bound to arise. There are now as many as a hundred brothels in Kosovo, each employing up to twenty women. Thousands more women are trafficked through Kosovo and on into Western Europe. In southern Macedonia, the town of Velesta has dozens of brothels under the control of a strongman named Leku, who has reportedly paid off the local police and operates in the open with complete impunity. When national authorities tried to crack down on his empire, he threatened to take to the hills and start his own private war. The highway south of the Macedonian town of Tetovo—long a hotbed of Albanian nationalism and organized crime—is lined with brothels as well.

Unable to use local women easily—they aren't so poor, and their families would come looking for them—men such as Leku have turned to the hundreds of thousands of illegal migrants fleeing the former Soviet Union. Young women who have been promised innocent-sounding jobs in Western Europe, particularly Italy, are typically escorted by Serb or Bulgarian gangsters into Kosovo and Macedonia and then sold to Albanian pimps. By the time they realize what is going on, it is too late. Deprived of their passports, gang-raped, often forced to take drugs, and disoriented by lack of food and sleep, these women find themselves virtual prisoners of whatever brothel they wind up in.

"Once, Leku told a Bulgarian girl to take off her bra when she was dancing," a Moldovan woman I will call Elena told me. Elena had managed to escape the Macedonian Mafia after months of bru-tality and servitude. "She didn't want to, because she was ashamed, so Leku took a belt from the bartender and started beating her. Then he made her go onstage bruised and bleeding and crying." Another bar Elena worked at was owned by a man she knew as Ayed. "Ayed put three new girls in a car and made the rounds of his friends—they all took turns raping them. They made the girls do things they'd never done before because they were very young. We all lived in one room and slept on mattresses next to each other. There wasn't enough room, so we had to sleep on our sides. We only ate once a day, and we had to beg toothpaste and soap from our clients. Ayed had a huge ring on his hand, which was shaped like a lion's head. One day he started beating us one by one in the face." According to Elena, if they fell down he kicked them, if they cried he beat them, if they looked at him he beat them, if they didn't look at him he beat them.

"I learned about good and evil," she says, "I saw so many evil people."

After an hour and a half Erol still had not come out, so Valon decided to look for him. He walked into the hotel lobby and heard men talking in the hallway and was spotted by them as he slipped closer. They wanted to know who the hell his friends in the car were. "They're from the United States," Valon said. For some rea-son he added, "One of them is a basketball coach."

That seemed to satisfy the thugs, who kicked him out and said Erol would be out in a few minutes. Erol emerged ten minutes later, smoking a cigarette and looking shaken. He got into the car and told Valon to get us out of there. "They found the tape recorder," he said. "They had a lot of questions." Valon pulled the car into the street, and we drove off through Ferizaj, keeping watch behind us to make sure no one was following. It was three in the morning, and Ferizaj was completely deserted. Erol said they'd found the tape recorder when they patted him down outside Niki's room, and five or six of them had gathered around and started yelling, demanding explanations. Erol said that it was just his tape recorder and that he took it everywhere with him.

They confiscated it and then wrote down his name from his passport. They were very angry and kept telling him not to fuck with them. "Listen," one of the men had finally said. "Go in the room, finish your job for one hour, or you can go, right here and now."

Erol screwed up his nerve and went into the room. There was one bed and a window with a narrow balcony and a shower but no toilet. Niki was sitting on the bed, and she started to undress when he walked in. "You don't have to do that—I'm not here for that," he said. "I just want to talk to you."

She'd probably had stranger requests before—they all must have. He asked her where she was from and how she'd gotten here, and she became very serious and told her story. This is what Erol could remember of it on the drive back to Priština:

Niki was from Moldova; her father was dead, and she had lived with her mother. She'd been promised a good job by a recruiter in Moldova who was actually in league with the Mafia, and she wound up trafficked to Banja Luka. Banja Luka was hell on earth, she said. Every customer was drunk and many were violent—one even grabbed her belly-button ring and ripped it right out. A month ago she had been trafficked to Ferizaj, where she wound up at Europe 2000. She sought refuge in the Apaci. Tonight her previous "owner"—Beqiri—had come looking for her at the Apaci and said he was going to kill her if he didn't get back her purchase price. She didn't have the money, and neither did the owner of the Apaci. That was the argument we had witnessed. She was the girl they'd been arguing over.

"I like life very much. I'm too young to die," Niki had told Erol. "I'm just eighteen years old."

Erol asked her if she was free to go home to Moldova if she wanted. She said that she was, but then admitted that she didn't actually have her passport. (In all likelihood, Beqiri did.) She wasn't even sure that any of the $150 Erol had paid for her would wind up in her pocket, so he gave her all the money he had on him, a 10 deutsche mark note (about $5). On it he wrote, "For Niki, the most beautiful girl." She gave him a cigarette lighter in return. His last question was whether she ever had feelings for the guys she was with, or were they all the same?

"Of course sometimes I have feelings," she said. "I'm human."

Erol told her he was sorry and said goodbye and walked out of the room.

The next day we went to the police station in Gnjilane to report what we'd seen. Not only was there plenty of evidence of trafficking and prostitution in Niki's case, but there was reason to believe her life was in danger. The deputy police chief in Gnjilane was an American named Bill Greer, who quickly organized a group of Kosovar police to raid the Apaci. (U.N. police officers are training local Albanians—many of them taken from the ranks of the disarmed Kosovo Liberation Army—and Serbs in basic police procedure.) The newly trained cops crowded into Greer's office and strapped on their guns and flak jackets while he explained through a translator: "We're going to get a young lady who's been threatened with being exterminated. She ran away from one pimp to the Apaci, and he came after her and demanded [$2,000] or she'd be killed."

The owner of the Apaci, Sevdush Veseli, was well-known to the authorities. He'd already been detained for trafficking a young Romanian woman, but when it came time to make a statement to the judge, she was too frightened to repeat what she'd said earlier to the police, so they had to let him go. Veseli was a former member of the KLA who wasn't known to be particularly violent, but Greer wasn't taking any chances. He sent half a dozen local police, backed up by a couple of U.N. officers, and they picked up reinforcements at the Ferizaj police station before bursting through the door at the Apaci. All they found was an old guy mopping the floor.

If Veseli hadn't been tipped off before, he certainly knew something was up now. Our little escapade the night before couldn't have escaped his notice, and he must have figured out that Niki had been the object of today's raid. Between the police and Beqiri, she was causing him more problems than she could possibly be worth. That meant that, one way or another, he would probably try to get her off his hands. That afternoon Ali Osman, a Turkish police officer who headed the Trafficking and Prostitution Investigation Unit in Gnjilane, sent word to Veseli that he was to appear at the police station the following morning with all of his dancers.

Technically the Apaci was just a strip joint on the outskirts of Ferizaj. And technically the police could round up the employees anytime they wanted to check their visas and work papers. At nine the next morning, Teun and I showed up at the police station to watch the interrogation of a dozen or so women employed by Sevdush Veseli at the Apaci.

The women were seated in a small room, smoking and looking annoyed. Teun and I walked in, glanced around, and told Osman that Niki was not among them. That was no surprise. We went into Osman's office; the next step was to question the women individually, where we could speak freely without the other girls or their bosses listening in. Not only might they know what happened to Niki, but some of them might want out. Those were the ones who could provide testimony of trafficking and prostitution at the Apaci, which was what Osman needed to put Veseli behind bars.

Since undercover investigations were not allowed at this time under the U.N. mandate, convicting someone like Veseli usually depends on testimony from the prostitutes. It's a delicate game, though. First there are plenty of prostitutes who—no matter how desperate their lives—have decided that anything is better than what they escaped from back home. Their pimp may be a violent alcoholic, but maybe their husband or father was, too, and at least here they have the possibility of making a little money. "You're fighting against the most appalling economic conditions," says Alison Jolly of the OSCE in Priština. "And one of the worst myths is that these women want to become prostitutes. I mean in a sense, yes, but how much of a choice is it when the alternative is to stand in a breadline trying to feed your child? You're a paid slave, but you're still a slave. I personally consider it a very clever ruse by the pimps to pay the women something. This is a recent development. These guys are very smart, and a little intimidation goes a long way."

Even for the ones who are desperate to escape, though, making the leap into police custody is risky. To begin with, the pimps have convinced their prostitutes that the police will simply throw them in jail for prostitution or visa violations—which was true until U.N. regulations were recently established that overrode the Yugoslav Criminal Code. Furthermore, the women know that—since they were recruited back home—the Mafia network extends into the smallest villages of their home country. When a pimp promises to harm a prostitute or her family, it is not an idle threat.

The first woman they brought into Osman's office was a short, dark-haired Moldovan who pretended barely to understand Serbian. She said she had come by taxi through Romania into Serbia, then across the internal border into Kosovo. She claimed she was just a stripper, not a prostitute, and made about $50 a month at the Apaci. "Tell her we are here to help her," Osman said to the translator. "She has no problem with the police." She said nothing, so Osman sent her out.

The next woman was Romanian, dressed in tight black pants, a purple spandex halter, and the same high-heeled white sandals as the previous girl. When she also claimed to be just a dancer, Osman told her that her owner had sold his girls to customers, had threatened them, had beaten them. She feigned surprise and said that her owner was very nice. "One day everything will change, you will see," Osman told her. He was playing tough cop, but I could see concern softening his eyes. Maybe he had a teenage daughter back home. "And when it does, I may not be able to do anything."

Finally a tall blond came in. I recognized her as the one who had sat with the American officer at the Apaci. She said that her name was Kristina and that she was from a small village in Moldova. She was wearing the same tight vinyl pants as the second woman but had different sandals and a lot less makeup. In the light of day she looked rougher, a more hardened version of her dance-floor self. I could see what she would look like as an old woman. She sat smirking with her legs spread and her feet cocked provocatively back on her high heels. She was smart and confident and said she spoke five languages well—all the countries she'd worked in. She said that she had come here by taxi from Moldova, and that her trip was paid for by a friend back home named Oleg. She had stayed in a house in Serbia for a while and then crossed the internal border into Kosovo two weeks ago.

"I heard about those houses with women waiting there," Osman said. "People come from Kosovo to pick you out." He pretended to be a buyer: "You, you, and you!"

"I don't know anything about it," Kristina said.

"I am sure you were trafficked. You were sold."

"No."

"Someone paid for you. Someone paid money for you."

"*Nyet.*"

"*Da.*"

"*Nyet.*"

"*Da.* You have no trouble with the police. Our job is to arrest the pimps, not you."

"I am telling you the truth, sir."

Before he let her go, Osman allowed me to ask her some questions. I described Niki and asked if she knew her. Kristina furrowed her brow in a parody of concentration and finally shook her head.

"Do you remember sitting at a table with an American officer at the back of the room two nights ago?"

"Yes."

"Do you remember four men at a table sitting close to the stage?"

"No."

"One more question," I said. "Have you ever seen me before in your life?"

We'd spent an hour about three feet from her—at one point she'd even given us a smile. Now, she looked straight at me, touched one hand to her hair, and laughed.

"No," she said. "Never."

Some do escape. The International Organization for Migration (IOM), which is charged with sheltering migrants and sending them back to their home countries, rescued more than 700 women from the Balkans and Italy during the year 2000. Elena, who was "owned" by Leku, escaped into police custody in a Macedonian town named Kumanovo, only to be sold by the police back to another bar owner. Through the help of a sympathetic client, she finally managed to make it to an IOM office in Macedonia, where she was taken care of and eventually put on a plane for home. There she was installed in an IOM safe house in Chişinău, the capital of Moldova, and given psychiatric counseling and job training.

Another Moldovan woman, whom I'll call Nina, left her husband to work in Italy as a waitress or cleaning lady because her son had a degenerative disease and she needed money to pay for his treatment. She wound up getting trafficked to Romania, where she was drugged and put on a train to Belgrade. Unable to buy her freedom, she wound up being sold again, this time to a brothel owner in the Bosnian town of Doboj, where she discovered that her husband had gotten her pregnant before she left. Her owner—unable to persuade her to have an abortion—took her to a corrupt doctor, who she suspects gave her an injection that induced miscarriage. A customer at the bar who found out what had happened slipped her the equivalent of $200 and offered his help. She eventually escaped to a local IOM office and made it back to Chişinău, though she never told her husband the details of what had happened to her.

Inevitably, the women who are driven to escape are the ones who have suffered the most trauma and are most urgently in need of care. But they are also the ones who have the most damning evidence against the traffickers and, theoretically, the most reason to want to put them in jail. This is where the agendas of the IOM and U.N. prosecutors diverge slightly. With no witness protection program yet in place to shelter the women, the IOM argues that their safety will be compromised if they are detained in Kosovo. Furthermore, there is insufficient funding to lodge them in safe houses for the duration of a criminal trial. For their part, U.N. prosecutors argue that in the long run the problem cannot be solved—in other words, the traffickers will never end up behind bars—if these women don't provide testimony.

The problem is made more complicated by the thicket of legal issues surrounding trafficking and prostitution. In the United States, gathering evidence of prostitution is fairly straightforward. Since it is nearly impossible to prove that a customer is not the prostitute's boyfriend, undercover cops pose as customers in order to prove prostitution charges. In Kosovo, however, the U.N. police force was until very recently prohibited from surreptitious intelligence gathering, and the Kosovo Police Service—the local police corps—has not yet been sufficiently trained in undercover work.

(KPS officers, who are paid only $230 a month, are also highly vulnerable to corruption, making security breaches almost unavoidable.) In addition, most of Europe has extremely rigorous standards for admitting into a trial evidence gained by an agent provocateur. A police action that in this country would be considered a standard "buy and bust" operation is more likely in Europe to be considered entrapment and therefore excluded as evidence.

As a result, the prostitutes themselves are needed to provide testimony against the pimps. Witness protection concerns aside, this raises legal issues. A woman who accuses someone of being her pimp is implicitly admitting to prostitution, which is in itself punishable by jail. To get around this, Section 8 of United Nations Regulation 2001/4 — which supersedes preexisting local laws — declares that providing evidence of trafficking protects the woman against charges of prostitution. "Section 8 understands that in many cases, but not all, a foreign woman in Kosovo finds herself a stranger in a strange land," says Michael Hartmann, an international prosecutor for the U.N. in Kosovo, "and that she was basically not given a choice. Even though she became a prostitute voluntarily, one could assume that she is someone who would not ordinarily do that."

Because she is at risk, it is not in her best interest to remain in Kosovo long enough to provide testimony against her owner in a criminal trial. As a result, U.N. regulations allow for videotaped testimony to be admitted in court. This has its own shortcomings, however. A good defense attorney can argue that his inability to cross-examine his client's accuser weakens the value of the evidence, and — more insidiously — video testimony can even be viewed skeptically by a biased judge. Major criminal trials in Kosovo have two international judges sit on a panel with three local, or "lay," judges. This panel hears all evidence and then comes to a verdict. The lay judges, however, occasionally display the prejudices of the highly patriarchal Kosovar culture. They tend to blame the woman for her troubles, in other words. "The majority of rape cases are fabricated by the alleged victims, seeking revenge, or trying to pressure the defendant to force a marriage proposal," one judge, according to an OSCE report, declared before a rape trial.

Even a perfect system, however, would face daunting enforcement challenges. New U.N. regulations have made trafficking itself a crime, apart from the related issues of assault, rape, forced prostitution, etc. Trafficking is defined, in part, by the level of deception involved: If a trafficker tells a woman she is going to be a waitress and then transports her across a border to sell her into prostitution, he is guilty of trafficking whether she went voluntarily or not. As a result, traffickers have changed their strategy to get around this new, looser definition of the crime. Instead of slipping across borders at night, for example, they pay off border guards so that the women have legitimate visas in their passports. They coach the women in what to say if they are questioned by the police—some of whom are corrupt and have been bought off in the first place. They have placed informants throughout the local and U.N. administrations. And they have started offering the trafficked women just enough money to keep them in the game.

"Ultimately the problem is the economic conditions that make prostitution the only thing these women can do," says Alison Jolly. "Even when jobs come onstream, it's not going to be the women who get them. For some countries it will be decades before the economic situation is such that you don't need to take the risks associated with trafficking. They think, Maybe, just maybe, I'll find something better out there."

In late March 2001, two women were arrested in Chişinău for selling illegal meat in plastic bags. Suspicious, the authorities tested it and confirmed their worst fears: The meat was human. The women said that they had gotten it at the state cancer clinic, and that they had been driven by poverty to sell it.

Only weeks earlier, the World Health Organization had warned that Moldova's economic collapse had created a thriving transplant market in human kidneys and other body parts. Some people were voluntarily selling their organs for cash, and others were being tricked into it in a ruse similar to the one used to lure women into prostitution. Moldova—pummeled by droughts, cold spells, and the 1998 Russian financial crisis—has become by far the poorest country in Europe. The average salary is $30 a month, unemployment is reportedly at 25 percent (though much higher in rural areas), and up to one million Moldovans—nearly a quarter of the country—have gone abroad to work. Some villages have lost half of their population, and virtually all their young people. Every year these migrants wire home an average of $120 million, which is equivalent to half the national budget. Two-thirds of the budget, however, is sent right back overseas to service the nation's foreign debt. With productivity only 40 percent of what it was under the Soviets, Moldova has voted back in a Communist government. It is the only former Soviet republic to have returned so unabashedly to its past.

Teun and I have left Kosovo. It is now several months later, and we're driving through the emptied and sullen countryside of Moldova. We have come to see this place where, according to a significant proportion of the trafficked women, life is even worse than in the brothels of Kosovo. It's a low, dark day that will soon deteriorate into a pounding rainstorm that will fill up the rivers and wash out the roads and force the villagers to take off their shoes and carry them under their jackets. That's what you do when you own only one pair.

Village after village stands nearly empty, the brightly painted wooden gates of the houses hanging open and the weeds growing up around the palings. Cornstalks are piled against the fences to dry, and an occasional horse cart rattles by with an old man at the reins. Sodden hills checkered with woods roll south toward the town of Kagul and the Romanian border. There are no workers in the fields, no cars on the roads, no children in the houses. It is as if a great plague had swept through, leaving behind a landscape out of medieval Europe, out of *Grimm's Fairy Tales*. Kagul is the center of trafficking in southern Moldova, and we are with a woman I'll call Natalia, who was trafficked through Kagul and just made it home a few weeks ago. Natalia's story is so horrendous that I'm tempted to think she has embellished it, but at this point I've heard and read so many accounts of trafficked women, and the brutality is so consistent, that I've given up looking for some other explanation. These are troubled, traumatized women who may have distorted, misremembered, or even fabricated details of their experience, but their testimonies are unfortunately too similar to be doubted.

Natalia grew up in a desperately poor village named Haragij, where people survived on whatever they could grow, and children had to bring their own firewood to school in the winter. At age 16 she was married against her will to a violent alcoholic who wound up beating her so badly that he fractured her skull and almost killed her. She says the police in her town were so corrupt that they had to be bribed in order to even consider arresting him, so she decided to leave and look for work in Chişinău instead. She had two young children, and she was determined to support them.

She wound up being trafficked twice. The first time she fell for the standard scam: A trafficker offered her a good job in Italy, but she was sold to a brothel in Macedonia. With the help of the IOM, she eventually escaped, but when she made it back to Moldova, she found out that her young sister had been trafficked as well. Now knowing that world inside out, she decided to go back to Chişinău and get herself sold into prostitution one more time. It was the only way she could think of to get back to the Balkans and bring her sister home.

It didn't take long. Within a few days she met a woman who passed her the phone number of a man who supposedly could get her work in Italy. She met with him—a well-dressed and impressive businessman of 35 or so—and he offered to put her up in his apartment. She soon found herself with about forty other women in an apartment somewhere in Chişinău. From this point on, her life would no longer be her own.

The women who didn't have passports were given fake ones and charged for them, which was the beginning of their debt. They were first taken by car to Constanţa, Romania, and from there to the banks of the Danube, which they crossed at night by boat. Now they were in Serbia. There they were forced to walk across fields at night to a road, where they were picked up by a man named Milos, who she says took them to the White Star café-bar in the town of Kraljevo. There were dozens of women—Moldovans, Ukrainians, Romanians—being held in the basement of the bar, waiting to be bought by brokers for the Albanian Mafia.

Natalia spent several weeks there and was then moved across the lightly guarded internal border from Serbia into Kosovo. There she was sold to a place called #1, in the town of Mitrovica. The women at #1 were all on drugs—pot, morphine, pharmaceuticals, coke—and fell into two categories: slaves and girlfriends of the owner, a Serb Natalia referred to as Dajan. The girlfriends were the most beautiful ones and were given a certain degree of privilege in exchange for keeping order among the regular prostitutes, whom they held in contempt. One girlfriend tried to force a new Moldovan girl to have sex with her, and when Natalia stood up for the girl, she was beaten by the owner. In revenge, Natalia says, she found some rusty thumbtacks and put them on the woman's office chair, and when the woman sat on them she got an infection that sent her to the hospital. Natalia never saw her again.

The schedule was brutal. They had to strip-dance from 8:00 P.M. until 6:00 A.M., taking time to go in back with clients if called upon, and they had to be up at 8:00 A.M. in case there were clients during the day. She says the customers were a mix of local Serbs and United Nations personnel. The prostitutes made around $30 per client and $1 for each drink the client bought, which was all put toward their debt. Natalia owed $1,500, but the owner deducted for food, lodging, clothes, and, of course, drugs, particularly cocaine, which the girls freebased in back. The new girls lived at the bar, and the ones who had repaid more than half their debt lived in an apartment, because the owner didn't want the experienced ones warning the new ones about what was going to happen to them. If a particular girl got close to repaying her debt, the owner sold her off to someone else, and she had to start all over again.

One day, according to Natalia, Dajan's brother killed an Albanian man at the bar, and the police finally came and shut the place down. The girls were hidden from the police before the raid, and Natalia was sold off to another bar in Mitrovica, but there her luck changed. The toilet had a small window in it, and she managed to crawl out and escape. She walked all night and made it to Priština, but instead of turning herself in to the IOM, she hitched a ride to Ferizaj. She had heard a rumor that her sister was in one of the Ferizaj bars, and she wanted to try to find her.

Natalia could not track down her sister, but at the Alo Bar she started talking to a beautiful and morose Moldovan woman named Niki. Niki was the girlfriend of the owner, an Albanian named Tus, and she said that she had been trafficked to Bosnia and then to the Apaci bar in Ferizaj, where she wound up in some kind of trouble.

"She told me that someone tried to help her and she thought that the owner noticed and so he sold her," Natalia says.

We are squeezed into the backseat of a Russian Lada on the way to Kagul. It has been raining hard all morning, and the creeks are up over the roads; the locals are using horses to drag cars through the washouts. "She told me there was something special on their faces," Natalia goes on. "She was afraid they were journalists and she didn't want to screw up her reputation back home. One of them questioned her, but he wasn't in love with her—she said he was either a journalist . . . or maybe the police."

Natalia spent hours talking to Niki, almost certainly the same woman we had tried to help. Either Natalia somehow heard about our experience and just repeated it to us, or the Kosovo underworld is so small and sordid—and the girls get shuffled around so much— that they just wind up meeting one another. Niki kept a diary, and during the time they were together she had let Natalia read it. I had told Niki my name when she came to our table, and in her journal she had referred to me as Sebastian Bach. She wrote that she must somehow have deserved the terrible things that happened to her, and so it didn't make sense that we were trying to help her. The owner had been tipped off that there was going to be a raid, and she had actually hidden herself when the police came looking for her after we left. She was scared of them because she knew that most of them were also customers at the bar. She knew that only the OSCE could help her, but she didn't want to escape before she had a little money to return home with. Also, she feared going to jail if she turned herself in to the police. In the meantime, she had taken some photos at the Alo Bar that she would try to send home to her mother. That way—however unrealistic the hope—her mother might be able to help her.

We arrive in Kagul in early afternoon, and Natalia takes us to the

Flamingo Bar, which is near the bus station. It's a cheap-looking place with Formica tabletops and louver blinds on the windows. This is where the traffickers try to pick up girls who are waiting for buses to Chişinău or Bucharest. Well-dressed men come and go from tables, and Natalia hides her face from them because she's afraid of being recognized. She got a crew cut a couple of weeks ago in an attempt to disguise herself, but she still lives in fear that they'll somehow find out she escaped. I ask her if she would testify against her traffickers if she had the chance.

"What would I do about my family?" she asks. "The police would lock up one guy, and there are ten more . . . We'd have to leave the country. It's better that I forget. I just pretend I don't see anything, and I go on with my life."

It was not until July 2001 that Moldova passed an anti-trafficking law. Recruiting for and organizing the trafficking of a human being abroad for the purpose of sexual exploitation, slavery, criminal or military activity, pornography, or "other loathsome purposes" is now punishable by up to fifteen years in jail. Traffickers can get up to twenty-five years if their crimes involve minors, groups of people, the use of violence, or the taking of internal organs.

The Moldovan law is modeled after U.N. regulations, but enforcing it is even more daunting here than in Kosovo. In a country where doctors make around $30 a month, buying off the entire justice system—from the police right on up to the judges on the bench—presents no particular difficulty for the Moldovan Mafia. There are honest cops and judges, but they face a trafficking system that is so fluid and hard to pin down that it is almost impossible to crack. The process often starts with a completely legal classified ad in the newspaper: "Hiring girls without complexes for the work abroad" is a common one. The ad includes a phone number, and the initial contact is usually a woman, often one who was trafficked and has been blackmailed or otherwise coerced into doing the job. From there, the recruits are handed over to the traffickers themselves, whose job it is to get them across the border into Romania. In many ways that is the smallest obstacle in the entire process. Passports can be bought or forged for just a few hundred dollars, border guards can be bribed for even less, and the border itself is so porous that until recently the authorities didn't even bother to keep records of who went back and forth. (The Moldovan government is still hoping for an international loan that will allow it to buy a computer system to handle that task.) Once the girls are in Romania, they're almost always beyond help.

Vastly adding to the problem is the psychology of both the new recruits and the ones who have made it back. Not only are they poor, uneducated, and desperate, but they have grown up in a society that tolerates such astronomical levels of domestic violence that almost any kind of abuse could be considered normal, even deserved. "During the Soviet times there weren't as many social problems," says Lilia Gorceag, an American-trained psychologist who treats women at the IOM safe house in Chişinău. "There was some kind of stability. Now that everything is gone, all our frustrations and fears have been converted to a fear about tomorrow, and it really increased the levels of violence."

According to Gorceag, one of the more common reactions to a violent childhood or marriage—not to mention a violent trafficking experience—is massive feelings of guilt. Niki's conviction that she somehow deserved her fate is a classic example of this sort of psychological defense. "Most trafficked women have very negative sexual experiences during childhood," says Gorceag. "Many were raped when they were young—I have many patients who had been raped by the age of twelve, sometimes by their own father. They adopt a perspective that they have been created to satisfy someone else's sexual needs. They consider themselves depraved, unacceptable to family and friends. And very few men here would tolerate it if they found out a woman had been trafficked. I know one nineteen-year-old woman who says her brother would kill her if he found out."

Such a woman is perfect prey for a trafficker, and a good candidate for relapsing into prostitution even if she makes it back to Moldova. Gorceag says that women who are trafficked to Turkey, Greece, and Italy generally survive their experiences psychologically intact, but the ones who wind up in the Balkans are utterly destroyed as people. They exhibit classic symptoms of severe post-traumatic stress disorder: They can't focus; they can't follow schedules; they're apathetic to the point of appearing somnambulistic; they fly into violent rages or plunge into hopeless depression; some even live in terror that someone will come and take them away. Their condition keeps them from functioning normally in a family or a job, and that puts them at even greater risk of being trafficked again.

"One of my patients ate napkins," says Gorceag. "When I took away the napkins, she started eating newspaper. She wasn't even aware of what she was doing. There is another patient who counts. She counts everything. When she can't find anything to count, she turns her sleeve and counts the stitching. These are people with completely destroyed psyches. It's a form of genocide. I know that's a very strong word, but I live with twenty-two of these women, and I see their suffering every day."

On our last day in Moldova, Teun and I meet Natalia to look at some photos she wants to show us. I have just received word from members of the U.N. anti-trafficking unit in Kosovo that they think they have found the bar where Niki is working, and they want me to fly back there to participate in a police raid. That way I can identify her so she can be sent home to Moldova, whether she wants to be or not. It's a beautiful fall day, and Natalia and Teun and I sit down at an outdoor café next to two puff-pastry blonds who are wearing maybe an ounce of fabric between them. Natalia—tough, smart, and battered by her experience in Kosovo—tosses them a dismissive look.

"What do those women want?" I ask her. "What are they looking for?"

"Men with money," Natalia says. "Moldovan women have become very cold, very callous. They don't want to fall in love. They just want to meet a rich guy, and most of the guys with money are thugs. It's their mothers who push them into this—that's the worst part."

The photos Natalia shows us were taken at a bar when she was working as a prostitute. One was taken a few days after she arrived; she's very drunk and her eyes are red from crying. She has long, glamorous hair and very red lipstick and a forced smile that says more about her situation than any expression of hate or fear. There is none of the wry sarcasm in her eyes that I have become so fond of. I tell her that Niki has been located, and that if I go back to identify her she in all likelihood will be repatriated to Moldova.

"What should we do?" I ask. "Would we just be making things worse for her?"

"Yes, I think so," Natalia says without hesitation.

"So we shouldn't go to the police?"

Natalia takes a drag on the cigarette we gave her and crushes it in the ashtray. For her this is clearly not a question of principle; it's a question of guessing what Niki herself would want. If Niki were tied up in a basement getting raped, the answer would be easy: Break down the door and save her. But she's not. She's imprisoned by a web of manipulation and poverty and threat and, much as I hate to admit it, personal choice. The answers aren't so obvious.

"She would just deny that she's a prostitute," says Natalia. "Look, there's nothing here for her. If you brought her home you'd have some sort of . . ." She casts around for the right words.

"Moral responsibility?"

"Yes," Natalia says, never taking her eyes off me. "Exactly."

THE KEYSTONE KOMMANDOS
GARY COHEN

The four men arrived by U-boat and landed on a deserted beach near Amagansett, Long Island, in the midnight darkness on Saturday, June 13, 1942, a mere six months after Japan's attack on Pearl Harbor. They had close to $80,000 (equivalent to nearly a million dollars today) in cash, four boxes of explosives, and a mission that had been planned at the highest levels of the Third Reich—namely, to halt production at key American manufacturing plants, create railroad bottlenecks, disrupt communication lines, and cripple New York City's water supply system. The mission, audacious in means and scope, had the potential to seriously impede America's military buildup, and perhaps even to affect the outcome of the war.

It was a spectacular failure. Within the month the operatives were arrested, along with the members of another team of four, who had landed in Florida four days later, under similar circumstances. Neither team had managed even to attempt an act of sabotage.

President Franklin Roosevelt, newly engaged in the war against Germany and eager to demonstrate successes, demanded that justice be swift and severe. To that end he ordered the creation of a military tribunal, using as precedents obscure cases from the Civil and Revolutionary Wars. Within a month all eight men had been sentenced to death and six had been executed. The other two, who had turned in their colleagues and cooperated with the U.S. government, had their sentences reduced—one to life in prison, the other to thirty years. Transcripts of the tribunal's proceedings, on which this article is based, ran to some 3,000 pages and were kept secret for eighteen years after the trial; a copy sits in the "Map Room files" at the Roosevelt Presidential Library, in Hyde Park, New York. Prior to the tribunal the FBI interviewed all eight of the would-be saboteurs, who provided details about their training in Germany, their arrival in the United States, and their capture. Transcripts of those interviews, on which this article also relies, can be found in Justice Department files at the National Archives.

This episode, though minor in the overall context of the war, is nevertheless of renewed interest today. The military tribunals proposed by the Bush administration in the wake of the September 11 attacks rely on the case of the captured Germans for precedent.

THE RECRUITS

The idea of sending saboteurs to the United States was the brainchild of Walter Kappe, a high-ranking Nazi official who had immigrated to America from Germany in 1925. Kappe took a job at a farm implement factory in Kankakee, Illinois; he later moved to Chicago, to write for a German-language newspaper, and by 1933 he had moved to New York and become a leader in the Friends of Hitler movement there. In 1937 he returned to Germany to serve in the Third Reich's propaganda office, where he spent the next four years giving pep talks to repatriated Germans like himself. By late 1941 Kappe had been transferred to German military intelligence, known as the Abwehr, where he was assigned to identify and train men for a sabotage campaign in America.

The Abwehr had studied U.S. military production and key transportation lines in great detail, and Kappe made use of this intelligence in his planning. To cripple the light-metals industry, critical in airplane manufacturing, he and the Abwehr targeted plants operated by the Aluminum Company of America in Alcoa, Tennessee; Massena, New York; and East St. Louis, Illinois. To disrupt the supply of important raw materials for aluminum production, they targeted the Philadelphia Salt Company's cryolite plant. They developed plans to sabotage certain U.S. waterways—focusing particularly on the Ohio River locks between Cincinnati and St. Louis and the hydroelectric power plants at Niagara Falls and in the Tennessee Valley. They also wanted to mangle the Horseshoe Curve, an important railroad site in Altoona, Pennsylvania, and the Hell Gate Bridge, which connected the rail lines of New England with New York City. They had designs on the Chesapeake and Ohio Railway, one of America's major coal carriers. They planned to bomb Jewish-owned department stores for general terror-inducing effect.

Kappe code-named his mission Operation Pastorius, after Franz Daniel Pastorius, the leader of the first group of Germans to settle in colonial America, in Germantown, Pennsylvania, in 1683. Kappe imagined that he would ultimately return to Chicago as the mastermind of the operation. He had plans that a U-boat with German saboteurs would arrive in the United States every six weeks until the war was won.

There was no shortage of candidates for Kappe's initial crew of operatives. The Nazis had recently repatriated thousands of Germans living in the United States by offering them one-way tickets home. But his requirements were exacting: He wanted men who spoke English, were familiar with the United States, and were skilled in a trade that could provide them with cover while they lived in America. That proved difficult.

George John Dasch was Kappe's first recruit. He had gone to America in October of 1922, as a stowaway on the S.S. *Schoharie*, and had been a dishwasher and a waiter in Manhattan and on Long Island. In August of 1926 he was arrested twice, for operating a brothel and for violating Prohibition laws. While working in a hotel he met and married an American. Later he spent time in Chicago selling sanctuary supplies for the Mission of Our Lady of Mercy before returning to waiting tables. Although he completed the requirements for U.S. citizenship in 1939, he never showed up in court to be sworn in.

In 1941 Dasch returned to Berlin, where the Nazi bureaucracy required that he fill out forms explaining the reason for his return to Germany. Dasch wrote that he intended "to partake in political life." This led to his being questioned further by a Gestapo agent, to whom he said, "Even if I have to work as a street cleaner and do my job cleaning streets right, I want to participate politically." His motives may have been more complicated, however: He was not, one of his fellows later observed, "the absolute Nazi he pretended to be." After his capture by the FBI, Dasch claimed that he had joined the sabotage mission in order to learn secrets that he could later use in the United States to fight against the Nazis.

On June 3, 1941, Dasch met Kappe, who cross-examined him about his life in the United States. When Dasch said he wanted to join the German army, Kappe said he believed that Dasch might serve the Third Reich to far better advantage in another, unspecified capacity. Kappe subsequently hired Dasch to monitor U.S. radio broadcasts in a listening station where fifty-three languages were spoken and where the news that was gathered was teletyped to all the members of the German cabinet.

In November, Kappe called on Dasch again and asked him if he would like to return to America, to help realize "the plan on which my office has been working for a long time." Dasch demurred, saying, "But that's a peaceful country, isn't it?" Kappe admitted that the United States was indeed neutral, but he characterized it as an indirect enemy, because it was a supplier and a supporter of Germany's enemies. "Therefore," he said, "it is time to attack them. We wish to attack the American industries by industrial sabotage." By mid-January of 1941 Dasch had been assigned permanently to the planning of the U.S. mission.

On March 1 Dasch reported to a secret officer of the Abwehr to review the personal histories of several other men whom Kappe had tentatively selected to make up two teams of saboteurs, one of which Dasch would lead. In a series of interviews Dasch identified and eliminated a number of what he called "nitwits," along with others who seemed interested simply in escaping Germany at any cost. In the end he selected the following men, who, if not "nitwits," were also not exactly the Nazi elite.

- Ernest Peter Burger, born in 1906, joined the Nazi Party at the age of 17. He immigrated to America in 1927 to work as a machinist in Milwaukee and Detroit. He became a U.S. citizen in February of 1933, but when he couldn't find work during the Depression, he returned to Germany. There he rejoined the Nazi Party and became an aide-de-camp to Ernest Roehm, the chief of the Nazi storm troopers. He went on to study at the University of Berlin, and he later wrote a paper critical of the Gestapo—a move that earned him seventeen months in a concentration camp. Upon his release from the camp, in July of 1941, Burger served as a private in the German army, guarding Yugoslav and British prisoners of war. The following February he appeared on a list of Germans who had lived in America, and soon after he was interviewed and—somewhat oddly, given his history—selected to attend sabotage school.

- Herbert Haupt, born in 1919, was the youngest of the recruits. He had also spent the most time in America, having moved to Chicago with his family when he was 6 years old. Haupt attended Chicago's Lane Technical High School and served in the German-American Bund's Junior League, but he fled to Mexico in June of 1941. The German consul in Mexico City gave him money and arranged for his passage to Japan; Haupt took a Japanese freighter to Yokohama, where he later boarded a German steamer that broke through the British naval blockade of Germany and landed him in Bordeaux 107 days later. He received the Iron Cross, second class, for sighting an enemy steamer while on lookout.

- Heinrich Heinck, born in 1907, entered the United States illegally in 1926. After working in New York City as a busboy, a handyman, an elevator operator, and a machinist, he leaped at the German government's return offer in 1939. He had a limited command of English and spoke with a thick German accent. The other recruits considered Heinck phlegmatic and unsure of himself.

- Edward Kerling, born in 1909, was among the first 80,000 men to join the Nazi Party. He joined at the age of 19 and maintained his membership after moving to America, in 1928. After a stint smoking hams for a Brooklyn meat-packing company, Kerling found work as a chauffeur and handyman in Mount Kisco, New York, and Greenwich, Connecticut. In 1940 he returned to Germany, where he ran the propaganda shows in movie theaters. With his puffy cheeks, heavy jaw, and dimpled chin, Kerling was, Burger thought, a "decidedly Irish type." He was chosen to lead the second team.

- Herman Neubauer, born in 1910, went to America in 1931; he worked as a cook in restaurants, on ships, and at the Chicago World's Fair, in 1933. In 1939 he moved to Miami, but in 1940, while visiting his family in Germany, he was drafted into the German army and sent to the Russian front, where he was wounded in the face and the leg by shrapnel. While recovering in an army medical center in Vienna, he received a note from Kappe inquiring whether he would "like to go on a special assignment to a country where you have been before."

- Richard Quirin, born in 1908, moved to the United States in 1927. He worked in maintenance at a General Electric plant in Schenectady, New York, but was laid off during the Depression. He then moved to New York City, where he joined the Friends of the New Germany and found work as a house-painter. He, too, returned to Germany in the repatriation program.

- Werner Thiel, born in 1907, traveled to America in 1927 to work as a machinist at a Ford plant in Detroit. He later moved to New York, where he took a job as a porter in a senior citizens' home. He subsequently moved to Hammond, Indiana, before taking various jobs in Illinois, California, and Florida. In 1939 Thiel returned to Germany in the repatriation program.

LIFE ON THE FARM

In April, Kappe and his recruits were dispatched to a farm in Brandenburg, forty miles west of Berlin. From the road all that was visible of the farm, formerly the home of a wealthy Jewish shoe manufacturer, was a large stone farmhouse and a few pigs and cows roaming the grounds. But back behind a stone wall armed guards and German shepherds were on patrol twenty-four hours a day. In the fields behind the farmhouse members of the Abwehr constructed sections of railroad track and bridges of various kinds and lengths. They also set up pistol and rifle ranges, a field for hand grenade practice, and a gymnasium for boxing and judo training. Classrooms and laboratories were situated above the garage, and a nearby greenhouse supplied fresh fruit, vegetables, and—incongruously, given the circumstances—flowers.

On their first day at the farm Kappe told the men that they were about to begin training for an important battle against U.S. production and manufacturing. Their training, he said, would include courses in the construction and use of explosives, primers, fuses, and timers, and in the workings and vulnerabilities of industrial plants, railroads, bridges, and canal locks. The men would also be given plausible new identities for use in the United States.

The recruits settled into a routine of classroom time, private study, practical training, and exercise. They began each day with calisthenics, attended lectures in the morning and the afternoon, and had regular breaks from the classroom for sports. They took walks in the countryside, during which they sang "The Star Spangled Banner" and "Oh, Susanna!" At meals and after hours they were required to read recently published American newspapers and magazines. In pairs they practiced blowing up the railroad tracks laid around the estate, determining by trial and error the exact amount of explosives required in a given situation. Occasionally their instructors tested their vigilance and their reactions by launching surprise attacks on them.

In the classroom the men were forbidden to take notes and were required instead to commit everything to memory. Using detailed photographs, plans, and drawings, their instructors discussed the major terminals of the U.S. railroad system, the various engines used, and average freight-train speeds. The men were briefed on railroad bottlenecks where sabotage would inflict the greatest disruption.

The primary objective of the missions, Kappe told his men, was simply to do enough harm to impede production. He warned them not to try to blow up large dams or iron bridges or bridges with girders—such jobs were too difficult for a small team to carry out. They should also avoid targeting passenger trains. The Abwehr wanted to minimize civilian casualties.

Kappe told his men that when they arrived in the United States, their first task would be to create suitable cover for themselves. He provided them with forged Social Security and Selective Service registration cards. Dasch and Kerling became George John Davis and Edward Kelly, respectively—both born in San Francisco before the 1906 earthquake and fire, which meant that no one could demand records to corroborate their papers. Thiel became John Thomas, and was identified as a Polish immigrant in order to explain his accent, which was heavy. Heinck became Henry Kayner, of Wilkes-Barre, Pennsylvania (a town name he was consistently unable to spell). Richard Quirin became Richard Quintas; Herman Neubauer became Henry Nicholas. Haupt kept his own identity, as did Burger. (Both had American citizenship.) Because Burger had worked as a commercial artist, Kappe developed the idea that Burger should move to Chicago, set up an art studio, and insert an ad for his services in the *Chicago Tribune* on the first and the fifteenth of each month—a plan that would give Burger visibility and credibility and would also provide all the men involved in the mission with an easy way to find him.

Kappe also made the men sign contracts obliging them to remain silent about their mission throughout their lives, on penalty of death, and stating that if they died during the mission, their wives would receive lump sums determined by the German government. Should their efforts prove successful, they would be given good jobs following the war. Kappe told them that they would be under constant observation in the United States by German intelligence—which, he claimed, had infiltrated the FBI.

On April 30, the last day of class, Kappe gave special instructions to Dasch and Kerling. Each was to lead three other men. The teams were to travel across the Atlantic by U-boat and land secretly in separate locations, carrying with them crates of explosives and other tools for sabotage. Dasch and Kerling would each be given $50,000 in cash for bribes and expenses, and their men would be given $9,000 apiece. Dasch and Kerling received white handkerchiefs that, when permeated with fumes from a bottle of ammonia, would reveal a message stating how to reach Kappe and several U.S.-based contacts. Kappe emphasized that the two men were to focus initially on establishing cover and to refrain from any sabotage activities whatsoever. Detailed instructions would come at noon on July 4, at the Hotel Gibson in Cincinnati.

Almost a month later, after his men had had a few weeks of

leave, Kappe gathered them together in Lorient, France, where the Germans based some of their U-boats, and gave them their final orders. Kerling, Neubauer, Haupt, and Thiel would depart for Florida on May 26; Dasch, Burger, Heinck, and Quirin would depart for New York on May 28.

FIRST CONTACT

On May 28 Dasch and his team boarded submarine U-202. Captain Hans-Heinz Lindner announced over the loudspeaker that the four men were on special assignment to America, and called on every crew member to treat them well and ask no questions. The sub carried forty men, fourteen torpedoes, a cannon, and an anti-aircraft gun. As the vessel approached the Long Island coast, on June 12, the captain switched from diesel to silent electric motors. Just before midnight the men heard a scraping sound: The sub had touched the ocean floor some fifty yards from shore.

Dasch and his team, accompanied by members of the U-boat's crew, were loaded into an inflatable rowboat along with four wooden crates full of explosives and supplies, and a giant canvas seabag containing civilian clothes and other gear. The men were dressed in German military uniforms; if they were apprehended immediately, they would become prisoners of war. Lindner ordered Dasch to subdue by violence any civilian or soldier who challenged his team, and to send the person back in the rowboat so that the sub's crew could "take care of him."

"It was pitch-dark, foggy night, made to order for landing," Dasch later recalled. The fog was so thick that the men could see barely fifty feet ahead. After rowing in circles for a time, the group finally made a landing, and Dasch quickly sought higher ground to survey his surroundings. To his horror, he saw beacons both left and right. Running back to the boat, he ordered his men to put on their civilian clothes. As soon as they had changed, Quirin and Heinck began burying the explosives in some high dunes. Burger, however, seemed already to be entertaining thoughts of betraying the mission. Out of sight of the others he placed an empty German cigarette tin in the sand, where it could later be easily discovered by a passing patrol. Farther up the beach he left a small schnapps bottle, some socks, a vest, and a bathing suit for good measure.

Also on the beach that night, on a six-mile foot patrol, was Coast Guardsman John Cullen, of Bayside, Queens, a 21-year-old former Macy's deliveryman who enlisted in the Coast Guard in 1940 and later became a "sand pounder," to keep watch at night for suspicious activity close to shore. For weeks on end Cullen had patrolled, unarmed, without ever encountering another person. But at about 12:30 that morning, through the fog, he saw a dark object in the water some twenty feet away, and three men standing nearby. "I thought they were fishermen, local residents," he recollected recently, at his home in Chesapeake, Virginia, "until I saw one of the guys dragging a seabag into the dunes and then speaking in German."

"What are you doing down here?" Cullen asked. "Who are you?"

"We're a couple of fishermen from Southampton who have run ashore," Dasch answered. "We will stay here until sunrise and we will be all right."

Cullen told them that sunrise was hours away and said that there was no reason Dasch couldn't come with him to the Coast Guard station until then. Dasch, concerned that the seabag might raise Cullen's suspicions, decided to pretend to go along with him. In the meantime, one of the Germans came running down the beach with the seabag and addressed Dasch in German, Dasch hollered, "You damn fool, why don't you go back to the other guys?" He then took Cullen's arm and asked menacingly how old he was, and if he had a father and a mother. Cullen said he did.

"Well," Dasch said, "I wouldn't want to have to kill you. Forget about this and I will give you some money and you can have a good time." He offered Cullen $100, which Cullen refused. Dasch then offered $300, and Cullen accepted. "I was afraid they were going to knock me off right there," Cullen later said. "But when he offered me the money, I knew that was a little encouragement."

Dasch took off his hat and shined a flashlight into his own face. "Take a good look at me," he said to Cullen. "Look in my eyes. You will hear from me in Washington." Dasch then turned around and joined his colleagues, and Cullen began walking cautiously backward before turning and racing toward the station, in the town of Amagansett.

Burger told the others that Dasch had been talking to an American sailor. The men were concerned, but Dasch said to them, "Now, boys, this is the time to be quiet and hold your nerves. Each of you get a box and follow me." Burger dragged the seabag, deliberately leaving a track that could be identified later, and then helped the others bury it, along with their army uniforms.

The team proceeded inland, almost crawling, for half a mile. They lay still in the dunes for an hour and then began walking until they found a road. Whenever a car passed, they dove into nearby bushes. Heinck, shivering like a dog, said over and over, "We're surrounded, boys!" Eventually, at just after five in the morning, they stumbled into the tiny train station in Amagansett. They were wet, grass-stained, and generally filthy.

When the station opened for business, at six-thirty, Dasch bought four tickets to Manhattan. "Fishing in this neighborhood has been pretty bad lately," he observed at the ticket window, in a feeble attempt at nonchalance. Not long after, he and his men boarded their train.

DOUBTS AND BETRAYAL

After moving out of sight of Dasch and his men, Cullen raced to the Coast Guard station and sounded the alarm. He and other officers quickly formed a search party and returned to the site of the encounter. "While I was standing there," Cullen recollected recently, "I saw the light from the sub. I could also smell diesel oil. I knew it had to be a sub, so we notified the main Coast Guard station at Napeague. The sub was stuck on a sandbar, and when they revved the engines, the ground where I was standing shook. We didn't know at the time whether the Germans were coming in or leaving."

At daybreak they found the cigarette tin and the bathing suit. After following the trail left by the seabag, a member of the search party poked a stick in the sand and struck something hard. The men dug the four crates of explosives out of the sand. Other members of the party followed footprints and soon found the buried German clothing, including a cap with a swastika sewn on it.

Sensing the gravity of what had been found, Coast Guard intelligence officers came and immediately took it all to Governor's Island, near Manhattan and the Statue of Liberty, where, at the area Coast Guard headquarters, they opened three of the crates. The fourth, hissing because the TNT inside had been exposed to salt water, was moved to the end of a dock and carefully opened there. At 11:00 A.M. the FBI was notified of the find, and by noon everything the Germans had brought with them, with the exception of their money and the clothes on their backs, had been impounded by the Bureau. Tension remained high, however: No one knew how many men had landed or what their plans were.

In Washington, J. Edgar Hoover, the director of the FBI, breathlessly informed Attorney General Francis Biddle of the news of the moment. Biddle later wrote, "All of Edgar Hoover's imaginative and restless energy was stirred into prompt and effective action. His eyes were bright, his jaw set, excitement flickering around the edge of his nostrils. He was determined to catch them all before any sabotage took place." The FBI worked with the Coast Guard to set up continuous surveillance of the area where the materials had been buried, hoping to apprehend the men when they returned for their stash. The Bureau commandeered a private bungalow on the beach and began interviewing local residents who fit the descriptions given by Cullen. Hoover also imposed a news blackout on the story.

Meanwhile, Dasch and his team had arrived at Jamaica Station in New York, at about 9:30 A.M., and had immediately bought themselves new sets of clothes. After changing in the men's room at a restaurant, they threw their old clothes in a trash can and split into two groups, agreeing to meet later. Dasch and Burger registered at the Hotel Governor Clinton—Dasch as George John Davis, and Burger as himself. Heinck and Quirin registered at the Hotel Martinique under their respective aliases. They all ate, washed, and rested.

The men found themselves completely on their own in the city. Free and loaded with money, they took full advantage of their situation by shopping, carousing in clubs, and seeking out prostitutes. Dasch later wrote, "There was nothing in the way of Nazi surveillance to prevent me from taking [all of the money] I'd been provided with and fading into a happy and luxurious obscurity."

But he didn't. Dasch and Burger began to have frank discussions about their mission and their motivations. Dasch admitted to Burger that he felt he didn't belong in Germany, and that he had in fact begun planning an escape back to America even as he had worked for Germany's propaganda division. Burger, for his part, talked of his troubles with the Gestapo. Dasch then told Burger that he "was not George John Davis, the group leader of a gang of saboteurs, but George John Dasch, the man who came here into this country for the opportunity to fight Hitler and his gang in my own fashion." Upon hearing this, Burger, according to Dasch, "broke out in a crying spell" and confessed to having left a trail of evidence on the beach, adding that he believed the crates of explosives must have been discovered by that time. The mission seemed botched before it had even begun.

Dasch told Burger it was critical that Dasch contact the FBI, because, he said, should any of the seven men—or even Dasch himself—fall into police hands, "it would be very difficult for me to prove the real reason I came here." First, however, Dasch and Burger needed to reassure Heinck and Quirin that all was proceeding according to plan. Burger met Heinck and Quirin several times during the next few days and persuaded the two to remain quiet in New York while Dasch supposedly pursued covert contacts for the team.

On Sunday, June 14, Dasch called the FBI. Agent Dean McWhorter answered, and Dasch introduced himself as Franz Daniel Pastorius, "a German citizen who has arrived in this country only yesterday morning." Dasch told McWhorter that he had information so important to report that "the only person who should hear it is J. Edgar Hoover." McWhorter suggested that Dasch come to his office, but Dasch mildly replied, "I, Franz Daniel Pastorius, shall try to get in contact with your Washington office either Thursday or Friday, and you should notify them of this fact." McWhorter indeed made note of the call, but rather than sending a message to Washington, merely wrote, "This memo is being prepared only for the purpose of recording the call made by [Pastorius]."

On the morning of June 18, Dasch packed for Washington. He divided the money Kappe had given him into several envelopes bound together with a rubber band and attached a note that said, in part, "Money from German [government] for their purpose, but to be used to fight the Nazis. George J. Dasch, alias George J. Davis, alias Franz Pastorius." He paid his and Burger's hotel bills and left Burger a note.

Dear Pete:

Sorry for not have been able to see you before I left. I came to the realization to go to Washington and finish that which we have started so far.

I'm leaving you, believing that you take good care of yourself and also of the other boys. You may rest assured, that I shall try to straighten everything out to the very best possibility. My bag and clothes I'll put in your room. Your hotel bill is paid by me, including this day. If anything extraordinary should happen, I'll get in touch with you directly.

Until later,

I'm your sincere friend,

George

Dasch arrived in Washington late Thursday and checked into the Mayflower Hotel. After breakfast the following morning he phoned the Information Service of the U.S. government and asked the young woman who answered to explain the difference between the FBI and the Secret Service. "She asked me what the purpose of my visit was," he later recalled, "and I told her that I had to make a statement of military as well as of political value." Directed to phone the FBI, Dasch ended up speaking to Agent Duane Traynor, who listened politely as Dasch identified himself as George John Dasch, the leader of a team of eight saboteurs who had just arrived from Germany. Traynor told him to remain in his room so that FBI agents could escort him to the Justice Department.

Dasch spoke with FBI special agents over the next five days. He told them he wanted to lead them to each of the seven other men and expressed an interest in "having the opportunity to meet your superior, and Mr. Hoover perhaps?" He told the agents all he knew about Kappe. He discussed his experiences after his return to Germany, his dissatisfaction with the Third Reich, and the circumstances of his amphibious return to the United States, including his encounter with John Cullen. He insisted that he had planned his betrayal long before. "This is an idea," he said, "that is eight months old."

Dasch also insisted that Burger was as staunchly anti-Nazi as he, having joined the mission "as a way to get even." Quirin and Heinck he dismissed as "a couple of Nazis who have only one duty to perform and that is to listen to the command." He said, "They have not to question the sincerity, truthfulness, and correctness. Their duty is to follow it, otherwise to die." By the end of the second day of interrogation, working with information provided by Dasch, the FBI had located and apprehended all three members of Dasch's team.

Rounding up the second team, which had landed near Jacksonville, Florida, during the night of June 16, was somewhat more difficult. All Dasch knew was that the two teams were to meet in Cincinnati on July 4, but he offered up the white handkerchief as a potential lead. At first he could not remember how to handle the invisible ink, but the FBI lab "broke the hankie," and agents were dispatched to shadow the contacts named on it. Within days the FBI had found all four members of Kerling's team, in New York and Chicago, and had them in custody.

Only after all the other men had been jailed, in New York, did the FBI officially arrest Dasch, on July 3. During his interrogation, Dasch later said, the FBI had told him to plead guilty and not to mention his betrayal—just to put on "the biggest act in the world" and "take the punishment," for which, after a few months in prison, he would receive a presidential pardon. After his arrest Dasch begged to be jailed with his colleagues, so that they would not suspect he had turned them in. The FBI obliged. Dasch was walked past the cells of his colleagues and then placed in his own cell. He was under the impression that his new friends at the FBI would soon come to release him. But not long after he arrived, he looked out the peephole of his cell and saw a guard reading the New York *Daily News:* Dasch's picture was on the front page, accompanied by the headline "CAPTURED NAZI SPY."

So it was that two weeks after the Long Island landing, all eight Germans found themselves in custody without having even tried to commit a single act of sabotage. Dasch consoled himself by remembering the FBI's promise of a presidential pardon.

HOMELAND DEFENSE

When the men had all been apprehended, Attorney General Biddle telephoned President Roosevelt with the good news. Roosevelt was determined that punishment be harsh, to discourage future infiltrations. In a memorandum to Biddle, Roosevelt wrote that the two American citizens among the eight were guilty of high treason and the other six were spies. All, he felt, deserved the death penalty. "I want one thing clearly understood, Francis," he told Biddle. "I won't hand them over to any United States Marshal armed with a writ of habeas corpus."

Meanwhile, Hoover and his aides at the FBI had decided that when the story was made public, Dasch's surrender and his and Burger's cooperation would go unmentioned, so as to give the German government the impression that the U.S. authorities were so efficient and so well-informed that additional landings would be a waste of time and manpower.

With the approval of the President and the Attorney General, Hoover broke the story at a press conference on June 27, making headlines nationwide the following day. "FBI CAPTURES 8 SABOTEURS" read the front page of *The New York Times*. The story itself, however, was remarkably light on the details of the men's capture. When pressed on how the FBI had broken the case, Hoover was quick and succinct. "That," he said, "will have to wait until after the war." Hoover did, however, reveal exactly which aluminum plants and railway bridges had been targeted, how much explosive material had been found on the beaches, and the fact that two of the men were American citizens.

Immediately after the arrests the FBI swung into action. Agents swarmed over the Swedish liner *Drottningholm*, for example, in search of German spies masquerading as refugees. They subjected the baggage and the mail of all 868 *Drottningholm* passengers to two days of intensive investigation—the most rigorous examination ever of a vessel docked in the Port of New York up to then. They questioned some 250 "enemy" aliens in Altoona, and seized many "powerful short-wave radio transmitters." When asked if these efforts were in any way connected to the eight Germans, the head of the FBI's Philadelphia field office responded, "Draw your own conclusions."

The public vilified the would-be saboteurs. *Life* magazine published FBI mug shots of the men, photographs of some of their equipment, and display type reading "THE EIGHT NAZI SABOTEURS SHOULD BE PUT TO DEATH." When the *South Bend* (Indiana) *Tribune* polled its readers on July 2, only one respondent wanted them set free. An overwhelming majority—1,097 people—were in favor of immediate execution. One reader went so far as to suggest that the men be fed to Gargantua, a giant circus gorilla—and enclosed money for Gargantua's funeral, writing that the gorilla would "surely . . . die of such poisonous eating."

On June 30 Biddle informed the President that a military tribunal would be preferable to a civil trial for handling the case, because it would be quick and secret and because the death penalty could be imposed with only a two-thirds majority among the judges. Biddle also feared that if the eight defendants were tried in a civil court, the jury might find that no sabotage had been committed, and the men might therefore receive sentences of only two or three years. He dredged up a seventy-six-year-old precedent, dating from the Civil War and involving Lambdin Milligan, a resident of Indiana and an outspoken opponent of Abraham Lincolns. Milligan had been charged with giving aid to and communicating with the enemy and violating the laws of war. He had been tried by a military commission and sentenced to death. The Supreme Court heard the case and unanimously granted him a writ of habeas corpus, citing a citizen's right to a trial in civil court unless "ordinary law no longer adequately secures public safety and private rights."

On July 2, less than a week after the men had been captured, Roosevelt issued a proclamation to the nation.

Whereas the safety of the United States demands that all enemies who have entered upon the territory of the United States as
part of an invasion or predatory incursion . . . should be promptly
tried in accordance with the Law of War; now, therefore, I,
Franklin D. Roosevelt, . . . do hereby proclaim that all persons
who are subjects, citizens or residents of any nation at war with
the United States or who give obedience to or act under the
direction of any such nation, and who during time of war enter
or attempt to enter the United States or any territory or possession thereof, through coastal or boundary defenses, and are
charged with committing or attempting or preparing to commit
sabotage, espionage, hostile or warlike acts, or violations of the
law of war, shall be subject to the law of war and to the jurisdiction of military tribunals; and that such persons shall not be priv-
ileged to seek any remedy or maintain any proceeding, directly
or indirectly, or to have any such remedy or proceeding sought
on their behalf, in the courts of the United States.

The wording of the proclamation was broad enough to cover
almost any remotely similar future offense.

Major General Frank R. McCoy was chosen to preside over the
tribunal (it was never to be called a court) that was hastily convened
to handle the case. Three other major generals and three brigadier
generals completed the commission. Attorney General Biddle was
assigned to lead the prosecution, assisted by Major General Myron
Cramer, the Army's judge advocate general. Brigadier General
Albert L. Cox was the tribunal's provost marshal. Among the many
lawyers working for Biddle was Lloyd Cutler, who went on to
become the White House counsel to Presidents Jimmy Carter and
Bill Clinton—and who has now been consulted by the Bush
administration as it attempts to set up military tribunals.

Colonel Cassius M. Dowell and Colonel Kenneth C. Royall

were ordered to serve as defense lawyers. Dowell, a forty-year Army veteran who had been wounded in World War I, handled a number of legal issues for the Army. Royall, a trial lawyer from North Carolina with a degree from Harvard Law School, had recently been appointed by Army Secretary Henry L. Stimson to head the Army's legal division in charge of military contracts. The two men came to the conclusion that it was best for their case if Dasch was defended separately, so Colonel Carl Ristine, of the Army Inspector General's Office, was appointed counsel for Dasch.

The votes of five of the commission's seven members were required for conviction and sentencing. As Commander in Chief, the President would be the final arbiter of all commission recommendations. There would be no appeal.

A MILITARY TRIBUNAL

On July 4 the eight Germans were moved in secret from New York to Washington, where they were incarcerated in the District of Columbia Jail. Each man was isolated in a tiled cell, with an empty cell on either side of him, and was under surveillance around the clock. Clad only in pajamas and paper slippers, the prisoners were denied writing materials. They were allowed to read old magazines and newspapers and to smoke cigarettes lit for them by their guards. Current newspapers were forbidden, so that the prisoners could not learn of their fate. No man was allowed to talk to any other. They were given only paper spoons and paper plates with which to eat their meals—there was to be no opportunity for suicide. The men never asked to see clergymen or relatives.

Room 5235 of the main Department of Justice building was ordinarily used by the FBI for lectures and films. On July 8, however, it became a military courtroom, its windows covered with heavy black curtains that blocked all daylight. At the front of the room that day, as the tribunal began, long tables were placed end to end to serve as the bench for the seven judges. To the left of the bench stood a witness chair, a small table for the court reporter, and tables for the prosecution and the defense. Behind the table for the defense sat all eight defendants, in alphabetical order, dressed in the clothing—suits and two-toned shoes—that they had bought during their brief time at large in the United States. Each man was flanked by guards. At the rear of the room were the buried clothing, the explosives, and the crates, all of which were to be entered as evidence.

Each day of the trial the prisoners were transported from the jail to the Justice Department and back, in two armored black vans. FBI agents led the procession, and nine police officers on motorcycles followed alongside. Behind the prisoners' vans were three Army scout cars with soldiers and machine guns at the ready. Each of the nineteen days that the men were summoned before the tribunal, the motorcade took a different, circuitous route to the Justice Department, where fifty soldiers stood guard outside the entrance. Hot-dog and ice-cream vendors set up stands to feed the curious.

Colonel Royall opened his defense with a statement to the tribunal. "In deference to the commission," he said, "and in order that we may not waive for our clients any rights which may belong to them, we desire to state that, in our opinion, the order of the President of the United States creating this court is invalid and unconstitutional. . . . Our view is based first on the fact that the civil courts are open in the territory in which we are now located and that, in our opinion, there are civil statutes governing the matters to be investigated."

Biddle was no less tough in his response. "This is not a trial of offenses of law of the civil courts, but is a trial of the offenses of the law of war, which is not cognizable by the civil courts. It is the trial, as alleged in the charges, of certain enemies who crossed our borders . . . and who crossed in disguise and landed here. . . . They are exactly and precisely in the same position as armed forces invading this country."

Royall argued that the articles of war cited in the charges applied solely to U.S. citizens caught aiding an enemy, and not to enemies themselves. He further contended that no evidence suggested that the men would have followed through with their plans for sabotage. They had not been trained for espionage, had only vague contacts through which to communicate with Germany, and had no plans to return home until after the war. In response Biddle cited the case of Major John André, the British officer executed during the Revolutionary War for passing through American lines with the intention of bribing an American officer.

Lloyd Cutler remembers the opening arguments as a harbinger of what was to come. "Royall stood up and made an objection—a perfectly good one. The president of the court banged his gavel and said, 'The court will rise.' Forty-five minutes later the court came back and said 'Objection overruled.' Then Biddle asked a second question, and the same thing happened. The court took another forty-five-minute break and overruled the objection. Royall got the message."

Coast Guardsman John Cullen was the first witness. After recalling the events of his encounter with the Germans, Cullen said he could identify Dasch only if allowed to hear his voice. When Dasch said, "What is your name?" Cullen positively identified him. In his cross-examination of Cullen, Colonel Ristine noted that Dasch had never attempted any violence against Cullen. After Cullen left the stand, Warren Barnes, the chief of the Amagansett Coast Guard station, identified all the objects found on the beach, including the clothes Dasch's men had buried. Next an FBI munitions expert testified as to the type of the explosives.

The next two FBI agents to testify seemed to strengthen Dasch's case. Special Agent Charles Lanham stated that Burger had confessed that he and Dasch had never planned to follow through on the sabotage but instead had wanted to fight Hitler. Special Agent Norval Wills testified to the promise of a presidential pardon for Dasch in return for pleading guilty.

Royall later called each of the Germans to testify in his own defense. Haupt testified that he had planned all along not to go through with the sabotage and to turn the others in on July 6, when he would know where they all were. Neubauer swore that he and Kerling had almost immediately come "to the conclusion that we would not have a chance to go through with our orders." Quirin claimed to have developed doubts about the mission "on the submarine." Thiel claimed that he would never have carried out acts of sabotage. During the trial, under interrogation by Biddle, Thiel and Neubauer claimed that they hadn't turned themselves in to the FBI for fear of the alleged Gestapo infiltration, which would have resulted in dire harm to their families in Germany. Heinck admitted that even before going to the training farm he had understood that the work he was about to do in America was definitely sabotage.

Meanwhile, the question of Dasch's and Burger's special status as collaborators with the U.S. government was also being discussed outside the tribunal. On July 16 Biddle wrote in a memorandum to Roosevelt,

Dasch and Burger were helpful in apprehending the others and in making out the proof. However, up to now, they have refused to testify. The Judge Advocate General and I intend to ask the Commission to impose the death penalty on them because we think they had some intention to go through with their plans when they landed and are therefore legally guilty. If the Commission sentences all eight to death, we will probably be prepared to recommend that you grant some clemency to Dasch and Burger. At the very least, however, they should be detained à la Rudolph Hess until after the war. Burger wants no publicity if he receives clemency. He prefers death to endangering his family. Dasch, however, seems to prefer the publicity, and it might be useful to make him somewhat of a hero, thus encouraging other German agents to turn in their fellows.

Dasch and Burger finally did testify. Dasch claimed that the sole reason he had entered sabotage school was to escape Germany, and Ristine again pointed out Dasch's failure to harm Cullen, despite the orders he was under to subdue and take back to the submarine anybody he encountered. Burger was the last to testify; he said that he was an American citizen who had served in two National Guard units, earning two honorable discharges. After his return to Germany, he said, he quickly became disillusioned with the Nazi Party and began to plot a return to the United States. The lawyers defending him pointed out that he had cooperated with the FBI agents when they came to his hotel room, and that his interrogation had actually been more useful than Dasch's, with far more detailed descriptions of the school for saboteurs and of his colleagues.

After sixteen days in session the defense rested on July 27, and the six men other than Dasch and Burger signed a statement expressing appreciation for having been given a fair trial. In it they wrote, "Before all we want to state that defense counsel has represented our case unbiased, better than we could expect and probably risking the indignation of public opinion. We thank our defense counsel."

But Royall wasn't finished. Determined to challenge the President's proclamation that the men should face a military tribunal, he sought to win his clients' freedom by demanding a writ of habeas corpus. Though the Supreme Court had been adjourned for the summer, it convened in a special session on July 29 to consider the matter.

Royall argued that Long Island and Florida beaches could not be characterized as "zones of military operation." There had been no combat there, and no plausible threat of invasion. Royall argued that the civil courts were functioning, and under the circumstances they were the appropriate venue for the case to be heard. Biddle argued that the United States and Germany were at war, and cited a law passed by Congress in 1798 that stated, "Whenever there is a declared war, and the President makes public proclamation of the event, all native citizens, denizens or subjects of the hostile nation shall be liable to be apprehended . . . as alien enemies."

On July 31 the Supreme Court unanimously denied Royall's appeal, writing, "The military commission was lawfully constituted . . . petitioners are held in lawful custody for trial before the military commission and have not shown cause for being discharged by writ of habeas corpus."

The members of the tribunal then deliberated for two days before reaching a verdict. Finally, on August 3, in accordance with instructions, the tribunal's verdict was delivered — by Army plane — directly to Roosevelt, at Hyde Park, in four thick manila envelopes. It found all eight men guilty and recommended death by electrocution, but added, "In view of the apparent assistance given to the prosecution by defendants Ernest Peter Burger and George John Dasch, the commission unanimously recommends that the sentence of each of these two defendants . . . be commuted from death to life imprisonment."

On August 7 General Cox, the tribunal's provost marshal, received instructions from President Roosevelt: All but Dasch and Burger were to be electrocuted at noon the following day.

THE END OF THE AFFAIR

Early in the morning of August 8, after the Germans had been fed a breakfast of scrambled eggs, bacon, and toast at the District of

Columbia Jail, General Cox and an Army chaplain entered the cells of the condemned men and informed them of their fate. Each man turned pale and seemed stunned. None said a word. Burger was reading a copy of *The Saturday Evening Post* when Cox and the chaplain entered and told him he had been spared. Burger responded simply "Yes, sir," and returned to his reading.

As the morning progressed, military officers, Army doctors, the city coroner, and Army ambulances arrived at the jail. People moved quickly and said little. The mood was somber. Final adjustments were made to the electric chair—a red-oak device situated in a 12-by-18-foot execution chamber located on the top floor of the jail. Each condemned man would face a glass panel that appeared to him to be opaque, behind which would sit representatives of the tribunal and other officials. The witnesses were to include Major General McCoy, Hoover, and representatives of the War and Justice Departments. In alphabetical order, beginning with Haupt, the condemned men would be walked into the chamber and executed with 4,500 volts of electricity.

The process began at noon. Each execution took no longer than fourteen minutes—the time required to administer the sentence, establish a time of death, remove the corpse, and ventilate the room for the arrival of the next man.

After the final execution the tribunal reported to President Roosevelt that his orders had been carried out. Just before 1:30 P.M. an announcement was made by the White House press secretary, Steve Early, who reported that six executions had taken place. The six bodies were buried in a pauper's cemetery at Blue Plains, in the District of Columbia, a site adjacent to the House for the Aged and Infirm and the Industrial Home School for Colored Children. Six wooden headboards—marked simply 276, 277, 278, 279, 280, and 281—identified the graves.

Early also announced that by "unanimous recommendation by the commission concurred in by the Attorney General and the

Judge Advocate General of the Army," the President had commuted the sentences of Dasch and Burger. "The commutation directed by the President in the case of Burger," Early said, "was to confinement to hard labor for life. In the case of Dasch, the sentence was commuted by the President to the confinement at hard labor for thirty years. The records in all eight cases will be sealed until the end of the war."

Dasch and Burger spent some six years in U.S. prisons and then were deported to Germany in April of 1948. Burger subsequently disappeared and is rumored to have fled to Spain. In 1959 Dasch published *Eight Spies Against America*, a self-promotional and little-noticed account of the whole affair. He spent his final years working as a travel agent and a tour guide in Germany and enduring regular harassment in the places he lived, because of his role in the betrayal of his colleagues. In 1983 he was tracked down by an American college student named Jonathan Mann, who reported that Dasch "got all teary-eyed talking about how he facilitated the deaths of 'those boys.'" Late in his life Dasch befriended Charlie Chaplin, who was living in exile in nearby Switzerland, and the two often compared notes on how J. Edgar Hoover had ruined their lives.

Until his death, in 1992, in Germany, Dasch remained hopeful that he would receive the presidential pardon promised to him decades before. It never came.

———

The editors at The Atlantic Monthly *commissioned the "Keystone Kommandos" just after Bush signed the order allowing military tribunals to try foreigners charged with terrorism after September 11. Bush copied some provisions straight from President Roosevelt's order, including closing the trials to the public, judgment by a two-thirds vote of the military commissioners, and no appeal.*

But legal scholars, members of Congress, and civil rights activists

*questioned whether Bush's order was constitutional, pointing out that
the legal precedent for tribunals is only during formally declared wars.*

*My story had no political motivation; it was just meant to be a his-
torical tale about the last time a military tribunal was convened. I
think what I found most compelling were some of the parallels
between the Al Qaeda terrorists and the hapless Nazis of 1942 — their
youth and inexperience, the rigorous training for the mission, even
the fact that both sets of men seemed to enjoy their brief time in America. But history does not always repeat itself.*

MURDER ON THE AMAZON
DEVIN FRIEDMAN

The *Seamaster* anchored in the wrong place. Claudio, on duty at the harbormaster's office, watched it pull right past him. It moved past Alvaro, who was sitting on an overturned canoe, enjoying a morning bottle of wine, and João, who was loading a boat with cases of Coke and was soaked in sweat. It was ten o'clock on the morning of December 5, 2001, and the sun was already bleaching out the world. The *Seamaster*'s sails were down, and its motor was churning up deep contrails of white water as the 112-foot aluminum schooner plowed through the Brazilian Amazon, past Rita as she pinned up laundry along the river, and a man known as the Pig Farmer, who was buying lima beans at the grocery near the port. The *Seamaster*, with a crew of nine plus the skipper, Sir Peter Blake, was supposed to motor on to Macapá, a few minutes downriver. But they didn't receive that message from the harbormaster because they were tuned to the wrong radio frequency. Instead they pulled into the port of Santana, the worst neighborhood in maybe two hundred miles. The *Seamaster* was anchored there for only a half hour before an officer from the port authority told them this was not a safe place to be, and the boat moved on to Macapá. But the *Seamaster*'s shipping agent, a fat and perpetually sweating man whose name is José Sansão Souza Batista, but who likes to be called Sam, says that their mistake changed the whole course of events.

"I would think, if I was a spiritual person, that everything was concurring for this boat to have an encounter with death," Sam says, with the benefit of hindsight.

"Everyone knows the boats that come in and out of here," says Alvaro, who was drinking the wine. "We all pay attention. This is what it is to live in this town." João, who was loading the Coke, says there was a lot of talk about the *Seamaster*. "We have yachts come through here all the time, but this was a strange-looking one. Everyone thought, This person is very rich."

Among the others who took an interest in the *Seamaster* were six men who would later be called pirates in newspapers all over the world: Ricardo, Isael, José, Reney, Rubens, and Josué. They were known to hang around the docks, where they'd pick up the odd job or smoke a few cigarettes or get drunk in the saloons at night. Ricardo, a 22-year-old from Santana, would later say, "We saw the boat and we were thinking, This is a rich tourist. There will be a lot of American dollars. And so we thought, Let's go see this boat."

Santana is not geared for tourists—there are lots of boats moving through the port, but almost none of them are yachts carrying foreigners looking for rum drinks and beaded necklaces. The only regular visitors are the crews of giant, rusty freighters that stop to load wood pulp or manganese. A bartender at one of the dirty saloons that crowd the port area says he makes a good deal of his money from Greek and Russian sailors. He says there are ten people ready to sell them a beer the second they descend the gangway, and at least as many ready to charge them for sex, rob them, or both. At night, you can see the whores congregate around the port wearing the international whore uniform: cheap, high plastic pumps and brightly colored short skirts.

Macapá, population 250,000, is the capital of Amapá, the most godforsaken of the Brazilian states. The only way in or out is by plane or boat. They tried to build a road to the city of Manaus, a thousand miles away, but a couple hundred miles out the thing sank into the Amazonian swamp. Santana is ten miles from downtown

Macapá, and the intrastate epicenter of crime. Most weeks, says a doctor at the Santana hospital, a dozen people are murdered. "Mostly it's by machete. I had to help a guy yesterday who had had seven hacks taken out of him. It was because he'd killed the attacker's brother the week before. Neither of them has been arrested."

On the Sunday after I arrive, my translator, Marcelo, and I are approached by a drunk guy with a puffy face and a T-shirt that says Santana will be AIDS-free by 2001. He asks for money, and when we say no, he pushes Marcelo. A shipping porter comes over and chases him away before anything else happens. The porter and Marcelo say this is by far the most common kind of robber: a sort of aggravated begging. Santana is a place where you need to know where you are all the time, Marcelo says, and it's good to be able to tell when the mood of a place is changing.

Late one night, I can't sleep and decide to take a walk around the neighborhood, though I've been warned against it. On the front porch of my hotel, I meet a woman named Rose, a Mormon missionary. She has soft lines on her face, gray hair, and a low-wattage beatific smile. As it turns out, she is a first-rate insomniac and has stood watch over the darkling streets of Johannesburg, Manila, and New York, among others. I ask her why Santana seems to be such a dangerous place and she says that poor rural villages the world over are pretty safe. It's the poor people in the cities, the transients, the have-nots in plain sight of the haves, who become antisocial.

When I leave for my walk (which lasts about thirty-seven seconds), Rose puts her hand on mine and says, "Careful, dear, they'll shoot you in the face."

When Sir Peter Blake pulled his boat into Macapá, it was the last day of the *Seamaster*'s two-month mission through the Amazon basin. The crew had sailed 1,200 miles upstream and back again, making a documentary about the Amazonian ecosystem to teach the world, as Blake said, that "the earth is a water planet: good water, good life; poor water, poor life." The size of the crew fluctuated between ten and twenty people throughout the expedition, but the core was men Blake had known for years—Don Robertson, his best friend; Errol Olphert, who had sailed with Blake on his America's Cup team—and for whom the *Seamaster* voyage was a kind of reward.

Things on the Amazon hadn't gone exactly as Blake had planned. He had hired a diver to do some filming, but the Amazon was so murky with silt that they'd been unable to get any good footage. Plus, says Robertson, "With wildlife, it's not like the zoo; the animals don't just line up so you can take their picture." But they did see a few pink dolphins—strange, shy animals that live more than a thousand miles from the ocean. Throughout, Blake ran the expedition with an abiding professionalism—the crew rose at dawn each morning to clean the boat, chart the course, set up for the filming.

Blake was possibly the greatest sailor who ever lived. There are people who would argue this point—some would say it was Dennis Conner, or maybe Sir Francis Drake—but there are about four million people who wouldn't. Blake was from New Zealand, and after winning the Whitbread around-the-world race in 1990, the Jules Verne Trophy in 1994 (in the process breaking the record for circumnavigating the globe), and, most famously, the America's Cup in 1995 and 2000, he became a national hero. "Most kids in New Zealand will have a bit of a grasp on who the heroes are," says Don Robertson. "And they'll tell you it's Edmund Hillary and Peter Blake."

Blake did not become the greatest sailor in the world by being the best technical sailor. It was a greatness achieved more by force of personality. He was an extraordinarily striking person to meet. He stood six feet four inches tall (his friends sometimes called him Six Four) and had worn his hair in a Beatles-esque mop since the sev-

enties. Steve Fossett, who holds world records for sailing and bal-
looning, says it made him look like a Viking. People who met Blake
say he possessed a spiritual energy, as if he were sprinkled with a
kind of fairy dust that could make almost anyone a true believer.
Michael Levitt, who's written eleven books on sailing, tells this
story: "I met him in Philadelphia when he took one of his early
Whitbread boats around. He'd put this project together, built this
boat, and he was off to win this race, and you could just *see* it in
him. You didn't know what to make of it then, because he hadn't
actually accomplished anything yet. But he just radiated."

Blake had an uncanny ability to get very rich men to give him
millions of dollars to build and race boats in exchange for a company logo painted on the hull, and to convince the best yachtsmen
in the world to sail with him. David Alan-Williams, who crewed
with Blake on his record-setting around-the-world voyage in 1994,
says, "There were a lot of us who used to say that if Peter came to us
and said he was going to sail a boat to the moon, we'd go, 'Okay,
when do we start?'" Levitt thinks people became devoted to Blake
partly because he acted as if he had never in his life experienced a
moment of doubt.

Blake endured a great deal to be a long-distance sailor. In an
ocean race, you are expected to shrink your existence to its smallest
and most portable form. Peter Blake was not designed for the quarters on racing yachts; the ceilings on the *ENZA New Zealand*, for
instance, were less than six feet high. So Blake spent thirty years of
his life on metal schooners and catamarans doing thirty knots, bent
at the waist, sleeping in beds in which maybe 80 percent of him fit
comfortably. And most of those races he did not win—he lost the
Whitbread four times before he won it. "Every time I've done a
round-the-world race, I've said it's the last," Blake said in 1987. "It's
the highlight of your life, but it's crazy." At some level, Blake was
carrying on a war of attrition against the Big Forces of the world:
weather, ocean, time. His greatest skill may have been his ability to

ignore conditions, failure, and, according to the sometimes dismal logs of his races, broken masts, disintegrated hulls, and spells of hypothermia. The will to move forward was possibly Blake's most basic impulse.

The *Seamaster* was a retirement from professional racing. Blake felt he'd accomplished everything he could. (As Don Robertson says, "Would Hillary climb Everest twice?") Instead of puttering about in the garden or sinking into a fit of drinking and self-pity, as some retired athletes do, he decided to launch the *Seamaster*. "I sailed all over the world," Blake said, "but I never got to slow down and look at anything." He was able to convince the Omega watch company to give him the money to buy a boat from the Cousteau Society, which he painted, stamped with the name SEAMASTER, after Omega's $3,000 flagship watch, and launched under the imprimatur of Blakexpeditions, which he figured on building into his own Cousteau Society. Not that retirement didn't have its benefits. Instead of eating freeze-dried soy protein, as he had when he raced, on the *Seamaster* he had a full-time cook, a Brazilian named Rizaldo. When they brought the boat to South America, the crew built canvas shades against the tropical sun, and stocked the fore freezer with loads of meat and the aft refrigerators with greens and tropical fruit and milk and cold beer. Robertson says, "The conditions were positively luxurious compared to the other boats we'd sailed on."

Because they didn't really have anything to document in Macapá (the main tourist activity is straddling the equator, which runs through town, at the visitors' center), the *Seamaster*'s crew had designated the day for running errands and generally screwing around. Sam, the shipping agent, drove them to the big grocery store in town, where they bought fruit, gas for the grill, and bottles of local rum. Blake and six of his crew spent a few hours at a restaurant at Fazendinha Beach, across from their new anchorage, eating fish and rice and drinking caipirinhas.

"Mr. Peter docked his dinghy right there and stayed from 5:30 P.M. until 8:00 P.M.," the waiter who served them tells me. "He was a very tall man, much taller than us, very white and very strong, much stronger than us. It was easy to see he was the leader. All the attention was on him."

Around Blake at the table were most of the crew of the *Seamaster*, who were also his good friends. Leon Sefton, the cameraman, was his longtime business partner's son. Blake had invited Robin Allen, because at 19 he was a promising young sailor, and Rodger Moore, an Auckland plumber with little sailing experience, because Blake had worked with his son. Don Robertson was staff photographer.

"We were all quite relaxed because it was the end of the trip," Robertson says, "and all we had to do was sail around the corner and up to Trinidad and Tobago, where some of us were going to have a Caribbean Christmas."

The waiter says, "They had a very good time, laughing always. They drank, too. They had ten caipirinhas and fourteen six-hundred-milliliter bottles of beer between seven of them. You see that waitress over there? She served him." He calls the waitress over. She's in her forties and wearing stained yellow spandex pants and a white shirt that laces up the front. "We danced together a little bit, and I gave him his last kiss, on his cheek, of course," she says.

When the crew got back to the boat that night, Blake and the others turned on the CD player, opened a few beers, and installed themselves in their hammocks. The cook began preparing a light dinner.

"The night in Macapá started so great," says Robin Allen, who lives near the Blakes' home in Hampshire, England, and is close with their children (James, 15, and Sarah-Jane, 18). He says, "You know, there was absolutely no alcohol allowed while we were under way. Peter would kick you off for that. The main partying took place when he would say, 'Okay, tonight is for having a good time.'"

"They had a nice party," Sam, the shipping agent, says. "They drank beer. If there was one thing they had a lot of, it was beer. When I came on the boat later, I saw a bucket with fifty empty beer cans in it. But this was a party, and we know we can't just have two beers when we are having a party."

At nine o'clock, six men met at the port in Santana: Ricardo, Isael, José, Reney, Rubens, and Josué. They were local guys, between 20 and 30 and mostly unemployed. Ricardo had been working as a receptionist at a computer school his cousin owned, until he was fired the month before. Reney sometimes helped his father with electrical work. Most of them had a history of crime, especially armed robbery. Isael had been out of prison for only two months and seven days.

Some of the men brought their motorcycle helmets to Santana. Others had cut their wives' and mothers' pantyhose to make masks. Rubens, 20, had gotten use of his boss's boat, a twenty-foot wooden *catraia*, the most common kind of boat on the Amazon. The men pooled their money, bought five reals' ($2.15) worth of gas, and then pointed the boat toward the ocean. At close to ten o'clock, Rubens drew the *catraia* flush with the far side of the *Seamaster*, away from the lights of Macapá so that only the monkeys and birds of the jungle could have seen the men climb on board. He killed the motor and lashed the *catraia* to Blake's boat. As always in Macapá, it was hot and windy, and the water, which carries so much silt it looks like roiling, molten peanut butter, was covered in baby whitecaps. The six of them sat quietly for a few minutes, observing the crew. Everyone on the *Seamaster* was listening to what Ricardo called "loud foreign music." Some of them were dancing, and many of them were talking in loud foreign voices.

The first two aboard were Ricardo and Isael, each with a 7.65-millimeter pistol; Reney, Josué, and José followed. Rubens stayed in the boat and waited for the getaway. Almost immediately, things got complicated. "This is a robbery!" Ricardo screamed. "Everyone get down on the floor!" But the crew did not speak any Portuguese and didn't seem to understand what these men were doing on their boat, wearing stocking masks and waving guns. One of the crewmen tossed a can of beer at the intruders. Someone else threw a jar of mayonnaise at them.

Later, none of the crew would talk specifically about what happened that night; they were worried about the effects it might have on the trial, which, when this story was written, was still in progress. According to one person on the boat, "The crew were totally out of their depth. When someone comes on board with a gun, there's a certain script you're supposed to follow, and they didn't follow it. It could have been worse than it was."

Rodger Moore, 55, decided to fight. He pushed Ricardo, and Ricardo shoved back. The operation seemed on the verge of chaos, so Ricardo pistol-whipped Moore and knocked him out. While Ricardo herded the rest of the crew together, he saw a tall white man run downstairs. He figured the man was going to radio for help and sent Isael to follow him.

As soon as he saw Moore being pistol-whipped, Blake had turned and gone downstairs. One of the crew members heard him saying, "Is this for real?" Blake was going for the Winchester .308 rifle he kept in his cabin. Before he and his wife, Pippa, had left on their honeymoon, sailing around the pirate-rich Red Sea in 1979, Blake had trained on a rifle range so he could protect them.

David Alan-Williams says, "Peter was always quick to identify a problem, and he'd often fix it himself. If something was wrong at the top of the mast, he was the first to go up there, even if the boat was pitching back and forth in storm conditions."

Leon Sefton had been below deck reading a book when he heard the commotion. He got up to investigate, and as he neared the stairs he saw Isael, short and taut, with a mask obscuring his face. Isael pointed his pistol at Sefton's head and Sefton got on the ground. Then Blake's cabin door opened, and he came out. He leveled his gun at Isael and said, "Get the fuck off my boat."

Sefton watched Isael break for the deck and, in a moment, Sefton heard shots. He can't say who shot first; he doesn't know the sounds of guns well enough. A spokesman for the federal police says, "Probably it was Peter Blake who shot the first time. Maybe if Mr. Blake did not shoot, maybe if he did not have a gun, maybe the criminals would not have shot anyone." But the prosecutor trying the case says, "Isael behaved as if he were leaving the boat, and Peter Blake followed him. Then, once he got to the top of the stairs, Isael turned and shot at Peter Blake."

One way or another, Isael and Blake began shooting at each other, Isael at the top of the stairs and Blake behind the wall at the bottom, turning to shoot upward. Rubens, in the *catraia*, heard the gunfire, jumped into the river, and hid beneath his boat. In the confusion, the Brazilian cook got into the control room, locked the door, and radioed for help, but the radio was still tuned to the wrong frequency and he could raise only the harbormaster in Manaus, nearly a thousand miles away.

Isael's bullets made holes in the aluminum walls of the cabin, and shots from Blake's Winchester tore through the canopy. Blake hit Isael in two places—piercing his forearm and blowing off two fingers. The prosecutor says this was a show of both Blake's restraint and, as he would write in the indictment, "utmost precision." A defense lawyer says that Blake shot at Isael point-blank, and would have killed him had he been sober. After Isael was hit, Ricardo ran to the stairway and began shooting into the cabin.

Sefton saw Blake banging his gun against the floor. He tried to give him some extra ammunition, but Blake said he didn't need it—his gun was jammed. Sefton went back down the hall again, and when he came back a minute later he found Blake on the floor, shot in the back. The police say Ricardo confessed to shooting Blake, but he later denied it.

A few of the criminals kept watch over the crew, who were lying on the deck, while Ricardo and Isael gathered what they could— some cameras, a couple of Omega Seamaster watches, CDs, and Blake's Winchester. They took one of the *Seamaster's* dinghies, a rigid-hull inflatable Zodiac, and made their escape in two boats. They fired back at the *Seamaster* (they claim someone was shooting at them with a second rifle) and grazed Geoff Bullock across the back. As they were making their getaway, Reney said to Ricardo, "Why did you shoot [Blake]!" and Ricardo said, "It was either me or him."

Peter Blake lay at the foot of the stairs, bleeding from twin holes in his back. The boat was quieter now, and the movement of water was audible. At its mouth, the Amazon is tidal, and the river was now flowing backward, raising the *Seamaster* five feet an hour. Sefton found Blake with his head cocked awkwardly to the side. He straightened it and watched as Blake took a few labored breaths. One bullet had traveled through his left lung and superior vena cava and come to rest just under the skin of his armpit; the other had pierced his lungs and aorta, and remained in his upper right chest. Either one would have been enough to kill him, says Dr. Carlos Marcos Santos, who arrived on the *Seamaster* at 10:40 and tried to resuscitate him. He estimates that it took Blake about fifteen minutes to die. He says that Blake had alcohol on his breath (though the crew says he wasn't drinking on the boat), and that the others seemed very drunk—unsteady on their feet, bleary-eyed, slurring.

"When I got there, Mr. Blake was faceup, below deck," Dr.

Marco says. "He was wearing shorts, either blue or khaki, I can't remember. And no shirt. You could tell he had a great deal of strength for a man his age. But he was out of shape. He had a prominent belly. His face had seen the sun, you could tell that. There were many deep, permanent lines around the eyes."

At near 11:00 P.M., Marcos pronounced Blake dead. As they were taking the body off the boat, Rizaldo, the cook, said to the doctor, "These guys have no idea what they have done. He is a national hero, like Pelé is to this country. Everybody loves him. They have no idea what they've done."

The news of Blake's death reached the rest of the world in the morning. In England, where Blake had been knighted for his accomplishments, *The Daily Telegraph* wrote that "Blake towered over the sport" of sailing. In New Zealand, Parliament was canceled for the day and the government flew at half-staff a pair of red socks — Blake had worn red socks nearly every time he raced. The prime minister, Helen Clark, speaking at a memorial two weeks later, said, "He put New Zealand on the map."

I asked Robertson if he had any regrets about the way things happened that night in Macapá. "No. There's no way any of us can replay the scenario and say, Well, we were responsible, or, We could have done more. Or could've done less. I'm sure people must have horrible experiences when somebody dies and the last thing they remember is that they had an argument. But we were having such a good time."

One well-known character in the yachting world, who didn't want his name used, says, "Blake was a tough guy. A very tough guy. The kind who wouldn't have handed over his wallet without a fight. Hearing the circumstances, it wasn't surprising. Like a lot of Kiwis, he didn't take a lot of crap. It was part of his skill as a leader, but it was also part of his downfall."

.   .   .

A week after the murder, when all six suspects have been arrested, Marcelo, the translator, takes me driving through the neighborhoods where they grew up. They are suburbs that have evolved organically, small wooden houses with which the electric/water/civil-service grid is struggling to keep up. The men are mostly in flip-flops and soccer shorts. But the women wear very stylish and sexy clothes. One girl looks particularly elegant, sitting sidesaddle on the back of a bike in a sheer black skirt, black shirt, and black stilettos, heading down a dirt road under the waning equatorial sun.

Another thing you notice is the kites. Big red kites and little black kites and even those cheap plastic bags dispensed at every shop the world over. Telephone wires holding the skeletons of old kites, frozen in their death like inmates zapped while trying to climb the electric fence. Maybe it's just that the conditions are perfect: It's always sunny, warm, and windy, and there are always plenty of little kids and plastic bags to go around.

José, one of the two so-called pirates who didn't have a record, lived in one of the better neighborhoods. His parents' house is just a few blocks from his, and they've agreed to be interviewed because they don't want people to think José is a hardened criminal.

We sit on the concrete patio in front of their house. There's a little plastic Christmas tree on a table in the corner, and the family Volkswagen has been pulled up onto the patio, blocking the front door. José's parents, a teacher and a retired government worker, sit on metal rocking chairs. His wife, Milene, leans against the car, holding their two daughters, Isadora, one, and Isabela, five, who has drawn a rainbow tattoo on her forearm. Across the street, some neighbors are building a brick wall around their house because someone keeps stealing the light fixtures on their porch. José's mother says she will not discuss anything about the case, because she is afraid of saying the wrong thing, but that she'd like to talk about José as a regular person.

"He treasured the motorbike his father gave him," his mother

says. "And his collection of Conan the Barbarian comic books."
Isabela runs inside and returns with a Conan the Barbarian comic
book written in Portuguese. "No one was allowed to touch them,"
his mother goes on. "And he had over a hundred magazines." On
the cover of the comic book, Conan is swinging onto the deck of a
ship with a sword between his teeth.

José, Ricardo, and Reney were arrested on December 6 after they
were given up by Isael, who was the first to be picked up, since he
was walking around with two stumps where fingers should have
been and was easy to identify. They found Josué and Rubens the following day, hiding out at a house in the jungle. At Ricardo's mother's
home, in the ceiling, they found a Canon camera, an Omega Seamaster watch, a pistol with a fitting for a silencer, a .38 revolver, a
bulletproof vest, and, as the police report indicates, thirty-seven "foreign music" CDs. José was arrested while having sex with his wife,
dragged naked out into the street, and beaten in front of the neighbors. They discovered another of the watches at his home, where
he'd shoved it inside a little red teddy bear in Isadora's room.

The first four, as well as three others who were eventually
released, were arrested by the local police before being turned over
to the federal authorities. While still in local-police custody, these
four were beaten in the presence of one of their lawyers (though the
police denied this). Later, in a cell, José claims, the officers played a
game called telephone, which involved smacking both his ears
simultaneously. A man named Jânio, a suspect who was later
released, says that they put a bag over his head until he almost
passed out, and then took it off. "And when we were in the car, the
policeman, he put a bullet in the gun and spun it," Jânio says, "then
pulled the trigger right in front of my face. I could see the bullet,
that it wasn't yet in the chamber, but I was still scared. They were
saying, 'The president of Brazil told us he doesn't care if you're alive
or dead. He said, "Do whatever you want to them."' I shit my pants."

In the few hours after they were arrested, the pirates came to realize that they'd been involved in an event of completely different proportions from what they'd thought. They left the boat having robbed and murdered a tourist, an anonymous victim, but they soon discovered they'd killed a person who might inspire large-scale consequences. And realizing this was, they all say, pretty bewildering.

"If this had been some regular guy," one of their lawyers says, "they wouldn't have even made arrests at this point."

The Amapá State Prison is on the outskirts of town. It's not a hulking, high-tech campus, like American prisons are. There are no monolithic sliding gates or remote locks or video cameras. It's just a few single-story buildings separated from the highway by a series of concrete walls. Between the buildings are a couple of bald fields where prisoners play soccer.

Marcelo, the translator, lives just across the road and says that every year a few inmates are killed by other prisoners or guards, and another half-dozen escape. "It's okay, I guess," Marcelo says. "They usually run into the woods and not toward my house."

A Franciscan friar who runs a mission at the prison agrees to take us to meet the six suspects. We arrive just after lunch. When you're done with your meal at the Amapá State Prison, you simply throw what remains out through the bars of your cell, so the hall is covered with rice and what appear to be bits of chicken. Beneath that odor is the funk of food rotted into concrete and the stink of fifty men in equatorial heat. Some of the inmates make noises as we walk past—quasi-menacing laughter, unintelligible grumbling, a convincing pig squeal.

All six of the accused are housed in the same cell, which looks to be about six feet across and twelve feet deep. When they hear our approach, they get up from their hammocks, which are slung across the middle of the room, and make some effort to clean up a bit. Ricardo, the shooter, puts on a shirt, and Rubens pushes some clothes into a corner. They all come to the cell door and look at me curiously. The friar says, "You're the first white reporter they've met." The guard tells us we have an hour to talk, then leads us to a concrete bench outside the cell block and waits at the gate.

In the pictures published all over the world two days after the murder, the pirates looked like a bunch of guys pulled in from a barbecue, wearing soccer shorts and sandals. In person, they look even less intimidating. Only Isael looks like someone you'd be scared of, with a big scar across his belly and a muscular body with a very low center of gravity. The gunshot wounds to the hand and forearm don't hurt, either. Reney, on the other hand, has delicate features and soft, velvety black eyes. He doesn't look so different from Ralph Macchio, circa *The Karate Kid*.

"We are being treated worse than anyone else here," Ricardo says. "We have been tortured. Show them, José." José stands up and pulls down his shorts. His ass is covered in big black-and-yellow bruises, which, he says, were administered with an iron bar wrapped in a towel. Isael puts his arm forward and says he hasn't been allowed to see a doctor in a week. The wound on his forearm, about eight inches long and closed crudely with some black thread, looks unnaturally wet. He unwraps the bandage on his hand and shows where the two fingers closest to his pinkie were shot off at the knuckle.

José, who's called Grande Blanco (roughly, "Big Whitey") and has remarkable jug ears and a prominent jaw, says, "It's not like the media is saying that we are used to doing this job. This is the first time we killed someone—" and then Ricardo cuts him off. The police say Ricardo was the mastermind, and he seems to control the group. He rarely allows any of the others to speak.

One thing I wanted to ask when I came to see them in prison was, given that they didn't set out to murder a man, how they felt when they realized they had. This was, after all, possibly *the* crucial moment in their lives. The group looks to Ricardo for an answer: "We did not know what happened. We never went down below deck to see him. We knew only that his shooting had stopped and so we left the boat." I don't point out that this can't be true, since they stole Blake's rifle.

I ask them if there is anything they want to ask me. Ricardo says, "What is the main religion in Peter Blake's country?" I say I think they are mainly Protestant, and ask why he wants to know. "I'm Catholic," he says, "so I would like to know. It's important."

José says, "I have a question. What did you think of us before? And how do you think of us now? We aren't what they say we are, right? We are not pirates, river rats." I tell him I hadn't known much about them other than that they'd killed Peter Blake while trying to rob him. "Well, I don't think it's right, what they're saying about us. You know, I've never been convicted of any crimes before." The criminals now find themselves infamous, cast in a role larger than they had before. Ricardo seems to see the appeal of it. José, though, is scared shitless that he's lost his former identity as simple local screwup, a feeling that thirty years in prison will probably relieve him of. José says, "I swear, I never could imagine that the story would end this way."

If things had gone according to script, it would have been the Southern Ocean that killed Peter Blake. The Southern Ocean is roughly eight million square miles spreading out from Antarctica. It was the most dangerous and crucial leg of his five Whitbreads and two Jules Vernes, and Blake liked to call it the loneliest place on earth. He said often, "If you get into trouble down there, well, no use crying to Mum." And trouble was inevitably what you'd find in the Southern Ocean. It was a wind-and-weather factory of unrivaled proportions, and Blake called the swells there "liquid Himalayas." "The real danger," he said, "is the bow digging in and the boat flipping end over end." He built little hatches on the hull of *ENZA New Zealand* so he could climb out if this happened, not that there'd be much he could have done, sitting on an upside-down boat in the middle of the loneliest place on earth. Blake's friends and colleagues paint the relationship between him and the Southern Ocean like the relationship between, say, Rocky and Apollo Creed—the chummy, mortal respect reserved for worthy adversaries. It's not that Peter Blake did not realize that he was, like everyone else, a pawn of fate; it's just that when fate showed up on his boat, dressed in a motorcycle helmet and a grimy T-shirt, he failed to recognize it.

——

I went to Brazil just before Christmas last year to report a story on the death of Peter Blake for Men's Journal, *where I was working at the time. I'd like to say I was drawn to the story because of some overarching theme it brought up for me. But the truth is that a story appeared in* The New York Times *one morning about a world-famous sailor who'd been killed by pirates on the Amazon. It was a kind of no-brainer* Men's Journal *story, plus I had not written a piece in a while and I was afraid I was going to be fired. I am usually afraid I'm going to be fired. So I flew to Macapá, Brazil, a town I had never heard of before, found a translator who spoke maybe fifth-grade English, and drove around Equatorial Brazil in a rented Fiat, almost always in danger of being robbed by drunk people with machetes.*

There was, nonetheless, plenty of adventure and discovery in the reporting of this story. The thrill of finding yourself in a town you've never heard of before, suddenly integrated into its community of policemen and lawyers and criminals, cannot be overstated. The editor of Men's Journal *largely wanted me to write about the life of Peter Blake. He was, after all, a* Men's Journal *kind of guy—intrepid adventurer, naturalist, celebrity. But to me, his life was just another example of bored rich people creating challenges for themselves where none naturally exist (if Blake wanted to circumnavigate the globe, British Airways would have done it more quickly and cheaply, and* with more free pretzels). I was more interested in the families of the killers, in the neighborhoods where they lived, in the concrete stadium built over the equator for dancing competitions, and in the masses of children flying kites at dusk. It's always reassuring to go to some distant outpost and discover just how enormous and varied and confusing the world is.

One night, in my hotel room, I became convinced that bandits with pistols were going to climb through my window, steal my stash of American currency and Clif Bars, and leave me bleeding on the floor. And suddenly just how obscene Peter Blake's death was seemed very real. Blake had simply been a curious man passing through a town that meant almost nothing to him, not so different from me. It was a humanizing moment. That it took my feeling threatened is, I know, kind of pathetic, but I blame fame; it can take away a person's personness and make him seem more like a brand. The more I drove around Macapá in my rented Fiat learning about the night Blake was murdered, about the people involved, the more I became fascinated with the confluence of lives, with the perfect-storm-like escalation of events, the loss of control, the spontaneous combustion that resulted in a tragedy that no one involved had wanted.

When I met Peter Blake's killers in jail, they were bewildered at having been part of something so large and violent. When I spoke to the men in the crew, they were likewise bewildered. It was the sort of event for which denial is the only sensible reaction. Since I've returned from Brazil, the "pirates" (more like petty thieves) have begun prison sentences many of them may not outlive; Peter Blake's widow just put up the family yacht for auction, since it's too big a boat for her to handle on her own and she could use the money; Blake's business partners are trying to make a go of Blakexpeditions as a Cousteau-ian nonprofit. In the movies, killers are calculating and the murders they commit are shot through with meaning and psycho-philosophical dilemma. In Macapá, though, as in most places, lives take violent, abrupt turns for almost no reason at all.

A WOMAN'S WORK

PETER LANDESMAN

Slaughter, and then worse, came to Butare, a sleepy, sun-bleached Rwandan town, in the spring of 1994. Hutu death squads armed with machetes and nail-studded clubs had deployed throughout the countryside, killing, looting, and burning. Road-blocks had been set up to cull fleeing Tutsis. By the third week of April, as the Rwanda genocide was reaching its peak intensity, tens of thousands of corpses were rotting in the streets of Kigali, the country's capital. Butare, a stronghold of Tutsis and politically moderate Hutus that had resisted the government's orders for genocide, was the next target. Its residents could hear gunfire from the hills in the west; at night they watched the firelight of torched nearby villages. Armed Hutus soon gathered on the edges of town, but Butare's panicked citizens defended its borders.

Enraged by Butare's revolt, Rwanda's interim government dispatched Pauline Nyiramasuhuko, the national minister of family and women's affairs, from Kigali on a mission. Before becoming one of the most powerful women in Rwanda's government, Pauline — as everyone, enemy and ally alike, called her — had grown up on a small farming commune just outside Butare. She was a local success story, known to some as Butare's favorite daughter. Her return would have a persuasive resonance there.

Soon after Pauline's arrival in town, cars mounted with loud-speakers crisscrossed Butare's back roads, announcing that the Red Cross had arrived at a nearby stadium to provide food and guarantee sanctuary. By April 25, thousands of desperate Tutsis had gathered at the stadium.

It was a trap. Instead of receiving food and shelter, the refugees were surrounded by men wearing bandoleers and headdresses made of spiky banana leaves. These men were Interahamwe, thuggish Hutu marauders whose name means "those who attack together." According to an eyewitness I spoke with this summer in Butare, supervising from the sidelines was Pauline, then 48, a portly woman of medium height in a colorful African wrap and spectacles.

Before becoming Rwanda's chief official for women's affairs, Pauline was a social worker, roaming the countryside, offering lectures on female empowerment and instruction on child care and AIDS prevention. Her days as minister were similarly devoted to improving the lives of women and children. But at the stadium, a 30-year-old farmer named Foster Mivumbi told me, Pauline assumed a different responsibility. Mivumbi, who has confessed to taking part in the slaughter, told me that Pauline goaded the Interahamwe, commanding, "Before you kill the women, you need to rape them."

Tutsi women were then selected from the stadium crowd and dragged away to a forested area to be raped, Mivumbi recalled. Back at the stadium, he told me, Pauline waved her arms and then observed in silence as Interahamwe rained machine-gun fire and hand grenades down upon the remaining refugees. The Hutus finished off survivors with machetes. It took about an hour, ending at noon. Pauline stayed on, Mivumbi told me, until a bulldozer began piling bodies for burial in a nearby pit. (When questioned about this incident, Pauline's lawyers denied that she took part in atrocities in Butare.)

Shortly afterward, according to another witness, Pauline arrived at a compound where a group of Interahamwe was guarding 70 Tutsi women and girls. One Interahamwe, a young man named Emmanuel Nsabimana, told me through a translator that Pauline

ordered him and others to burn the women. Nsabimana recalled
that one Interahamwe complained that they lacked sufficient gasoline. "Pauline said, 'Don't worry, I have jerry cans of gasoline in my
car,'" Nsabimana recalled. "She said, 'Go take that gasoline and
kill them.' I went to the car and took the jerry cans. Then Pauline
said, 'Why don't you rape them before you kill them?' But we had
been killing all day, and we were tired. We just put the gasoline in
bottles and scattered it among the women, then started burning."

Around the same time, some Interahamwe arrived at the local hospital, where a unit of Doctors Without Borders was in residence.
Rose, a young Tutsi woman who had sought refuge at the hospital,
watched in terror as soldiers stormed the complex. (Rose, who is
now under military protection, requested that her last name not be
printed.) "They said that Pauline had given them permission to go
after the Tutsi girls, who were too proud of themselves," Rose told
me. "She was the minister, so they said they were free to do it."
Pauline had led the soldiers to see rape as a reward.

Chief among the Interahamwe at the hospital was Pauline's only
son, a 24-year-old student named Arsène Shalom Ntahobali.
Shalom, as he was known, was over six feet tall, slightly overweight
and clean-shaven. He wore a tracksuit and sneakers; grenades dangled from his waist. Rose said that Shalom, who repeatedly
announced that he had "permission" from his mother to rape Tutsis, found her cowering in the maternity ward. He yanked her to her
feet and raped her against the wall. Before leaving Rose to chase
after some students who had been hiding nearby, he promised that
he'd return to kill her. But before Shalom could do so, she fled the
hospital and ran home to her family.

A few days later, Rose recalled, a local official knocked on her
door. Rose told me that the official informed her that even though
all Tutsis would be exterminated, one Tutsi would be left alive—

one who could deliver a progress report to God. Rose was to be that witness. And her instruction on her new role began that moment. "Hutu soldiers took my mother outside," Rose told me, "stripped off her clothes and raped her with a machete." On that first day, twenty family members were slaughtered before her eyes.

Rose told me that until early July, when the genocide ended, she was led by Interahamwe to witness atrocity after atrocity. She said that even though the Interahamwe's overarching objective was to kill, the men seemed particularly obsessed by what they did to women's bodies. "I saw them rape two girls with spears, then burn their pubic hair," she said. "Then they took me to another spot where a lady was giving birth. The baby was halfway out. They speared it." All the while, Rose repeatedly heard the soldiers say, "We are doing what was ordered by Pauline Nyiramasuhuko."

I met Rose in Butare this summer. She is 32 now, a pretty woman with high cheekbones and small features. Speaking in an airless hotel room, Rose pitched slightly forward in a red business suit, her gaze direct. She explained that since the genocide she has suffered from stomach ulcers, and occasionally slips into semiconsciousness, racked with delirium and pain. "People think I'm possessed," she said. These fits, she said, frighten her children—her two born before 1994 and the four genocide orphans she adopted afterward. As we spoke, it was clear that Rose was telling her horrific story as carefully as possible, to finally fulfill, in a way much different from intended, her role as witness.

Rose said that during the months the genocide was carried out, she saw Pauline Nyiramasuhuko three times. The minister was an unforgettable sight. She'd exchanged her colorful civilian wraps for brand-new military fatigues and boots. She was seen carrying a machine gun over her shoulder. Other survivors told me they heard the minister for women and family affairs spit invectives at Tutsi women, calling them, "cockroaches" and "dirt." She advised the men to choose the young women for sex and kill off the old. By one account, women were forced to raise their shirts to separate the mothers from the "virgins." Sometimes, I was told, Pauline handed soldiers packets of condoms.

Much of the violence took place in the scrubby yard in front of Butare's local government offices, or prefecture, where at one point hundreds of Tutsis were kept under guard. Witnesses recalled that Pauline showed up at night in a white Toyota pickup truck, often driven by Shalom, and supervised as Interahamwe loaded the truck with women who were driven off and never seen again. Often, when a woman at the prefecture saw Pauline, she appealed to her, as a fellow woman and mother, for mercy. But this, claimed survivors, only enraged Pauline. When one woman wouldn't stop crying out, a survivor recalled, the minister told the Interahamwe to shut her up. They stabbed the pleading woman and then slit her throat.

There will never be a precise accounting of how many Rwandans were massacred between April and July 1994. Human Rights Watch calculates the number to be at least 500,000, while the United Nations estimates that between 800,000 and one million Rwandans died during that period. Whatever the total, the rate of carnage and the concentration of the killing (Rwanda is roughly the size of New Jersey) give it the distinction of being the most ferocious mass slaughter in recorded history. Three-quarters of the Tutsi population was exterminated. Today, Rwanda's common greeting, the Kinyarwanda expression *mwaramutse*—which translates as "did you wake?"—is less an expression of "good morning" than it is of relief that one is breathing at all.

Understandably, the world's attention subsequently focused on the sheer volume of the Rwandan slaughter. But the prosecutors and judges of the International Crime Tribunal for Rwanda in Arusha, Tanzania, are now coming to recognize the equally alarming and cynical story of what was left behind. Though most women were killed before they could tell their stories, a U.N. report has concluded that at least 250,000 women were raped during the genocide. Some were penetrated with spears, gun barrels, bottles or the stamens of banana trees. Sexual organs were multilated with machetes, boiling water, and acid; women's breasts were cut off. According to one study, Butare province alone has more than 30,000 rape survivors. Many more women were killed after they were raped.

These facts are harrowing. More shocking still is that so many of these crimes were supposedly inspired and orchestrated by Pauline Nyiramasuhuko, whose very job was the preservation, education, and empowerment of Rwanda's women.

In July 1994 Pauline fled Rwanda in a mass exodus of more than one million Hutus fearing retribution by the advancing Tutsi rebel army, the Rwandan Patriotic Front. After finding safety in a refugee camp in Congo, she eventually slipped into Kenya, where she lived as a fugitive for almost three years. On July 18, 1997, however, Pauline was apprehended in Nairobi by Kenyan and international authorities. (Shalom was seized six days later, in a Nairobi grocery store he was running.) After interrogation by investigators, Pauline was transferred with Shalom to Tanzania, where both were delivered to the International Tribunal in Arusha.

At the tribunal, Pauline faces eleven charges, including genocide, crimes against humanity, and war crimes. She is the first woman ever to be charged with these crimes in an international court. And she is the first woman ever to be charged with rape as a crime against humanity. (Her son, Shalom, faces ten charges, to which he has pled innocence.)

For the last five years mother and son have spent their days at the U.N. Detention Facility in Arusha in nearby 16-by-19 cells. They have access to a gym and a nurse. Pauline often spends time tending flowers and singing to herself in a common open-air courtyard.

Since June 2001, when their trials began, Pauline and Shalom have spent most of their weekdays in a courtroom inside Arusha's dilapidated conference center. The U.N. Security Council established the Arusha tribunal in November 1994, eighteen months after establishing a tribunal for the former Yugoslavia at The Hague. With all of Rwanda's judicial and law enforcement personnel dead or in exile, and the country's physical infrastructure reduced to rubble, the U.N. chose to house the tribunal in this tourist hub near the base of Mount Kilimanjaro. Fifty-three Rwandan *genocidaires* are in custody in Arusha; twenty more have been indicted and are on the lam, most likely in Kenya and Congo.

This summer, I attended sessions of Pauline's trial. In court, her appearance suggested a schoolteacher. Now 56, she favored plain high-necked dresses that showed off the gleaming gold crucifix she usually wears. According to observers, at the beginning of the trial she shook her head and smirked as charges were read out. But as more and more survivors have come from Butare to testify against her, she has grown subdued. During my visit, Pauline mostly looked blankly around the courtroom past a pair of scholarly bifocals, taking copious notes on a legal pad and avoiding the gaze of witnesses. Sometimes, I was told, she wears wild hairstyles and headdresses and slumps behind a computer screen that sits in front of her, as if she were trying to disguise herself from witnesses asked to identify her. On one such day eleven months ago, she didn't show up at all, preferring, her attorneys told the court, to worship in chapel; that morning, when asked to identify the defendant, the witness could point only to Pauline's chair. The courtroom is typically crowded with three judges, twelve defense attorneys and prosecutors, clerks, interpreters, and other staff. Most days there are only a handful of spectators watching all this in a narrow gallery behind bulletproof glass—and frequently there are none at all.

Pauline and Shalom are being tried together with four other Hutu leaders from Butare who are also accused of genocide. Fourteen witnesses for the prosecution have testified so far, with seventy-three more still to go, most of whom will have something to say against Pauline, who faces life imprisonment. In most cases, she is accused of inciting crimes rather than carrying them out herself. However, according to a document prepared by tribunal investigators in preparation for the trial, one witness, code-named Q.C., saw a Tutsi community leader die "at the hands of Nyiramasuhuko." (The report does not specify what weapon Pauline used.) Attorneys for each of the six accused will most likely open their defenses in 2004 and will probably call more than a hundred witnesses of their own as the trial creeps along for at least another two years. Justice at the tribunal has moved at a glacial pace, with only eight convictions and one acquittal handed down in seven years.

Pauline has consistently denied the charges against her. In 1995, before she was arrested, she gave an interview to the BBC in a squalid Hutu refugee camp across the Congo border, where she had been leading the camp's social services; her job duties included the reuniting of separated parents and children. When asked what she did during the war, Pauline replied: "We moved around the region to pacify. We wrote a pacification document saying people shouldn't kill each other. Saying it's genocide, that's not true. It was the Tutsi who massacred the Hutu." Told that witnesses had accused her of murder, Pauline shot back: "I cannot even kill a chicken. If there is a person who says that a woman—a mother—killed, then I'll confront that person."

Over lunch during a break in court this summer, one of Pauline's attorneys, Nicole Bergevin, accused the Tribunal of making her client a scapegoat of the vindictive current government in Rwanda and of an international community guilt-ridden over its failure to stop the bloodletting. "I'm sure there were some rapes," Bergevin said, "but Pauline never ordered any rapes." Later she added: "She was never known to be anti-Tutsi. I'm not saying that no one wanted the Tutsis to be exterminated. Probably there were, but it was not a plan. It was never the government's intention. If it was, Pauline was not aware of it." Bergevin then told me that Pauline didn't have any knowledge about the rapes taking place in Rwanda during the genocide.

Pauline has only one concern, Bergevin said, and it is for Shalom, who, like his mother, faces life imprisonment. "She feels helpless," Bergevin said.

My many requests to see Pauline were denied. The tribunal bars prisoners from contact with anyone other than family and friends (and even these visits are limited). I did, though, reach Pauline's husband, Maurice Ntahobari, who at the time of the genocide was the rector of National University in Butare. He now lives in Antwerp, Belgium; his Rwandan passport has been taken away. Though he admits to being in Butare during the genocide, Ntahobari insists he didn't see or hear any killing. As for the charges against Pauline, he reminded me that she had been a social worker: "She was committed to promoting equality between men and women," he said defiantly. "It is not culturally possible for a Rwanda woman to make her son rape other women. It just couldn't have taken place." Pauline's only error, he insisted, was in belonging to the side that lost.

Pauline Nyiramasuhuko was born in 1946 amid lush banana groves and green, misty valleys. Her parents were subsistence farmers in Ndora, a small, neat roadside settlement six miles east of Butare. Her family and friends remember her as more ambitious and disciplined than bright. Her sister, Vineranda Mukandekaze, who is 60, told me that Pauline was "good but not generous. She kept everything to herself." Juliana Niyirora, an old friend of Pauline's, said: "From her childhood Pauline had political ambition. She always wanted to achieve high. If she saw someone build a house, she wanted a bigger house. If she saw someone do well, she wanted to do better."

In high school, Pauline became friends with Agathe Kanziga, the eventual wife of the Hutu president Juvenal Habyarimana. It was a crucial connection. After graduating, Pauline left Butare for Kigali to join the Ministry for Social Affairs, which was then establishing a network of centers teaching women how to take care of their families, providing instruction on such basics as cooking and supervising children. When Pauline was only 22, Agathe helped her skip up the bureaucratic ladder to become national inspector of the ministry.

In 1968 Pauline married Maurice Ntahobari, who later became president of the Rwanda National Assembly, then minister of higher education and later rector of National University in Butare. By all accounts, however, Pauline was the dominant force in the family. "Maurice was like the woman; he didn't say anything," said Jean-Baptist Sebukangaga, a professor of art at National University who has known Pauline since her childhood. "Pauline directed everything. She got Maurice his job as rector at the university." A friend and neighbor told me that she once saw Pauline screaming at Maurice for not being more committed to the politics of the MRND, the ruling Hutu extremist party.

At 24, nine months pregnant, Pauline, already the mother of a little girl, traveled to Israel on a government mission and gave birth to a son there. (Hence, Shalom.) She returned to Kigali, where in the years that followed she had two more daughters. But Pauline never gave up her job and eventually enrolled in law school, one of the few women in Rwanda to do so. "She had four children, but she still wanted to go back to school," her friend Niyirora marveled. Already a local MRND party boss, in 1992 she was appointed minister of family and women's affairs.

Pauline's brother-in-law, Matthias Ngiwijize, told me that when

Pauline became a government minister, she changed. "She stopped coming to her family's homes," he said. "She didn't talk to anybody. She was only close to herself. She resented the poor part of the family. She even stopped visiting her mother."

A woman eager to prove herself in a party structure built around men and Rwanda's patriarchal society, Pauline soon found that the road to political success led her back to her birthplace. Butare had become the government's biggest headache. Home to National University and a scientific research institute—and with the highest concentration of Tutsis in Rwanda—Butare had the most enlightened citizens in the country. The town had been largely immune to Hutu extremism; the MRND never gained a foothold there. But Pauline tried to change all that through a program of intimidation. She would convoy through town with party thugs, setting up barricades in the streets, paralyzing traffic, and disrupting town life. Pauline's periodic invasions of the town became known as Ghost Days, days when Butare stood still.

Pauline was soon caught up in the anti-Tutsi ideology of her party. "Before 1994 there was no racism in Butare," said Leoncie Mukamisha, an old schoolmate of Pauline's who worked under her at the ministry. "Then Pauline came and organized demonstrations in town. The local papers described her as a frenzied madwoman." Leoncie said that Pauline's actions won the favor of the president, who recognized her obedience and anti-Tutsi virulence, and assigned to her a number of extremist Hutu ideologues as advisers.

Other friends I spoke with claimed that Pauline's anti-Tutsi conversion was a purely careerist move meant only to please the higher-ups. It was an echo of the old argument that many Nazis were "just following orders." Her sister told me that even in 1994, just before the genocide, Pauline had many Tutsi friends, and that a number of Tutsis worked peacefully under Pauline at the ministry.

Leoncie portrayed her differently. She said Pauline's racism was ardent; at the ministry, she said, Pauline was "horrified at having to be in daily contact with Tutsis." And a former Hutu political figure who met Pauline in 1992 says that in private discussions, her antipathy toward Tutsis was chillingly clear. "When one spoke with her, one became aware that the Tutsi were people to be destroyed," he said.

It may never be possible to answer what motivated Pauline's actions. She may have genuinely felt rage toward Tutsis; she may have been a simple opportunist, hungering for power. But certainly by 1994, her anti-Tutsi zealousness was public. During the genocide Pauline delivered admonishing speeches over Radio Rwanda. A witness recalled one speech: "We are all members of the militia," Pauline said. "We must work together to hunt down members of the Rwandan Patriotic Front."

In his confession to genocide and crimes against humanity, former Hutu Prime Minister Jean Kambanda identifies the members of his inner sanctum, where the blueprint of the genocide was first drawn up. The confession names only five names. Pauline Nyiramasuhuko's is one of them.

During my visit to Butare this summer, two young women, Mary Mukangoga, 24, and Chantal Kantarama, 28, led me into the center of Butare to the prefecture, where they first met and became friends. "I went to the prefecture because other refugees were there," Mary said in a near whisper. "I preferred to be killed when we were all together."

In the first weeks of the genocide, Chantal said, she had been abducted and raped by two Hutu men. She escaped and took refuge at a school near the prefecture. One day, Chantal recalled, she heard Pauline announcing through a microphone: "I have a problem. The cockroaches are now near my house. Tomorrow come and help me. Help me get rid of them." Chantal fled to the prefecture. The next day, Chantal said, Pauline visited the prefecture with Shalom. Mother and son came with the young men of the Interahamwe and selected girls to rape.

In silence, Mary and Chantal led me to the ruins of what was once a plastics factory, in a shady grove of trees 200 yards from the prefecture office. They explained that the Interahamwe used to store their ammunition in the factory, and that many evenings they were taken from the prefecture, led there, and raped. "Pauline would come and say, 'I don't want this *dirt* here, get rid of this dirt,'" Chantal recalled.

The two young women became part of a group of five sex slaves who were kept at the prefecture and raped, repeatedly and together, every night for weeks. Then one day, the women were thrown into a nearby pit that was full of corpses. The pit, about 400 feet square, is now half filled in with rubble and weeds. Chantal took me there, stepping to the edge; at that point she turned aside, refusing to look in. "They used machetes to kill the ones who resisted and dumped them into the hole," she explained. She began to weep. She remained inside the pit for a night and a day, she said; then, on the second night, she climbed the jumbled corpses to pull herself out.

I took Chantal back to her home, a neat mud hut in a bustling, dusty neighborhood of shops and wandering livestock. Chantal is married with two children; she was the only genocidal-rape survivor I met who was married. Her husband knows what happened to her. But for thousands of Rwandan survivors, one of the most insidious legacies of the rapes is the stigma—and the inevitable isolation. In Rwandan society, it is almost impossible for a woman who is known to have been raped to marry. One witness who testified against Pauline in Arusha had been engaged to be married a month later. When her fiancé heard about the testimony, he broke off the engagement.

Then there is the generation of children born of the rapes. As many as 5,000 such children have been documented, and most likely, there are many more than that who haven't. These children will most likely never know their fathers—in most cases, the mother was raped so many times that the issue of paternity was not only pointless but emotionally perilous: In effect, all of her attackers had fathered that child.

Compounding the dishonor, the mere sight of these children— those who aren't abandoned—can bring on savage memories to survivors. Two women I met who gave birth to their rapists' children named the children with words that translate as "Blessing from God" as a way to ease the pain. But others in the community gave them names that put them in the same category as their fathers: "Children of Shame," "Gifts of the Enemy," "Little Interahamwe."

"Did you ever see the look in a woman's eyes when she sees a child of rape?" asked Sydia Nduna, an adviser at the International Rescue Committee Rwanda who works for a program in Kigali aimed at reducing gender violence. "It's a depth of sadness you cannot imagine." The impact of the mass rapes in Rwanda, she said, will be felt for generations. "Mass rape forces the victims to live with the consequences, the damage, the children," Nduna explained.

Making matters worse, the rapes, most of them committed by many men in succession, were frequently accompanied by other forms of physical torture and often staged as public performances to multiply the terror and degradation. So many women feared them that they often begged to be killed instead. Often the rapes were in fact a prelude to murder. But sometimes the victim was not killed but instead repeatedly violated and then left alive; the humiliation would then affect not only the victim but also those closest to her. Other times, women were used as a different kind of tool: Half dead, or even already a corpse, a woman would be publicly raped as a way for Interahamwe mobs to bond together.

But the exposure—and the destruction—did not stop with the act of rape itself. Many women were purposely left alive to die later, and slowly. Two women I met outside Butare, Francina Mukamazina and Liberata Munganyinka, are dying of AIDS they contracted through rape. "My biggest worry is what will happen to my children when I'm gone," Francina told me. These children are as fragile as Francina fears: A U.N. survey of Rwandan children of war concluded that 31 percent witnessed a rape or sexual assault, and 70 percent witnessed murder. Francina's and Liberata's daughters survived but watched their siblings slaughtered and their mothers violated. They will grow up beside children born of rape, all of them together forced to navigate different but commingling resentments.

During my visit to Chantal's home, I asked her how she coped with her savage memories. She replied: "I just want to forget. My children are my consolation. Most rape survivors have nothing. We're poor, but I have my family. It's all I want."

I found Mary later that afternoon a few miles of dirt track away. She was sitting alone in her home, a stifling mud hut about twenty feet square with one small window. Mary told me that the rapes were her first and only sexual experience. Then, eyes averted, twisting her hands, she told me that five months ago she discovered she had AIDS. She said that two of the other young women she and Chantal were kept with are already dead. Their fate is not the exception but the rule. According to one estimate, 70 percent of women raped during the Rwanda genocide have HIV; most will eventually die from it.

In an interview at the State House in Kigali, Rwanda's president, Paul Kagame, talked about the mass rapes in measured, contemplative sentences, shaking his head, his emotions betraying him. "We knew that the government was bringing AIDS patients out of the hospitals specifically to form battalions of rapists," he told me. He smiled ruefully, as if still astonished by the plan.

The most cynical purpose of the rapes in Butare was to transmit a slower, more agonizing form of death. "By using a disease, a plague, as an apocalyptic terror, as biological warfare, you're annihilating the procreators, perpetuating the death unto the generations," said Charles B. Strozier, a psychoanalyst and professor of history at John Jay College of Criminal Justice in New York. "The killing continues and endures."

The use of AIDS as a tool of warfare against Tutsi women helped prosecutors in Arusha focus on rape as a driving force of the genocide. "HIV infection is murder," said Silvana Arbia, the Rwanda Tribunal's acting chief of prosecutions. "Sexual aggression is as much an act of genocide as murder is."

During my visit with Mary, I learned that she had been "murdered" in just this way. This young woman has only one relative who lived through the genocide, a younger brother who lives in Kigali. "All of my friends have AIDS," she told me in June. "But I'll die of loneliness before I die of AIDS," she whispered, choking on her tears. "All I wanted was to marry and have a family." Today, she lies gravely ill in her hut, cared for by Chantal, withering away.

Mass rape has long been a weapon of war. According to legend, ancient Rome was united after Romulus and his soldiers terrorized their rivals, the Sabines, by raping their women. Widespread sexual assault has been documented in conflicts ranging from the Crusades to the Napoleonic Wars.

It was Abraham Lincoln who approved the laws that eventually established the modern understanding of rape as a war crime. In 1863, he commissioned Francis Lieber, an expert jurist, to develop a set of instructions for governing armies during the Civil War. Lieber specifically named rape as a crime serious enough to be subject to the death penalty. "The Lieber code was revolutionary," said Kelly Askin, director of the International Criminal Justice Institute. "Before, gender crimes had been very much ignored."

International law was more reticent about the problem. "Rape was considered a kind of collateral damage," said Rhonda Copelon, a professor of law at the City University of New York. "It was seen as part of the unpreventable, fundamental culture of war." After World War II, the rapes of Chinese women by Japanese soldiers in Nanking were prosecuted as war crimes by an international tribunal. However, rape was prosecuted only in conjunction with other violent crimes. The same tribunal, moreover, failed to prosecute the most institutionalized form of sexual violence, the enslavement of "comfort women" by the Japanese army. In 1946, rape was named a crime against humanity by an Allied statute governing German war crimes trials, but the law was never implemented. It was not until 1995, at the International Criminal Tribunal for the former Yugoslavia, that rape was prosecuted as a grave crime tantamount to torture.

The defendant in that 1995 case was a Serbian policeman named Dusan Tadic. The tribunal charged him with various crimes, including the rape of a Muslim woman in a Bosnian prison camp. The rape was labeled a crime against humanity. So was another sexual crime, this one perpetrated against men. Tadic tortured two male Muslim prisoners, forcing one man to bite off the testicles of another, who then bled to death. The tribunal's indictments set an important precedent. Disappointingly, tribunal prosecutors were forced to drop the rape charge after Tadic's victim refused to testify—she was afraid of reprisal if she did so. The prosecutors were successful, however, with the sexual mutilation charge. Convicted of torture, among other crimes, Tadic was sentenced to twenty years in prison.

Individual stories of rape in Rwanda had begun to accumulate as soon as the genocide ended, mostly through interviews collected by groups like Human Rights Watch. But because Rwandan culture discourages women from talking about sexual matters—and also because the idea that rape was merely "collateral damage" remained ingrained in the judicial community—the prosecutors in Arusha did not initially connect the dots between rape and the Hutus' genocide blueprint. The legal breakthrough came by a willful accident, during the 1998 trial in Arusha of Jean Paul Akayesu, mayor of Taba, a Rwandan commune.

Initially, Akayesu had been charged only with genocide. Among the survivors who testified against him was a woman code-named H. (The identities of tribunal witnesses are shielded.)

"H. disclosed to me prior to her going on the stand that she was raped out in the bush," explained Pierre-Richard Prosper, the current U.S. ambassador-at-large for war crimes issues, who led the tribunal's prosecution against Akayesu. "She said that the Interahamwe would come in at the end of the day and start raping the women, and that Akayesu was there." Sensing a window into not just the act of H.'s rape but the intention of her rapists, Prosper dispatched investigators to Rwanda, specifically to find women who were raped in Taba during the third and fourth weeks of April. Of the 500 or so women they knew had been held captive, investigators discovered that almost all had been killed and dumped in a mass grave. Witness H. was one of about a dozen who was able to escape. So was a woman code-named J.J.

Prosper put J.J. on the stand. Her tale was sickeningly familiar: She said she had been dragged away by Interahamwe and raped repeatedly. Then she mentioned that Akayesu watched her being raped from the doorway and goaded the Interahamwe, saying with a laugh, "Never ask me again what a Tutsi woman tastes like."

The indictment against Akayesu was amended to include the first-ever charge of rape as a crime against humanity. Prosper argued that Akayesu, in making that flip remark as the Interahamwe proceeded with raping J.J., was effectively ordering them to continue raping others.

On September 2, 1998, Akayesu was convicted of genocide and crimes against humanity, including rape. He was sentenced to three life sentences, plus eighty years imprisonment, and transferred to a U.N.-sponsored prison in Mali, in West Africa.

"The intention in Rwanda was an abstraction: to kill without killing," said Arbia, the tribunal prosecutor. She described the case of a 45-year-old Rwandan woman who was raped by her 12-year-old son—with Interahamwe holding a hatchet to his throat—in front of her husband, while their five other young children were forced to hold open her thighs. "The offense against an individual woman becomes an offense against the family," Arbia said, "which becomes an offense against the country, and so, by deduction, against humanity."

On August 10, 1999, a year after Akayesu's conviction, Pauline Nyiramasuhuko's indictment was amended to include rape as a crime against humanity. According to prosecutors and witnesses, her frequent instructions to Interahamwe at the prefecture to rape before they killed, or to rape women instead of killing them, had triggered a collective sadism in Butare—one that had even inspired violence in the local peasants.

One Tutsi rape survivor I met in Butare, a farmer named Suzanne Bukabangwa, had never met Pauline, but became her victim by extension all the same. Her neighbors, uneducated farmers, had kept her as a sex slave during the genocide, she said, torturing her nightly. She remembered two things most of all: the stamens from the banana trees they used to violate her, leaving her body mutilated, and the single sentence one of the men used: "We're going to kill all the Tutsis, and one day Hutu children will have to ask what did a Tutsi child look like."

In Butare, I spoke to a local peasant, Lucien Simbayobewe, who was caught up in this cycle of humiliation. Now 40, he was being held prisoner in the local prison. (Only leaders of the genocide have been sent to Arusha.) He wore the pink shorts and matching pink shirt of the Rwandan inmate's uniform. Wringing his hands in his lap, he told me about one woman he killed who still comes to him every night in his dreams. He couldn't remember this apparition's name, but he said he'd killed her when Pauline first organized the Butare Interahamwe. Choking on emotion, he said, "She comes in the night dancing and gesturing with her hands invitingly, like a lover." My translator gyrated her arms to show me the motion. "The woman smiles, and says, 'How are you?' But before I can answer, she says, 'Goodbye,' and then she vanishes—and I wake up." Lucian then told me in detail about killing her. But when I asked Lucien if he'd raped the woman, he fell silent and fought back tears. Every prisoner I spoke with described explicitly whom he killed and how. Not a single one admitted to raping a Tutsi woman.

Perhaps this is because after the war, Rwanda's legislature declared the rapes committed during the genocide were the highest category of crime; those convicted are sentenced to death. Or maybe these men could somehow justify to themselves having murdered but not raped. In any event, the weight of that level of confession was obviously too much to bear, and if there could be any tangible proof that rape was considered the more shameful crime, it was this.

Some scholars are beginning to share this opinion. "Rape sets in motion continuous suffering and extreme humiliation that affects not just the individual victim but everyone around her," said the philosopher and historian Robert Jay Lifton, who in books like *The Nazi Doctors* has explored the psychology of genocide. "A woman is seen as a symbol of purity. The family revolves around that symbol. Then here is the brutal attack on that, stigmatizing them all. All this perpetuates the humiliation, reverberating among survivors and their whole families." He paused. "In this way, rape is worse than death."

Gerald Gahima, Rwanda's prosecutor general, agrees. "Rape was the worst experience of victims of the genocide," he said. "Some people paid to die, to be shot rather than tortured. Their prayers were for a quick and decent death. Victims of rape did not have that privilege."

The case against Pauline further cements the precedent established in the Akayesu trial: namely, that inciting mass rape is a crime against humanity. But Pauline's case transcends jurisprudence. She presents to the world a new kind of criminal. "There is a shared concept across cultures that women don't do this kind of thing," said Carolyn Nordstrom, an anthropologist at the University of Notre Dame. "Society doesn't yet have a way to talk about it, because it violates all our concepts of what women are."

I found Pauline's mother, Theresa Nyirakabue, on the same plot of land in Ndora where Pauline was born and reared. Directly across the road is one of the many orderly settlements of sturdy homes the government built for Tutsi survivors of the genocide. Theresa is 86, diminutive, and half-blind, and keeps upright by grasping a tall staff. But her milky eyes are electric, her smile is quick, and she was eager to invite strangers into her home to talk about her daughter.

She hadn't seen Pauline since the genocide began and was hungry for news of her. I asked her if she knew that Pauline was in detention in Arusha, and she nodded. I asked her if she knew why, and she nodded again. Then I said that I saw Pauline three weeks before in the courtroom and that she looked healthy enough. Smiling broadly, Theresa said: "Pauline wanted to teach at the health center. She liked to teach good health." She paused, still smiling, and said, "Pauline's ministership was the joy of my heart."

I asked her if she thought her daughter was innocent of the charges against her. Theresa sobered instantly. "It is unimaginable that she did these things," she said. "She wouldn't order people to rape and kill. After all, Pauline is a mother." Then Theresa leaned forward, her hands outstretched. "Before the war, Hutu and Tutsi were the same," she said. She told me that Pauline had many Tutsi friends. Theresa added that during the genocide, she herself had hidden a Tutsi boy in her home.

At first, Theresa's story took me by surprise. But then, Rwanda's lethal racialism could never be as starkly delineated as, say, Nazi Germany's. Whether Hutus and Tutsis are separate ethnic groups is a subject of debate, but it was only after European colonists arrived in Rwanda that any political distinction was made between them. Intermarriage had long been common, and both groups spoke the same language and practiced the same religion. Around the turn of the twentieth century, however, German and Belgian colonists used dubious racialist logic—namely, that Tutsis had a more "Caucasian" appearance—to designate the minority Tutsi the ruling class, empowering them as their social and governing proxy.

In the 1930s, the Belgians, deciding to limit administrative posts and higher education to the Tutsi, needed to decide exactly who was in Rwanda. The most efficient procedure was simply to register everyone and require them to carry cards identifying them as one or the other. Eighty-four percent of the population declared themselves Hutu and 15 percent Tutsi. Considering the degree of intermarriage in Rwandan history, this accounting was hardly scientific. What's more, Rwandans sometimes switched ethnic identities, the wealthy relabeling themselves as Tutsis and the poor as Hutus.

"Identity became based on what you could get away with," said Alison Des Forges, a senior adviser to the African Division of Human Rights Watch who has studied Rwanda for thirty years. "Half of the people are not clearly distinguishable. There was significant intermarriage. Women who fit the Tutsi stereotype—taller, lighter, with more Caucasian-like features—became desirable. But it didn't necessarily mean that the women were one or the other."

With desire comes its emotional alter ego, resentment. A revolution in 1959 brought the majority Hutus to power. As tensions increased around 1990, politicians began disseminating propaganda denouncing Tutsi females as temptresses, whores, and sexual deviants. Before the 1994 genocide began, Hutu newspapers ran cartoon after cartoon depicting Tutsi women as lascivious seducers.

Unlike the Nazis, who were fueled by myths of Aryan superiority, the Hutus were driven by an accumulated rage over their lower status and by resentment of supposed Tutsi beauty and arrogance. "The propaganda made Tutsi women powerful, desirable—and therefore something to be destroyed," Rhonda Copelon told me. "When you make the women the threat, you enhance the idea that violence against them is permitted."

This pernicious idea, of course, came to full fruition during the genocide. The collective belief of Hutu women that Tutsi women were shamelessly trying to steal their husbands granted Hutu men permission to rape their supposed competitors out of existence. Seen through this warped lens, the men who raped were engaged not only in an act of sexual transgression but also in a purifying ritual. "Once women are defiled as a group, anything one does to them is done in some kind of higher purpose," Robert Jay Lifton said. "It become a profound, shared motivation of eliminating evil. Tutsis must be killed down to the last person in order to bring about utopia. They are seen, in a sense, as already dead."

This explanation conformed with my sense of Pauline's view of the Tutsis; like many of her countrymen, she seemed able to view individual Tutsis as abstractions. But in my conversations with Pauline's mother, things became even more complicated. After Theresa told me about the Tutsi boy she had hidden, she paused, looked at me intently, and told me, matter-of-factly, that Pauline's great-grandfather was a Tutsi. The great-grandfather had been redesignated a Hutu, Theresa explained, because he became poor. Stunned, and knowing that in Rwanda kinship is defined patrilineally—through the blood of fathers—I asked Theresa if that didn't mean that Pauline was a Tutsi. "Yes, of course," she said eagerly. And would Pauline have known that she came from Tutsi lineage? Theresa pursed her lips and gave a firm, affirmative nod.

The young man Theresa hid was not difficult to find. His name is Dutera Agide, 36, a jobless handyman in Ndora. He told me that he is Pauline's second cousin, and that he is a Tutsi. He said he had spent one week hiding in Theresa's house, listening to the slaughter going on outside. Then he said something even more surprising. At one point, he said, he was hidden in Pauline's house. "I saw Pauline twice a week during the genocide," Dutera told me. "One day she came home, and she said: 'The war is not ending. I'm starting to get afraid. I don't know what will happen.' Then she came back again with her husband, loaded things from the house into a car, and left. She looked scared."

After my conversation with Dutera, I went back to Theresa's home one more time. Her exuberance had all but gone. She seemed to have settled into the truth, or a form of it. "People killed people because of fear to be also killed by the perpetrators of the genocide," she said. "My daughter, who was also a minister in the government, could have participated in the killing not because she wanted to kill but because of fear." Theresa then used the Kinyarwanda expression *Mpemuke ndamuke*: "to be dishonest in order to escape death."

I spoke again with Pauline's sister, Vineranda. "In 1959, when the Tutsi regime changed, our family changed with the situation," Vineranda explained. "Because she was a Tutsi, Pauline was afraid that maybe the government would find out. And she was among many men in the government. And she had money and a position. She didn't want to lose that."

Robert Jay Lifton was intrigued by the revelation that Pauline was of Tutsi descent. "Part of Pauline Nyiramasuhuko's fierceness had to do with eliminating the Tutsi in her," he hypothesized. "She was undergoing an individual struggle to destroy that defiled element in herself."

Pauline's husband, Maurice Ntahobari, denied irritably that there were Tutsi roots in either his or Pauline's family. After being asked repeatedly about Pauline's and Shalom's actions during the genocide, he sighed and said: "Try to understand, try to be in my shoes. This is about my wife and my son."

When I spoke again with Pauline's attorney, Nicole Bergevin, in July, and told her what Pauline's mother had told me about Pauline being of Tutsi descent, Bergevin said she knew. (In an odd reversal, she later denied that Pauline was Tutsi.) Bergevin's demeanor had changed since we had last spoken. This time around, she sounded defeated. Though she still insisted that Pauline knew nothing of the mass raping or murdering, she said, "I'm sure she's going to be found guilty." Then she paused and said with resignation, "When you do murder trials, you realize that we are all susceptible, and you wouldn't even dream that you would ever commit this act." There was a short silence. "But you come to understand that everyone is. It could happen to me, it could happen to my daughter. It could happen to you."

The crimes Pauline Nyiramasuhuko are accused of are monstrous. Her capacity for pity and compassion, and her professional duty to shield the powerless, deserted her, or collapsed under the irresistible urge for power. But in seeking a reasonable explanation for Pauline's barbarity, I remembered something that Alison Des Forges of Human Rights Watch told me.

"This behavior lies just under the surface of any of us," Des Forges said. "The simplified accounts of genocide allow distance between us and the perpetrators of genocide. They are so evil we couldn't ever see ourselves doing the same thing. But if you consider the terrible pressure under which people were operating, then you automatically reassert their humanity—and that becomes alarming. You are forced to look at these situations and say, 'What would I have done?' Sometimes the answer is not encouraging."

Pauline did possess humanity, but it was in short supply, and she reserved it for her only son, Shalom, whom she had helped turn into a rapist and a killer. In one of her last moments as an engineer of the genocide, however, she returned to her role as woman and mother.

It was in July 1994, right when the Hutu army was collapsing.

Butare had descended into mayhem, and Pauline's side had lost. One of Pauline's neighbors, Lela, spotted the minister in the streets. "I saw Pauline and Shalom at a roadblock," she said. "Pauline was wearing military fatigues, and she was still trying to separate Tutsis and Hutus, but the confusion was massive. There were people running everywhere. The Rwandan Patriotic Front was coming." A short time later, Lela saw Pauline again. This time she was standing alone outside her home, looking worried.

"I was shocked," Lela said. "She was wearing camouflage. She was standing upright in her uniform like a soldier, trying to see what was happening up and down the road. She just looked furious. She was looking everywhere for Shalom. He was her pet. She loved Shalom so much."

How odd and in some ways appropriate that the reporting of this profoundly disturbing story about Rwanda began on the Pakistan-Afghanistan border, and not with me but with my wife. Ten days after September 11, I was on a plane to Islamabad and beyond, and my wife, Kimberlee Acquaro, was on her way to Kigali on a Pew Fellowship for International Journalism. We spoke nightly by satellite phone, relating the horrors before us, the ones before me unfolding and the ones before Kimberlee surviving as living memories. I was exhausted. I had been on one intensive assignment after another for nearly eighteen months, and when I returned from South Asia I almost immediately left on still another story. I was out of gas.

But Kimberlee, a photographer as well as a writer, insisted we return to Rwanda together, to make an attempt to force an Afghanistan-centered readership to pay attention to a critical, as-yet-untold story that continues to reflect the worst of us. The Rwandan genocide, all things considered, may have been human history's most awful moment. And the woman at the heart of this particular angle, a woman mandated to care after the lives of women and children, who helped orches-

trate and personally carry out a campaign of unprecedented sexual torture and mass murder, in some ways reflects the demon sleeping in us all.

I entered the reporting reluctantly. But once in Rwanda, Kimberlee and I realized that this story was emblematic of a form of warfare and human behavior that has not been addressed honestly. One million dead in ten weeks, not in a hail of gunfire and not in rooms of gas, but hacked to pieces and sexually mutilated at the hands of neighbors, friends, priests, and relatives. I became obsessed, and remain so, by the angle that in this one 8,000-word article I could not make the room to fully address: What is the source of bloodlust? Rwanda was an orgiastic frenzy of almost joyful slaughter. What in us—in me and you—permits us to slough off what we know to be true, and to allow us to club to death a best friend or skewer a baby niece?

The first drafts of this story were too upsetting to read. My editor told me that he could hardly get through them. As difficult as the details are to digest, please do know that the most difficult job in the writing of this story was to cull the imagery enough to allow the typical brunch-time reader of The New York Times Magazine to turn the page.

But this story, more than any I have written, became a Pandora's box. It is about the relationship between the West and Africa, between white and black, between man and woman, and between a reporter and his own conscience. It took me nearly six months to accumulate the will to move on to another story. But the questions that the Minister of Rape raised (there are no answers) echo loudly and every day.

CONTRIBUTORS

Born in Cleveland, Ohio, the son of a newspaper editor/publisher, **ROBERT SAM ANSON** was educated at the University of Notre Dame. He began working for *Time* while still a college student and served as correspondent in the Chicago, Los Angeles, Saigon, and New York bureaus. Taken captive by North Vietnamese/Khmer Rouge forces while on assignment in Cambodia in August 1970, he was released after several weeks.

He served as chief anchorman/executive producer for special events at WNET/13 and was a senior writer for *New Times* magazine, a special correspondent for *Life*, a contributing editor for *Esquire*, and editor in chief of *Los Angeles Magazine*. At present a contributing editor at *Vanity Fair*, he is the author of six books and has written for, among others, *The New York Times*, *New York*, the *London Sunday Times*, *U.S. News & World Report*, and the *Los Angeles Times*.

Regarded as an investigative specialist, he covered Bosnia, organized crime, race riots, national politics, the New Left, the civil rights movement, and the sixties. He thinks of himself as the Susan Lucci of the National Magazine Awards.

MARIE BRENNER is writer at large of *Vanity Fair* and the author of five books, including the best-selling *Great Dames: What I Learned from Older Women* (Crown 2001) and *House of Dreams: The Bingham Family of Louisville* (1988).

"The Man Who Knew Too Much," her investigation of the life of Big Tobacco whistle-blower Jeffrey Wigand, inspired the Michael Mann movie, *The Insider*, starring Al Pacino and Russell Crowe, which was nominated for nine Academy Awards, including Best Picture. She is the winner of three Front Page Awards and her articles have appeared in *The New Yorker*, *New York*, *Vogue*, and *The New York Times Magazine*. Her reporting on the Enron case was used as the basis for questioning during the Senate hearings on the matter.

RENE CHUN is a New York–based writer who has written for numerous publications including *The New York Times, Esquire, GQ*, and *New York*. He is currently working on a book about the former World Chess Champion Bobby Fischer, which is based on an article of his that appeared in *The Atlantic Monthly*.

GARY COHEN lives in Washington, D.C., and writes for *The Atlantic Monthly* and *Vanity Fair* magazines.

DEVIN FRIEDMAN is a senior writer at *GQ* magazine. He has also been on staff at *Men's Journal* and *Esquire*. He would appreciate your not making any men's magazine jokes. He's written for *Rolling Stone, The New York Times Magazine*, and *The New Yorker*, among others, and he was nominated for a National Magazine Award and was a finalist for the Livingston Award. He was raised by a criminal defense attorney and used to work for the public defender's office; it's not surprising that he often has somewhat more compassion for criminals than normal people do.

JOSHUA HAMMER has been *Newsweek's* Jerusalem bureau chief since January 2001. Before that, he was the magazine's bureau chief in Nairobi, Buenos Aires, and Berlin. He is the author of *Chosen by God: A Brother's Journey*, a finalist for the 2000 Los Angeles Times Book Award, and the forthcoming *A Season in Bethlehem: Unholy War in a Sacred Place*.

SKIP HOLLANDSWORTH has been writing crime stories for *Texas Monthly* for fifteen years. He has been nominated for the National Magazine Award four times and several of his articles have been optioned by film producers. He is now working on a nonfiction book for HarperCollins on the mysterious murders of seven women in Austin, Texas, in the late nineteenth century.

SEBASTIAN JUNGER, the author of the international bestseller *The Perfect Storm* and *Fire*, has been awarded a National Magazine Award and an SAIS-Novartis Prize for his journalism. He lives in New York.

TOM JUNOD is a two-time winner of the National Magazine Award. He is a writer at large for *Esquire*, and lives in Marietta, Georgia.

JESSE KATZ is a senior writer for *The Los Angeles Magazine*. His work has appeared in *The Los Angeles Times Magazine, The New York Times Magazine*, and *Texas Monthly*. He received a 2002 gold medal in reporting from the national City and Regional Magazine Association for his investigation into the murder of former Los Angeles police chief Bernard Parks's granddaughter. As a *Los Angeles Times* reporter from 1985 to 2000, he was a member of the Metro staff that twice won Pulitzer Prizes in the spot news category, for the 1992 LA riots and for the 1994 Northridge earthquake.

JAY KIRK has written for *Harper's Magazine, The New York Times Magazine,* the *Chicago Reader,* Nerve.com, and other publications. This story was nominated for a National Magazine Award.

ROBERT KURSON is a graduate of the University of Wisconsin and Harvard Law School. He is a senior editor at *Chicago* magazine, a frequent contributor to *Esquire,* and has written for *Rolling Stone, The New York Times Magazine,* and other publications.

PETER LANDESMAN is a journalist, novelist, and screenwriter. His nonfiction appears frequently in *The New York Times Magazine.* His first novel, *The Raven,* was awarded the American Academy of Arts and Letters prize for best first fiction in 1996. He lives in Los Angeles and New York with his wife, photographer and journalist Kimberlee Acquaro.

DOUG MOST is a senior editor at *Boston Magazine* and a freelance writer whose work has appeared in *Sports Illustrated* and *The New York Times Magazine.* He's had pieces chosen to appear in *Best American Sports Writing* and the first edition of *Best American Crime Writing.* He's the author of *Always in Our Hearts: Amy Grossberg, Brian Peterson, and the Baby They Didn't Want.*

Award-winning journalist **MAXIMILLIAN POTTER** has been on staff at GQ since 2000, covering sports, business, politics, and crime. He's written for *Outside, Premiere, Details,* and *Philadelphia Magazine.* He lives with his wife and two sons in Pennsylvania.

PETER RICHMOND is a staff writer for GQ magazine, a commentator for NPR's *Morning Edition,* and the author of three books. His fourth, a biography of the late singer Peggy Lee, will be published by Henry Holt in 2005. His work has appeared in *The New Yorker, The New York Times Magazine,* and *Rolling Stone.*

JEFF TIETZ has written for *The New Yorker, Harper's Magazine, The Atlantic Monthly,* and *Rolling Stone.* He lives in Texas.

PAIGE WILLIAMS is a native of Tupelo, Mississippi, and has written for *The New York Times Magazine, Men's Journal, Playboy,* and *Atlanta,* and before that wrote for *The Charlotte Observer.* Now she lives in New York and is a first-year MFA candidate in fiction at Columbia University.

EVAN WRIGHT is a contributing editor to *Rolling Stone,* where he has been dubbed "ambassador to the underbelly" for his coverage of the West Coast's peculiar underworld of porn magnates, celebrity drug addicts, anarchist environmentalists, Internet scam artists, punk skateboarder gangs, and unrepentant murderers. He previously worked for Larry Flynt as the entertainment editor at *Hustler* magazine. He has also contributed to *Time Asia*, *Men's Journal*, *ESPN* magazine, and *LA Weekly*. During the past eighteen months he has reported from the Middle East on the conflicts in Afghanistan and Iraq. A native of Cleveland, Ohio, Evan Wright lives in Southern California.

LAWRENCE WRIGHT is a writer of books, magazine articles, and screenplays, both fiction and nonfiction. His screenplay, *Siege*, coauthored with Menno Meyjes and its director, Edward Zwick, based on Wright's original story, was called by *Panorama* "the most chillingly prescient terrorism film of them all." He lives in Austin, Texas.

PERMISSIONS ACKNOWLEDGMENTS

THOMAS H. COOK is the author of eighteen books, including two works of true crime. His novels have been nominated for the Edgar Allan Poe Award, the Macavity Award, and the Dashiell Hammett Prize. *The Chatham School Affair* won the Edgar Allan Poe Award for Best Novel in 1996. His true crime book, *Blood Echoes*, was nominated for the Edgar Allan Poe Award in 1992, and his story "Fatherhood" won the Herodotus Prize in 1998 and was included in *Best American Mystery Stories* of 1998, edited by Otto Penzler and Ed McBain. His works have been translated into fifteen languages.

OTTO PENZLER is the proprietor of The Mysterious Bookshop in New York City. He was the founder of the Mysterious Press and created the publishing firm Otto Penzler Books. He is a recipient of an Edgar Award for *The Encyclopedia of Mystery and Detection* and the Ellery Queen Award and a Raven by the Mystery Writers of America for his many contributions to the field. He is the series editor of *The Best American Mystery Stories of the Year*. His other anthologies include *Murder for Love, Murder for Revenge, Murder and Obsession, The 50 Greatest Mysteries of All Time,* and *The Best American Mystery Stories of the Century*. He wrote *101 Greatest Movies of Mystery and Suspense*. He lives in New York City.

JOHN BERENDT is the author of *Midnight in the Garden of Good and Evil*, which spent four years on *The New York Times* bestseller list. He has been the editor of *New York* magazine and an *Esquire* columnist. He lives in New York.